Ordnance Survey Ireland

National Mapping Agency
www.osi.ie

GW00514851

Route Plann	
M50 Map	II
Garda Road Safety Information	III-IV
Dart, Luas and Suburban Rail Network	V
Dublin Bus Information	VI
Dublin City and District Maps	1-68
City Centre Maps	69-76
Town Maps	77-92

77	Ashbourne	**86**	Dunshaughlin
79	Balbriggan	**87**	Kilcock
81	Blessington	**88**	Lusk
82	Clane	**89**	Rush
83	Delgany/Greystones	**91**	Ratoath
85	Donabate	**92**	Skerries

Tourist Information	93-94
Embassies	95
List of Hospitals	96
Industrial Estates and Business Parks	97-98
Street Index	99

Kardiff
045-866
337

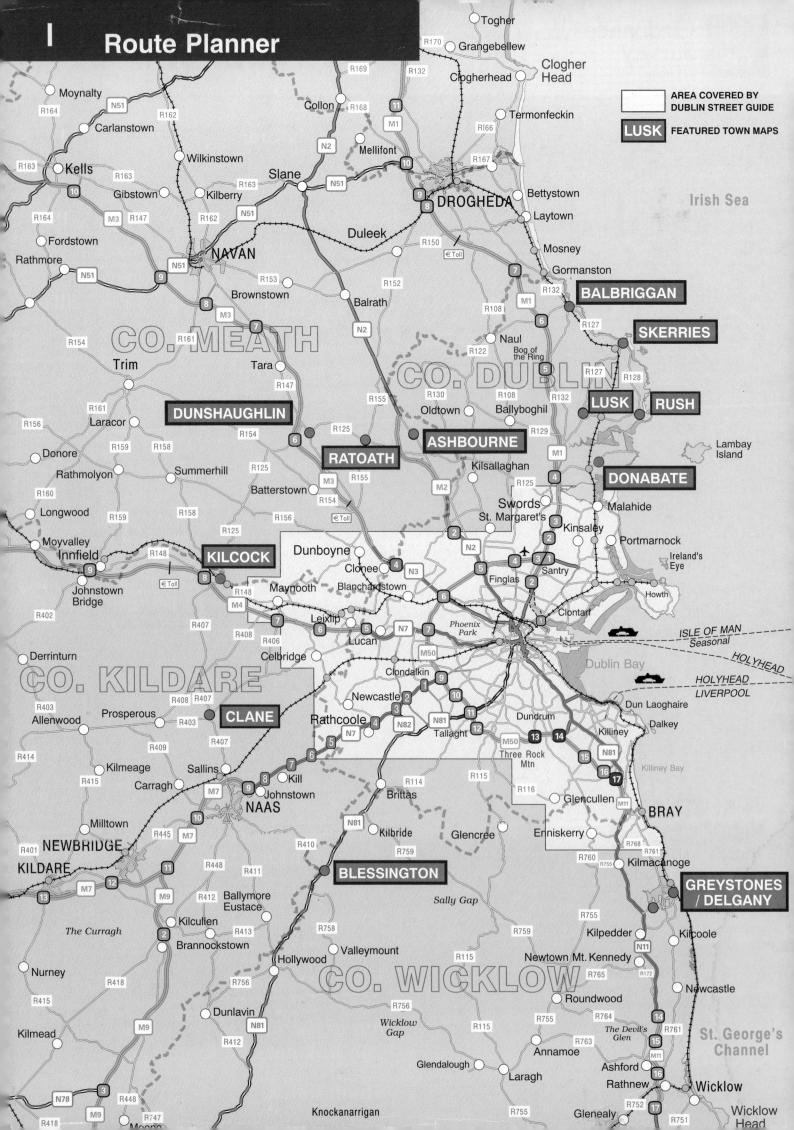

Bray to Ballymount

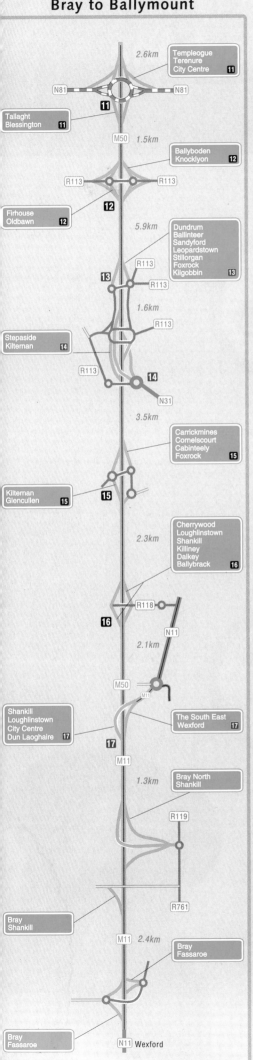

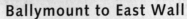

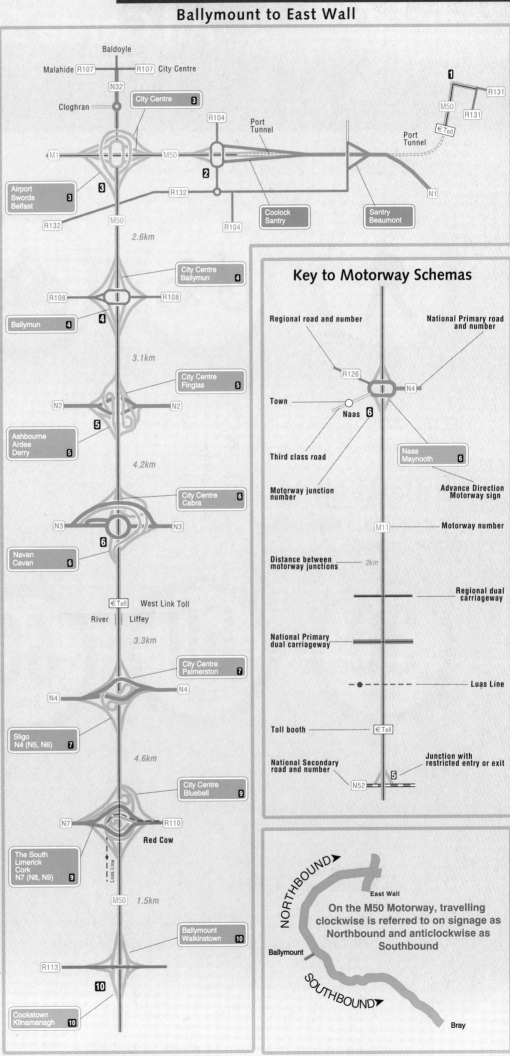

Key to Motorway Schemas

Regional road and number

National Primary road and number

R126

N4

Town

Naas 6

Third class road

Naas Maynooth 6

Motorway junction number

Advance Direction Motorway sign

Distance between motorway junctions — 2km

M11 — Motorway number

Regional dual carriageway

National Primary dual carriageway

Luas Line

Toll booth — € Toll

National Secondary road and number

N52

Junction with restricted entry or exit

5

NORTHBOUND

East Wall

On the M50 Motorway, travelling clockwise is referred to on signage as Northbound and anticlockwise as Southbound

Ballymount

SOUTHBOUND

Bray

An Garda Síochána
Ireland's National Police Service

Vulnerable Road Users

1 in 3   1 in 6   1 in 10

Since 2001, approximately 60% of Dublin's fatalities have been pedestrians, cyclists or motorcyclists. Watch out for vulnerable road users

Speed Limits

To protect our Vulnerable Road Users, the following speed Limits apply within the Greater Dublin Area

High risk to Vulnerable Road Users   General built up areas   Primary approach roads to the city

Know your Speed Limits, know YOUR Speed!

Speed Detection

Speed checkpoints are carried out in "collision prone zones". These locations may be found at www.garda.ie/ traffic

They may be static, mobile or fixed camera. Penalties include fines, and/ or penalty points. Take heed- do not speed!

5+ Axle HGV Ban

A 5+ axle HGV ban operates in certain areas of Dublin City at certain time periods. A limited permit scheme is in operation for those that need to load/ unload during the restricted time period.

When you CANNOT enter the restricted zone: During the hours of 07.00 – 19.00, seven days a week, HGVs with 5+ axles are not allowed to enter the restricted zone during these times unless you have a **valid permit**.

When you CAN enter the restricted zone: During the hours 19.00 – 07.00, seven days a week HGVs with 5+ axles are allowed to enter the restricted zone, even without a permit. HGVs with 4 axles or less are allowed to enter the restricted zone at any time, day or night. **For more details see www.dublincity.ie**

 # Crime Prevention Advice

It pays to be careful. To reduce your chances of becoming a victim of crime, consider the following -

- » Be aware of your surroundings
- » Avoid travelling alone, where possible
- » Avoid walking alone at night
- » Keep cash on your person to the minimum required
- » Keep wallets / purses out of sight
- » Keep hand or shoulder bags close to the body and not dangling by the straps
- » Where possible, take a mobile phone with you when out & about
- » If travelling by public transport, sit as close as possible to the driver or exit
- » If travelling by car, keep all doors locked
- » Be alert when parking and getting out of your vehicle
- » Be alert to pickpockets

- » Ideally, do not leave property in cars or other vehicles
- » Be especially careful with small electronic equipment e.g. Sat Navs, digital cameras, mobile phones, music players etc.
- » Close all windows and lock all doors
- » Do not leave property on view in your vehicle
- » Do not leave cash, cheque books, credit/debit cards in your vehicle
- » Do not leave personal/valuable documents in your vehicle e.g. utility bills, bank statements etc.
- » Avoid parking in isolated places and, at night-time, park with care in a well-lit area
- » Always secure bicycles to an immovable object

V Dart, Luas and Suburban Rail Network

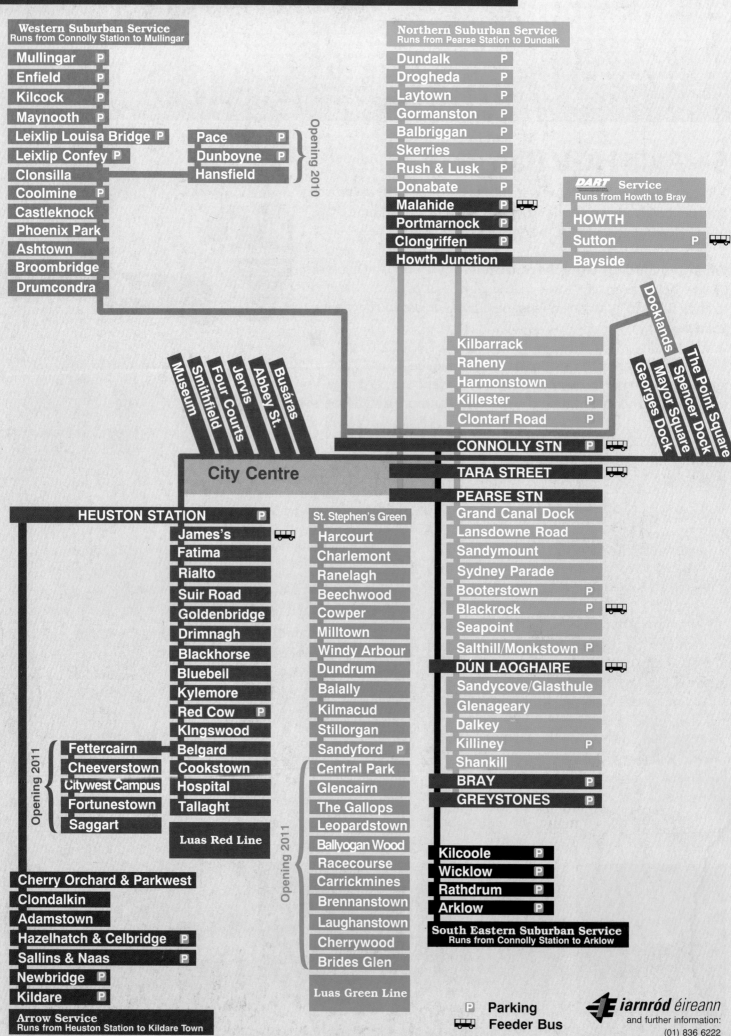

Western Suburban Service
Runs from Connolly Station to Mullingar

- Mullingar **P**
- Enfield **P**
- Kilcock **P**
- Maynooth **P**
- Leixlip Louisa Bridge **P**
- Leixlip Confey **P**
- Clonsilla
- Coolmine **P**
- Castleknock
- Phoenix Park
- Ashtown
- Broombridge
- Drumcondra

Opening 2010
- Pace **P**
- Dunboyne **P**
- Hansfield

Northern Suburban Service
Runs from Pearse Station to Dundalk

- Dundalk **P**
- Drogheda **P**
- Laytown **P**
- Gormanston **P**
- Balbriggan **P**
- Skerries **P**
- Rush & Lusk **P**
- Donabate **P**
- Malahide **P**
- Portmarnock **P**
- Clongriffen **P**
- Howth Junction

DART Service
Runs from Howth to Bray
- HOWTH
- Sutton **P**
- Bayside

- Kilbarrack
- Raheny
- Harmonstown
- Killester **P**
- Clontarf Road **P**
- CONNOLLY STN **P**
- TARA STREET
- PEARSE STN

Docklands
- The Point Square
- Spencer Dock
- Mayor Square
- Georges Dock

Museum
Smithfield
Four Courts
Jervis
Abbey St.
Busáras

City Centre

- HEUSTON STATION **P**

St. Stephen's Green
- Harcourt
- Charlemont
- Ranelagh
- Beechwood
- Cowper
- Milltown
- Windy Arbour
- Dundrum
- Balally
- Kilmacud
- Stillorgan
- Sandyford **P**

Opening 2011
- Central Park
- Glencairn
- The Gallops
- Leopardstown
- Ballyogan Wood
- Racecourse
- Carrickmines
- Brennanstown
- Laughanstown
- Cherrywood
- Brides Glen

Luas Green Line

- James's
- Fatima
- Rialto
- Suir Road
- Goldenbridge
- Drimnagh
- Blackhorse
- Bluebell
- Kylemore
- Red Cow **P**
- Kingswood
- Belgard
- Cookstown
- Hospital
- Tallaght

Opening 2011
- Fettercairn
- Cheeverstown
- Citywest Campus
- Fortunestown
- Saggart

Luas Red Line

- Grand Canal Dock
- Lansdowne Road
- Sandymount
- Sydney Parade
- Booterstown **P**
- Blackrock **P**
- Seapoint
- Salthill/Monkstown **P**
- DÚN LAOGHAIRE
- Sandycove/Glasthule
- Glenageary
- Dalkey
- Killiney **P**
- Shankill
- BRAY **P**
- GREYSTONES **P**

- Kilcoole **P**
- Wicklow **P**
- Rathdrum **P**
- Arklow **P**

South Eastern Suburban Service
Runs from Connolly Station to Arklow

Opening 2011
- Cherry Orchard & Parkwest
- Clondalkin
- Adamstown
- Hazelhatch & Celbridge **P**
- Sallins & Naas **P**
- Newbridge **P**
- Kildare **P**

Arrow Service
Runs from Heuston Station to Kildare Town

P Parking
Feeder Bus

iarnród éireann
and further information:
(01) 836 6222

River Liffey

You'll find your way quicker with Dublin Bus

Thanks to improved bus priority such as Quality Bus Corridors and the College Green Bus Corridor, the bus now gets you into and around Dublin City quicker and easier than ever before - and with the new Interactive Maps facility on www.dublinbus.ie you can see exactly what route your bus will take and where you'll find your nearest bus stop.

So whether you want to go into town shopping or simply want to get to work faster, find all the route, timetable and ticket information you need at www.dublinbus.ie

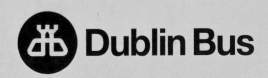

D

E

F

Corballis Golf Links

18

Strand

1

IRISH SEA

2

COAST ROAD

Biscayne

Castle
Robbswall

The
Lighthouse

Sports
Ground

ROBSWALL
WALK PATH

THE
CRESCENT

The Anchorage
The Spinnaker

THE
CRESCENT

R106

230
32a/x

102
42n

3

MONKS
MEADOW

32

32B

LIMETREE
AVENUE

EMER COURT

CONVENT LANE

Martello
Tower

ASHLEY RISE

HEATHER
GARDENS

HEATHFIELD
GROVE

WHEATFIELD ROAD

BRACKEN DRIVE

BRIAR WALK

42n

KELVIN CLOSE

BLACKTHORN CLOSE

DEWBERRY
PARK

HEATHER WALK

STRAND ROAD

WENDELL AVENUE

32x

WENDELL AVE

4

MARTELLO COURT

CARRICKHILL RISE

CARRICKHILL WALK

PORTMARNOCK CRESCENT

2/a/b

CARRICKHILL
CLOSE

RRICKHILL
CLOSE

PORTMARNOCK CLOSE

2

PARKVIEW

RISE

HOPE AVE

PORTMARNOCK DRIVE

BURROW LCT

42n
102

PINE
CT

D

CARRICKHILL HTS

E

F

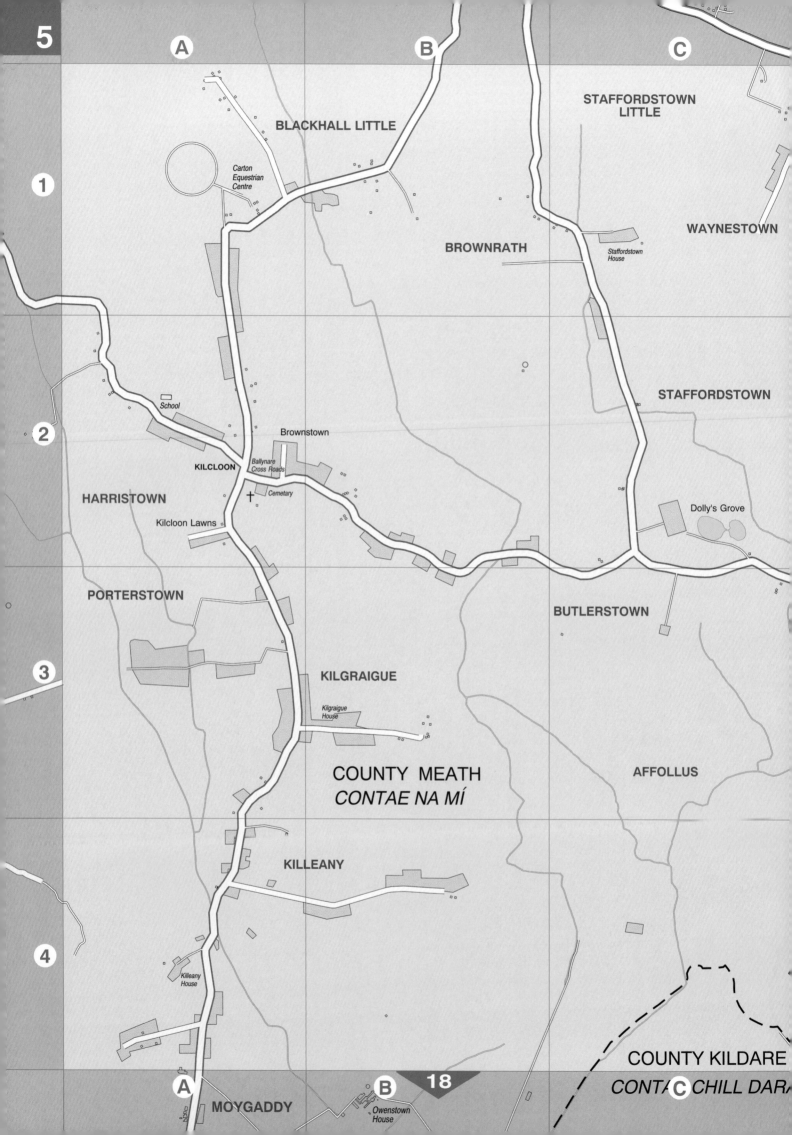

A B C

1

STAFFORDSTOWN
LITTLE

BLACKHALL LITTLE

Carton
Equestrian
Centre

BROWNRATH

Staffordstown
House

WAYNESTOWN

STAFFORDSTOWN

School

2

Brownstown

KILCLOON

Ballynare
Cross Roads

Cemetary

Dolly's Grove

HARRISTOWN

Kilcloon Lawns

BUTLERSTOWN

PORTERSTOWN

3

KILGRAIGUE

Kilgraigue
House

COUNTY MEATH
CONTAE NA MÍ

AFFOLLUS

KILLEANY

4

Killeany
House

COUNTY KILDARE
CONTAE CHILL DARA

MOYGADDY

Owenstown
House

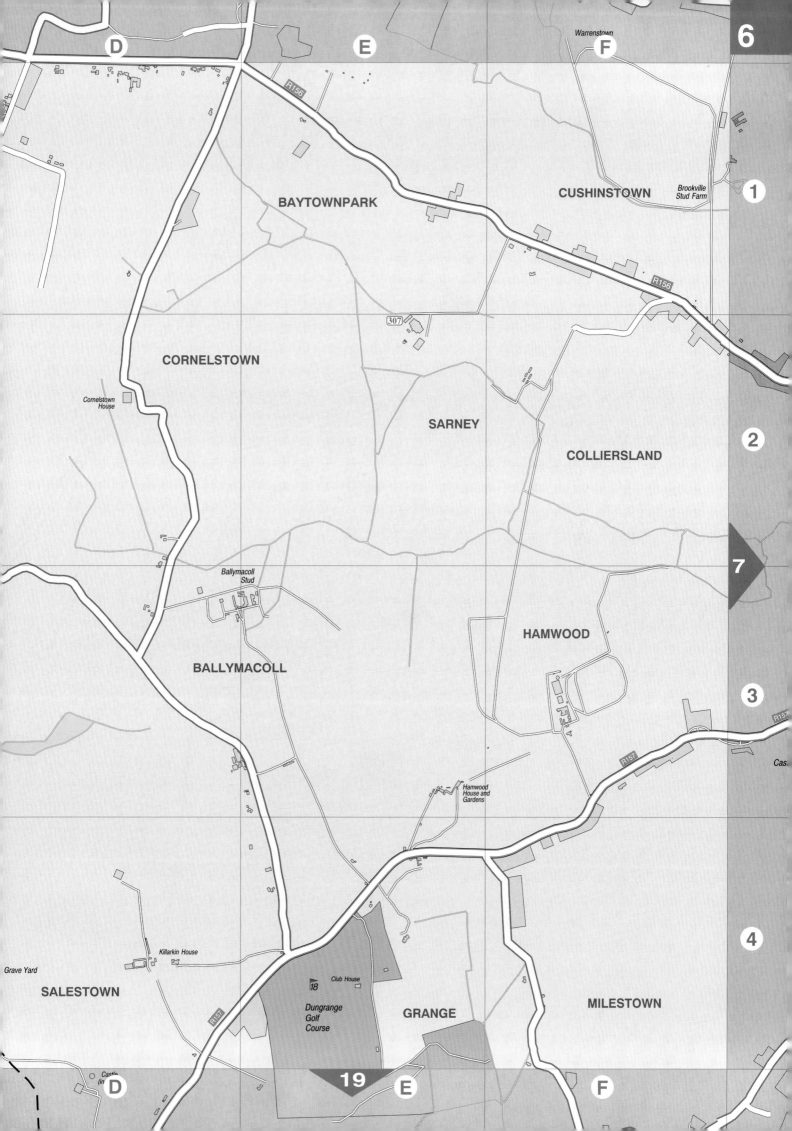

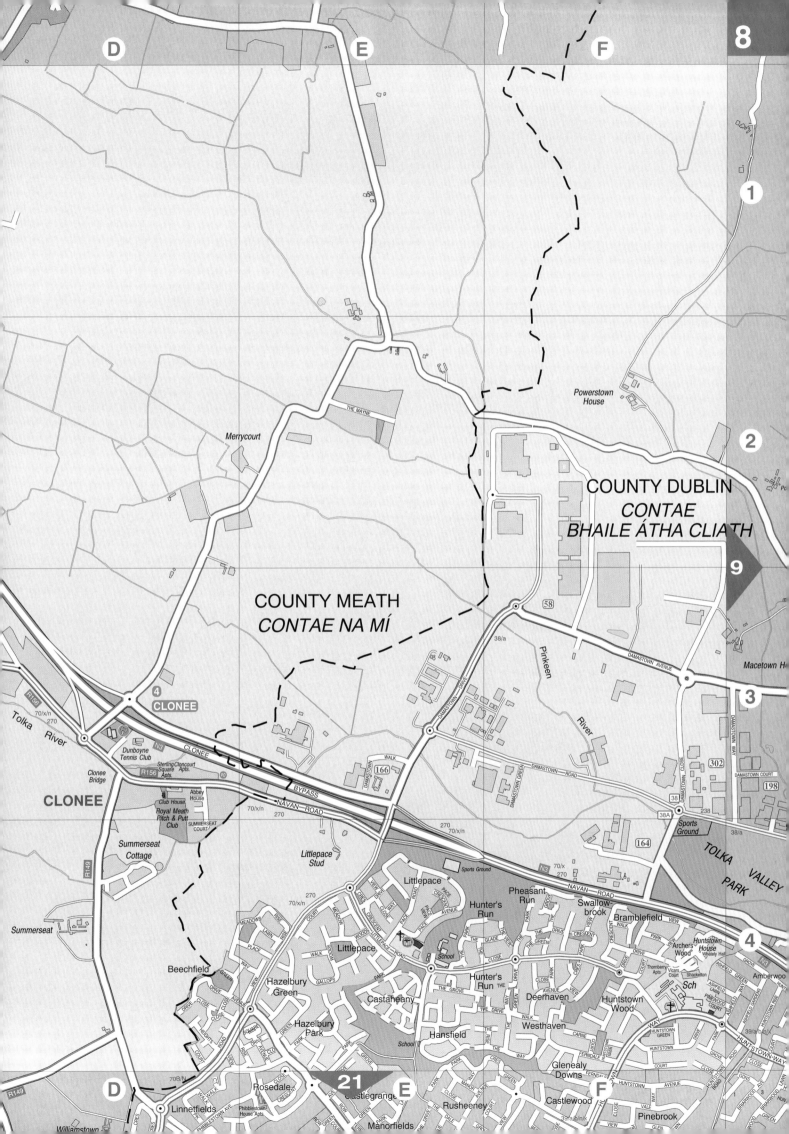

D   E   F

1

2

11

3

4

D   23   E   F

KILSHANE

CAPPOGE

Broghan
New Br.

Broghan House

Pitch
and
Putt

Dunsoghly
Castle

Newtown C

Cement Works

Kilmore House

Woodlands

Kilshane
Cross

Kilshane
House

88N

NORTH   ROAD

N2

N2

KILSHANE AVENUE

Stable Campus

Mitchelstown   Old Quarry

KILSHANE VIEW

Old Quarry Campus

KILSHANE PARK

Sports
Ground

Primeside Park

KILSHANE DRIVE

KILSHANE ROAD

Sand &
Gravel Pit

Burial
Gd

KILSHANE WAY

201

Cloghran House

236

238
236

13

38b

220

40d

220

ROSEMOUNT PARK ROAD

BALLYCOOLIN ROAD

133

ROSEMOUNT PARK DRIVE

202

CAPPAGH   ROAD

203

Cappoge
Cottages

Kildonan House

Electricity
Station

M50

88n

285

40a

Marine
Institute

Spo
Grou

2

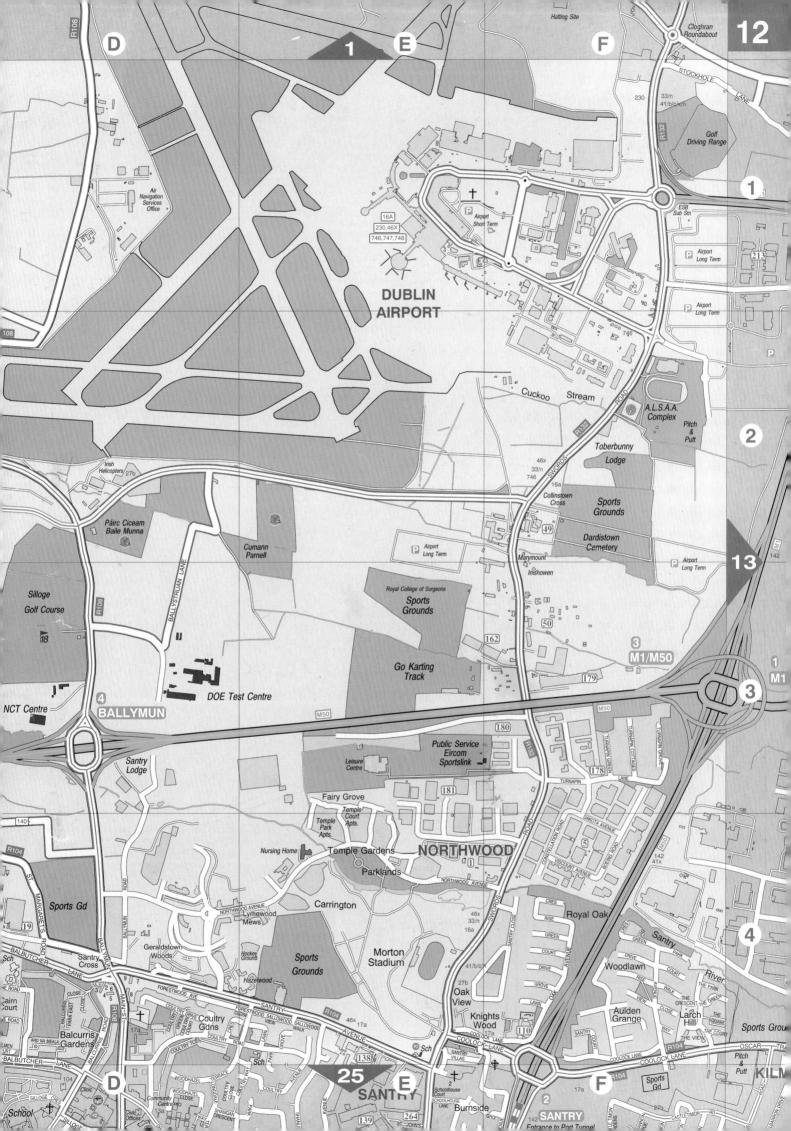

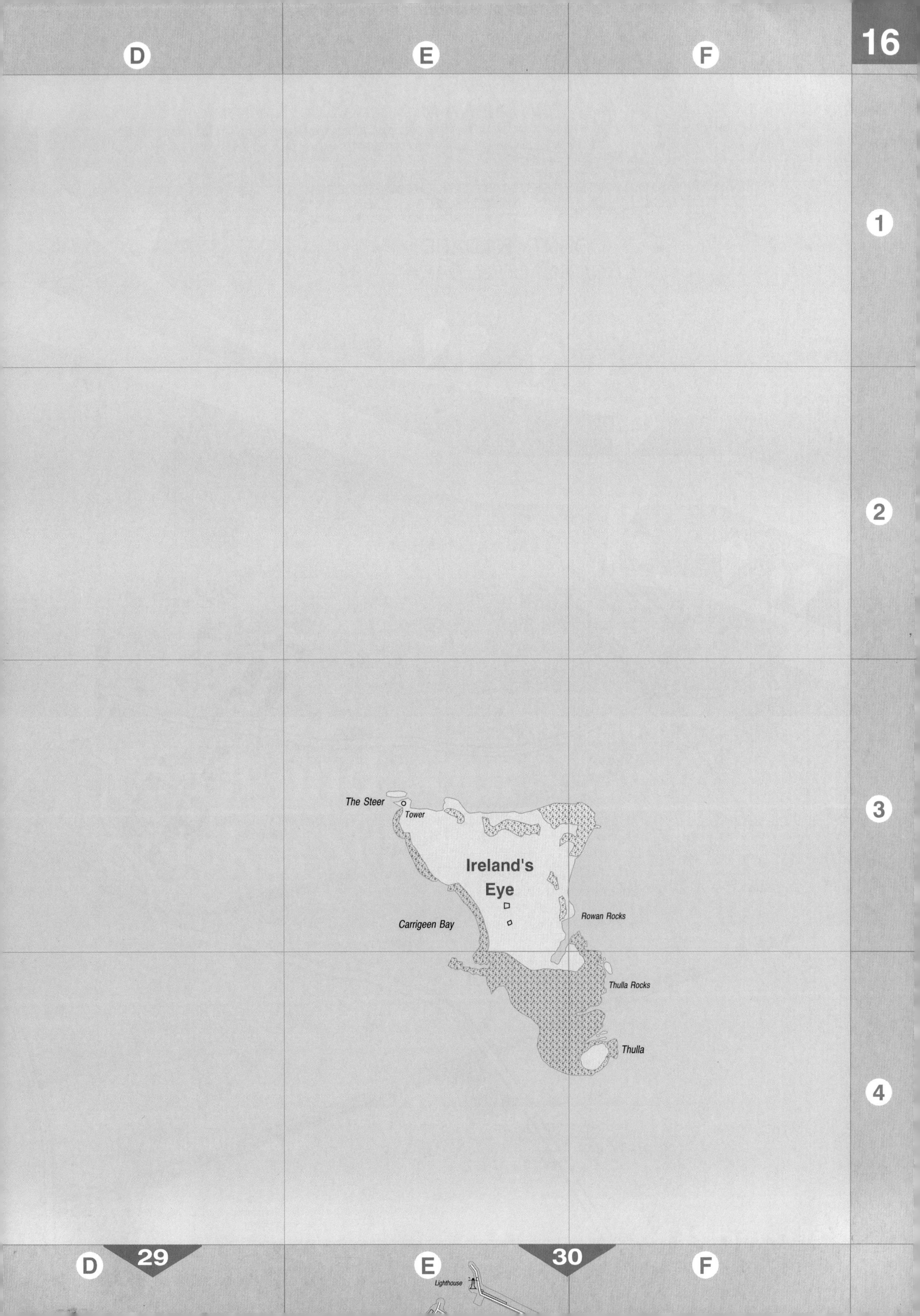
D
E
F
1
2
3
4
The Steer
Tower
Ireland's Eye
Rowan Rocks
Carrigeen Bay
Thulla Rocks
Thulla
Lighthouse

29
30

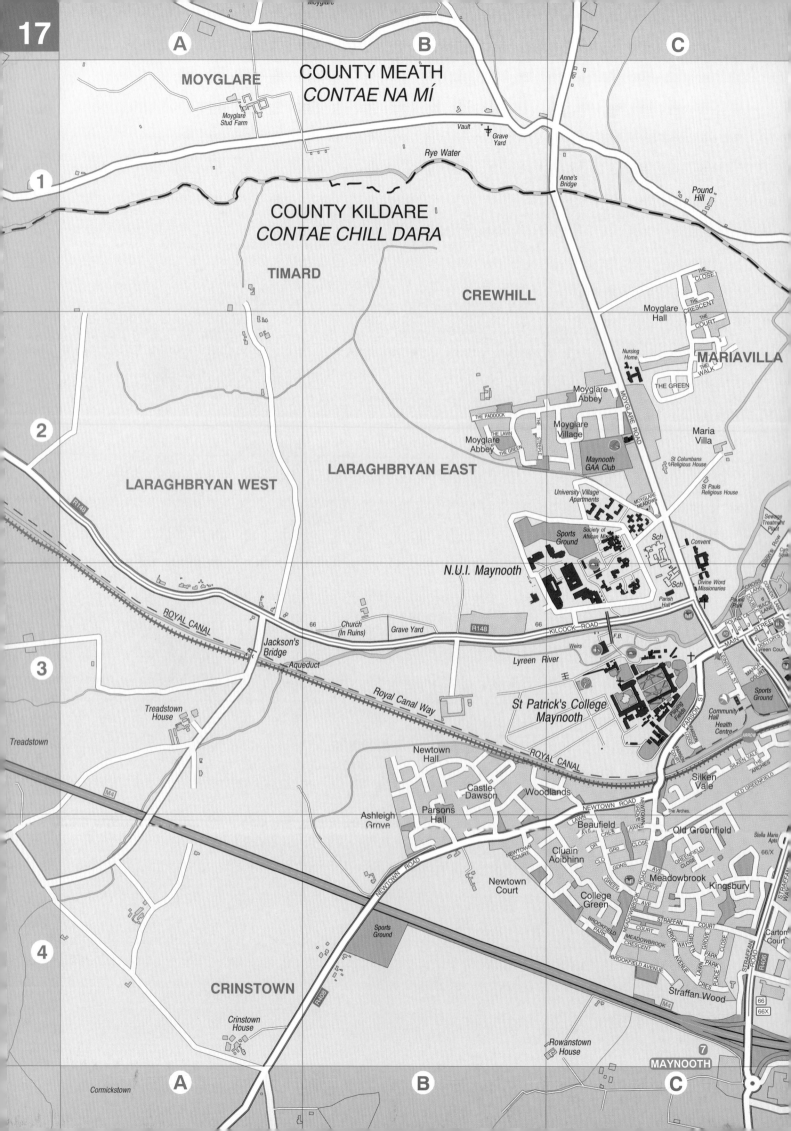

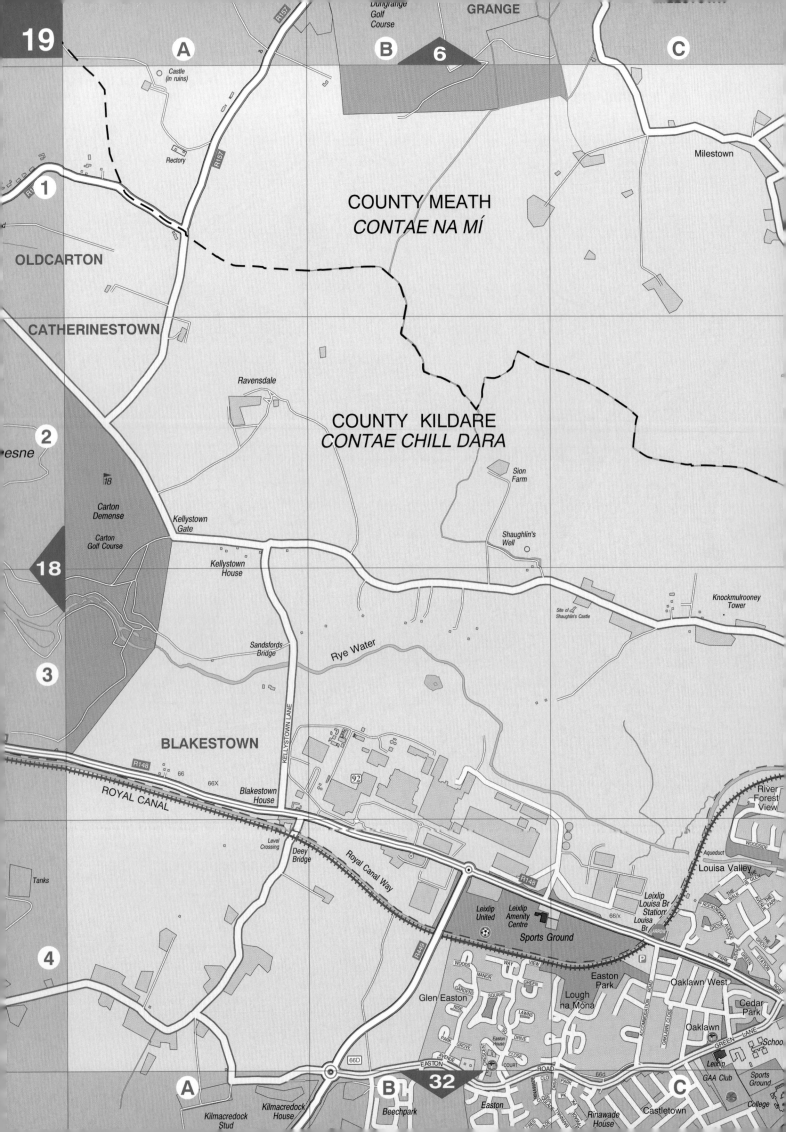

19

A   B   **6**   C

GRANGE

Dungrange
Golf
Course

R157

Castle
(in ruins)

Rectory

R157

1

OLDCARTON

Milestown

COUNTY MEATH
CONTAE NA MÍ

CATHERINESTOWN

Ravensdale

esne

2

COUNTY KILDARE
CONTAE CHILL DARA

Sion
Farm

18

Carton
Demense

Kellystown
Gate

Shaughlin's
Well

Carton
Golf Course

18

Kellystown
House

Site of
Shaughlin's Castle

Knockmulrooney
Tower

3

Sandsfords
Bridge

Rye Water

BLAKESTOWN

R148

66

66X

Blakestown
House

KELLYSTOWN LANE

92

ROYAL CANAL

Level
Crossing

Deey
Bridge

Royal Canal Way

River
Forest
View

Aqueduct

WOODSIDE

Louisa Valley

Tanks

Leixlip
United

Leixlip
Amenity
Centre

Sports Ground

R148

Leixlip
Louisa Br
Station

66/X

Louisa
Br

ARROW

4

R149

WOODS

MANOR

WAY

VIEW

GREEN

SQUARE

Easton
Park

Oaklawn West

Cedar
Park

Glen Easton

GARDENS

RISE

LAWNS

Lough
na Móna

Oaklawn

Schoo

A   66D   B   **32**   C

Kilmacredock
Stud

Kilmacredock
House

Beechpark

Easton

Rinawade
House

Castletown

Leixlip
GAA Club

Sports
Ground

College

D
7
E
F
1
2
21
3
4

The Cottage

Stirling House
Stirling Stud
R149
Sunny Bank

Hilltown House

COUNTY MEATH
CONTAE NA MÍ

COUNTY KILDARE
CONTAE CHILL DARA

Westmanstown Park

R149

Confey Abbey

Confey Park

Allenswood House

Mount Thunder

Confey Castle (in ruins)

Church (in ruins)
Leavalley

Cemetery

Confey House

COUNTY DUBLIN
CONTAE
BHAILE ÁTHA CLIATH

River Forest View
River Forest

Royal Canal Way

Leixlip Confey Station

Cope Bridge
Creighton Park
Confey

Royal Canal Amenity Group

R149

ROYAL CANAL

Collins Bridge

School
66A
66X

River Forest

River Forest

Glendale

NEWTOWN GLENDALE
66a/x/n

ST CATHERINE'S VIEW

Glendale Meadows

Sports Grounds

Rye Water

Sch

Newtown Park

Ryevale Lawns
Ryevale House

CONFEY

Ryevale Nursing Home

DISTILLERY

Avondale

66a/x/n

St Catherines Park
Lucan Demesne

Ryemont Abbey

Ryevale Lawns

St Mary's Park

Mandalay

Riverdale

St Catherines

66/x

66/n/b

Sports Ground

Schs

KNOCKAULIN

OLD HILL

CELBRIDGE ROAD
HIGHFIELD PARK

POUND ST

Rye River

CAPTAINS HILL

GROVE
CRES
PK GARDENS
CLO
AVENUE COURT

R149

MILL LANE

D
The Mall
MAIN STREET
232
33
LEIXLIP
E
Sewage Treatment Works
RIVER
F

Health Centre
Graves Yard
P
CASTLE PARK

Rye Bridge

THE BLACK

Glenwood
Laraghcon

DUBLIN BAY

15

29

Georgian Hamlet
School
Turnberry
Parkvale
SEAGRANGE PARK
Sports Ground
School
Tuscany Park
Turnberry Square
Sutton Park
SUTTON PARK
Cypress House
Sycamore House
Kilbarrack Cemetery
Sutton Downs
Sailing Club
Nursing Home
Warrenhouse Road
Strand Road
Warren Green
Moyclare Road
Moyclare Ave
Moyclare Close
Baldoyle Road
Railway Ave
Burrowfield
Level Crossing
Crescent
Court
Binn Eadair
Binn Eadair View
Nursing Home
Astro Pitch
Club House
Sutton RFC
School
Tramway Court
Sutton Station
Level Crossing
FB
DART
SUTTON
Dublin Road
R105
R106
R106
R105
Sutton Strand
Slipway
Slipway
Bayside Station
Sports Ground
School
Nursing Home

Cush Point
Club House
Sutton Golf Links
Lifeguard Station
Burrow Road
Claremont Road
Level Crossing
School
Clarer
Howth Road
R105
Glencarraig
Corr Castle
Church Road
Conv
School
Santa Sabina Manor
Greenfield Road
Offington Park
Offington Drive
Offington Avenue
Offington
Offington Court

Sutton Creek
Strand Road
Carrickbrack Road
Duncarraig
Carrickbrack Heath
Carrickbrack Hill
Carrickbrack Lawn
Sch
Howth Celtic
St. Fintans Cemetery
Old Castle Ave
La Vista Avenue
Old Quay
Old Quay Terrace
Old Quay Mews
St Fintans Park
Crescent
Sports Ground
Sutton Sailing Club
Slipway
St. Fintan's Grove
St Fintan's Crescent
School
South Hill
Shiel Martin Drive
Shiel Martin Road
Bottle Quay
Sutton Castle Apts.
Sutton House
Martello Tower
Cliff Walk
Barren Cross R Middle Mot

BEACH

31b

31b/n

1

2

3

4

D E F

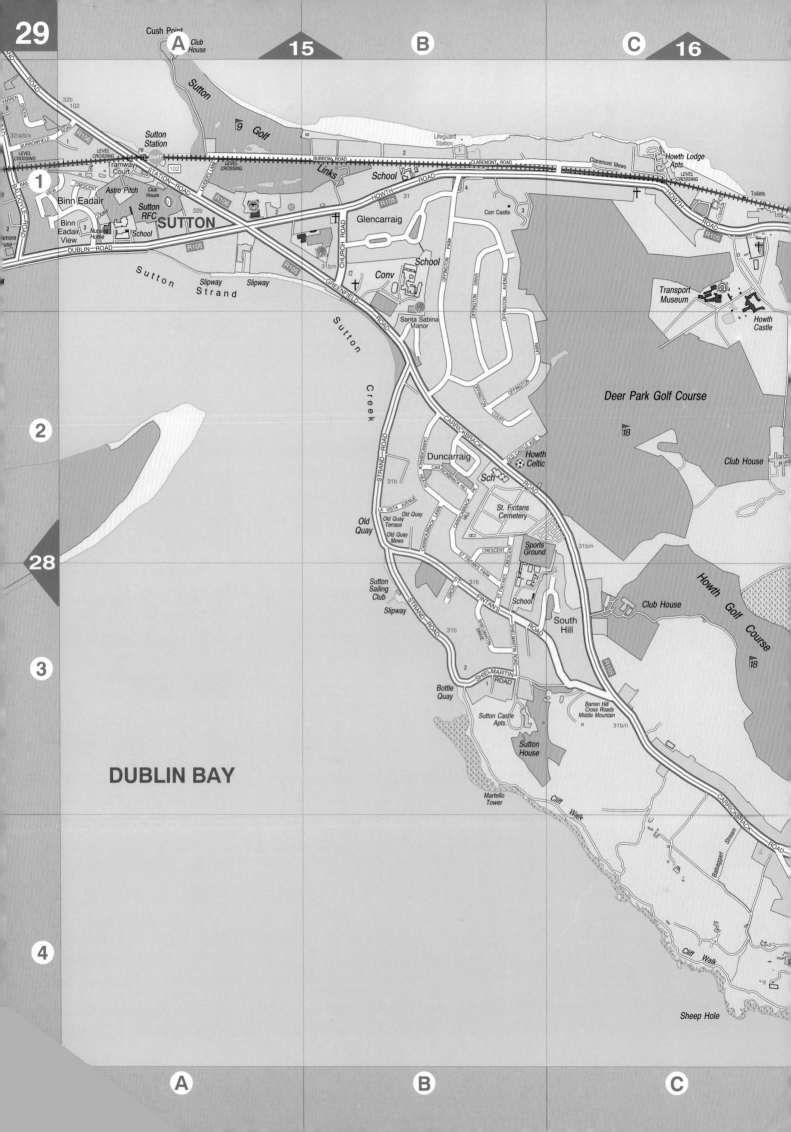

Lighthouse

WEST PIER

HOWTH
HARBOUR

Slipway
Slipway

EAST PIER

Slipway
Slipway
Lifeboat
Station
Yacht
Club

Howth
Station
DART

Slipway

Toilets

31n

HARBOUR
3 14 16
15.

CHURCH ROAD

Tower

Asgard
Apts.

Balscadden Bay

Baths

STREET
ABBEY STREET
ST LAWRENCE
EVORA PARK
GRACE O'MALLEY RD
GRACE O'MALLEY DRIVE

Health
Centre

BALSCADDEN

Sports
Ground
School

HOWTH

Puck's Rocks

ASGARD PARK

KILROCK ROAD
NASHVILLE PARK

Kilrock

Nose of Howth

Park Golf Course

Deer Park

Reservoir

TUCKETTS
ST PETER'S TERRACE
BALKILL GROVE
BALKILL PARK
BALKILL PARK

27
18

Beann Éadair
G.A.A. Club

Club
House

Woodside

BALGLASS RD
MAIN STREET

Sch

NASHVILLE ROAD

R105

ASGARD ROAD

CORRBOETER LANE

THORMANBY

Cannon Rock Estate

THORMANBY LAWNS

THORMANBY ROAD

DUNGRIFFAN ROAD

GREY'S LANE

WOODCLIFF HEIGHTS

BALKILL ROAD

Rockstown

Thormanby
Woods

MARINERS COVE

OSANA VIEW

Cannon Rock

Gull
Cottage

Cannon Rock
Cottage

Cliff Walk

Casana Rock

Green Ivy

Thormanby Lodge

WINDGATE ROAD

BALKILL ROAD

Ben
of
Howth

Loughoreen Hills
Green Hallows Quarries

The Green
Hallows

Howth Hill
Lodge Nursing
Home
Blakeney
House
(Mews)

KILESTOWN RD

31/n

The
Gate
Lodge

Piper's Gut

Fox Hole

Reservoir

WINDGATE RISE

NEW RD

BAILEY GREEN ROAD

31 31b

The
Summit

Reservoir

Tower
Baily
Green

Highroom Bed

Lough Leven

Carrickbrack
Reservoir
(Disused)

THORMANBY ROAD

Gaskin's Leap

Whitewater Brook

OLD CARRICKBRACK ROAD

CARRICKBRACK

R105 31b/n

CEANCHOR ROAD

Sisters of Charity -
Stella Maris

Cliff Walk

Glenaveena

The Great
Baily

Webb's Castle Rock

Helipad
The Little
Baily

Doldrum Bay

Lion's Head

Hippy
Hole

The Needles or
Candlesticks

Baily Lighthouse

Drumleck Point

Oaklawn

Park

Schools

Leixlip

GAA Club

Sports Ground

College

Kilmacredock Stud

Kilmacredock House

Beechpark

Easton

Easton House

Rinawade House

Castletown

CELBRIDGE — RIVER ROAD

Sports Grour

COU
KILD
COM
CHILL

6 CELBRIDGE

R449

Leixlip Gate

M4

Wonderful Barn

Barnhall

Elton Court

Leixlip Park

KILCOCK MAYNOOTH LEIXLIP BYPASS

CELBRIDGE ROAD

R404

RIVER

Crodaun Forest Park

COUNTY KILDARE
CONTAE CHILL DARA

234

Alensgrove

Reservoir

Oaklee Sheltered Housing

Castletown House

The Walled Gardens

Barnhall Rugby Club

Club House

66B

Salmon Leap Canoe Club

Sports Ground

New Bridge

Tearmannmhuire Centre

R403

67/A/N/X

Backweston State Laboratory Campus

LIFFEY

Convent

St. Wolstan's Abbey
(in ruins)

RIVER

Donaghcumper

Rock Bridge

Shinkeen Bridge

67/A/N/X

Celbridge Football Park

Bellebrook

Dara Court

Burial Ground

Community Centre

Riding School

R403

CELBRIDGE

DUBLIN ROAD

Cemetery

Church (in ruins)

Ballyoulster Park

Celbridge Golf Driving Range

St Patrick's Park

Conv School

Celbridge Lodge

Ashbrook

Shinkeen Stream

Ballyoulster Utd

Club House

Stacummy

CHURCH ROAD

Riverview Apts.

St. Wolston's Abbey

R405

Primrose Gate

Celbridge Abbey

School

Health Centre

PRIMROSE HILL

Primrose Hill

Grove Ho

Temple Lawns

The Grove

Simmonstown Park

Primrose Gate

WILLOW CRESENT

WILLOW GREEN

WILLOW DRIVE

WILLOW RISE

WILLOW VIEW

WILLOW AVENUE

Stacummy Bridge

Simmonstown Manor

Simmonstown House

Chandlers Mill

Hazelhatch Park

The Cottage

Celbridge G.A.A.

Elm Hall

Club House

Pitch and Putt Course

9

Celbridge Elm Hall Golf Club

NEWTOWN

ock Bridge

Celbridge Lawn Tennis Club

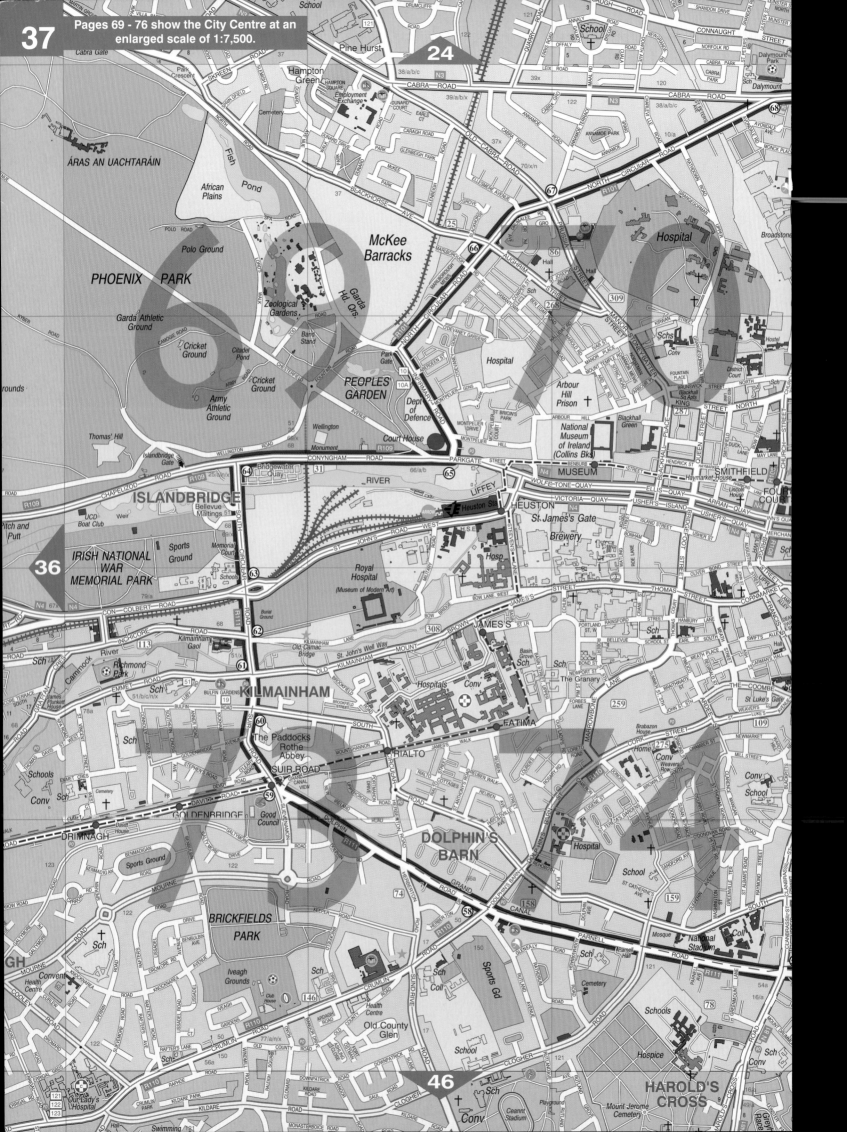

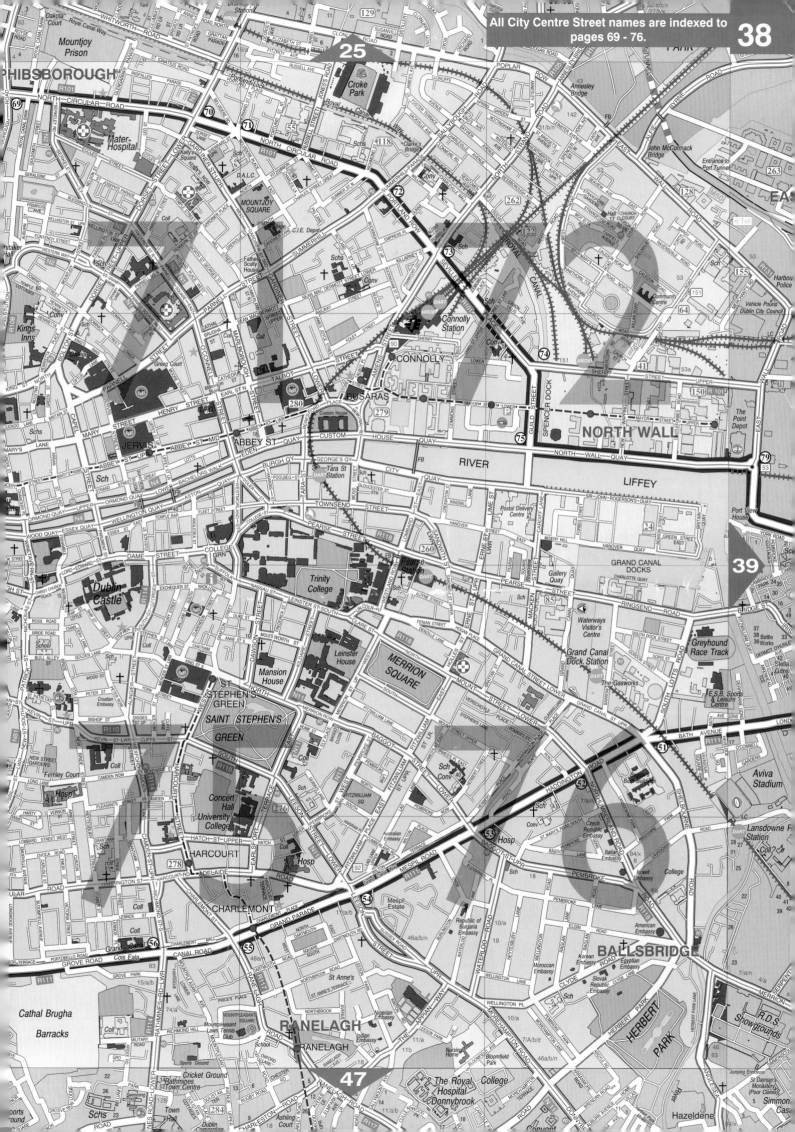

D

Wooden
Bridge

Seascout Den
Bull Wall Cottages

Bull Wall

Lighthous

A

Park
The Cottage

Mill

41

helmsford

SIMMONSTOWN

1

**COUNTY KILDARE
CONTAE CHILL DARA**

32

B

Elm Hall

Club
House

Celbrid

Celbridge Lawn
Tennis Club

R405

STRALEEK

The Laurels

Ha

COMMONS LOWER

DANG

2

KE A

DUBLIN   BAY

4

D

49

E

F

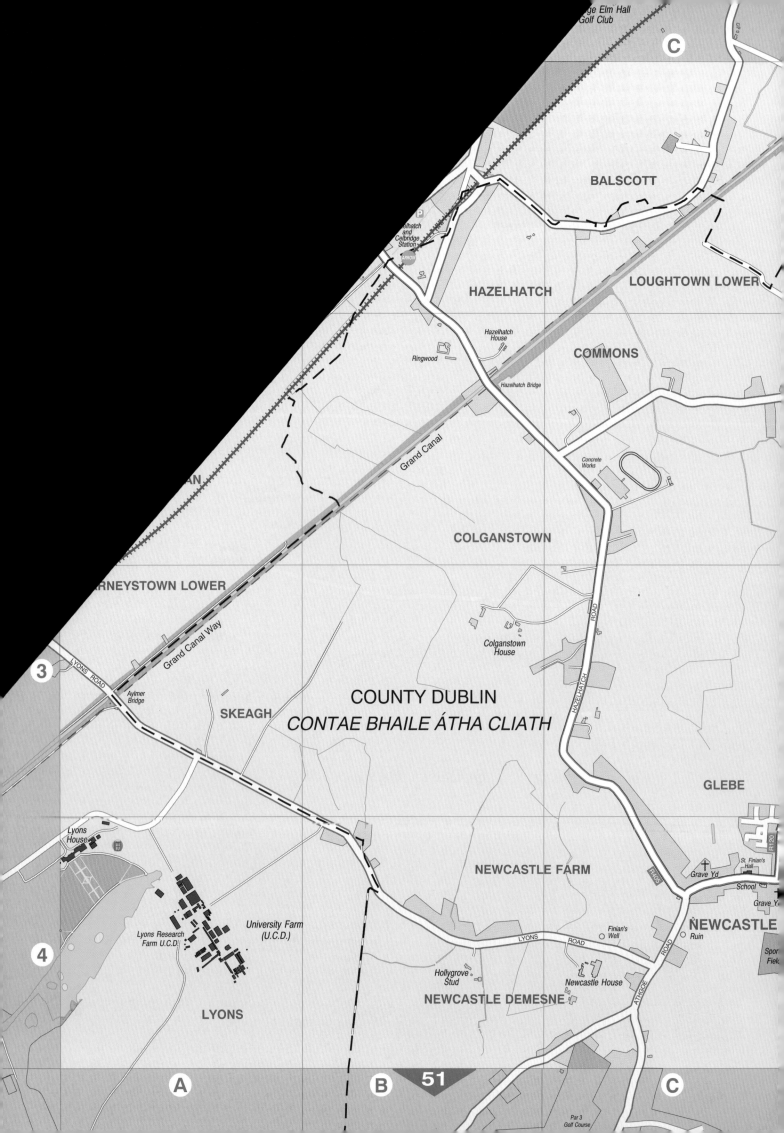

ge Elm Hall
Golf Club

BALSCOTT

P

zelhatch and
Celbridge
Station

ARROW

HAZELHATCH

LOUGHTOWN LOWER

Hazelhatch
House

Ringwood

COMMONS

Hazelhatch Bridge

Grand Canal

Concrete
Works

COLGANSTOWN

ROAD

Colganstown
House

HAZELHATCH

RNEYSTOWN LOWER

AN

Grand Canal Way

LYONS ROAD

Aylmer
Bridge

SKEAGH

COUNTY DUBLIN
CONTAE BHAILE ÁTHA CLIATH

GLEBE

R120

Lyons
House

St. Finian's
Hall

Grave Yd

School

Grave Y

NEWCASTLE FARM

R405

NEWCASTLE

Finian's
Well

Ruin

University Farm
(U.C.D.)

Lyons Research
Farm U.C.D.

LYONS
ROAD

Spor
Fiel

Hollygrove
Stud

Newcastle House

ATHGOE ROAD

NEWCASTLE DEMESNE

LYONS

Par 3
Golf Course

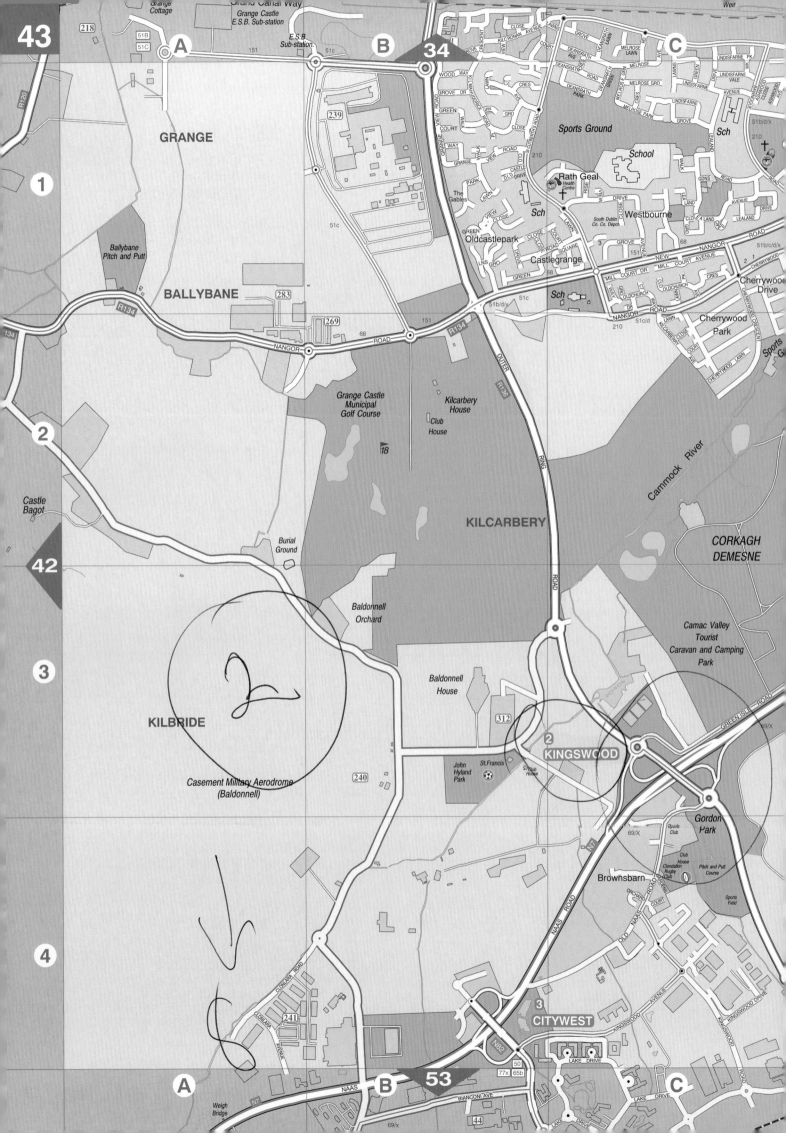

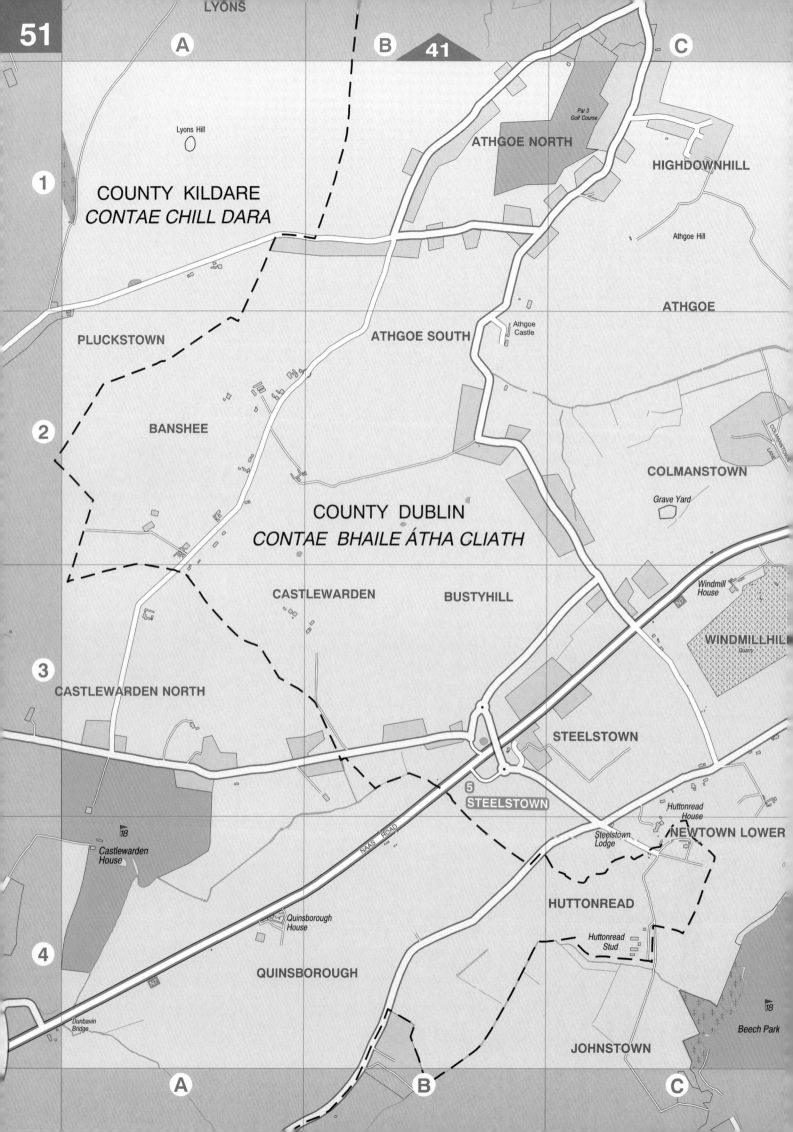

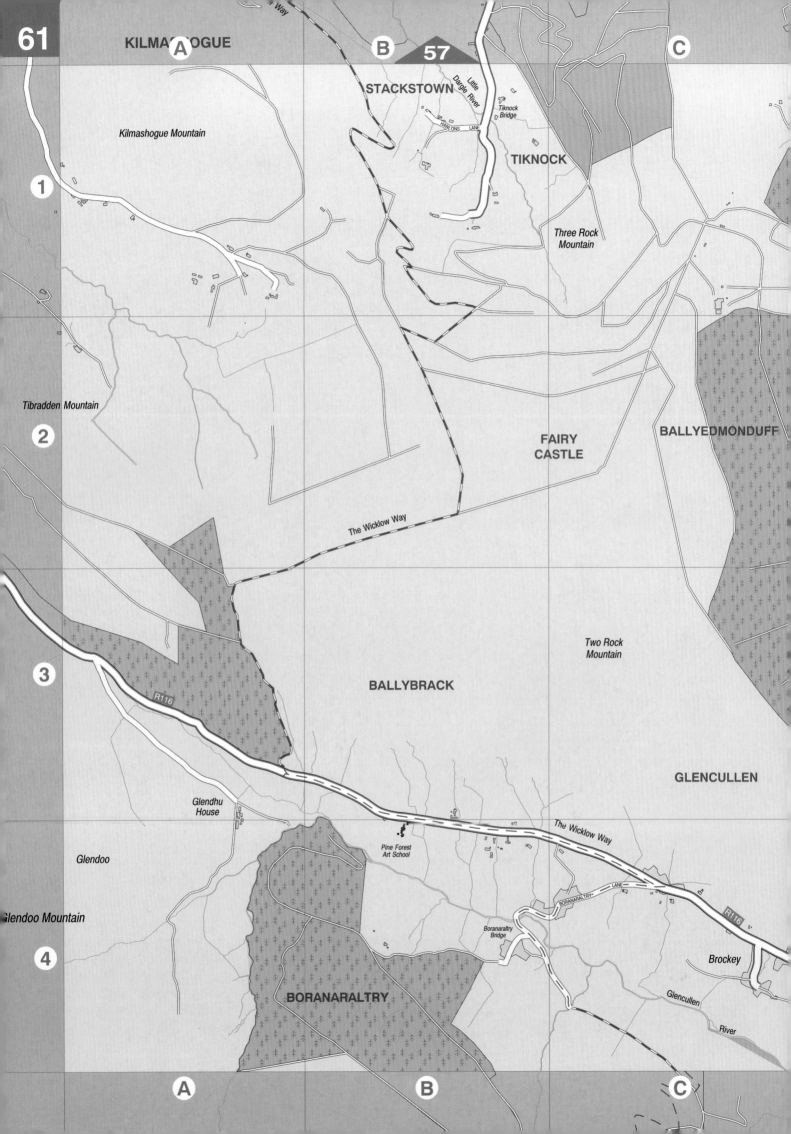

BARNACULLIA

Stepaside Village
Par 3 Golf Course
Kilgobbin Lawn

Cruagh Wood
Wingfield
Cairnfort

Stepaside Public Golf Course
18

Jamestown Cottages

STEPASIDE

Ballyedmonduff

Jamestown Par 3 Golf Course

Driving Range

Stepaside Golf Centre

Jamestown House

Pinecroft

Bridon

Club House

De la salle Palmerston F.C.

JAMESTOWN

Sports Ground

GLENAMUCK NORTH

Club House
Sch

Glebe

Grave Yard
44
Sch

Shaldon Grange

Rectory

Long Meadow

Greenmount Lodge

Cromlech Close

Golden Ball

Glenamuck

63

Rockville

Quarry

Quarry

Quarry

Brackloon House

Cruagh

Filter Weir

Barnacullia Water Works

Taylors Folly

Knockbracken

Cromlech Lodge

Water Works

Kilternan Abbey

KILTERNAN

Wayside Cottages

Sports Gd

Sports Gd

44

118
63

BALLYCORUS ROAD

R116

Sch

Bishop's Lane

Grave Yard

Kilternan Lodge

Adult Education School

Mill House

Kilternan Bridge

Cuckoo Field

Carrowkeel Stud

Ballyedmonduff House

Newtown House

Kestrel Lodge

Evesham

Sunnyside

Verny House

44

Pinefield House

Giants Grave

Glencullen Pitch & Putt

Stone

NEWTOWN

BALLYEDMONDUFF ROAD

R116

BALLYBETAGH ROAD

Ballybetagh House

Ballybetagh Wood

9

Glencullen Golf Course

Old Grave Yard

Grave Yard

Sch

GLENCULLEN

Glenacre

Dinish

BALLYBETAGH

R116

FIERY LANE

Par 3 Golf Course

44

The Moors

Butter Well

Glencullen House

Eagle Lodge

COUNTY DUBLIN
CONTAE BHAILE ÁTHA CLIATH

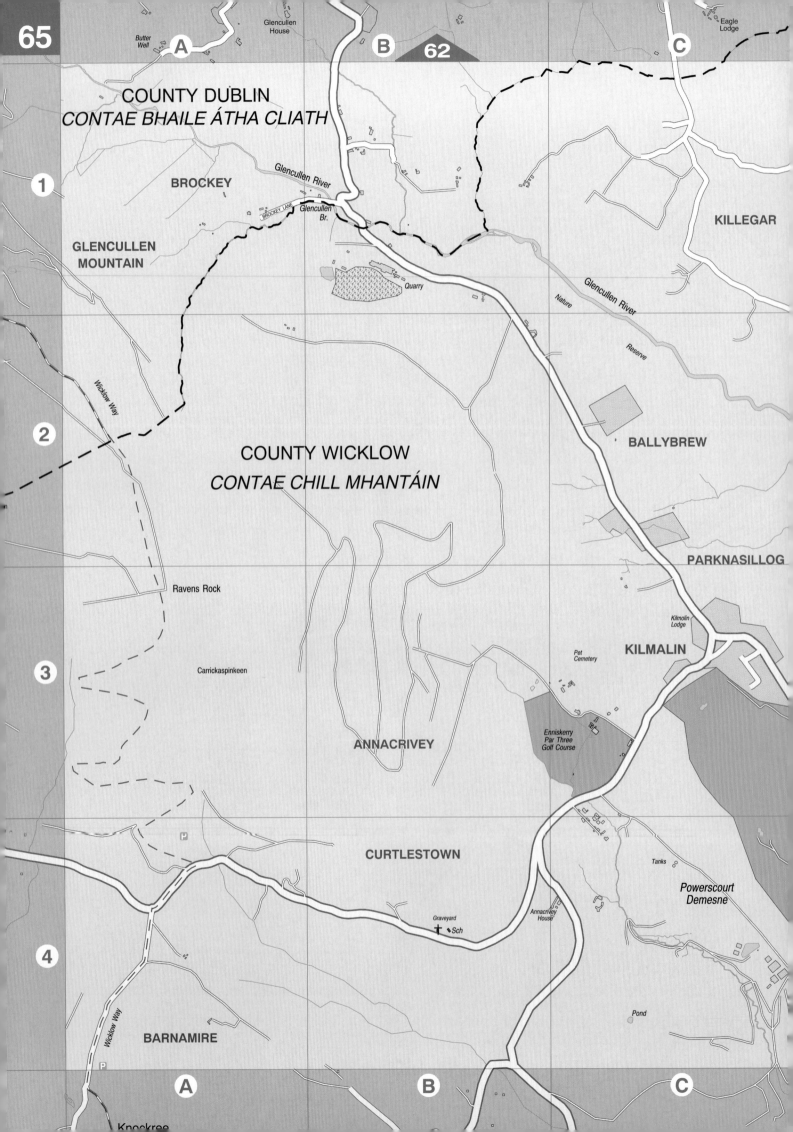

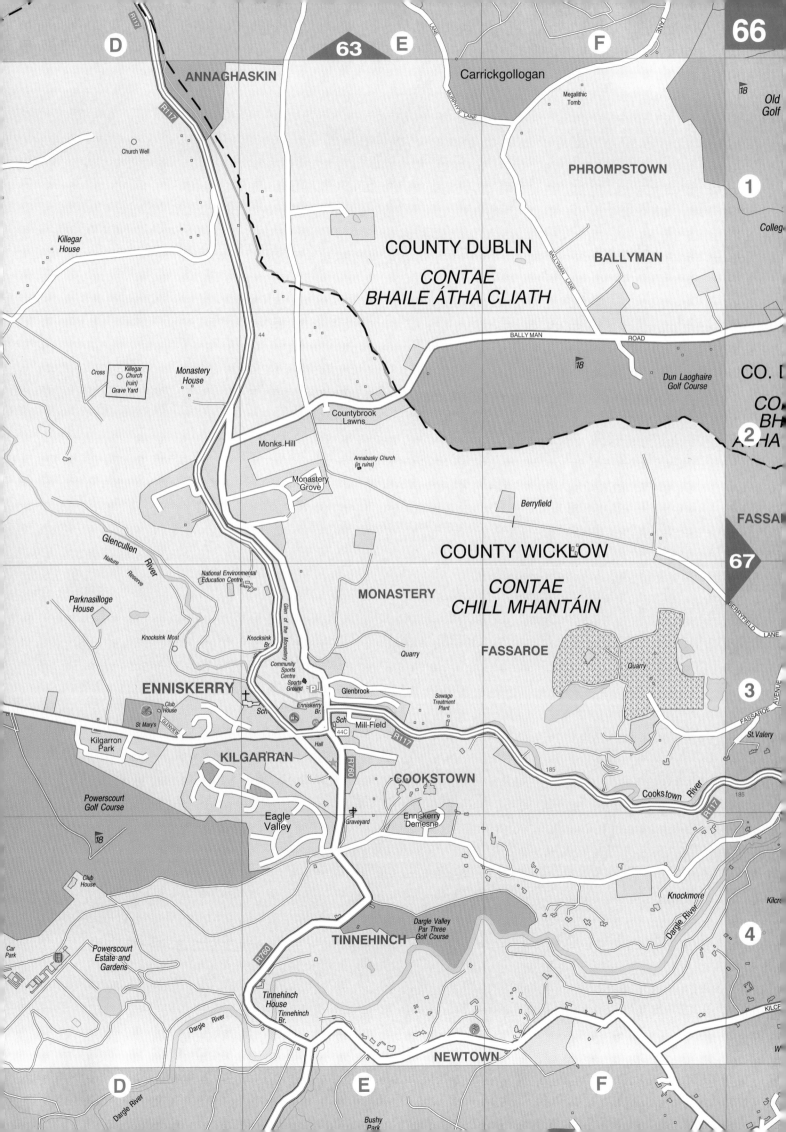

D E F

1

BRAY

National
Sea Life
Aquarium

2

Naylor's Cove

Fontenoy
Terrace

RAHEEN PARK

Raheenacluig Church
(in Ruins)

Golf Course

3

Briar
Wood

Bray
Head

Tunnel

NEWCOURT

COUNTY WICKLOW

4

18 Bray Golf Club

CONTAE
CHILL MHANTÁIN

Tunnel

184
84/X/N

Tunnel
Tunnel

D E F

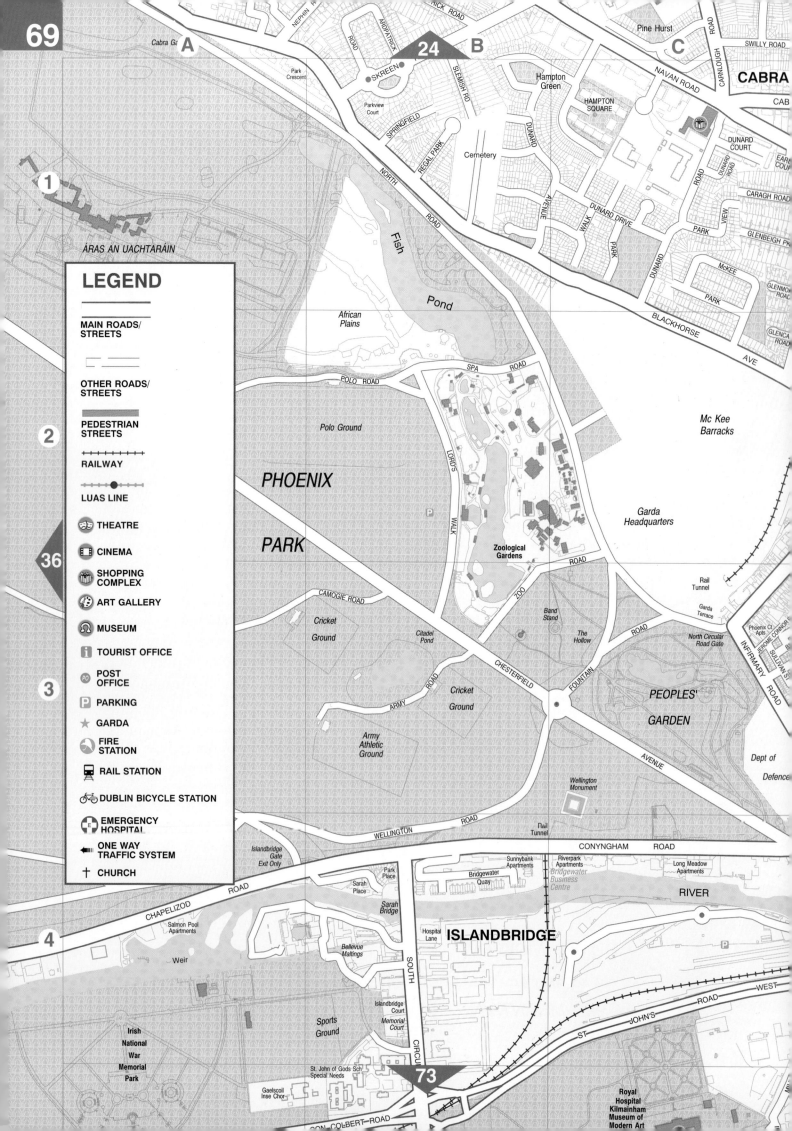

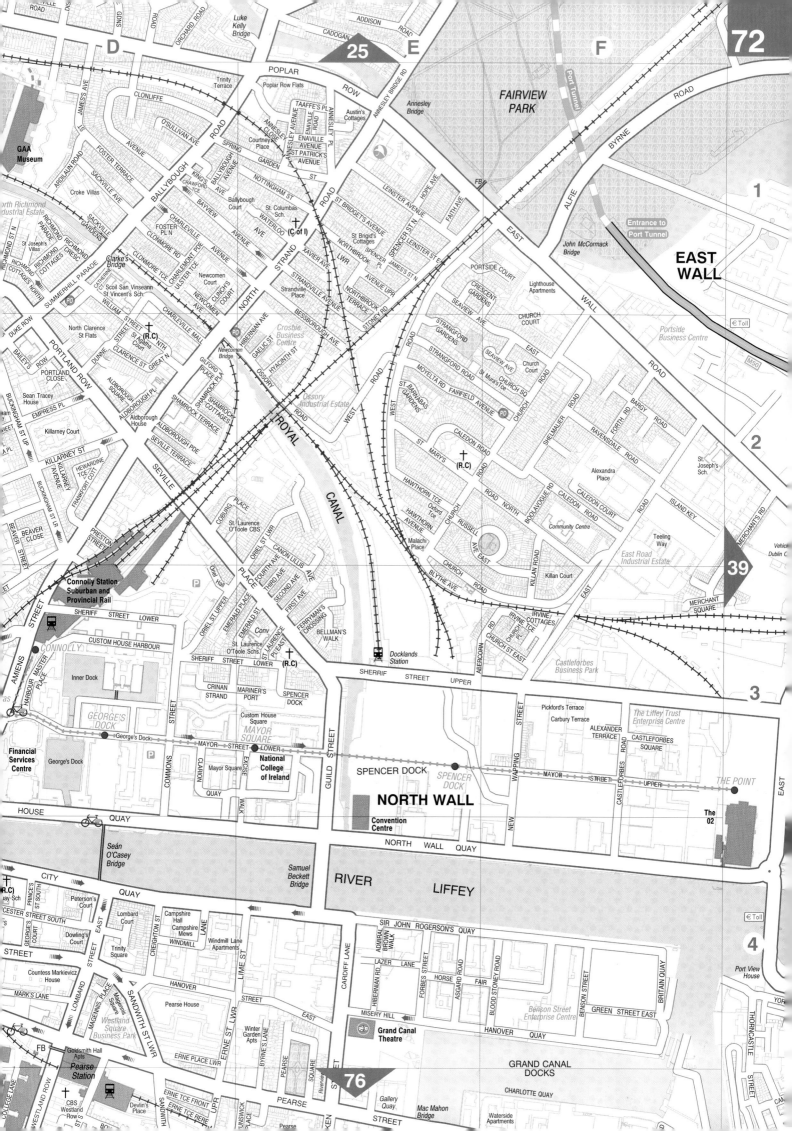

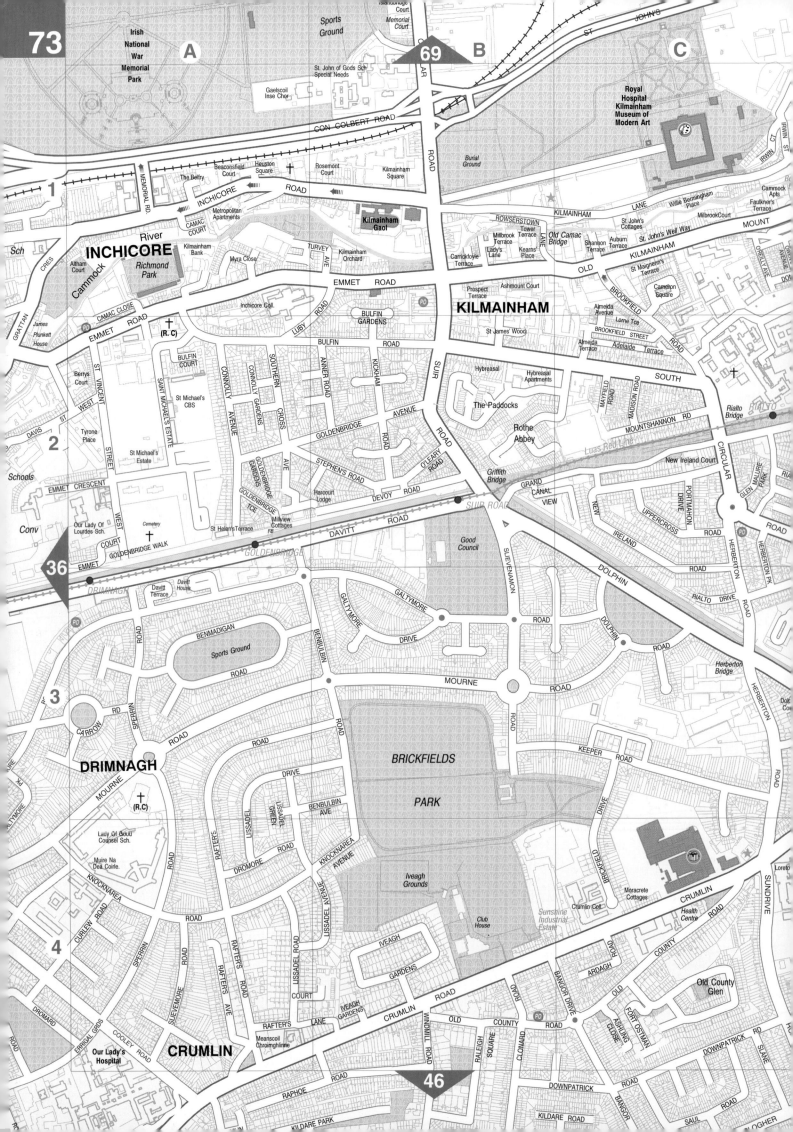

A

69

B

C

Irish
National
War
Memorial
Park

Sports
Ground

Islandbridge
Court

Memorial
Court

ST. JOHN'S

Royal
Hospital
Kilmainham
Museum of
Modern Art

St. John of Gods Sch
Special Needs

Gaelscoil
Inse Chor

CON COLBERT ROAD

Burial
Ground

IRWIN

Cammock Apts

1

The Beltry

Beaconsfield
Court

Heuston
Square

Rosemont
Court

Kilmainham
Square

ROAD

KILMAINHAM

LANE

Willie Bermingham
Place

Milbrook Court

Faulkner's
Terrace

INCHICORE

ROAD

ROWERSTOWN
LANE

St John's
Cottages

MOUNT

CAMAC
COURT

Metropolitan
Apartments

Millbrook
Terrace

Tower
Terrace

Old Camac
Bridge

Auburn
Terrace

St. John's Well Way

River
Cammock

Kilmainham
Bank

Kilmainham
Gaol

Carrickfoyle
Terrace

Lady's
Lane

Kearns
Place

Shannon
Terrace

KILMAINHAM

O'REILLY AVE

INCHICORE

Altham
Court

Richmond
Park

Kilmainham
Orchard

OLD

St Maignenn's
Terrace

Cameron
Square

Sch

CRES

Myra Close

EMMET ROAD

Prospect
Terrace

Ashmount Court

BROOKFIELD

Almeida
Avenue

James
Plunkett
House

CAMAC CLOSE

Inchicore Coll.

St James' Wood

KILMAINHAM

Lorne Tce

Rialto

PO

BULFIN
GARDENS

PO

BROOKFIELD STREET

GRATTAN

EMMET

ROAD

LUBY

ROAD

BULFIN

ROAD

Almeida
Terrace

Adelaide Terrace

ROAD

(R. C)

Hybreasal

SOUTH

Rialto Bridge

2

Berrys
Court

BULFIN
COURT

CONNOLLY

KICKHAM

Hybreasal
Apartments

MAYFIELD
ROAD

MADISON ROAD

WEST

ST VINCENT

St Michael's
CBS

CONNOLLY GARDENS

ANNER ROAD

The Paddocks

MOUNTSHANNON RD

Tyrone
Place

SAINT MICHAEL'S ESTATE

SOUTHERN

AVENUE

Rothe
Abbey

Luas Red Line

DAVIS

ST

St Michael's
Estate

CROSS

GOLDENBRIDGE

ROAD

New Ireland Court

CIRCULAR

GLEN MAURE PARK

ROAD

Schools

EMMET CRESCENT

GOLDENBRIDGE GARDENS

AVE

STEPHEN'S ROAD

O'LEARY

SUIR

Griffith
Bridge

GRAND
CANAL
VIEW

NEW

PORTMAHON

UPPERCROSS

DRIVE

HERBERTON

Conv

WEST

Cemetery

GOLDENBRIDGE
TCE

Harcourt
Lodge

ROAD

ROAD

IRELAND

ROAD

Our Lady Of
Lourdes Sch.

COURT

St Helen's Terrace

Millview
Cottages
FB

DEVOY

ROAD

Good
Council

DOLPHIN

HERBERTON PK

36

EMMET

GOLDENBRIDGE WALK

DAVITT

ROAD

ROAD

RIALTO DRIVE

ROAD

GOLDENBRIDGE

SLIEVENAMON

Herberton
Bridge

DRIMNAGH

Davitt
Terrace

Davitt
House

ROAD

GALTYMORE

ROAD

DOLPHIN

Dolpt
Cot

3

CARROW

RD

SPERRIN

ROAD

BENMADIGAN

Sports Ground

ROAD

GALTYMORE

DRIVE

GALTYMORE

MOURNE

ROAD

KEEPER

ROAD

ROAD

BENBULBIN

BRICKFIELD

DRIMNAGH

MOURNE

ROAD

(R. C)

LISSADEL

DRIVE

BENBULBIN

BENBULBIN
AVE

ROAD

BRICKFIELDS

PARK

CRUMLIN

Lady Of Good
Counsel Sch.

LISSADEL
GREEN

KNOCKNAREA

Moracrete
Cottages

CRUMLIN

Muire Na
Dea Coirle.

ROAD

DROMORE
ROAD

AVENUE

Iveagh
Grounds

Crumlin Cott.

Health
Centre

Loreto

KNOCKNAREA

RAFTER'S

LISSADEL AVENUE

Club
House

Sunshine
Industrial
Estate

ROAD

SUNDRIVE

4

CURLEW ROAD

SLIEVEMORE

ROAD

RAFTER'S ROAD

LISSADEL ROAD

IVEAGH

GARDENS

BANGOR DRIVE

ARDAGH

ROAD

Old County
Glen

DROMARD

ERRIGAL GRDS

ROAD

RAFTER'S
COURT

RAFTER'S
LANE

IVEAGH
GARDENS

CRUMLIN

ROAD

WINDMILL ROAD

OLD

COUNTY

ROAD

FORT OSTMAN

ASHLING CLOSE

ROAD

GALTYMORE

Our Lady's
Hospital

COOLEY ROAD

CRUMLIN

Meánscoil
Chroimghlinne

RAPHOE

RAFTER'S

ROAD

RALEIGH
SQUARE

CLONARD

BANGOR
ROAD

SAUL

SLANE

DOWNPATRICK

46

DOWNPATRICK

ROAD

KILDARE PARK

KILDARE ROAD

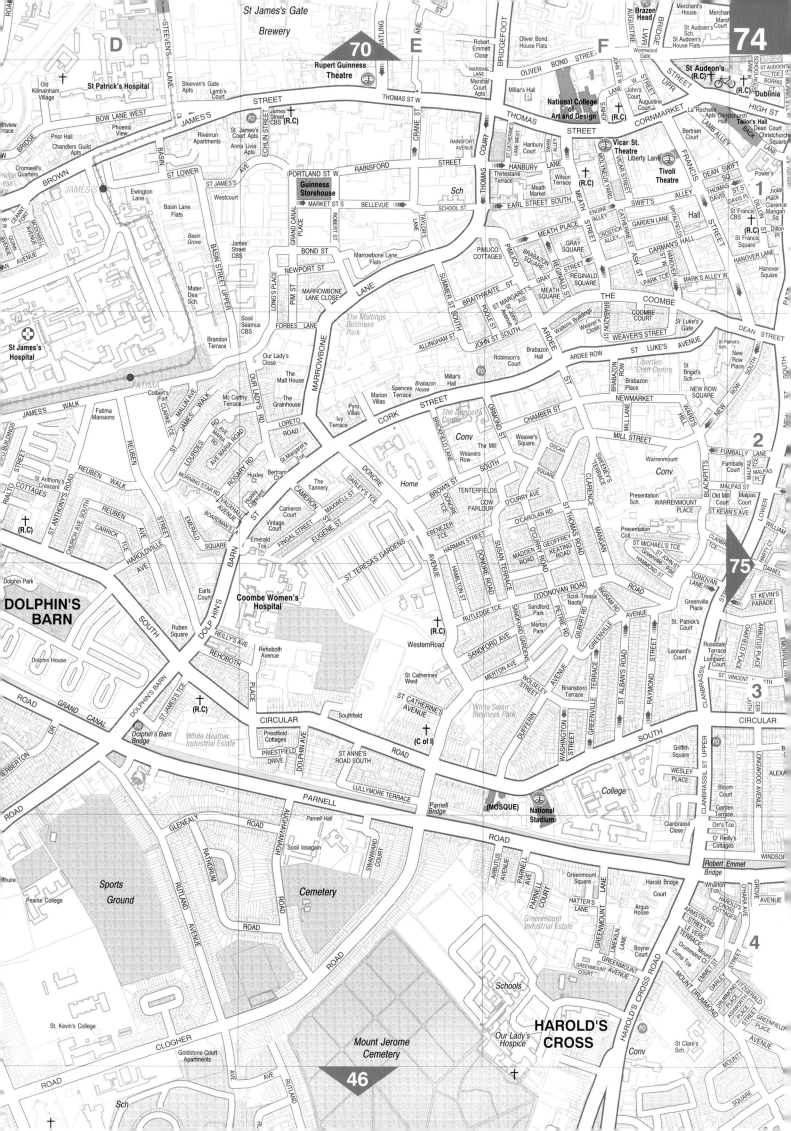

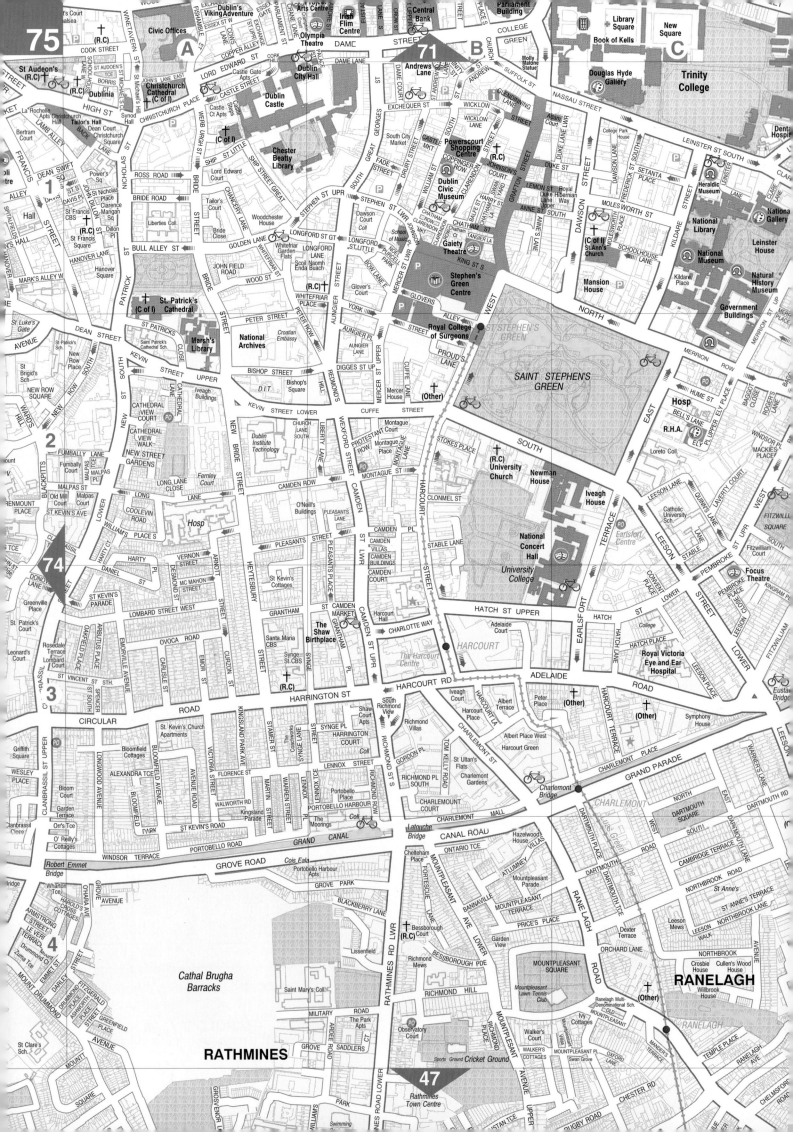

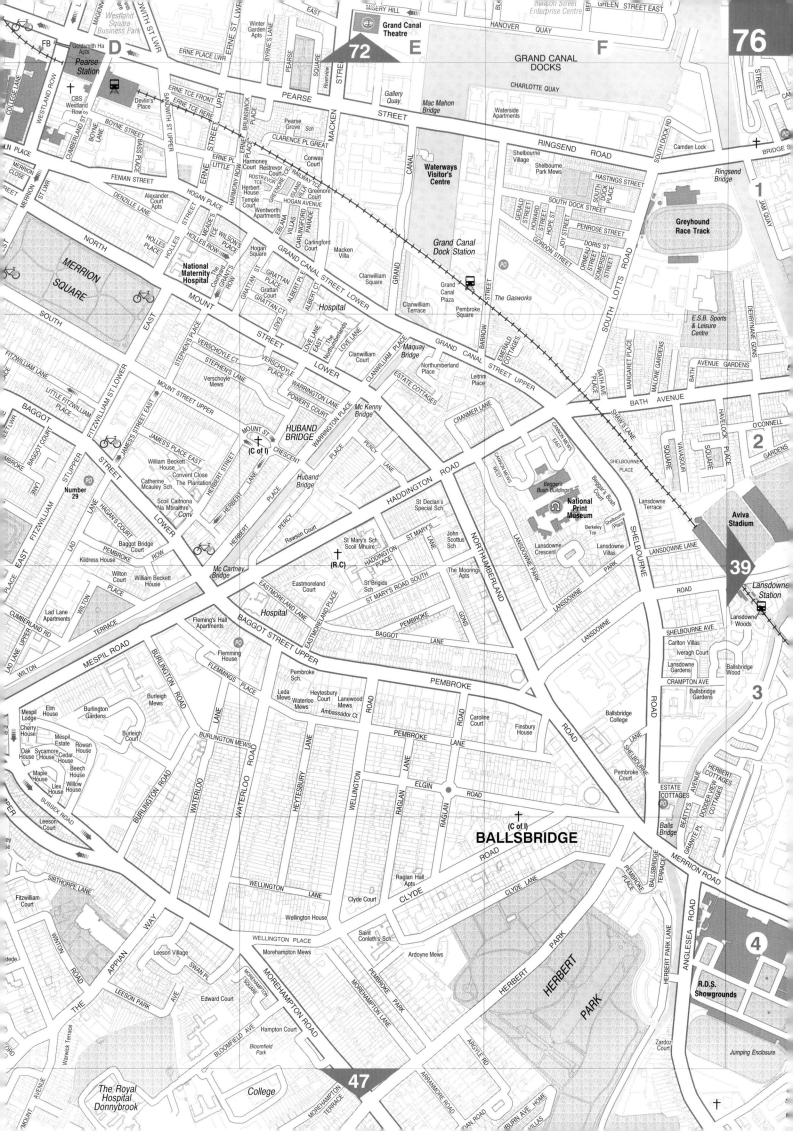

ASHBOURNE

LEGEND

M1	MOTORWAY
N9	NATIONAL PRIMARY ROAD
N81	NATIONAL SECONDARY ROAD
R683	REGIONAL ROAD
	MAIN ROADS/ STREETS
	OTHER ROADS/ STREETS
	NARROW / STREET PRIVATE ROADS
	ROAD UNDER CONSTRUCTION
	PEDESTRIAN STREETS
	BUILT UP AREA
	GREEN AREA
	WOODED AREA
	COMMERCIAL / INDUSTRIAL
	HOSPITAL / SCHOOL
	WATER
✚	HOSPITAL
	FIRE STATION
★	GARDA
P	PARKING
PO	POST OFFICE
†	CHURCH
▪	MONUMENT / STATUE
	LIGHTHOUSE
←	ONE WAY STREETS
	MAINLINE RAIL STATION
	ART GALLERY
	SAMPLE LANDMARK BUILDING
	CINEMA
	GAELIC GROUND
	LIBRARY
	MUSEUM
	RUGBY GROUND
i	TOURIST OFFICE
	SHOPPING COMPLEX
	SCHOOL / COLLEGE
	SOCCER GROUND
	THEATRE
	VISITOR CENTRE
⚑	GOLF COURSE
▲	CAMPING SITE
	CARAVAN SITE
	RAIL LINE

L C
(Level Crossing)

1

2

3

A

B

To Slane

To Slane

R135

Ashbourne Industrial Park

Monument

Rath Cross Roads

Ashbourne Retail Park

Rath Cross Business Park

Rath Lodge

BALLYBIN ROAD

Ashbourne Industrial Park

Tudor Grove

Westfield Green

Tudor Close

GROVE

Westfield View

GREEN

Saint Johns Wood Court

Tudor Crescent

Brindley Park

SQUARE

CRESCENT

Saint Johns Wood Park

KILDERRY HALL

Ashbourne Business Park

ROAD

St Johns Wood Drive

CLUAIN RI

Healt Centre

COURT

Cookstown Bridge

CRESCENT

GROVE

RISE

PARK

AVENUE

Killegland Park

Millbourne

HALL

Club House

Donaghmore Ashbourne GLC

KILLEGLAND

BOURNE VIEW

WESTVIEW

To Ratoath

Factory

R125

Factory

To Finglas

A

B

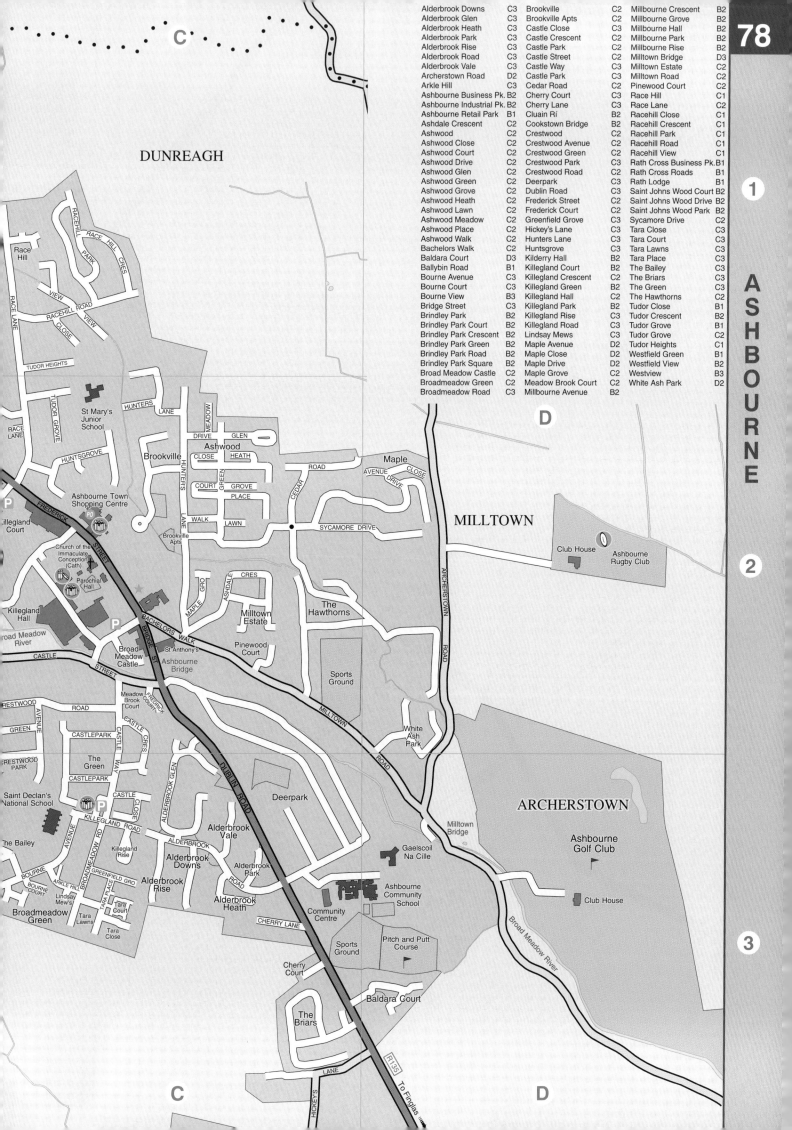

Street	Grid	Street	Grid	Street	Grid
Alderbrook Downs	C3	Brookville	C2	Millbourne Crescent	B2
Alderbrook Glen	C3	Brookville Apts	C2	Millbourne Grove	B2
Alderbrook Heath	C3	Castle Close	C3	Millbourne Hall	B2
Alderbrook Park	C3	Castle Crescent	C2	Millbourne Park	B2
Alderbrook Rise	C3	Castle Park	C2	Millbourne Rise	B2
Alderbrook Road	C3	Castle Street	C2	Milltown Bridge	D3
Alderbrook Vale	C3	Castle Way	C3	Milltown Estate	C2
Archerstown Road	D2	Castle Park	C3	Milltown Road	C2
Arkle Hill	C3	Cedar Road	C2	Pinewood Court	C2
Ashbourne Business Pk.	B2	Cherry Court	C3	Race Hill	C1
Ashbourne Industrial Pk.	B2	Cherry Lane	C3	Race Lane	C2
Ashbourne Retail Park	B1	Cluain Rí	B2	Racehill Close	C1
Ashdale Crescent	C2	Cookstown Bridge	B2	Racehill Crescent	C1
Ashwood	C2	Crestwood	C2	Racehill Park	C1
Ashwood Close	C2	Crestwood Avenue	C2	Racehill Road	C1
Ashwood Court	C2	Crestwood Green	C2	Racehill View	C1
Ashwood Drive	C2	Crestwood Park	C3	Rath Cross Business Pk.	B1
Ashwood Glen	C2	Crestwood Road	C2	Rath Cross Roads	B1
Ashwood Green	C2	Deerpark	C3	Rath Lodge	B1
Ashwood Grove	C2	Dublin Road	C3	Saint Johns Wood Court	B2
Ashwood Heath	C2	Frederick Street	B2	Saint Johns Wood Drive	B2
Ashwood Lawn	C2	Frederick Court	C2	Saint Johns Wood Park	B2
Ashwood Meadow	C2	Greenfield Grove	C3	Sycamore Drive	C2
Ashwood Place	C2	Hickey's Lane	C3	Tara Close	C3
Ashwood Walk	C2	Hunters Lane	C3	Tara Court	C3
Bachelors Walk	C2	Huntsgrove	C3	Tara Lawns	C3
Baldara Court	D3	Kilderry Hall	B2	Tara Place	C3
Ballybin Road	B1	Killegland Court	B2	The Bailey	C3
Bourne Avenue	C3	Killegland Crescent	C2	The Briars	C3
Bourne Court	C3	Killegland Green	B2	The Green	C3
Bourne View	B3	Killegland Hall	C2	The Hawthorns	C3
Bridge Street	C3	Killegland Park	B2	Tudor Close	B1
Brindley Park	B2	Killegland Rise	C3	Tudor Crescent	B2
Brindley Park Court	B2	Killegland Road	C3	Tudor Grove	B1
Brindley Park Crescent	B2	Lindsay Mews	C3	Tudor Grove	C2
Brindley Park Green	B2	Maple Avenue	D2	Tudor Heights	C1
Brindley Park Road	B2	Maple Close	D2	Westfield Green	B1
Brindley Park Square	B2	Maple Drive	D2	Westfield View	B2
Broad Meadow Castle	C2	Maple Grove	C2	Westview	B3
Broadmeadow Green	C2	Meadow Brook Court	C2	White Ash Park	D2
Broadmeadow Road	C3	Millbourne Avenue	B2		

BALBRIGGAN

1
2
3

BREMORE

To Drogheda

Dublin-Belfast Railway

Cardy Rock

Sports Ground

FLEMINGTOWN

R132

COURT

WALK

CLOSE

AVE

CRES

SQUARE

O'Dwyers GAA Club

Club House

St Molaga's Church (in Ruins)

Castle

Sports Ground

Saint Molaga's National School

Lambeeche

FLEMINGTON LANE

VIEW

GROVE

DRIVE

Mount Rochford

CLOSE

AVE

PARK

HAMLET

CLO

ROAD

RISE

New Haven

COURT

RISE

AVE

CRESCENT

Clonuske

CLOSE

W

DROGHEDA ROAD

Baths

ROAD

Dún Saithne

CLO

PARK

COURT

GREEN

GREEN

HAMLET

LANE

GREEN

Bremore Castle

RISE

RISE

DRIVE

GREEN

Neilsfield Court

Flemington Park

PLACE AVE

ROW

BREGA

HAMLET

Ashfield

BREMORE CT

BREMORE DRIVE

New Haven Bay

Trimleston

HAMLET

AVENUE

Chieftain's

BREMORE CASTLE GATE

HAMLET LANE

CLOSE

WAY

Hampton Woods

RISE

CLOSE

GREEN

COVETOWN

Hastings

AVENUE

HAMLET

LANE

MEWS

ROAD

TEMPLE VILLE

Chapel Gate

Oakleigh

CLOSE

LAWN

COURT

DRIVE

GREEN

Barons Hall Rise

HAMLET SQ

DRIVE

PLACE

CRES

ROAD

Moylaragh Park

CHAPEL GROVE

Brecan Close

Balbriggan Community College

Brackenwood

Castlemill

Barons Hall Park

CRESCENT

Moylaragh

CRESCENT

CHAPEL CLOSE

CHAPEL AVENUE

AVENUE

PLACE

Balbriggan Educate Together National School

Barons Hall Grove

DRIVE

AVENUE

GATE

Bremore Pastures

GREEN

WAY

LANE

MOYLARAGH GDNS

MEWS

Moylaragh

DRIVE

GROVE

Moylaragh Walk

Westbrook

GROVE

CHAPEL

PINE RIDGE

Saint Peter and Paul's Junior School

CRESCENT

AVENUE

MEWS

LANE

WAY

AVENUE

RISE

CLOSE

DRIVE

CHAPEL

Martello

RISE

ROAD

VIEW

PARK

WALK

CLOSE

TCE

MEWS

CLOSE

HEIGHTS

GREEN

PARK

LN

GREEN

AVENUE

PROSPECT

TARA COURT

FULLAM TCE

CRESCENT

St. Peter and Paul's Cemetery

RISE

CLONARD

TARA COVE

CLONARD ROAD

Saint George's National School

CLOGHEDER

HARRY REYNOLDS ROAD

Balbriggan Business Park

Fingal Bay Business Park

CLONARD or FOLKSTOWN GREAT

Stephenstown Business Park

R122

To M1 and Naul

M1

STEPHENSTOWN

Halting Site

FOLKSTOWN LITTLE

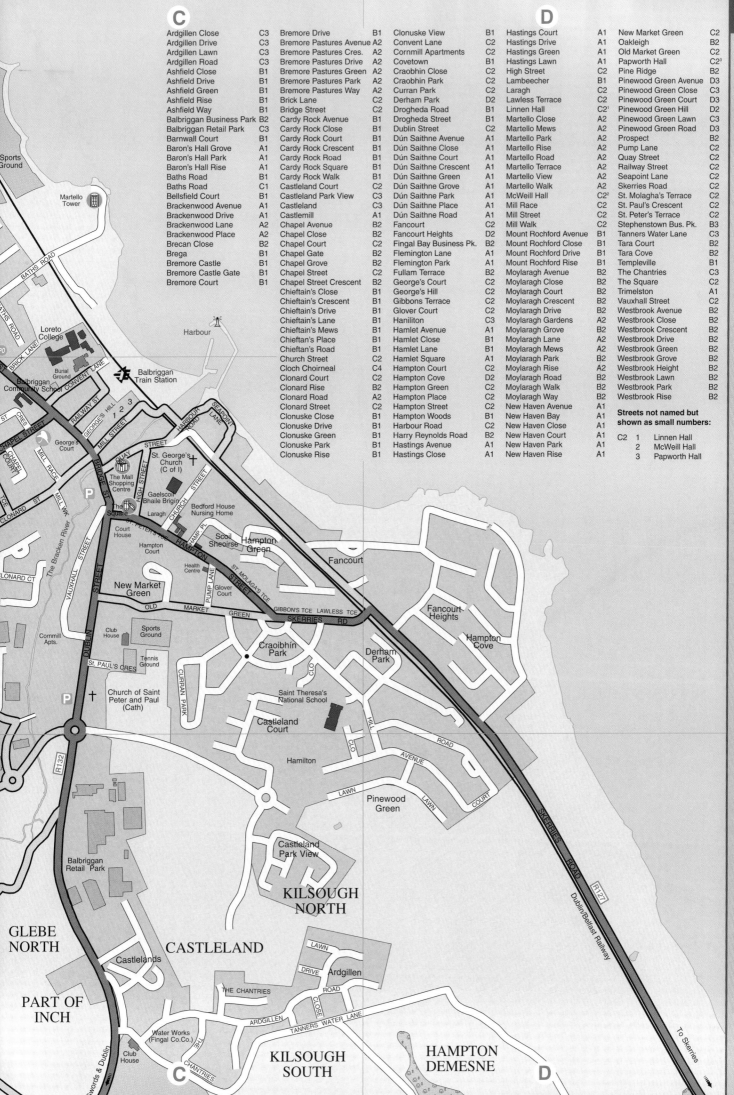

Ardgillen Close	C3	
Ardgillen Drive	C3	
Ardgillen Lawn	C3	
Ardgillen Road	C3	
Ashfield Close	B1	
Ashfield Drive	B1	
Ashfield Green	B1	
Ashfield Rise	B1	
Ashfield Way	B1	
Balbriggan Business Park	B2	
Balbriggan Retail Park	C3	
Barnwall Court	B2	
Baron's Hall Grove	A1	
Baron's Hall Park	A1	
Baron's Hall Rise	A1	
Baths Road	B1	
Baths Road	C1	
Bellsfield Court	B1	
Brackenwood Avenue	A1	
Brackenwood Drive	A1	
Brackenwood Lane	A2	
Brackenwood Place	A2	
Brecan Close	B2	
Brega	B1	
Bremore Castle	B1	
Bremore Castle Gate	B1	
Bremore Court	B1	

Bremore Drive	B1	
Bremore Pastures Avenue	A2	
Bremore Pastures Cres.	A2	
Bremore Pastures Drive	A2	
Bremore Pastures Green	A2	
Bremore Pastures Park	A2	
Bremore Pastures Way	A2	
Brick Lane	C2	
Bridge Street	C2	
Cardy Rock Avenue	B1	
Cardy Rock Close	B1	
Cardy Rock Court	B1	
Cardy Rock Crescent	B1	
Cardy Rock Road	B1	
Cardy Rock Square	B1	
Cardy Rock Walk	B1	
Castleland Court	C2	
Castleland Park View	C3	
Castleland	C3	
Castlemill	A1	
Chapel Avenue	B2	
Chapel Close	B2	
Chapel Court	C2	
Chapel Gate	B2	
Chapel Grove	B2	
Chapel Street	C2	
Chapel Street Crescent	B2	
Chieftain's Close	B1	
Chieftain's Crescent	B1	
Chieftain's Drive	B1	
Chieftain's Lane	B1	
Chieftain's Mews	B1	
Chieftan's Place	B1	
Chieftan's Road	B1	
Church Street	C2	
Cloch Choirneal	C4	
Clonard Court	C2	
Clonard Rise	B2	
Clonard Road	A2	
Clonard Street	C2	
Clonuske Close	B1	
Clonuske Drive	B1	
Clonuske Green	B1	
Clonuske Park	B1	
Clonuske Rise	B1	

Clonuske View	B1	
Convent Lane	C2	
Cornmill Apartments	C2	
Covetown	B1	
Craobhin Close	C2	
Craobhin Park	C2	
Curran Park	C2	
Derham Park	D2	
Drogheda Road	B1	
Drogheda Street	B1	
Dublin Street	C2	
Dún Saithne Avenue	A1	
Dún Saithne Close	A1	
Dún Saithne Court	A1	
Dún Saithne Crescent	A1	
Dún Saithne Green	A1	
Dún Saithne Grove	A1	
Dún Saithne Park	A1	
Dún Saithne Place	A1	
Dún Saithne Road	A1	
Fancourt	C2	
Fancourt Heights	D2	
Fingal Bay Business Pk.	B2	
Flemington Lane	A1	
Flemington Park	A1	
Fullam Terrace	B2	
George's Court	C2	
George's Hill	C2	
Gibbons Terrace	C2	
Glover Court	C2	
Haniliton	C3	
Hamlet Avenue	A1	
Hamlet Close	B1	
Hamlet Lane	B1	
Hamlet Square	A1	
Hampton Court	C2	
Hampton Cove	D2	
Hampton Green	C2	
Hampton Place	C2	
Hampton Street	C2	
Hampton Woods	B1	
Harbour Road	C2	
Harry Reynolds Road	B2	
Hastings Avenue	A1	
Hastings Close	A1	

Hastings Court	A1	
Hastings Drive	A1	
Hastings Green	A1	
Hastings Lawn	A1	
High Street	C2	
Lambeecher	B1	
Laragh	C2	
Lawless Terrace	C2	
Linnen Hall	C2¹	
Martello Close	A2	
Martello Mews	A2	
Martello Park	A2	
Martello Rise	A2	
Martello Road	A2	
Martello Terrace	A2	
Martello View	A2	
Martello Walk	A2	
McWeill Hall	C2²	
Mill Race	C2	
Mill Street	C2	
Mill Walk	C2	
Mount Rochford Avenue	B1	
Mount Rochford Close	B1	
Mount Rochford Drive	B1	
Mount Rochford Rise	B1	
Moylaragh Avenue	B2	
Moylaragh Close	B2	
Moylaragh Court	B2	
Moylaragh Crescent	B2	
Moylaragh Drive	B2	
Moylaragh Gardens	A2	
Moylaragh Grove	A2	
Moylaragh Lane	A2	
Moylaragh Mews	A2	
Moylaragh Park	B2	
Moylaragh Rise	A2	
Moylaragh Road	B2	
Moylaragh Walk	B2	
Moylaragh Way	B2	
New Haven Avenue	A1	
New Haven Bay	A1	
New Haven Close	A1	
New Haven Court	A1	
New Haven Park	A1	
New Haven Rise	A1	

New Market Green	C2	
Oakleigh	B2	
Old Market Green	C2	
Papworth Hall	C2³	
Pine Ridge	B2	
Pinewood Green Avenue	D3	
Pinewood Green Close	C3	
Pinewood Green Court	D3	
Pinewood Green Hill	D2	
Pinewood Green Lawn	C3	
Pinewood Green Road	D3	
Prospect	B2	
Pump Lane	C2	
Quay Street	C2	
Railway Street	C2	
Seapoint Lane	C2	
Skerries Road	C2	
St. Molagha's Terrace	C2	
St. Paul's Crescent	C2	
St. Peter's Terrace	C2	
Stephenstown Bus. Pk.	B3	
Tanners Water Lane	C2	
Tara Court	B2	
Tara Cove	B2	
Templeville	B1	
The Chantries	C3	
The Square	C2	
Trimelston	A1	
Vauxhall Street	C2	
Westbrook Avenue	B2	
Westbrook Close	B2	
Westbrook Crescent	B2	
Westbrook Drive	B2	
Westbrook Green	B2	
Westbrook Grove	B2	
Westbrook Height	B2	
Westbrook Lawn	B2	
Westbrook Park	B2	
Westbrook Rise	B2	

Streets not named but shown as small numbers:

C2	1	Linnen Hall
	2	McWeill Hall
	3	Papworth Hall

BALBRIGGAN

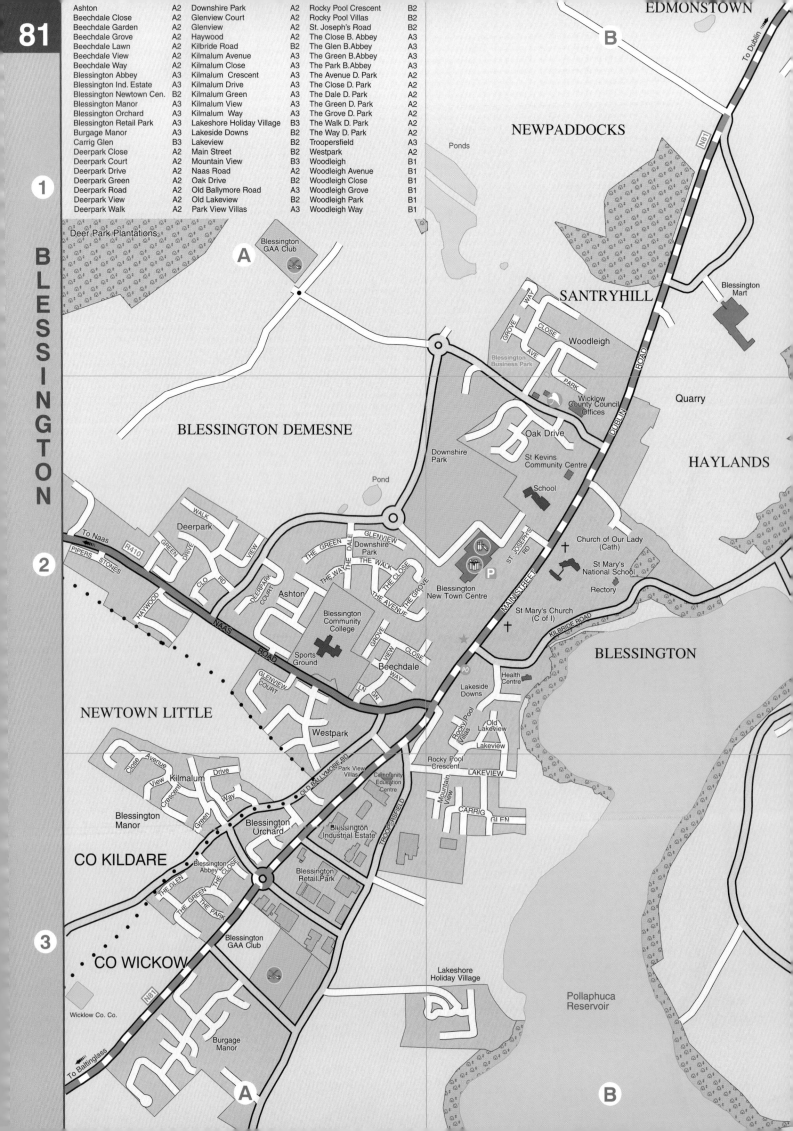

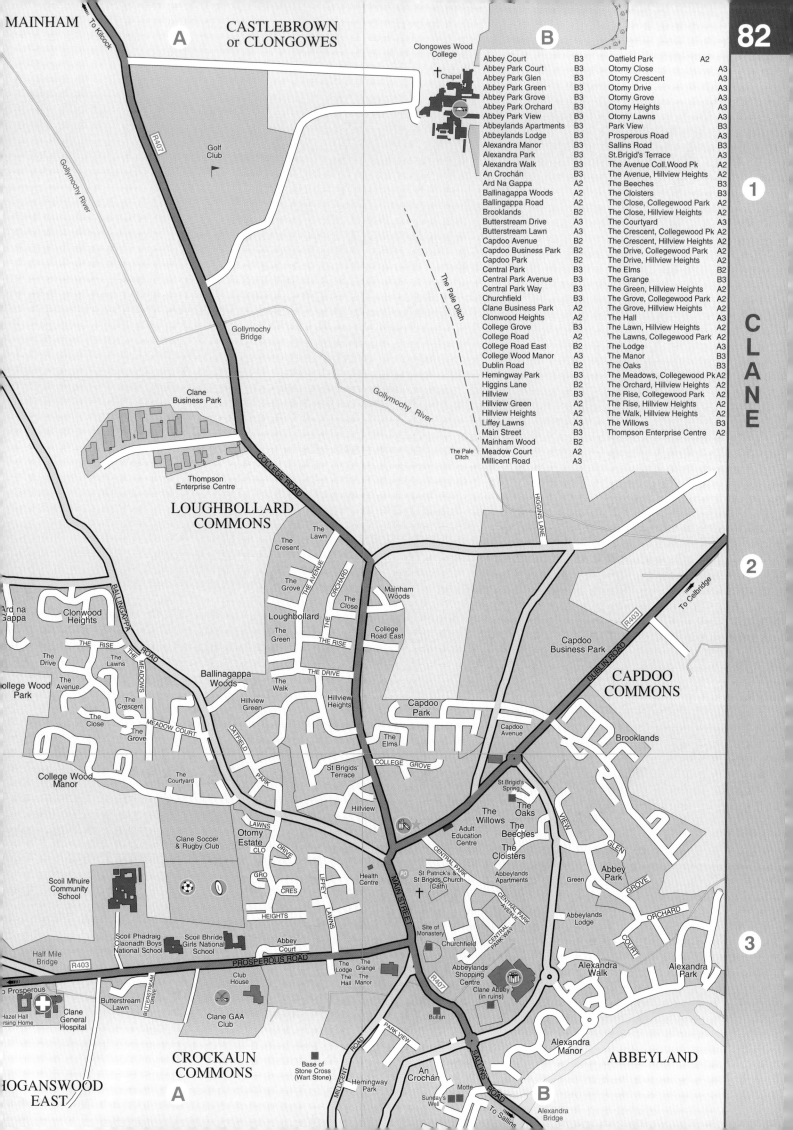

Abbey Court	B3	Oatfield Park	A2
Abbey Park Court	B3	Otomy Close	A3
Abbey Park Glen	B3	Otomy Crescent	A3
Abbey Park Green	B3	Otomy Drive	A3
Abbey Park Grove	B3	Otomy Grove	A3
Abbey Park Orchard	B3	Otomy Heights	A3
Abbey Park View	B3	Otomy Lawns	A3
Abbeylands Apartments	B3	Park View	B3
Abbeylands Lodge	B3	Prosperous Road	A3
Alexandra Manor	B3	Sallins Road	B3
Alexandra Park	B3	St.Brigid's Terrace	A3
Alexandra Walk	B3	The Avenue Coll. Wood Pk	A2
An Crochán	B3	The Avenue, Hillview Heights	A2
Ard Na Gappa	A2	The Beeches	B3
Ballinagappa Woods	A2	The Cloisters	B3
Ballingappa Road	A2	The Close, Collegewood Park	A2
Brooklands	B2	The Close, Hillview Heights	A2
Butterstream Drive	A3	The Courtyard	A3
Butterstream Lawn	A3	The Crescent, Collegewood Pk	A2
Capdoo Avenue	B2	The Crescent, Hillview Heights	A2
Capdoo Business Park	B2	The Drive, Collegewood Park	A2
Capdoo Park	B2	The Drive, Hillview Heights	A2
Central Park	B3	The Elms	B2
Central Park Avenue	B3	The Grange	B3
Central Park Way	B3	The Green, Hillview Heights	A2
Churchfield	B3	The Grove, Collegewood Park	A2
Clane Business Park	A2	The Grove, Hillview Heights	A2
Clonwood Heights	A2	The Hall	A3
College Grove	B3	The Lawn, Hillview Heights	A2
College Road	A2	The Lawns, Collegewood Park	A2
College Road East	B2	The Lodge	A3
College Wood Manor	A3	The Manor	B3
Dublin Road	B2	The Oaks	B3
Hemingway Park	B3	The Meadows, Collegewood Pk	A2
Higgins Lane	B2	The Orchard, Hillview Heights	A2
Hillview	B3	The Rise, Collegewood Park	A2
Hillview Green	A2	The Rise, Hillview Heights	A2
Hillview Heights	A2	The Walk, Hillview Heights	A2
Liffey Lawns	A2	The Willows	B3
Main Street	B3	Thompson Enterprise Centre	A2
Mainham Wood	B2		
Meadow Court	A2		
Millicent Road	A3		

Clongowes Wood College

Chapel

Golf Club

Gollymochy River

Gollymochy Bridge

Gollymochy River

The Pale Ditch

The Pale Ditch

Clane Business Park

Thompson Enterprise Centre

LOUGHBOLLARD COMMONS

COLLEGE ROAD

The Lawn

The Cresent

The Grove

THE AVENUE

THE ORCHARD

The Close

Loughbollard

Mainham Woods

The Green

THE RISE

College Road East

Ballinagappa Woods

THE DRIVE

The Walk

Hillview Green

Hillview Heights

Capdoo Business Park

R403

Capdoo Park

Capdoo Avenue

CAPDOO COMMONS

DUBLIN ROAD

To Celbridge

Brooklands

Ard na Gappa

Clonwood Heights

BALLINGAPPA ROAD

THE RISE

The Drive

The Lawns

College Wood Park

The Avenue

The Crescent

THE MEADOWS

The Close

The Grove

MEADOW COURT

The Courtyard

OATFIELD PARK

The Elms

St Brigids' Terrace

COLLEGE GROVE

Hillview

St.Brigid's Spring

The Willows

The Oaks

The Beeches

The Cloisters

Abbey Park

GLEN

GROVE

ORCHARD

COURT

VIEW

Green

Abbeylands Apartments

Abbeylands Lodge

College Wood Manor

LAWNS

Otomy Estate

CLO

DRIVE

GRO

CRES

HEIGHTS

LIFFEY LAWNS

Clane Soccer & Rugby Club

Health Centre

Adult Education Centre

PO

MAIN STREET

CENTRAL PARK AVENUE

CENTRAL PARK WAY

St Patrick's & St Brigids Church (Cath)

Site of Monastery

Churchfield

Scoil Mhuire Community School

Scoil Phadraig Claonadh Boys National School

Scoil Bhríde Girls National School

Abbey Court

PROSPEROUS ROAD

Club House

Clane GAA Club

The Lodge
The Grange
The Hall
The Manor

R407

Abbeylands Shopping Centre

Clane Abbey (in ruins)

Alexandra Walk

Alexandra Park

Half Mile Bridge

R403

To Prosperous

Hazel Hall Nursing Home

Clane General Hospital

Butterstream Lawn

BUTTERSTREAM DRIVE

MILLICENT ROAD

PARK VIEW

Base of Stone Cross (Wart Stone)

Bullán

An Crochán

Hemingway Park

Sunday's Well

Motte

SALLINS ROAD

To Sallins

Alexandra Bridge

Alexandra Manor

ABBEYLAND

DELGANY

GREYSTONES

INSET FOR PAGE 84

KINDLESTOWN UPPER

1

2

3

A

B

Saint Crispins

Church (In Ruins)

Rathdown Castle (Site of)

Redford

Redford Court

SEA VIEW

RATHDOWN ROAD

Redford Park

Willowmere

Mount Haven

Redford Rise

Sports Ground

Dromont

Kindlestown Rise

Kindlestown Heights

Kindlestown Castle (In Ruins)

CONVENT ROAD

Meado Court

CHAPEL ROAD

Conver Court

Bellevue Cottages

St Mary's Church (Cath)

Bellevue Lawns

Monastery

Church (In Ruins)

Cross

Hunter's Brook

Valley View

Bellevue Court

Delgany Golf Course

Club House

Reservoir

Priory Gate

PRIORY ROAD

Chris Chur (C of I

To Bray & Dublin

N11

Glen of the Downs

Woodlands Church (In Ruins)

Fair Green

R762

DRUMMIN WEST

To Wicklow Town & Arklow

N11

STILEBAWN

Reservoir

BLACKBERRY LANE

R762

To Bray

R761

Adare Close	C2	Cherry Green	C2	Kindlestown Lower	C2	Rathdown Lawn	C1
Applewood Drive	C1	Cherry Grove	C2	Kindlestown Park	C2	Rathdown Park	C1
Applewood Heights	C1	Cherry Lane Nurseries	C2	Kindlestown Rise	B1	Rathdown Road	INSET
Bayswater Terrace	D1	Cherry Orchard	C2	Kinlen Road	D2	Rathdown Road	C1
Beechbrook Park	C1	Cherry Rise	C2	La Touche Close	D1	Redford	INSET
Belleview Demesne	C1	Church Gate	D1	La Touche Park	C1	Redford Court	INSET
Bellevue Cottages	B2	Church Lane	C1	La Touche Place	D1	Redford Park	INSET
Bellevue Court	B3	Church Road	D1	La Touche Road	D1	Redford Rise	INSET
Bellevue Heights	C2	Churchfields	C2	Lower Grattan Park	C1	Rivendell Grove	C2
Bellevue Lawns	B2	Cliff Road	D1	Manor Avenue	D2	Riverfield	C2
Bellevue Park	D1	Convent Court	B3	Marine Road	D1	Saint Crispins	INSET
Bellevue Road	D1	Convent Road	B2	Marine Terrace	D1	Saint Vincent Road	D2
Blackberry Lane	B3	Delgany Glen	C2	Meadow Court	B3	Salem Vale	C3
Blacklion Manor	C1	Delgany Park	C3	Mill Road	D2	Sea View	INSET
Burnaby Avenue	D3	Delgany Wood	C3	Mill Road	D3	Sidmonton Place	D1
Burnaby Court	D3	Dromont	B2	Millbrook	D3	Somerby Road	D2
Burnaby Heights	C2	Drummin Rise	C3	Millgrove	INSET	South Place	D2
Burnaby Lawns	D3	Eden Gate	C3	Millgrove Close	C3	St. Bridget's Park	C1
Burnaby Manor	D1	Eden Road	D1	Mount Haven	INSET	The Arch	D1
Burnaby Mews	D1	Elsinore	C3	Mountain View Park	C1	The Bawn	D1
Burnaby Mill	D3	Erskine Avenue	D2	New Road	C3	The Manor	D1
Burnaby Park	D2	Fair Green	A3	New Road	D1	The Nurseries	C2
Burnaby Road	D2	Fairfield Park	D1	Oaklands	C1	The Poplars	C2
Burnaby Woods	D2	Glen of the Downs	A3	Oaklands Court	C1	Thornbury	C3
Carraig Orchard	C2	Glenair Manor	C3	Old Mill Road	D2	Trafalgar Court	D1
Carrick Villas	C2	Glenbrook Park	C3	Orchard View	C2	Trafalgar Road	D1
Carrig Villas	C3	Harbour Court	D1	Park Lane	D2	Turn Pike Lane	D1
Castle Villas	C2	Hawkins Lane	D2	Pavilion Road	D2	Upper Grattan Park	C1
Castlefield Terrace	C2	Hethervue	D1	Portland Place	D2	Valley View	B3
Chapel Road	C1	Hillcrest Avenue	C2	Portland Road	D2	Victoria Road	D1
Chapel Road	C2	Hillside	D1	Portland Road North	D2	Wendon Brook	C3
Chapel View	C1	Hillside Road	D1	Priory Gate	B2	Wendon Drive	C3
Charlesland Court	D3	Hunter's Brook	B3	Priory Rise	C2	Wendon Park	C3
Charlesland Grove	D3	Kenmare Heights	C2	Priory Road	B3	Whitshed Road	D2
Charlesland Park	D3	Killincarrick Road	D1	Priory Way	C2	Willow Bank	C1
Charlesland Wood	D3	Kimberley Court	D1	Quarry Road	D2	Willowmere	INSET
Cherry Court	C2	Kimberley Road	D1	Rathdown Close	D1	Woodlands	D2
Cherry Drive	C2	Kindlestown Heights	B2	Rathdown Court	C1		

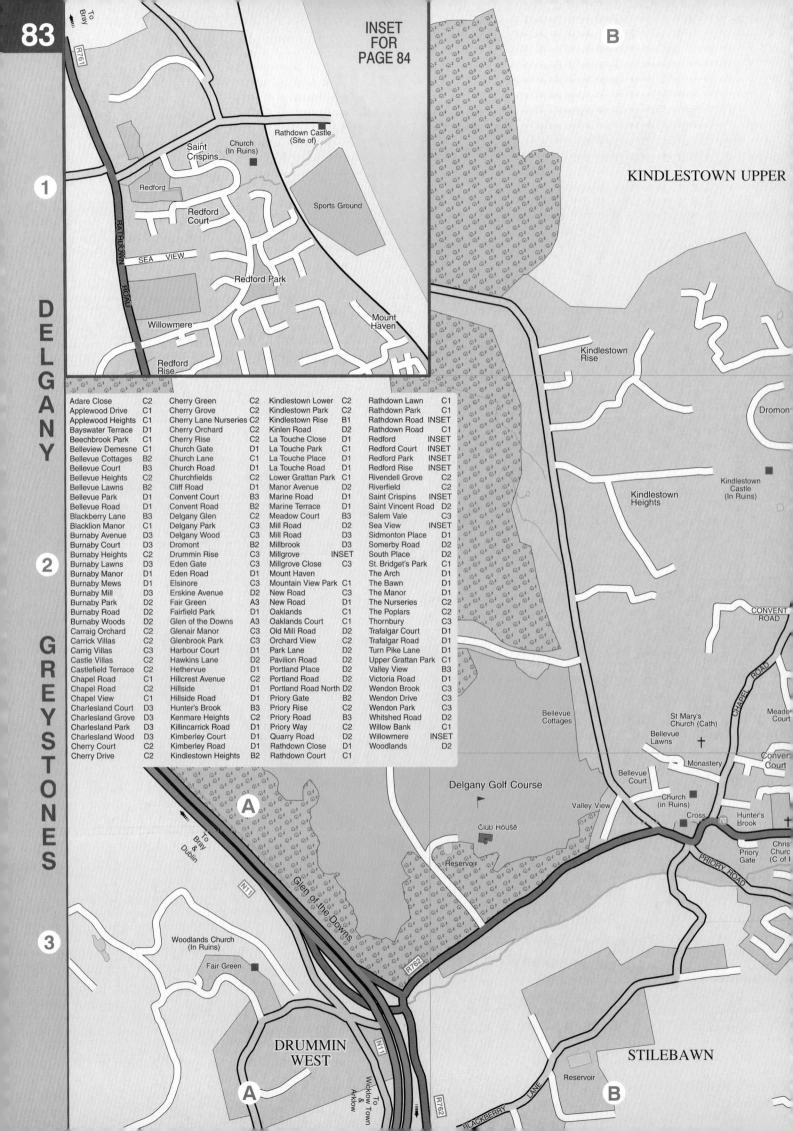

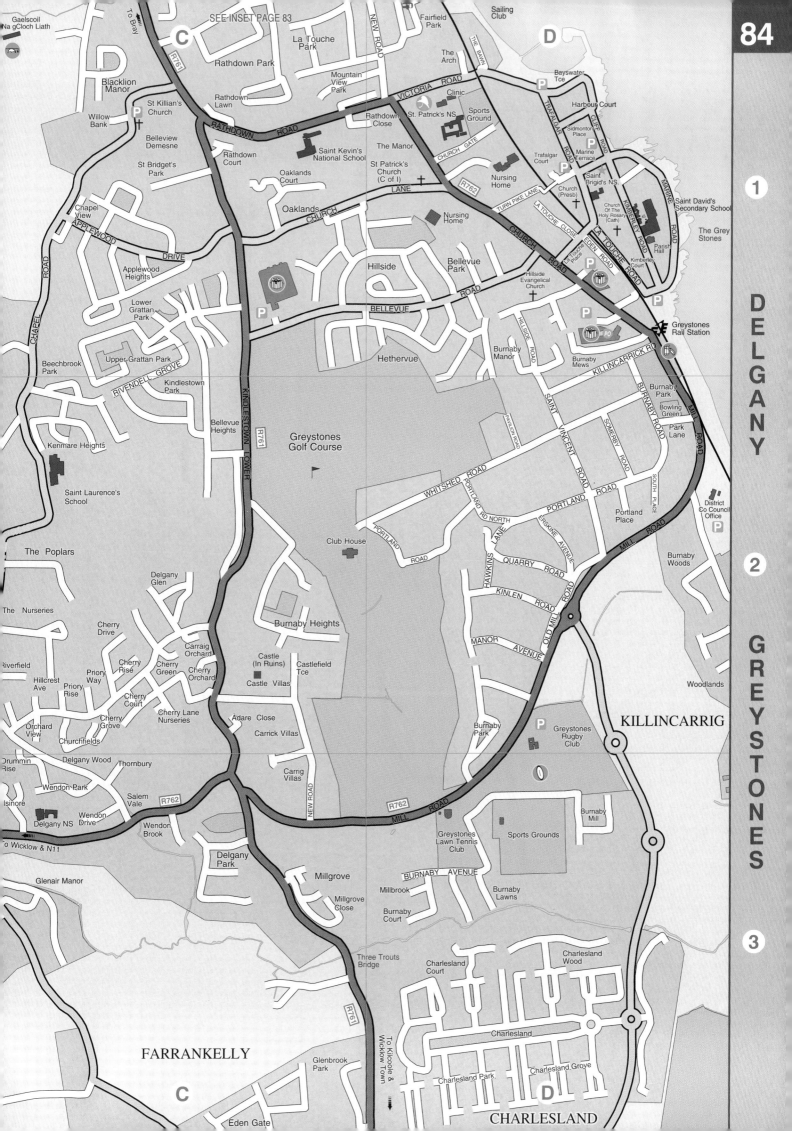

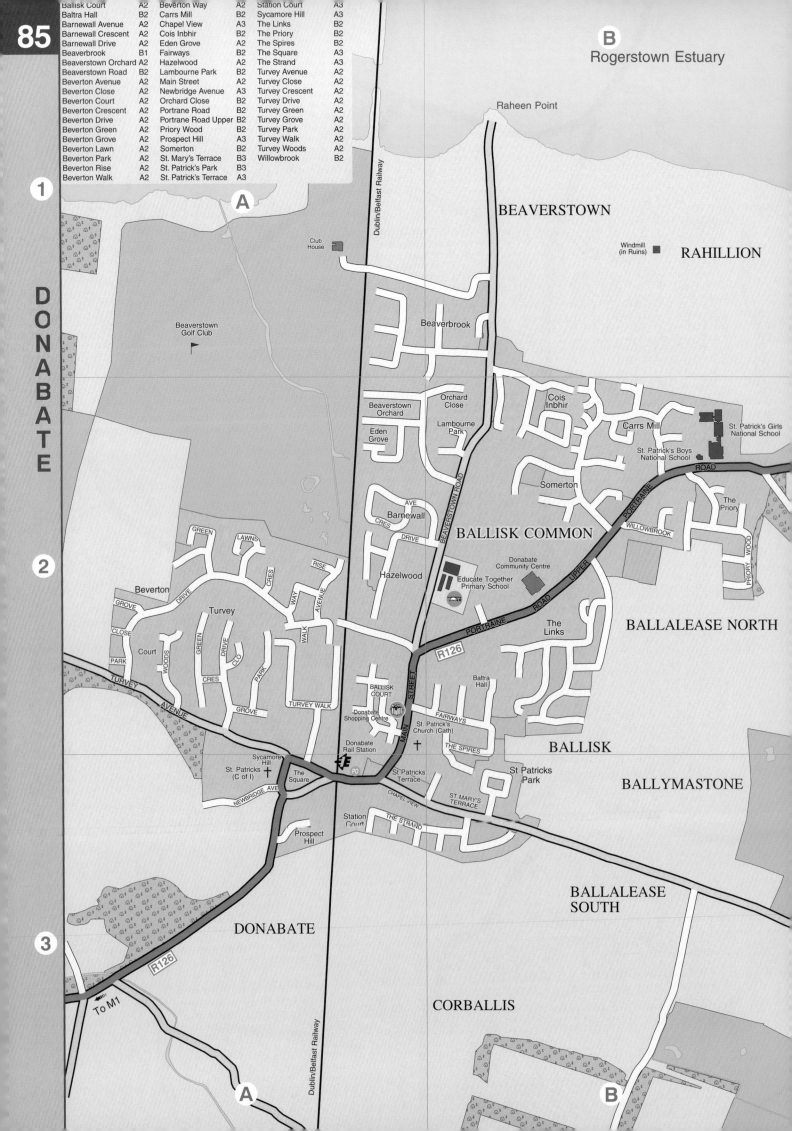

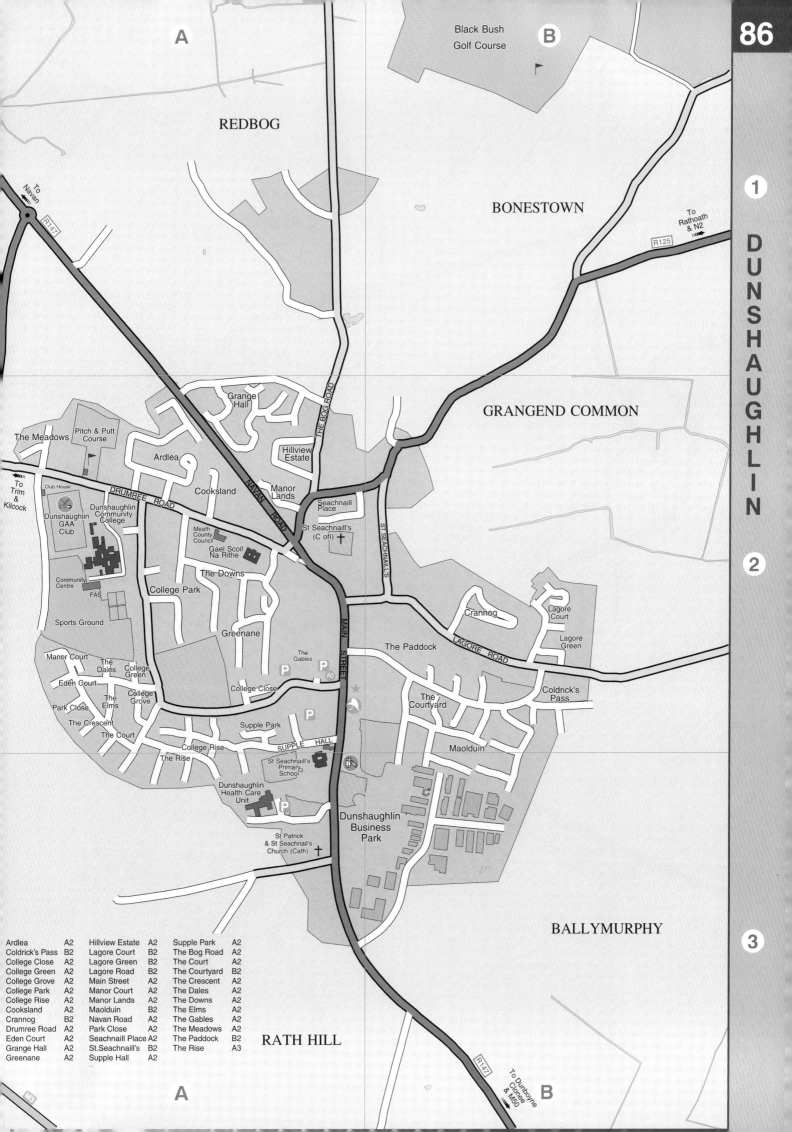

A

B

REDBOG

Black Bush
Golf Course

BONESTOWN

To
Navan

R147

To
Rathoath
& N2

R125

GRANGEND COMMON

Grange
Hall

The Meadows

Pitch & Putt
Course

Hillview
Estate

Ardlea

Cooksland

Manor
Lands

Seachnaill
Place

To
Trim &
Kilcock

Club House

DRUMREE ROAD

NAVAN ROAD

St Seachnaill's
(C of I)

Dunshaughlin
GAA Club

Dunshaughlin
Community
College

Meath
County
Council

ST SEACHNAILL'S

Gael Scoil
Na Rithe

Community
Centre

FÁS

The Downs

College Park

Sports Ground

Greenane

Crannog

Lagore
Court

The Paddock

Lagore
Green

Manor Court

The Dales

College
Green

The Gables

LAGORE ROAD

Coldrick's
Pass

Eden Court

The Elms

College
Grove

College Close

P

P

PO

The
Courtyard

Park Close

The Crescent

The Court

College Rise

P

Supple Park

SUPPLE HALL

MAIN STREET

Maolduin

The Rise

St Seachnaill's
Primary
School

Dunshaughlin
Health Care
Unit

P

Dunshaughlin
Business
Park

St Patrick
& St Seachnaill's
Church (Cath)

BALLYMURPHY

RATH HILL

To Dunboyne
& M50

R147

M3

A

B

Ardlea	A2	Hillview Estate	A2	Supple Park	A2		
Coldrick's Pass	B2	Lagore Court	B2	The Bog Road	A2		
College Close	A2	Lagore Green	B2	The Court	A2		
College Green	A2	Lagore Road	B2	The Courtyard	B2		
College Grove	A2	Main Street	A2	The Crescent	A2		
College Park	A2	Manor Court	A2	The Dales	A2		
College Rise	A2	Manor Lands	A2	The Downs	A2		
Cooksland	A2	Maolduin	B2	The Elms	A2		
Crannog	B2	Navan Road	A2	The Gables	A2		
Drumree Road	A2	Park Close	A2	The Meadows	A2		
Eden Court	A2	Seachnaill Place	A2	The Paddock	B2		
Grange Hall	A2	St.Seachnaill's	B2	The Rise	A3		
Greenane	A2	Supple Hall	A2				

1

2

3

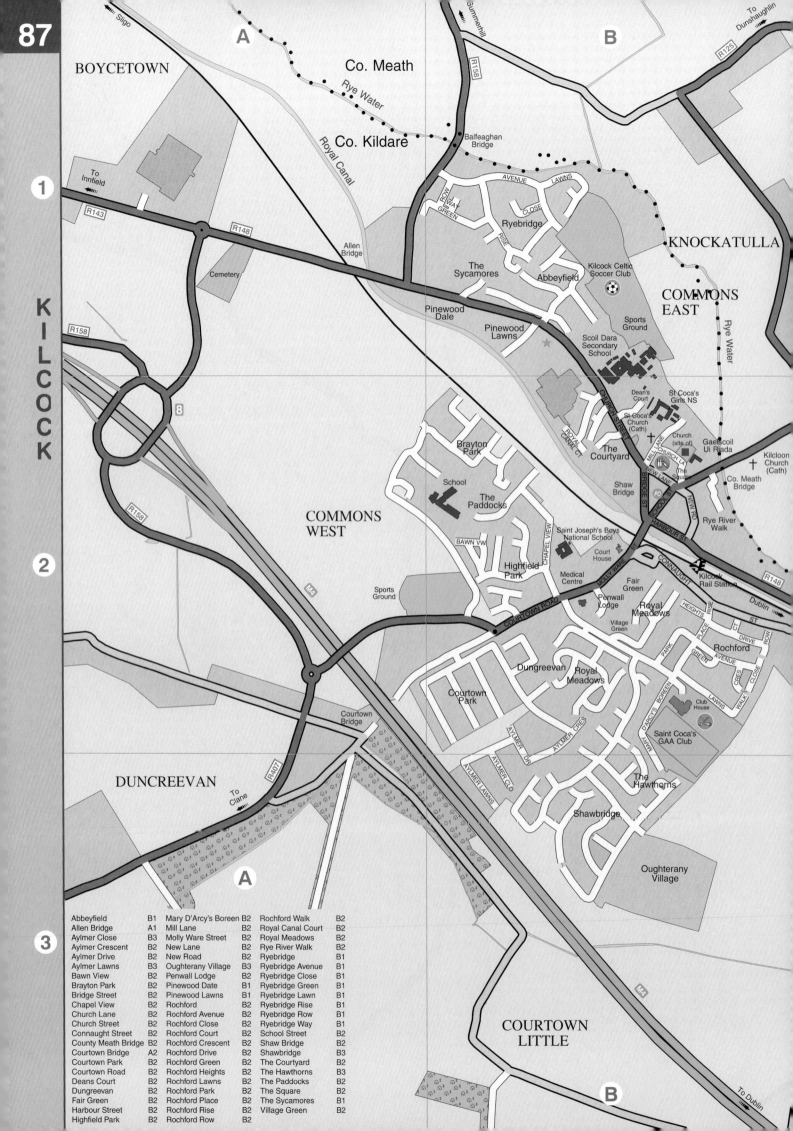

BOYCETOWN

Co. Meath

Rye Water

Royal Canal

Co. Kildare

Balfeaghan Bridge

To Dunshaughlin

R125

R158

KILCOCK

To Innfield

R143

R148

Allen Bridge

Cemetery

R158

8

R158

M4

AVENUE

LAWNS

ROW

WAY

GREEN

CLOSE

RISE

Ryebridge

The Sycamores

Abbeyfield

Kilcock Celtic Soccer Club

Sports Ground

KNOCKATULLA

COMMONS EAST

Rye Water

Pinewood Dale

Pinewood Lawns

Scoil Dara Secondary School

CHURCH STREET

ROYAL CANAL CT

Dean's Court

St Coca's Girls NS

St Coca's Church (Cath)

Church (site of)

The Courtyard

Gaelscoil Ui Riada

Kilcloon Church (Cath)

Co. Meath Bridge

COMMONS WEST

Brayton Park

School

The Paddocks

Shaw Bridge

MILL LANE

CHURCH LA

The Square

NEW LANE

BRIDGE ST

SCHOOL ST

HARBOUR ST

Chapel View

BAWN VW

Highfield Park

Saint Joseph's Boys National School

Court House

Medical Centre

Penwall Lodge

Fair Green

CONNAUGHT ST

Kilcock Rail Station

Rye River Walk

R148

To Dublin

Dublin ST

Sports Ground

COURTOWN ROAD

Village Green

Royal Meadows

HEIGHTS

RISE

PLACE

CT

DRIVE

ROW

Rochford

AVENUE

GREEN

CRES

CLOSE

WALK

Dungreevan

Royal Meadows

Courtown Park

AYLMER CRES

AYLMER DR

AYLMER CLO

AYLMER LAWNS

MARY DARCY'S BOREEN

PARK

LAWNS

Saint Coca's GAA Club

Club House

The Hawthorns

Shawbridge

Oughterany Village

COURTOWN LITTLE

Courtown Bridge

R407

To Clane

DUNCREEVAN

To Dublin

Abbeyfield	B1	Mary D'Arcy's Boreen	B2	Rochford Walk	B2
Allen Bridge	A1	Mill Lane	B2	Royal Canal Court	B2
Aylmer Close	B3	Molly Ware Street	B2	Royal Meadows	B2
Aylmer Crescent	B2	New Lane	B2	Rye River Walk	B2
Aylmer Drive	B2	New Road	B2	Ryebridge	B1
Aylmer Lawns	B3	Oughterany Village	B3	Ryebridge Avenue	B1
Bawn View	B2	Penwall Lodge	B2	Ryebridge Close	B1
Brayton Park	B2	Pinewood Date	B1	Ryebridge Green	B1
Bridge Street	B2	Pinewood Lawns	B1	Ryebridge Lawn	B1
Chapel View	B2	Rochford	B2	Ryebridge Rise	B1
Church Lane	B2	Rochford Avenue	B2	Ryebridge Row	B1
Church Street	B2	Rochford Close	B2	Ryebridge Way	B1
Connaught Street	B2	Rochford Court	B2	School Street	B2
County Meath Bridge	B2	Rochford Crescent	B2	Shaw Bridge	B2
Courtown Bridge	A2	Rochford Drive	B2	Shawbridge	B3
Courtown Park	B2	Rochford Green	B2	The Courtyard	B2
Courtown Road	B2	Rochford Heights	B2	The Hawthorns	B3
Deans Court	B2	Rochford Lawns	B2	The Paddocks	B2
Dungreevan	B2	Rochford Park	B2	The Square	B2
Fair Green	B2	Rochford Place	B2	The Sycamores	B1
Harbour Street	B2	Rochford Rise	B2	Village Green	B2
Highfield Park	B2	Rochford Row	B2		

To Sligo

Summerhill

A

B

1

2

3

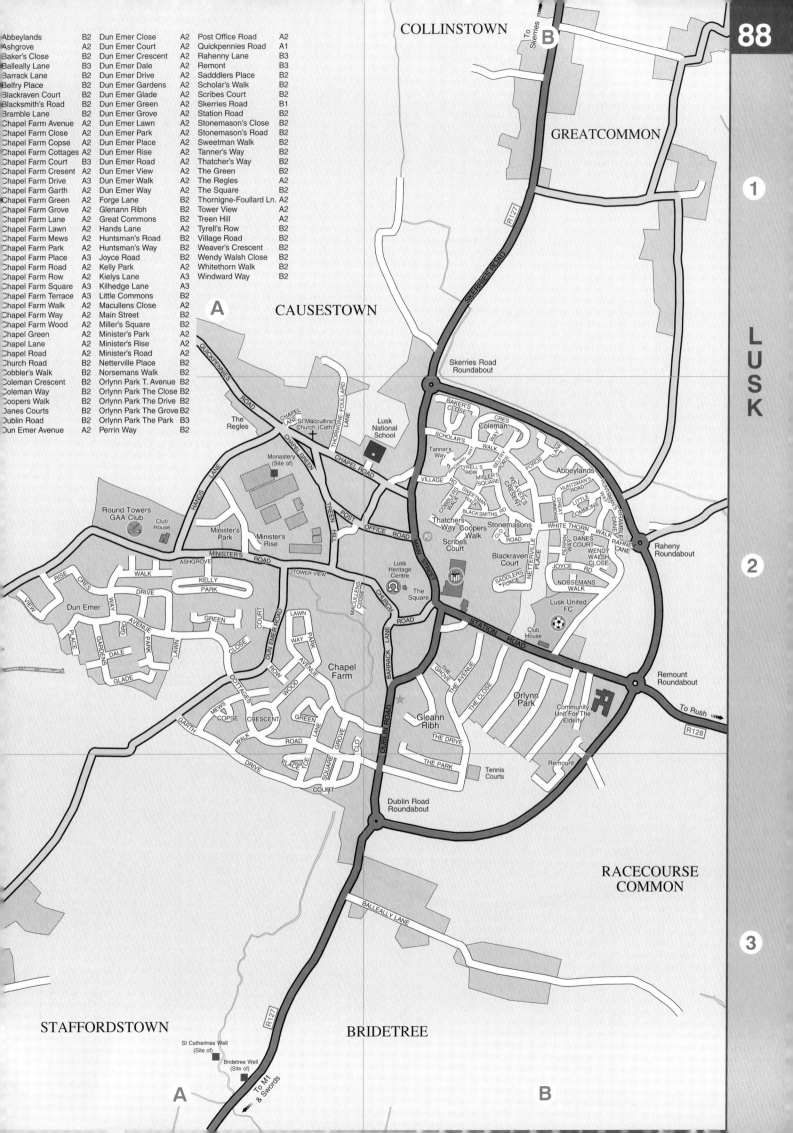

Abbeylands	B2	Dun Emer Close	A2	Post Office Road	A2
Ashgrove	A2	Dun Emer Court	A2	Quickpennies Road	A1
Baker's Close	B2	Dun Emer Crescent	A2	Rahenny Lane	B3
Balleally Lane	B3	Dun Emer Dale	A2	Remont	B3
Barrack Lane	B2	Dun Emer Drive	A2	Sadddlers Place	B2
Belfry Place	B2	Dun Emer Gardens	A2	Scholar's Walk	B2
Blackraven Court	B2	Dun Emer Glade	A2	Scribes Court	B2
Blacksmith's Road	B2	Dun Emer Green	A2	Skerries Road	B1
Bramble Lane	B2	Dun Emer Grove	A2	Station Road	B2
Chapel Farm Avenue	A2	Dun Emer Lawn	A2	Stonemason's Close	B2
Chapel Farm Close	A2	Dun Emer Park	A2	Stonemason's Road	B2
Chapel Farm Copse	A2	Dun Emer Place	A2	Sweetman Walk	B2
Chapel Farm Cottages	A2	Dun Emer Rise	A2	Tanner's Way	B2
Chapel Farm Court	B3	Dun Emer Road	A2	Thatcher's Way	B2
Chapel Farm Cresent	A2	Dun Emer View	A2	The Green	B2
Chapel Farm Drive	A3	Dun Emer Walk	A2	The Regles	A2
Chapel Farm Garth	A2	Dun Emer Way	A2	The Square	B2
Chapel Farm Green	A2	Forge Lane	B2	Thornigne-Foullard Ln.	A2
Chapel Farm Grove	A2	Glenann Ribh	A2	Tower View	A2
Chapel Farm Lane	A2	Great Commons	B2	Treen Hill	A2
Chapel Farm Lawn	A2	Hands Lane	A2	Tyrell's Row	B2
Chapel Farm Mews	A2	Huntsman's Road	B2	Village Road	B2
Chapel Farm Park	A2	Huntsman's Way	B2	Weaver's Crescent	B2
Chapel Farm Place	A3	Joyce Road	B2	Wendy Walsh Close	B2
Chapel Farm Road	A2	Kelly Park	A2	Whitethorn Walk	B2
Chapel Farm Row	A2	Kielys Lane	A3	Windward Way	B2
Chapel Farm Square	A3	Kilhedge Lane	A3		
Chapel Farm Terrace	A3	Little Commons	B2		
Chapel Farm Walk	A2	Macullens Close	A2		
Chapel Farm Way	A2	Main Street	B2		
Chapel Farm Wood	A2	Miller's Square	B2		
Chapel Green	A2	Minister's Park	A2		
Chapel Lane	A2	Minister's Rise	A2		
Chapel Road	A2	Minister's Road	A2		
Church Road	B2	Netterville Place	B2		
Cobbler's Walk	B2	Norsemans Walk	B2		
Coleman Crescent	B2	Orlynn Park T. Avenue	B2		
Coleman Way	B2	Orlynn Park The Close	B2		
Coopers Walk	B2	Orlynn Park The Drive	B2		
Danes Courts	B2	Orlynn Park The Grove	B2		
Dublin Road	B2	Orlynn Park The Park	B3		
Dun Emer Avenue	A2	Perrin Way	B2		

LUSK

RUSH

An Tearmann	B3	Finistere	D2	Linn Beag	B2	St Catherines Close	C1
Barrack Lane	C2	Golden Ridge Avenue	C2	Linn Cuin	B2	St Catherines Crescent	C1
Bawn Road	C2	Golden Ridge Court	C2	Linn Dubh	B2	St Catherines Drive	C1
Bayview Villas	C2	Golden Ridge Close	C2	Lower Main Street	C2	St Catherines Green	C1
Bollum Lane	C2	Golden Ridge Crescent	C2	Melbourne Gardens	C3	St Catherines Grove	C1
Brookfield Park	C2	Golden Ridge Drive	C2	Mill Bank	B2	St Catherines Lawn	C1
Brookford Park	B2	Golden Ridge Green	C2	Mill Bank Court	B2	St Catherines Park	C1
Brookford	B2	Golden Ridge Lodge	C2	Old Barrack Road	D3	St Catherines View	C1
Brookside Gardens	B2	Golden Ridge Square	C2	Old Haystown	B2	St Catherines Way	C1
Carthy's Lane	A3	Golden Ridge View	C2	Old Road	B2	St. Joseph's Road	C3
Ceol na Mara	C2	Golden Ridge Walk	C2	Old Road Court	B2	St. Maur's Park	C2
Channel Road	A3	Golden Ridge Way	C2	Old Road Grove	B2	Sundrive Road	B3
Chapel Green	B2	Golf Road	B3	Palmer Court	C1	Sundrive Road	C3
Clann Beag	B3	Hand Park	D2	Palmer Road	C1	Sunlock Court	C2
Clifflands	C1	Hands Lane	C3	Park Road	C2	Sunset Court	C2
Clifflands Court	C1	Harbour Road	D2	Quay Road	D2	Tayleurs Point	D3
Clifflands Rise	C1	Haystown	B2	Ravenswell	C1	The Cairn	C1
Cois Tra	C2	Haystown Road	B2	Rogerstown Court	B3	The Forge	D2
Congress Gardens	C3	Healy's Lane	B3	Rogerstown Park	B3	The Mall	C2
Convent Lane	C3	Kenure Crescent	C2	Sandy Lane	C3	Thorn Chase	C1
Cooper's Bank	C2	Kenure Lawns	C1	Sandy Road	C2	Thornleigh	C2
Cooper's Lane	C2	Kenure Park	C2	Sea Brook	B2	Tower Street	D2
Coopersfield	C2	Kilbush Lane	C2	Seafield Court	D2	Upper Main Street	C2
Crescent Road	B3	Kilbush View	C2	Skerries Road	C2	Whitestown Road	A3
Daly's Lane	B3	Knockabawn	D2	South Shore Road	C3	Woodbury	C3
Doctor's Lane	B2	Lady Cove	C1	South Shore Cove	B3	Woodland Court	C2
Echlin Court	C2	Lambay View	C1	South Strand	C3	Woodland Park	C2
Eden Terrace	C2	Linkside	INSET	Spout Road	A3	Woodvale Road	C1
Farran's Lane	C2	Linn Ban	B2	St Catherines Avenue	C1		

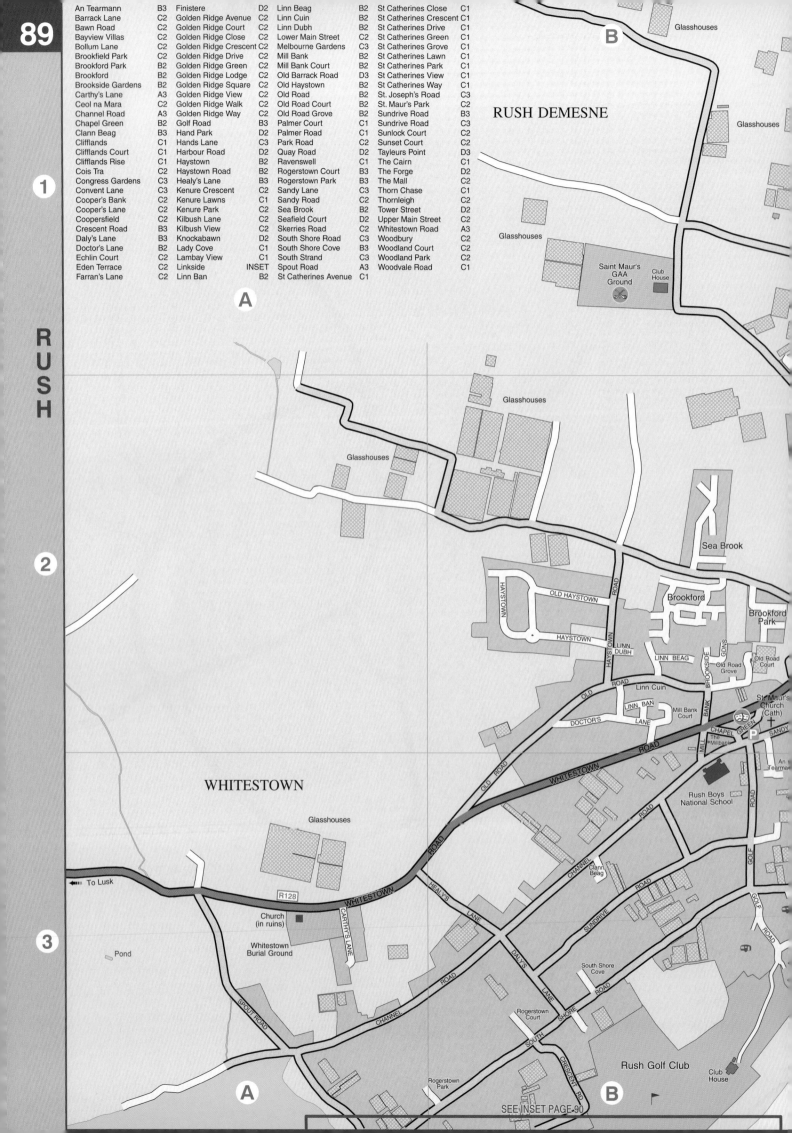

SEE INSET PAGE 90

D

1

2

3

IRISH SEA

To Skerries

R128

C

Church
(in ruins)

Lambay
View

CRESCENT
AVENUE
PARK
GREEN
DRIVE
WAY
CLOSE
GROVE
LAWN
THE CAIRN
RISE
CLIFFLANDS COURT
VIEW

Saint Catherine's
National School

WOODVALE RD

St Catherine's Estate

THORN CHASE

Clifflands

Ravenswell

PALMER

ROAD

Palmer
Court

Lady
Cove

Glasshouses

Brooks's End

Megolithic Tomb
(Site of)

Kenure
Lawns

KENURE
CRESCENT

Rush
Nursing
Home

WOODLAND PARK

Woodbury

Kenure
Park

ST MAUR'S PARK

CLOSE
Square
WALK
AVENUE
GREEN

Golden
Ridge

Rush
Cricket
Club

Kenure Church
(C of I)

North Beach

PARK
ROAD

WAY
LODGE
DRIVE
COURT
VIEW
CRESCENT
SKERRIES ROAD

FARRAN'S LANE
COOPERS LANE

Brookfield
Park

Kilbush
View
Sunset
Court

Coopersfield

Thornleigh

SOUTH

KILBUSH LANE

KILBUSH

LANE

Cois
Tra

Woodland
Court

Ceol Na
Mara

Seafield
Court

The
Forge

P

Pier

P

HARBOUR

ROAD

QUAY RD

UPPER
MAIN
STREET

P

The
Mall

Barrack
Lane

LOWER
MAIN

OLD STREET

Finistere

QUAY ROAD

TOWER STREET

Martello
Tower

Glasshouses

Bayview
Villas

ROAD

P

Echlin
Court

BOLLUM LANE

P.O
Cooper's
Bank

LANE

St Catherines
Well

Sunlock
Court

Rush Vocational
School

BAWN

HSE

EDEN
TCE

Knockabawn

Hand
Park

SANDY

LANE

St Catherines
Well

Sisters of Mercy
Convent

ST JOSEPH'S RD

Congress
Gardens

Melbourne
Gardens

BARRACK

Tayleurs
Point

Glasshouses

SUNDRIVE

ROAD

HANDS

CONVENT

Saint Joseph's
Secondary
School

ROAD

ROAD

South Strand

P

SOUTH

SHORE

ROAD

South Beach

C

Pier

Rush Sailing
Club House

LINKSIDE

INSET
FOR
PAGE 89

D

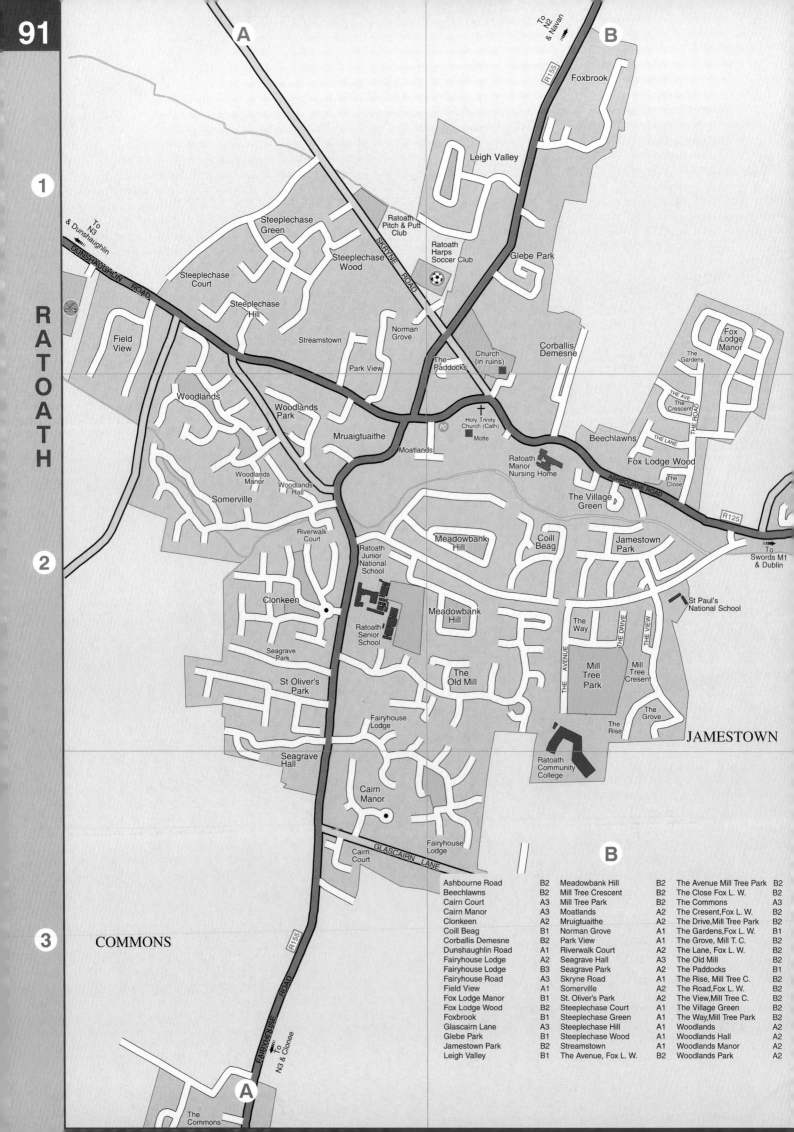

RATOATH

Ashbourne Road	B2	Meadowbank Hill	B2	The Avenue Mill Tree Park	B2
Beechlawns	B2	Mill Tree Crescent	B2	The Close Fox L. W.	B2
Cairn Court	A3	Mill Tree Park	B2	The Commons	A3
Cairn Manor	A3	Moatlands	A2	The Cresent, Fox L. W.	B2
Clonkeen	A2	Mruigtuaithe	A2	The Drive, Mill Tree Park	B2
Coill Beag	B1	Norman Grove	A1	The Gardens, Fox L. W.	B1
Corballis Demesne	B2	Park View	A1	The Grove, Mill T. C.	B2
Dunshaughlin Road	A1	Riverwalk Court	A2	The Lane, Fox L. W.	B2
Fairyhouse Lodge	A2	Seagrave Hall	A3	The Old Mill	B2
Fairyhouse Lodge	B3	Seagrave Park	A2	The Paddocks	B1
Fairyhouse Road	A3	Skryne Road	A1	The Rise, Mill Tree C.	B2
Field View	A1	Somerville	A2	The Road, Fox L. W.	B2
Fox Lodge Manor	B1	St. Oliver's Park	A3	The View, Mill Tree C.	B2
Fox Lodge Wood	B2	Steeplechase Court	A1	The Village Green	B2
Foxbrook	B1	Steeplechase Green	A1	The Way, Mill Tree Park	B2
Glascairn Lane	A3	Steeplechase Hill	A1	Woodlands	A2
Glebe Park	B1	Steeplechase Wood	A1	Woodlands Hall	A2
Jamestown Park	B2	Streamstown	A1	Woodlands Manor	A2
Leigh Valley	B1	The Avenue, Fox L. W.	B2	Woodlands Park	A2

An Claddagh	A2	Kelly's Bay Parade	INSET	Shalloch Hill Grove	A2	
Arcadia Court	B2	Kelly's Bay Pier	INSET	Shenick Avenue	B3	The Haven	B2
Ardgillan View	A2	Kelly's Bay Promenade	INSET	Shenick Drive	B3	The Heights, Skerries Rk.	A2
Balbriggan Road	A2	Kelly's Bay Rise	INSET	Shenick Grove	B3	The Hoar Rock	A2
Balbriggan Street	A2	Kelly's Bay Rocks	INSET	Shenick Park	B3	The Kybe	B2
Beau-Piers Lane	B2	Kelly's Bay Shore	A2	Shenick Road	B3	The Lawn, Skerries Rock	A2
Brookville Lane	B2	Kelly's Bay Strand	INSET	Sherlock Park	B3	The Maltings	B2
Cabra Hill	B3	Kelly's Bay Tide	INSET	Sherlock Terrace	B3	The Park	A2
Callaghan's Lane	B2	Kelly's Bay Tower	INSET	South Strand	B2	The Park, Skerries Rock	A2
Chapel Lane	B2	Kelly's Bay View	A1	St. Patrick's Close	A3	The Quays	A2
Church Street	B2	Kelly's Bay Weir	INSET	Station Road	A3	The Rise, Skerries Rock	A2
Churchfield Close	B3	Little Strand Street	B2	Strand Street	B2	The Square	B2
Churchfield Lawns	B3	Manning's Opening	B2	Tennis Courts Lane	B2	The Stableyard	B2
College Court	B2	Martine Court	B2	The Avenue, Skerries Rock	A2	The Vale, Skerries Rock	A2
Convent Lane	B2	Marywell	B3	The Brambles	A2	The View, Skerries Rock	A2
Downside Heights	B3	McLoughlin's Lane	B2	The Brock	B2	The Walk, Skerries Rock	A2
Downside Park	B3	Miller's Lane	B3	The Close, Skerries Rock	A2	The Way, Skerries Rock	A2
Dublin Road	A3	Millhill Park	B2	The Court, Skerries Rock	A2	Thomas Hand Street	B2
Friar's Lane	B2	Millview	B2	The Crescent, Skerries RK.	A2	Townparks	A2
Fox Grove	A2	Mooring Cove	A2	The Cross	B2	Weldon's Lane	B3
Golf Links Road	B3	Mourne Close	A2	The Drive, Skerries Rock	A2	Windmill Lane	B3
Greenlawns	A3	Mourne Court	A2	The Green	A2		
Hacketstown Park	C4	Mourne Drive	A2	The Grove, Skerries Rock	A2		
Harbour Road	B2	Mourne Grove	A2				
Harrison's Cove	A2	Mourne Park	A2				
Heeney's Lane	B2	Mourne View	A2				
Hillside Close	B3	New Street	B2				
Hillside Gardens	A3	New Townparks	A2				
Holmpatrick	B2	North Strand	A2				
Holmpatrick Terrace	B3	Northcliffe Heights	A2				
Kelly's Bay Beach	INSET	Quay Street	B2				
Kelly's Bay Cliffs	INSET	Red Island	B1				
Kelly's Bay Cove	INSET	Rush Road	B3				
Kelly's Bay Drive	INSET	Sandy Banks	B2				
Kelly's Bay Harbour	INSET	Seacrest	B2				
Kelly's Bay Heights	INSET	Selskar Avenue	A2				
Kelly's Bay Inlet	INSET	Selskar Court	A2				
Kelly's Bay Jetty	INSET	Selskar Rise	A2				
Kelly's Bay Moorings	INSET	Selskar Road	A2				

Talk to the Experts on Dublin!

Our travel advisors can point you in the right direction

Suffolk Street Dublin 2
Mon-Sat 09:00-17:30. Sun 10.30-15.00

O'Connell Street Dublin 1
Mon-Sat 09:00-17:00

Dublin Tourism
DUBLIN REGIONAL TOURISM AUTHORITY

...the official Tourist Information Office for Dublin

Offices also located at **Dublin Airport Arrivals Hall** and **Ferry Terminal Dun Laoghaire Harbour**
For more information go to **visitdublin.com**

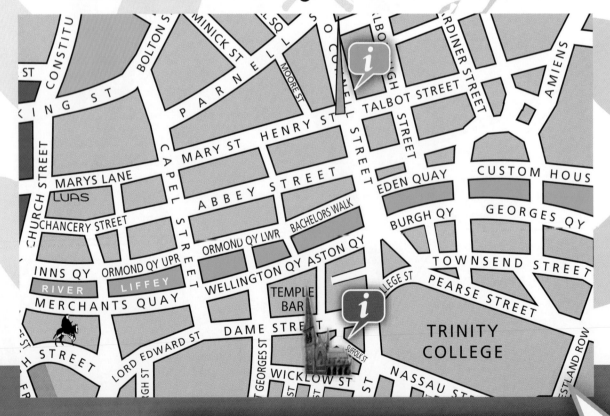

Get in the know on
visitdublin.com

DUBLIN'S TOP 10

1. Visit the Dublin Tourism Centre in the former Saint Andrews Church on Suffolk Street (just off Grafton Street) in the city centre. Apart from giving you the opportunity to view this beautifully restored building, we have a wide range of services to assist you in planning your visit to Dublin City, Dublin County. Alternatively, click on www.visitdublin.com (or dublin.mobi from your mobile phone!) the official online tourist office for Dublin to begin planning your day in and around Dublin. Here, you will find information on events and attractions; or even download walking tours to your MP3 player.

2. See more for less with The Dublin Pass - your passport to Dublin giving you loads of great features in one great value package, including; FREE entry to visitor attractions, FREE airport transfer to Dublin city with Aircoach and special offers for eating, shopping, entertainment and tours. All this and a guidebook to Dublin…and you can jump the queues too!

3. Tour Dublin - Discover more of the city on one of the hop-on-hop-off bus tours. If you want to get away from the hustle and bustle, coach tours will take you to the surrounding countryside or coastal villages, just a 20-minute drive from the city centre. If you prefer to discover the city for yourself, download an iWalk to your MP3 player and take things at your own pace.

4. Visit a Castle –Step back in time and visit a selection of ancient and historic fortifications situated both in the city and throughout Dublin County e.g. Malahide Castle.

5. Discover the story of Dublin - A wealth of museums hold an array of information and artefacts recounting to you the history of this ancient capital.

6. Visit Georgian Dublin - The Georgian door is a well recognised symbol of 'Welcome' in Dublin. In the 18th century (Georgian Era) the city acquired this beautiful and distinctive style of architecture. Stroll through the elegant streets of Merrion and Fitzwilliam Squares, as fine examples of the great Georgian period.

7. Eat Out - Dubliners like to eat, and the last ten years has seen the emergence of a cosmopolitan and chic food culture, which is mirrored in the hundreds of restaurants you will find throughout the Dublin region.

8. Sample some local brews - Have a pint of Guinness or a shot of whiskey in one of Dublin's 1000 pubs! Discover how our world-famous brews are made with visits to the Guinness Storehouse and Old Jameson Distillery. Or why not visit Bewleys Café, Bar, Restaurant – Dublin's oldest coffee house?

9. Shop 'til you drop! - Dublin offers a wonderful array of products ranging from the traditional to the contemporary in its many shops, boutiques and department stores.

10. Party the night away! - Dublin has one of Europe's most vibrant and exciting nightlife cultures. So whether it's the traditional pubs with Irish music, or the hip and trendy bar and club scene that you're after, you'll find it all here in Dublin!

Dublin is also famous for its playwrights and choice of theatres so if drama's your thing why not check out what's on?

Truly Madly Deeply
Dublin
visitdublin.com

Apostolic Nunciature
183 Navan Road
Dublin 7
Tel: 838 0577   24 D4

Argentine Embassy
15 Ailesbury Drive
Dublin 4
Tel: 269 1546   48 D1

Australian Embassy
7th Floor,
Fitzwilton House
Wilton Terrace, Dublin 2
Tel: 664 5300   38 E4

Austrian Embassy
15 Ailesbury Court Apts.
93 Ailesbury Road
Dublin 4
Tel: 269 4577   48 D1

Belgian Embassy
2 Shrewsbury Road
Dublin 4
Tel: 205 7100   48 D1

Embassy of the Federative Republic of Brazil
Block 8 Sixth Floor
Harcourt Centre,
Charlotte Way.
Dublin 2.
Tel: 475 6000   38 D4

British Embassy
29 Merrion Road
Dublin 4
Tel: 205 3700   48 D1

Bulgarian Embassy
22 Burlington Road
Dublin 4
Tel: 660 3293   38 E4

Canadian Embassy
7/8 Wilton Terrace.
Dublin 2
Tel: 234 4000   38 E4

Chilean Embassy
44 Wellington Road
Ballsbridge
Dublin 4
Tel: 667 5094   38 F4

Embassy of the People's Republic of China
40 Ailesbury Road
Ballsbridge, Dublin 4
Tel: 260 1707   48 D1

Embassy of the Republic of Croatia
Adelaide Chambers
Peter Street
Dublin 8
Tel: 476 7181   38 D3

Embassy of the Republic of Cuba
2 Adelaide Court,
Adelaide Road,
Dublin 2
Tel: 475 0899   38 D4

Embassy of Republic of Cyprus
71 Lower Leeson Street
Dublin 2
Tel: 676 3060   38 E3

Embassy of Czech Republic
57 Northumberland Road
Dublin 4
Tel: 668 1135   38 F4

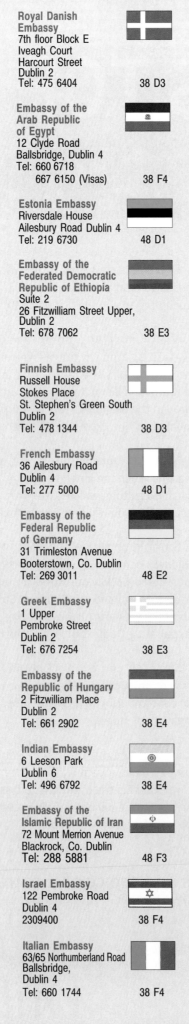

Royal Danish Embassy
7th floor Block E
Iveagh Court
Harcourt Street
Dublin 2
Tel: 475 6404   38 D3

Embassy of the Arab Republic of Egypt
12 Clyde Road
Ballsbridge, Dublin 4
Tel: 660 6718
    667 6150 (Visas)   38 F4

Estonia Embassy
Riversdale House
Ailesbury Road Dublin 4
Tel: 219 6730   48 D1

Embassy of the Federated Democratic Republic of Ethiopia
Suite 2
26 Fitzwilliam Street Upper,
Dublin 2
Tel: 678 7062   38 E3

Finnish Embassy
Russell House
Stokes Place
St. Stephen's Green South
Dublin 2
Tel: 478 1344   38 D3

French Embassy
36 Ailesbury Road
Dublin 4
Tel: 277 5000   48 D1

Embassy of the Federal Republic of Germany
31 Trimleston Avenue
Booterstown, Co. Dublin
Tel: 269 3011   48 E2

Greek Embassy
1 Upper
Pembroke Street
Dublin 2
Tel: 676 7254   38 E3

Embassy of the Republic of Hungary
2 Fitzwilliam Place
Dublin 2
Tel: 661 2902   38 E4

Indian Embassy
6 Leeson Park
Dublin 6
Tel: 496 6792   38 E4

Embassy of the Islamic Republic of Iran
72 Mount Merrion Avenue
Blackrock, Co. Dublin
Tel: 288 5881   48 F3

Israel Embassy
122 Pembroke Road
Dublin 4
2309400   38 F4

Italian Embassy
63/65 Northumberland Road
Ballsbridge,
Dublin 4
Tel: 660 1744   38 F4

Japanese Embassy
Nutley Building
Merrion Centre
Nutley Lane, Dublin 4
Tel: 202 8300   48 E1

Embassy of the Republic of Kenya
11 Elgin Road
Ballsbridge, Dublin 4
Tel: 613 6380   38 F4

Embassy of the Republic of Korea
15 Clyde Road
Ballsbridge, Dublin 4
Tel: 660 8800   38 F4

Embassy of the Republic of Latvia
92 St Stephen's Green
Dublin 2
Tel: 428 3320   38 E4

Embassy of Lesotho
2 Clanwilliam Square,
Grand Canal Quay,
Dublin 2.
Tel: 676 2233   38 F3[41]

Embassy of the Republic of Lithuania
47 Ailsbury Road,
Ballsbridge, Dublin 4.
Tel: 678 1025   48 D1

Embassy of Malaysia
Level 3A-5A
Shelbourne House
Shelbourne Road
Ballsbridge Dublin 4.
Tel: 667 7280   38 F3

Maltese Embassy
15 Leeson Street
Dublin 2
Tel: 6762340   38 E4

Mexican Embassy
19 Raglan Road
Dublin 4
Tel: 667 3105   38 F4

Embassy of the Kingdom of Morocco
39 Raglan Road
Dublin 4
Tel: 660 9449   38 F4

Netherlands Embassy
160 Merrion Road
Dublin 4
Tel: 269 3444   48 D1

Embassy of the Federal Republic of Nigeria
56 Leeson Park
Dublin 6
Tel: 660 4366   38 E4

Royal Norwegian Embassy
Hainault House
34 Molesworth Street,
Dublin 2
Tel: 662 1800   38 E3

Embassy of the Islamic Republic of Pakistan
1B Ailesbury Road
Ballsbridge Dublin 4
Tel: 261 3032   48 D1

Embassy of the Republic of The Philippines
77 Sir John Rogerson's Quay
Dublin 2
Tel: 640 1946   72 F4

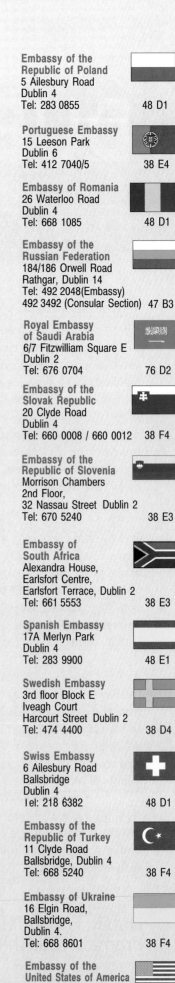

Embassy of the Republic of Poland
5 Ailesbury Road
Dublin 4
Tel: 283 0855   48 D1

Portuguese Embassy
15 Leeson Park
Dublin 6
Tel: 412 7040/5   38 E4

Embassy of Romania
26 Waterloo Road
Dublin 4
Tel: 668 1085   48 D1

Embassy of the Russian Federation
184/186 Orwell Road
Rathgar, Dublin 14
Tel: 492 2048(Embassy)
492 3492 (Consular Section)   47 B3

Royal Embassy of Saudi Arabia
6/7 Fitzwilliam Square E
Dublin 2
Tel: 676 0704   76 D2

Embassy of the Slovak Republic
20 Clyde Road
Dublin 4
Tel: 660 0008 / 660 0012   38 F4

Embassy of the Republic of Slovenia
Morrison Chambers
2nd Floor,
32 Nassau Street Dublin 2
Tel: 670 5240   38 E3

Embassy of South Africa
Alexandra House,
Earlsfort Centre,
Earlsfort Terrace, Dublin 2
Tel: 661 5553   38 E3

Spanish Embassy
17A Merlyn Park
Dublin 4
Tel: 283 9900   48 E1

Swedish Embassy
3rd floor Block E
Iveagh Court
Harcourt Street Dublin 2
Tel: 474 4400   38 D4

Swiss Embassy
6 Ailesbury Road
Ballsbridge
Dublin 4
Tel: 218 6382   48 D1

Embassy of the Republic of Turkey
11 Clyde Road
Ballsbridge, Dublin 4
Tel: 668 5240   38 F4

Embassy of Ukraine
16 Elgin Road,
Ballsbridge,
Dublin 4.
Tel: 668 8601   38 F4

Embassy of the United States of America
42 Elgin Road
Ballsbridge, Dublin 4
Tel: 630 6200   38 F4

For further information contact:
Dept of Foreign Affairs,
80 St. Stephen's Green, Dublin 2.
Tel: 478 0822 / www.foreignaffairs.gov.ie

Adelaide & Meath (A&E)
Hospital & The National
Childrens Hospital
Tallaght
Dublin 24
Tel: 01-414 2000 **54 F1**

Beaumont Hospital (A&E)
Beaumont Road
Beaumont Dublin 9
Tel: 01-809 3000 **26 D1**

Cherry Orchard Hospital
Ballyfermot
Dublin 10.
Tel: 01-620 6400 **35 C3**

Cheeverstown House
Kilvare
Templeogue
Dublin 6W
Tel: 01-499 3700 **46 D4**

City Of Dublin
Skin & Cancer Hospital
Hume St.
Dublin 2
Tel: 01-676 6935 **38 E3**

Connolly Hospital (A&E)
Blanchardstown
Dublin 15.
Tel: 01-646 5000 **22 F2**

Dublin Dental
School & Hospital
Lincon Place
Dublin 2
Tel: 01-612 7200 **38 E3**

National Orthopaedic
Hospital
Cappagh
Finglas
Dublin 11
Tel: 01-814 0400 **23 C1**

National Rehabilitation
Hospital
Dun Laoghaire
Co.Dublin
Tel: 01-235 5000 **59 C2**

ncorporated Orthopaedic
Hospital Of Ireland
Castle Ave.
Clontarf
Dublin 3.
Tel: 01-833 2521 **26 E4**

Peamount Hospital
Newcastle
Co. Dublin
Tel: 01-601 0300 **42 E2**

Royal Hospital
Donnybrook
off Morehampton Rd.
Dublin 4
Tel: 01-406 6600 **47 B1**

Royal Victoria
Eye & Ear Hospital
Adelaide Road
Dublin 2.
Tel: 01-664 4600 **38 E4**

St. Bricins Military Hospital
Infirmary Road
Dublin
Tel: 01-677 6112 **37 B2**

St.Columcilles Hospital (A&E)
Loughlinstown
Co . Dublin
Tel: 01-282 5800 **64 D2**

St. James's Hospital (A&E)
James's St.
Dublin 8.
Tel: 01-410 3100 **37 B3**

St. Joseph's Hospital
Clonsilla
Dublin 15
Tel: 01-821 7177 **21 B2**

St. Joseph's Hospital
Springdale Road
Raheny
Dublin 5
Tel: 01 877 4900 **27 A2**

St. Luke's Hospital
Highfield Road.
Rathgar
Dublin 6.
Tel: 01-406 5000 **47 A2**

St. Mary's Hospital
Phoenix Park
Dublin 20
Tel: 01-625 0300 **36 E2**

St. Michael's Hospital (A&E)
Lower George's St.
Dun Laoghaire
Co. Dublin.
Tel: 01-280 6901 **50 D4**

St. Vincent's Hospital (A&E)
Elm Park
Dublin 4.
Tel: 01-221 4000 **48 E1**

Stewart's Hospital
Palmerston
Dublin
Tel: 01-626 4444 **35 C1**

The Mater Hospital (A&E)
Eccles St.
Dublin 7.
Tel: 01-803 2000 **38 D1**

MATERNITY HOSPITALS

Coombe Women's Hospital
Dolphin's Barn
Dublin 8
Tel: 01-408 5200 **37 C4**

National Maternity Hospital
Holles Street
Dublin 2.
Tel: 01-637 3100 **38 E3**

Rotunda Hospital
Parnell St.
Dublin 1
Tel: 01-817 1700 **38 D1**

CHILDRENS HOSPITALS

Childrens University
Hospital (A&E)
Temple Street
Dublin 1
Tel: 01-878 4200 **38 D1**

National Childrens
Hospital
Tallaght
Dublin 24
Tel: 01-414 2000 **54 F1**

Our Lady's Hospital
for Sick Children (A&E)
Crumlin
Dublin 12
Tel: 01-409 6100 **46 D1**

PSYCHIATRIC HOSPITALS

Central Mental Hospital
Dundrum
Dublin 14
Tel: 01-298 9266 **47 C3**

St. Brendan's Hospital
Rathdown Road
Dublin 7
Tel: 01-869 3000 **37 C1**

St. Ita's Hospital
Portrane
Donabate
Co. Dublin
Tel: 01-843 6337

St. John of God Hospital
Stillorgan
Co. Dublin
Tel: 01-288 1781 **58 F1**

St. Vincent's Hospital
Richmond Road
Fairview
Dublin 3
Tel: 01-884 2400 **25 B4**

St. Patrick's Hospital
James's St.
Dublin 8
Tel: 01-249 3200 **37 B3**

PRIVATE HOSPITALS

Beacon Hospital
Sandyford
Dublin 18
Tel: 01-293 6600 **58 D2**

Blackrock Clinic
Rock Road
Blackrock
Co. Dublin
Tel: 01-283 2222 **48 F3**

Bon Secours Hospital
Glasnevin
Dublin 9
Tel: 01-837 5111 **25 A3**

Hermitage Medical Clinic
Old Lucan Road
Dublin 20.
Tel: 01-645 9000 **35 A1**

Clane General Hospital
Prosperous Road
Clane
Co. Kildare
Tel: 045-982 300 **82 A3**

Name	Page	Grid/ Ref. No.	Name	Page	Grid/ Ref. No.	Name	Page	Grid/ Ref. No.
Abbey Business Park	14	F4 112	Bray Business Park	67	C4 255	Cranford Centre, Stillorgan	48	D2 274
Advance Business Park	12	F3 179	Bray Ind Est	67	C4 30	Croke Park Ind Est	38	E1 55
Aerodrome Business Park	52	F1 60	Bridges Ind Est	45	A1 32	Crosbie Business Centre	38	F1 262
Airport Business Park	13	A1 213	Bridgewater Business Centre	37	B2 31	Crossbeg Ind Est	45	A2 56
Airport Industrial Campus	12	E4 1	Brookfield Enterprise Centre	54	D1 247	Crosslands Business Park	45	A2 297
Airside Business Park	2	D3 266	Broombridge Ind Est	24	E3 33	Crosslands Ind Park	45	A2 57
Airside Retail Park	1	C3 295	Broomfield Business Park	3	B4 271	Cruiserath Business Park	9	C3 199
Airton Business Park	45	A4 2	Broomhill Bus Pk Close	45	A4 35	Crumlin Business Park	46	E1 292
Airton Business Park	45	A4 3	Broomhill Bus Pk Drive	45	A4 36	Damastown Ind Est	8	F3 58
Airton Business Park	45	A4 4	Broomhill Bus Pk Road	45	A4 37	Damastown Ind Park	8	F3 302
Airton Coporate Park	45	A4 38	Broomhill Business Park	45	A4 84	Damastown Technology Park	8	E3 166
Airways Industrial Estate	12	F4 5	Burton Hall Campus	58	E2 39	Dartmouth House Ind Centre	36	E3 217
Allied Industrial Estate	36	E4 6	Butterly Business Park	26	D2 66	Deansgrange Business Park	59	B2 59
Alltech Technology Park	6	E2 307	Calmount Business Park	45	B2 197	Docklands Innovation Park	39	A1 155
Ardee Court	67	B2 7	Carrigalea Ind Est	45	B1 40	(The)Donnelly Centre		
Ashgrove Industrial Estate	59	C1 8	Cashel Business Centre	46	E2 293	Cork Street	37	C3 275
Aughrim Lane Ind Est	37	C1 268	Castleforbes Business Park	38	F2 41	Dublin Ind Est		
Avonbeg Enterprise Centre	55	A1 85	Cedar Ind Park	67	B4 258	/ Glasnevin/Broombridge	24	E3 61
Avonbeg Ind Est	45	B1 277	Celbridge Ind Est	31	C3 238	Dun Laoghaire Ind Est	59	B2 63
Avondale	49	A4 167	Central Park Business Park	58	E2 253	Dunboyne Ind Est	7	B2 62
Baldonnel Business Park	43	A4 241	Century Business Park	11	B4 206	Dundrum Business Park	47	C3 231
Baldoyle Ind Est	27	C1 10	Chapelizod Ind Est	36	E2 90	Earlscourt Industrial Estate	47	B4 224
Balfe Road Ind Est	45	C1 196	Charlestown Centre	11	A4 160	Earlsfort Centre	38	E3 276
Balheary Ind Park	2	D1 11	Cherry Orchard Ind Est	35	C2 42	East Point Business Park	39	A1 263
Ballyboggan Ind Est	24	D3 12	Cherrywood Business Park	64	D1 251	East Road Ind Est	38	F1 64
Ballycoolin Business Park	10	D4 13	Churchtown Business Park	47	B4 225	Elmfield Ind Est	44	E1 65
Ballymount Business Centre	45	B2 14	Cian Park Ind Est	25	B4 43	Fashion City	45	A3 69
Ballymount Court			City Junction Business Park	13	C4 212	Feltrim Industrial Park	2	E3 67
Business Centre	45	B2 72	City Link Business Park	36	E4 215	Finches Industrial Park	45	B1 68
Ballymount Cross Ind. Est.	45	A2 15	City West Business Campus	53	B1 44	Finglas Business Centre	11	B4 140
Ballymount Ind Est	45	B2 16	Clondalkin Business Centre	35	B4 46	Finglas Business Park	24	E3 23
Ballymount Road Ind. Est.	45	B2 17	Clondalkin Commercial Park	35	B4 45	Finglas Business Park	9	C3 210
Ballymount Trading Centre	45	B2 18	Clondalkin Enterprise Centre	35	A3 177	Fonthill Retail Park	35	A2 176
Ballymun Ind Est	12	D4 19	Clonshaugh Business			Frank Fahey Centre	45	B1 9
Barbeque Poultry			& Technology Park	13	A4 311	Furry Park Ind Est, Santry	12	E3 181
Business Park	64	E3 300	Clonshaugh Ind Est	13	A4 47	Gaywood Ind Est	9	B3 70
Base Enterprise Centre	9	A4 301	Clonskeagh House Office Park	47	C2 226	Glasnevin Business Centre	24	D3 220
Beech Hill Office Campus	47	C2 228	Clonskeagh Square			Glasnevin Business Park	24	D3 221
Beechlawn Industrial Complex	45	B2 20	Office Park	47	C2 227	Glen Abbey Complex	44	F4 71
Beechwood Close Ind Est	67	C4 21	Cloverhill Ind Est	35	B4 48	Glen Ind Est	24	E3 73
Belfield Office Park	47	C2 229	College Business			Glenageary Office Park	60	D2 291
Belgard Ind Est	44	F4 22	& Technology Park	9	C4 200	Glenview Ind Est	37	B4 74
Bellevue Industrial Park	24	E3 86	Collinstown Cross Ind Est	12	F2 49	Glenville Ind Est	48	E3 75
Benson Street			Collinstown Ind Est	12	F3 50	Goldenbridge Ind Est	36	F4 76
Enterprise Centre	38	F2 24	Collinstown Ind Park (Intel)	19	B3 92	Grange Castle Business Park	34	D4 218
Blackhorse Ind Est	37	B1 25	Concord Ind Est, Naas Road	36	E4 272	Grange Castle		
Blackrock Business Park	49	A3 169	Cookstown Business Centre	44	F4 245	International Business Park	43	B1 239
Blanchardstown			Cookstown Enterprise Park	44	F4 51	Great Keppel Business Centre	15	A1 296
Corporate Park	9	C3 165	Cookstown Ind Est	44	F4 52	Green Isle Business Park	44	D3 242
Blanchardstown Ind Park	9	C4 26	Cookstown Ind Est			Greenhills Business Centre	45	B4 193
Bluebell Business Centre	36	E4 273	The Extension	44	E4 243	Greenhills Business Park	45	B4 192
Bluebell Business Park	36	E4 27	Cookstown Square	44	F4 244	Greenhills Centre	45	B4 191
Bluebell Ind Est	36	D4 28	Coolmine Industrial Est	22	D2 53	Greenhills Ind Est	45	A4 77
Bow Bridge Business Centre	37	B3 308	Courtyard Business Park	43	B2 269	Greenmount Ind Est	37	C4 78
Bracetown Business Park	7	C1 29	Crag Avenue Ind Centre	35	B4 219	Greenogue Business Park	42	E4 235

Name	Page	Grid/Ref.	No.
Grove Ind Est Dubber Cross	11	B3	79
Grove Ind Est, Finglas	24	E1	80
Harbour Ind Est	67	C1	81
(The) Harcourt Centre,	38	D4	278
Hewlett Packard Ind Park	32	F2	234
Hibernian Industrial Estate	45	A4	82
Hillcrest Industrial Estate	45	B2	93
Hills Ind Est	34	D1	83
Hollywood Business Park	9	C3	303
Horizon Logistics	11	B2	204
Howth Junction Business Park	27	B1	270
I.D.A.Tallaght Business Park	54	F2	89
Industrial Yarns Complex	67	C1	91
International Financial Services Centre (IFSC)	38	E2	279
Irish Life Centre	38	E2	280
J.F.K. Ave	45	A1	96
J.F.K. Drive	45	B1	97
J.F.K. Park	36	D4	98
J.F.K. Road	36	D4	99
Jamestown Business Park	11	A4	208
Jamestown Ind Centre	36	F4	95
Jamestown Ind Estate	36	E4	94
Jamestown Little Ind Estate	11	A4	298
KCR Ind Est	46	E2	100
Kilbarrack Ind Est	27	B1	101
Kilcarberry Ind Park	43	A1	283
Kileen Ind Park	36	D4	216
Killarney Road Business Park	67	B3	257
Killinardin Enterprise Park	54	F2	246
Kingswood Business Park	43	B3	312
Kinsealy Business Park	14	D1	281
Knockmitten Business Park	44	F1	282
Kylemore Ind Est	36	D4	102
Kylemore Park North	36	D3	103
Kylemore Park South	36	E4	104
Kylemore Park West	36	D4	105
Landys Ind Est	56	D1	106
Lansdown Valley	45	C1	107
Leopardstown Office Park	58	E2	261
Leopardstown Retail Park	58	E2	108
Liberties Craft & Small Industries Centre	37	C3	109
(The)Liffey Trust Enterprise Centre	38	F2	150
Lilmar Ind Est	12	F4	110
Loughlinstown Ind Est	64	D1	111
(The)Maltings Business Park	37	C3	259
Manor Street Business Park	37	C1	309
Maynooth Business Campus	17	C4	211
Merrywell Business Park	45	A2	188
Merrywell Ind Est	45	A2	182
Metropolitan Ind Est	37	A3	113
Mill Lane Business Park	33	B1	232
Millbank Business Park	34	D1	87
Millenium Business Park	10	E3	202

Name	Page	Grid/Ref.	No.
Monarch Ind Est	44	F4	114
Montone Business Park	44	F1	248
Mount Pleasant Ind Est	47	A1	284
Mulcahy Keane Est	45	C2	115
Mygan Industrial Estate	11	B4	207
Naas Road Business Park	36	E4	132
Naas Road Ind Park	36	F4	170
Nangor Road Business Centre	35	C4	174
Newcastle Business Centre	42	E1	88
Newcourt Business Park	11	A2	205
Newlands Business Centre	44	E2	116
Newtown Ind Est	13	C4	117
North Park Business & Office Park	11	A4	209
North Richmond Ind Est	38	E1	118
North Ring Business Park	12	F3	180
Northern Cross Business Park	11	A4	285
Northwest Business Park	10	D3	201
Nutgrove Enterprise Park	57	A1	252
Nutgrove Office Park	47	A4	223
Oak Road Business Park	44	F1	250
Oakfield Ind Est	35	A4	119
Old Court Ind Est	67	B4	120
Old Sawmills Ind Est	45	B2	121
Ossory Ind Est	38	F1	122
Palmgrove Ind Est	25	B2	265
Park West Business Park	35	C4	173
Park West Enterprise Centre	35	C4	172
Park West Ind Park	36	D4	171
Parkmore Ind Est	45	B1	123
Parkway Business Centre	45	A2	183
Phoenix Ind Est	23	B3	124
Pineview Ind Est	55	C1	125
Pinewood Close Ind Est	67	C4	126
Plato Business Park	9	A3	198
Poppintree Ind Est	11	B4	127
Port Tunnel Business Park	13	A4	310
Portside Business Centre	38	F1	128
Red Cow Business Park	45	A1	184
(The)Red Cow Interchange Est	44	F2	233
Richmond Road Ind Est	25	B4	129
Richview Park	47	C2	230
Riversdale Ind Est	36	E4	130
Riverview Business Centre	35	C4	175
Robinhood Business Park	45	A1	294
Robinhood Ind Est	45	B1	131
Rock Enterprise Centre	43	B3	240
Rosemount Business Park	10	D4	133
Royal Liver Retail Park	36	E4	214
Sandyford Business Centre	58	E2	137
Sandyford Ind Est	58	E2	135
Sandyford Office Park	58	E2	136
Sandyford Park	58	E2	163
Santry Avenue Ind Est	12	E4	138

Name	Page	Grid/Ref.	No.
Santry Hall Ind Est	25	B1	139
Shankhill Business Centre	64	E2	141
Shanowen Ind Est, Santry	25	B1	142
Sitecast Ind Est	45	B4	194
Solus Retail Park, Bray	67	C1	254
South City Business Park	54	F2	306
South City Executive Park	46	E1	288
South County Business Park	58	F2	143
Southern Cross Business Park	67	B4	256
S.P.A.D.E. Unemployment Enterprise Centre	37	C2	287
(The)Square Industrial Complex	54	F1	289
St. Joans Ind Est	45	A2	134
St. John's Court Office Park	25	B1	264
St. Margaret's Business Park	11	A4	286
St. Anthony's Business Park	45	A2	54
Stadium Ind Est	10	E4	203
Stillorgan Ind Park	58	D2	144
Sunbury Ind Est	45	B2	145
Sunshine Ind Est	37	A4/B4	146
Swanward Business Centre	45	A2	185
Swiftbrook Ind Est	53	A2	147
Swords Business Campus	2	D1	267
Swords Business Park	2	E1	148
Tallaght Enterprise Centre	55	A1	149
Taurus Business Park	45	B4	195
Terenure Business Park	46	F2	290
Terenure Enterprise Centre	46	F2	304
Tolka Ind Parks	24	D3	34
Tolka Valley Business Park	24	D3	222
Turnpike Ind Est see Ballymount Cross	45	A2	151
Unidare/Jamestown Business Park	24	E1	152
Weatherwell Ind Est	35	A4	153
West Pier Business Campus	49	C4	168
Westend Retail Park	22	E2	237
Western Business Park	44	F1	249
Western Ind Est	45	A1	156
Western Office Park	22	E1	236
Western Parkway Business Centre, Ballymount Road	45	B2	157
Western Parkway Business Park	45	B2	190
Westgate Business Park	45	A3	186
Westland Square Business Park	38	E2	260
Westlink Ind Est	36	E3	154
Westpoint Buisness Park	8	F4	164
Westway Centre	45	B2	189
White Heather Ind Est	37	B4	158
White Swan Business Park	37	C4	159
Whitestown Ind Est	54	F1	305
Willow Business Park	45	A1	187
Woodford Business Park	12	F3	178
Woodlawn Ind Est	12	F3	162

Due to the limitations imposed by scale it has not been possible to include all street names on the maps. Unnamed streets have been given small numbers which appear after their grid reference in this index. A list of such streets, by grid reference, is given on page 140.

Streets not named or indicated by number on map pages are prefixed by * and are given their appropriate location and grid reference.

STREET NAME	PAGE/GRID REFERENCE
A	
1 Branch Road North	39 A2
1 Branch Road South	39 A2
2 Branch Road North	39 B2
2 Branch Road North Extension	39 B1
2 Branch Road South	39 A2
3 Branch Road South	39 A2
4 Branch Road South	39 B2
A.W. Pugin House	46 F4[19]
(off Stonepark Court)	
Abberley	64 E1
Abberley Square Apartments	54 F1[2]
Abbey Cottages	71 B4
Abbey Court (Killester)	26 E3
Abbey Court (Celbridge)	31 C4
Abbey Court	59 B1[7]
(off Abbey Road Monkstown)	
Abbey Drive	24 D4
Abbey Green	31 C4
Abbey House	8 D3
Abbey Lane	31 C4
Abbey Park (Killester)	26 E3
Abbey Park (Baldoyle)	27 C1
Abbey Park (Celbridge)	31 C4
Abbey Park (Kill O'The Grange)	59 B1
Abbey Road	59 B1
Abbey Street (Howth)	30 D1
Abbey Street Lower	71 C3
Abbey Street Middle	71 B4
Abbey Street Old	71 C3
Abbey Street Upper	71 B4
Abbey Terrace	30 D1[11]
(off Abbey Street)	
Abbey View	59 B1
Abbeydale	34 F3
Abbeydale Close	34 F3
Abbeydale Crescent	34 F3
Abbeydale Gardens	34 F3
Abbeydale Park	34 F3
Abbeydale Rise	34 F3
Abbeydale Walk	34 F3
Abbeyfarm	31 C4
Abbeyfield (Killester)	26 E3
Abbeyfield (Clonskeagh)	47 B2
Abbeylea Avenue	1 C1
Abbeylea Close	1 C1
Abbeylea Drive	1 C1
Abbeylea Green	1 C1
Abbeyvale Avenue	1 B1
Abbeyvale Close	1 B1
Abbeyvale Court	1 B1
Abbeyvale Crescent	1 B1
Abbeyvale Drive	1 B2
Abbeyvale Green	1 B2
Abbeyvale Grove	1 B1
Abbeyvale Lawn	1 B1
Abbeyvale Place	1 B1
Abbeyvale Rise	1 B1
Abbeyvale View	1 B2
Abbeyvale Way	1 B2
Abbeywood	34 F3
Abbeywood Avenue	34 F3
Abbeywood Close	34 F3
Abbeywood Court	34 E3
Abbeywood Crescent	34 F3
Abbeywood Park	34 F3
Abbeywood Way	34 F3
Abbots Hill	3 C3
Abbotstown Avenue	23 C2
Abbotstown Drive	23 C1
Abbotstown Road	24 D2
Abby Well	14 D1
Abercorn Road	72 E3
Abercorn Square	36 F3[19]
(off Inchicore Terrace South)	
Abercorn Terrace	36 F3[10]
(off Inchicore Terrace South)	
Aberdeen Street	70 D3
Abington	2 F3
Accommodation Road	19 C4
Achill Road (Drumcondra)	25 B3
Achill Road (Loughlinstown)	64 E1
Acorn Drive	57 B1
Acorn Road	57 B1
Acres Road	36 F2
Adair (off Sandymount Avenue)	39 A4[14]
*Adair Lane (off Aston Place)	71 B4
*Adair Terrace	71 A1
(on St Joseph's Parade)	
Adam Court (off Grafton Street)	75 B1
Adams Town Court	34 D2[2]
(off Adamstown Road)	
Adamstown Avenue	33 C4
Adamstown Road	34 D2
Adare Avenue	26 E1
Adare Drive	26 E1
Adare Green	26 E1
Adare Park	26 E1
Adare Road	26 E1
Addison Avenue (off Addison Lane)	24 F3[8]
Addison Drive	24 F3
Addison Hall (off Addison Lane)	24 F3[6]
Addison Lane	24 F3
Addison Park	24 F3
Addison Place (off Botanic Avenue)	25 A3[9]
Addison Road	25 C4
Adelaide Court	75 B3
Adelaide Mews	48 E1
Adelaide Road (Dún Laoghaire)	60 E1
Adelaide Road (Bray)	67 C2
Adelaide Road (Leeson Street)	75 B3
Adelaide Street	50 D4
Adelaide Terrace (off Adelaide Road Dún Laoghaire)	60 E1[28]
Adelaide Terrace	73 C2
(off Brookfield Road)	
Adelaide Villas	60 E1[27]
(off Adelaide Road Dún Laoghaire)	
Adelaide Villas (Bray)	67 C2
Admiral Brown Walk	72 E4
Admiral Court	15 A4[9]
(off Willie Nolan Road)	
Admiral Park	15 A4
Adrian Avenue	46 F1
Aengus Hall	54 F1[3]
(off Belgard Square West)	
Affollus	5 C3
Aideen Avenue	46 E2
Aideen Drive	46 E2
Aideen Place	46 E2
Aikenhead Terrace	39 A3
Aiken's Village	58 D3
Ailesbury (off Shanowen Road)	25 B1[1]
Ailesbury Close	48 D1[4]
(off Ailesbury Road)	
Ailesbury Drive	48 D1
Ailesbury Gardens	48 E1
Ailesbury Grove (Donnybrook)	48 D1
Ailesbury Grove (Dundrum)	57 B1
Ailesbury Lane (off Ailesbury Road)	48 D1
Ailesbury Lawn	57 B1
Ailesbury Mews	48 E1
Ailesbury Park	48 E1
Ailesbury Road	48 D1
Ailesbury Wood	48 D1
Airfield Court	48 D2
Airfield Drive	47 B4[13]
(off Churchtown Road)	
Airfield Park	48 D2
Airfield Road	46 F2
Airlie Heights	33 B2
Airpark Avenue	56 E2
Airpark Close	56 E2
Airpark Court	56 E2
Airpark House	56 E2
Airpark Rise	56 E2
Airside	2 D3
Airton Close	45 A4
Airton Road	45 A4
*Airton Terrace (off Greenhills Rd)	45 A4
Albany Avenue	49 B4
Albany Court	64 E1
Albany Road	47 B1
Albert Avenue	68 D2
Albert College Avenue	25 A2
Albert College Court	25 A2
Albert College Crescent	25 A2
Albert College Drive	25 A2
Albert College Grove	25 A2
Albert College Lawn	25 A2
Albert College Park	25 A2
Albert Court (Sandycove Road)	60 E1
Albert Court	76 E1
(Grand Canal St. Lower)	
Albert Court (off Grand Canal St)	76 E1
Albert Park (off Hudson Road)	60 E1[3]
Albert Place East	76 E1
Albert Place West	75 B3
Albert Road Lower	60 E1
Albert Road Upper	60 E2
Albert Terrace	50 D4[27]
(off Crofton Road)	
Albert Terrace (Charlemont Street)	75 B3
Albert Walk	67 C2
Aldborough House	72 D2
Aldborough Parade	72 D2
Aldborough Place	72 D2
Aldborough Square	72 D2
(off Aldborough Place)	
Aldemere	21 B2
Alden Drive	27 C1
Alden Park	27 C1
Alden Road	27 C1
Alder Court	4 D4[1]
Alder Lodge	23 A4
Alderpark Court	54 F1
Alderwood Avenue	54 E1
Alderwood Close	54 E1
Alderwood Court	54 E1
Alderwood Drive	54 F1
Alderwood Green	54 E1
Alderwood Grove	54 F1
Alderwood Lawn	54 E1
Alderwood Park	54 E1
Alderwood Rise	54 E1
Alderwood Way	54 F1
Aldrin Walk	26 E1
Alen Hall	54 F1[4]
(off Belgard Square West)	
Alensgrove	32 F2
Alexander Court Apartments	76 D1
Alexander Terrace (Bray)	67 C2[43]
Alexander Terrace (North Wall)	72 F3
Alexandra Court	47 C4
Alexandra Place	72 F2
Alexandra Quay	39 A2[2]
(off York Road, Ringsend)	
Alexandra Quay (Alexandra Basin)	39 A2
Alexandra Road	39 A2
Alexandra Road Extension	39 C2
Alexandra Terrace (Terenure)	46 F2
Alexandra Terrace (Dundrum)	47 C4
Alexandra Terrace (Portobello)	75 A3
Alexandra Villas	47 C4[3]
(off Dundrum Road)	
Alfie Byrne House	71 B2
Alfie Byrne Road	72 F1
All Hallows Green	25 B3
All Hallows Lane	25 B3[7]
(off All Hallows Square)	
All Hallows Square	25 B3
All Saint's Close	27 A3
All Saints Drive	27 A3
All Saints Park	27 A3
All Saints Road	26 F3
Allen Park Drive	58 E1
Allen Park Road	58 E1
Allen Terrace	70 F1
(off Avondale Avenue)	
Allendale Close	21 B2
Allendale Copse	21 B1
Allendale Court	21 B1
Allendale Drive	21 B1
Allendale Elms	21 B1
Allendale Glen	21 B1
Allendale Green	21 B1
Allendale Grove	21 B1
Allendale Heath	21 B1
Allendale Lawn	21 B1
Allendale Place	21 B1
Allendale Rise	21 B1
Allendale Square	21 B2
Allendale Terrace	21 B1
Allendale View	21 B1
Allendale Walk	21 B1
Allenton Avenue	55 A3
Allenton Crescent	55 A2[3]
(off Allenton Road)	
Allenton Drive	55 A3
Allenton Gardens	55 A3
Allenton Green	55 A3
Allenton Lawns	55 A2
Allenton Park	55 A2
Allenton Road	55 B3
Allenton Way	55 A3
Allies River Road	67 A1
Allingham Street	74 E2
Alma Park	49 C4[30]
(off Carrickbrennan Road)	
Alma Place	49 C4[14]
(off Carrickbrennan Road)	
Alma Road	49 B4
Alma Terrace	47 A1[13]
(off Mountpleasant Avenue Upper)	
Almeida Avenue	73 C1
Almeida Terrace	73 C2
Alone Walk	26 E2
Alpine Heights	44 D1
Alpine Rise	44 E4
Altadore	60 D2
Altamont Hall	47 C4
Alverno (off Castle Avenue)	39 B1[1]
Ambassador Court	76 E3
(off Herbert Road)	
Amber Vale	44 E4
Amberwood	9 A4
Amiens Street	72 D3
An Crannog	60 D3
Anastasia Lane (off Sorrento Road)	60 F2[1]
Anglers Rest	47 C1
Anglesea Avenue	49 A3
Anglesea House	39 A4[40]
(off Serpentine Avenue)	
Anglesea Lane (off Corrig Avenue)	50 D4[20]
Anglesea Park	60 E2
Anglesea Road	47 C1
Anglesea Row	71 A3
Anglesea Street	71 B4
Anley Court	34 E1
Ann Devlin Avenue	46 E4
Ann Devlin Drive	46 E4
Ann Devlin Park	56 E1
Ann Devlin Road	46 E4
Anna Livia Apartments	74 E1
Anna Villa	47 B1
Annabeg (off Wyattville Road)	60 D4[1]
Annacrivey	65 B3
Annadale	47 B4[16]
(off Churchtown Road Upper)	
Annadale Avenue	25 C4[1]
(off Philipsburgh Avenue)	
Annadale Crescent	25 C3
Annadale Drive	25 C3
Annagh Court	22 F1
Annaghaskin	66 D1
Annaly Close	21 B1
Annaly Court	21 B1
Annaly Drive	21 B1
Annaly Grove	21 B1
Annaly Road	24 F4
Annaly Terrace	21 B1
Annamoe Drive	70 E1
Annamoe Parade	70 E1
Annamoe Park	70 E1
Annamoe Road	70 D1
Annamoe Terrace	70 E1
Annaville Avenue	59 A1
Annaville Close	47 C4
Annaville Grove	47 C3[1]
(off Annaville Park)	
Annaville Lodge	47 C4
Annaville Park	47 C4
Annaville Terrace	47 C3
Anne Street North	71 A3
Anne Street South	75 B1
Anner Road	73 B2
Anne's Bridge	17 C1
Anne's Lane	75 B1
Annesley Avenue	72 E1
Annesley Bridge (Tolka River)	72 F1
Annesley Bridge Road	72 F1
Annesley Close	72 E1
Annesley Park	47 B1
Annesley Place	72 E1
Annfield	22 D3
Annfield Court	22 D3
Annfield Crescent	22 D3
Annfield Drive	22 D3
Annfield Lawn	22 D4
Annsbrook	47 C2
Annville Drive	58 E1
Apollo Way	26 D1
*Appian Close (on Leeson Park)	76 D4
Apples Road	58 D2
Applewood Avenue East	1 Inset
Applewood Birch	1 Inset
Applewood Crescent	1 Inset
Applewood Drive	1 Inset
Applewood Main Street	1 Inset
Applewood Mews	1 Inset
Applewood Place	1 Inset
Applewood Square	1 Inset
Aranleigh Court	56 F1
Aranleigh Dell	57 A1
Aranleigh Gardens	56 F1
Aranleigh Mount	56 F1

STREET NAME	PAGE/GRID REFERENCE
Aranleigh Park	57 A1
Aranleigh Vale	56 F1
Arás na Cluaine	35 B4
Aravon Court	68 D2
Arbour Hill	70 E3
Arbour Place	70 E3
Arbour Terrace	70 D3
Arbutus Avenue	74 F4
Arbutus Grove	67 B1 [4]
Arbutus Place	75 A3
Archers Wood	8 F4
*Archway Court	71 A2
(off Mountjoy Street)	
Ard Lorcain	58 F1
Ard Lorcain Villas	58 F1 [2]
(off Ard Lorcain Stillorgan)	
Ard Mhacha	54 F2
Ard Mhuire Park	60 E2
Ard Mor Avenue	53 C1
Ard Mor Close	53 C1
Ard Mor Court	53 C1
Ard Mor Crescent	53 C1
Ard Mor Dale	53 C1
Ard Mor Drive	53 C1
Ard Mor Green	53 C1
Ard Mor Lawn	53 C1
Ard Mor Park	53 C1
Ard Mor Walk	53 C1
Ard na Glaise	48 F4
Ard Na Gréine	47 A3 [11]
(off Orwell Road Rathgar)	
Ard Na Gréine (Ballymorris)	67 B4
Ard na Mara	3 A3
Ard na Meala	12 D4
Ard Ri Place	70 E3
Ard Ri Road	70 E3
Ardagh Avenue	59 A1
Ardagh Close	59 A1 [6]
(off Ardagh Park Road)	
Ardagh Court	58 F1
Ardagh Crescent	59 A1
Ardagh Drive	59 A1
Ardagh Grove	59 A1
Ardagh Park	59 A1
Ardagh Park Road	59 A1
Ardagh Road	73 C4
Ardara Avenue	14 D4
Ardbeg Crescent	26 E2
Ardbeg Drive	26 E2
Ardbeg Park	26 E2
Ardbeg Road	26 E2
Ardbrugh Close	60 F2 [31]
(off Ardbrough Road)	
Ardbrugh Road	60 F2
Ardbrugh Villas	60 F2 [21]
(off Ardbrough Road)	
Ardcian Park	1 C1
Ardcollum Avenue	26 E2
*Ardee Court (Ardee Row)	74 F2
Ardee Grove	75 B4
Ardee Road	75 B4
Ardee Row	74 F2
Ardee Street (Bray)	67 B2
Ardee Street (The Coombe)	74 F2
Ardeen	33 C2
Ardeevin Avenue	33 C2
Ardeevin Court	33 C2
Ardeevin Drive	33 C2
Ardeevin Road	60 F2
*Ardeevin Terrace	60 F2
(off Ardeevin Road)	
Ardenza Park	49 B3 [3]
(off Seapoint Avenue)	
Ardenza Terrace	49 B3 [1]
(off Seapoint Avenue)	
Ardglas Estate	57 C1
Ardilaun	14 F1
Ardilaun Road	72 D1
*Ardilaun Square	72 D1
(off Sackville Avenue)	
Ardilea Downs	48 D4
Ardlea Road	26 E2
Ardlui Park	59 A1
Ardmeen Park	59 A1
Ardmore Avenue	70 D1
Ardmore Close	26 D2
Ardmore Crescent (Artane)	26 D2
Ardmore Crescent (Bray)	67 B2
Ardmore Drive	26 D1
Ardmore Grove	26 D1
Ardmore Lawn	67 B3
Ardmore Park (Artane)	26 D2
Ardmore Park	59 C1
(Kill O'The Grange)	
Ardmore Park (Bray)	67 B2
Ardmore Wood	67 B3
Ardoyne Mews	76 E4
(off Claremont Road)	
Ardpatrick Road	24 D4
Ardtona Avenue	47 B4 [6]
(off Churchtown Road Lower)	
Arena Road	58 E2
Argus House	74 F4
Argyle House Apartments	39 A4 [37]
(off Claremont Road)	
Argyle Road	76 E4
Argyle Square	47 C1 [25]
(off Marlborough Road)	
Arkendale Court	60 E1 [26]
(off Arkendale Road)	
Arkendale Road	60 E1
Arkendale Woods	60 E1 [25]
(off Arkendale Road)	
Arkle Road	58 E2
Arkle Square (off Brewery Road)	58 F2 [6]
Arklow Street	70 D2
Armagh Road	46 D1
Armstrong Street	74 F4
(off Harold's Cross Road)	
Armstrong Walk	26 E1
Army Road	69 B3
Arnold Grove	60 D2
Arnold Park	60 D2
Arnott Street	75 A2
Arran Avenue	64 E1
Arran Close	64 E1
Arran Court	22 F1
Arran Drive	64 E1
Arran Green	67 C2
Arran Quay	70 F4
Arran Quay Apartments	70 F4
*Arran Quay Terrace (Arran Quay)	70 F4
Arran Road	25 B3
Arran Square Apartments	70 F4
Arran Street East	71 A4
Arran Street West	70 F4
Arranmore Avenue	71 A1
Arranmore Road	47 C1
Artane	26 E2
Artane Cottages Lower	26 E2 [2]
(off Malahide Road)	
Artane Cottages Upper	26 E2 [3]
(off Malahide Road)	
Arthur Griffith Court	34 D2 [1]
(off Esker Road)	
Arthur Griffith Park	34 D3
Arundel (off Monkstown Valley)	49 B4 [19]
Asdill's Row (off Temple Bar)	71 B4
Asgard Apartments	30 D1
Asgard Park	30 D2
Asgard Road (Howth)	30 D2
Asgard Road	72 E4
*Ash Grove (Meath Street)	74 F1
Ash Park Avenue	34 E3
Ash Park Court	34 E3
Ash Park Grove	34 E2
Ash Park Heath	34 E2
Ash Street	74 F1
Ashberry	34 D3
Ashbrook (Ashtown)	23 C3
Ashbrook (Clontarf)	26 D4
Ashbrook (Bray)	67 C2
*Ashbrook Terrace (Ranelagh)	47 B1
*Ashbrook Villas (Ranelagh)	47 B1
Ashbury Park	67 C2
Ashcroft	27 A2
Ashcroft Court	22 D1 [5]
(off Briarwood Lawn)	
Ashcroft Grove	22 D1 [4]
(off Briarwood Lawn)	
Ashdale Avenue	46 F2
Ashdale Close	2 E3
Ashdale Gardens	46 F2
Ashdale Park (off Ashdale Road)	46 F2 [1]
Ashdale Road (Swords)	2 E3
Ashdale Road (Terenure)	46 F2
Ashe Court	2 E2
Ashfield	46 D4
Ashfield Avenue (Clondalkin)	44 F3
Ashfield Avenue (Ranelagh)	47 B1
Ashfield Close (Clondalkin)	44 F3
Ashfield Court (Mulhuddart)	9 A4
Ashfield Court (Ballymorris)	67 B4
Ashfield Drive	44 F3
Ashfield Gardens	9 A4
Ashfield Green	8 F4
Ashfield Grove	9 A4
Ashfield Lawn	8 F4
Ashfield Park	9 A4 [2]
(off Blakestown Road)	
Ashfield Park (Clondalkin)	44 F3
Ashfield Park (Terenure)	46 F2
Ashfield Park (Booterstown)	48 E2
Ashfield Road (Ranelagh)	47 B1
Ashfield Way	8 A4
Ashford Cottages	70 D2
Ashford Place	70 D2
Ashford Street	70 D2
Ashgrove (Baskin Lane)	13 C1
Ashgrove (Celbridge)	31 C2
Ashgrove (Tallaght)	54 E1
Ashgrove (Kill O'The Grange)	59 C1
Ashgrove Court	57 C1 [8]
(off Sandyford Road)	
Ashgrove Terrace	57 C1 [2]
(off Sandyford Road)	
Ashington Avenue	24 D3
Ashington Close	24 D3
Ashington Court	24 D3
Ashington Crescent	23 C3
Ashington Dale	24 D3
Ashington Gardens	24 D3
Ashington Green	24 D3
Ashington Grove	24 D3
Ashington Heath	24 D3
Ashington Mews	24 D3
Ashington North	24 D3
Ashington Park	24 D3
Ashington Rise	23 C3
Ashlawn	57 C1
Ashlawn Court	67 B2
Ashlawn Park	60 D4
Ashleigh Court	22 F3 [3]
(off Castleknock Road)	
Ashleigh Green	22 F3
Ashleigh Grove (Maynooth)	17 B4
Ashleigh Grove (Blanchardstown)	22 F3
Ashleigh Lawn	3 B3
Ashley Avenue	2 D2
Ashley Drive	2 D2
Ashley Grove	2 D2
Ashley Heights	67 B2 [4]
Ashley Rise	4 D4
Ashling Close	73 C4
Ashling Court	47 B1
Ashling Heights	22 E1
Ashmount (off Blakestown Road)	9 A4 [1]
Ashton Avenue	1 Inset
Ashton Avenue	56 D1
Ashton Close	1 Inset
Ashton Close	56 D1
Ashton Court	1 Inset
Ashton Drive	1 Inset
Ashton Green	1 Inset
Ashton Grove	1 Inset
Ashton Grove	56 D1
Ashton Lawn	56 D1
Ashton Lawns	1 Inset
Ashton Park	49 B4
Ashton Rise	1 Inset
Ashton Wood	67 A3
Ashtown	23 C3
Ashtown Court	23 C4
Ashtown Gate (Phoenix Park)	23 B4
Ashtown Gate Road	23 B4
Ashtown Grove	23 C4
Ashtown Lodge	23 C4 [4]
(off Ashtown Grove)	
Ashtown Road	23 B3
Ashtowngate	23 C3
Ashurst	48 E4 [3]
(off Mount Merrion Avenue)	
Ashurst	60 E4
Ashurst (Ballybrack)	64 E1
Ashville Close	34 E1
Ashwood Avenue	43 C1
Ashwood Close	43 C1
Ashwood Drive	44 D1
Ashwood Lawns	44 D1
Ashwood Park	44 D1
Ashwood Road	44 D1
Ashwood Way	44 D1
Ashworth Place	75 A4
(off Mount Drumond Avenue)	
Aspen Drive	2 E3
Aspen Park (Kinsealy Court)	2 E3
Aspen Park (off Carriglea Avenue)	59 C1 [11]
Aspen Road	2 E3
Aspen Wood	22 D2
Aspin Avenue	21 C2
Aspin Lawns	22 D2
Assumpta Park	64 E3
Aston Place	71 B4
Aston Quay	71 B4
Astor Hall	71 C4
Athgoe	51 C1
Athgoe Drive	64 E2 [4]
Athgoe North	51 B1
Athgoe Road (Newcastle)	41 C4
Athgoe Road (Shankill)	64 E2
Athgoe South	51 B2
Atlumney Villas	75 B4
Atmospheric Road	60 E1 [29]
(off Castlepark Road)	
Aubrey Grove	64 E3
Aubrey Park	64 E3
Auburn	26 D4
Auburn Avenue (Castleknock)	23 A3
Auburn Avenue (Donnybrook)	47 C1
Auburn Avenue (Cabinteely)	60 D3
Auburn Avenue Roundabout	23 A3
Auburn Close (Castleknock)	23 A3
Auburn Close (Cabinteely)	60 D3
Auburn Drive (Castleknock)	23 A3
Auburn Drive (Cabinteely)	60 D3
Auburn Green	23 A3
Auburn Grove	3 A3
Auburn Road (off Victoria Avenue)	47 C1 [11]
Auburn Road	60 D3 [1]
(off Churchview Road)	
Auburn Road	60 D3
(off Woodlands Road)	
Auburn Street	71 A2
Auburn Terrace	73 C1
(Old Kilmainham)	
Auburn Villas (Rathgar)	47 A2
Auburn Villas (Bray)	67 B2
Auburn Walk	70 D2
Aughavannagh Road	74 E4
Aughrim Court	70 E3
Aughrim Lane	70 E2
Aughrim Place	70 D2
Aughrim Street	70 D2
Aughrim Villas	70 D2
Augustine Court	74 F1
(St Margaret's Terrace)	
Augustine Villas	67 C2 [30]
Aulden Grange	12 F4
Aungier Lane	75 B2
Aungier Place	75 B2
Aungier Street	75 B1
Austin's Cottages	72 E1
Avalon	59 A3 [3]
(off Brighton Road Foxrock)	
Avalon Apartments	29 B1 [2]
(off Claremont Road)	
Ave Maria Road	74 D2
Avenue Road	75 A3
Avila Apartments	59 A1 [10]
(off Carysfort Avenue)	
Avila Park	23 C1
Avila Park Gardens	23 C1
Avoca Apartments	32 D3
Avoca Avenue (Stillorgan)	48 F4
Avoca Avenue (Dún Laoghaire)	67 C3
Avoca Court	48 F4
Avoca Hall (off Avoca Park)	49 A4 [10]
Avoca Park	48 F4
Avoca Place	49 A3
Avoca Road	48 F4
Avoca Terrace	48 F4
Avoca Wood	48 F4
Avonbeg Court (off Avonbeg Drive)	55 A1 [3]
Avonbeg Drive	55 A1
Avonbeg Gardens	55 B1
Avonbeg Park	55 A1
Avonbeg Road	55 B1
Avondale	20 D4
*Avondale Apartments	71 A3
(Lurgan Street)	
Avondale Avenue	70 F1
Avondale Court (Blackrock)	49 A4
Avondale Court	60 E1 [31]
(off Albert Road Lower)	
Avondale Crescent	60 E2
Avondale House	71 C2
Avondale Lawn	49 A4

STREET NAME	PAGE	GRID
Avondale Mews (off Kirkwood)	39	A4 [55]
Avondale Park (Raheny)	27	A2
Avondale Park (off Carysfort Avenue Blackrock)	49	A4 [1]
Avondale Park (Dalkey)	60	E2
Avondale Park (Dún Laoghaire)	67	B3
Avondale Road (Dalkey)	60	D2
Avondale Road (Phibsborough)	70	F1
Avondale Square	7	B2 [2]
Avondale Terrace	45	C2
Avonmore	59	A2
Avonmore Avenue (off Avonmore Road)	55	B1 [5]
Avonmore Close	55	B1
Avonmore Drive	55	B1
Avonmore Grove	55	B1
Avonmore Park	55	B1
Avonmore Road	55	B1
Aylesbury	55	A2
Aylmer Ave	42	D4
Aylmer Heath	42	D4
Aylmer Road	42	D4
Ayrefield Avenue	26	F1
Ayrefield Court	26	F1
Ayrefield Drive	26	F1
Ayrefield Grove	26	F1
Ayrefield Park (off Ayrefield Road)	26	F1 [2]
Ayrefield Place	26	F1
Ayrefield Road	26	F1
Ayward Green	24	D2

B

STREET NAME	PAGE	GRID
Bachelor's Walk	71	B4
Bachelors Walk Apartments	71	B4
Bachelors Way	71	B4
Back Lane (off College Street Baldoyle)	15	A4 [3]
Back Lane (Maynooth)	17	C3
Back Lane (High Street)	75	A1
*Back Lane (off Sandwith St Upper)	76	D1
Back Road	3	B4
Baggot Bridge Court	76	D2
Baggot Close	75	C2
Baggot Court	76	D2
Baggot Lane	76	E3
Baggot Rath House (off Newbridge Avenue)	39	A3 [48]
Baggot Road	23	C4
Baggot Street Lower	76	D2
Baggot Street Upper	76	E3
Baggot Terrace (off Blackhorse Avenue)	23	C4 [1]
Baggotrath Place	76	D2
Bailey Green	30	E3
Bailey Green Road	30	E3
Bailey View (off Harbour Road)	60	F1 [15]
Bailey's Row	72	D2
Balally Avenue	58	D1
Balally Close	58	D1
Balally Drive	58	D1
Balally Grove	58	D2
Balally Hill	58	D2
Balally Park	58	D1
Balally Road	57	C1
Balally Terrace (off Sandyford Road)	58	D2 [1]
Balbutcher Drive	11	C4
Balbutcher Lane	11	C4
Balbutcher Lane Lower	11	C4
Balbutcher Way	11	C4
Balcurris Close	12	D4
Balcurris Gardens	12	D4
Balcurris Park East	12	D4
Balcurris Road	12	D4
Baldoyle	15	A4
Baldoyle Road	28	D1
Balfe Avenue	45	C1
Balfe Road	45	C1
Balfe Road East	46	D1
Balfe Street	75	B1
Balgaddy Road	34	F3
Balglass Road	30	D2
Balgriffin	14	D3
Balgriffin Cottages	14	D3
Balgriffin Park	14	D3
Balgriffin Road	14	D3
Balheary Road	2	D1
Balkill Grove	30	D2
Balkill Park	30	D2
Balkill Road	30	D2
Ballawley Court	57	C2
Ballentree	9	B2
Ballentree Avenue	9	B2
Ballentree Close	9	B2
Ballentree Crescent	9	B2
Ballentree Drive	9	B2
Ballentree Grove	9	B3
Ballentree Lodge Apartments	9	B2
Ballentree Villa	9	B3
*Ballinakelly Edge (off Newcastle Boulevard)	42	D4
*Ballinakelly Mews (off Newcastle Boulevard)	42	D4
*Ballinakelly Rise (off Newcastle Boulevard)	42	D4
Ballinakelly Village	42	D4
Ballinclea Heights	60	E3
Ballinclea Road	60	D3
Ballinteer	57	B2
Ballinteer Avenue	57	B2
Ballinteer Close	57	B2
Ballinteer Court (off Ballinteer Avenue)	57	B2 [2]
Ballinteer Crescent	57	B2
Ballinteer Drive	57	B2
Ballinteer Gardens	57	C2
Ballinteer Grove	57	B2
Ballinteer Park	57	B2
Ballinteer Road (Dundrum)	57	C1
Ballinteer Road (Delbrook Park)	57	C2
Ballintrane Wood	1	C2
Ballintyre Demesne	57	B2
Ballintyre Downs	57	B2
Ballintyre Lane	57	B2
Ballintyre Meadows	57	B2
Ballintyre Square	57	B2
Ballintyre Terrace	57	B2
Ballintyre Walk	57	B2
Ballintyre Woods	57	B2
Ball's Lane	71	A3
Ballsbridge (River Dodder)	76	F4
Ballsbridge Avenue (off Merrion Road)	39	A4 [26]
Ballsbridge Court	76	F3
Ballsbridge Gardens (off Merrion Road)	76	F3
Ballsbridge Park (off Merrion Road)	39	A4 [23]
Ballsbridge Terrace (off Sandymount Avenue)	76	F4
Ballsbridge Wood	76	F3
Ballybetagh	62	F4
Ballybetagh Road	62	E4
Ballyboden	56	E1
Ballyboden Crescent	56	E1
Ballyboden Road	56	E1
Ballyboden Way	56	E1
Ballyboggan Road	24	E3
Ballybough Avenue	72	D1
Ballybough Court	72	D1
*Ballybough Lane (King's Avenue)	72	D1
Ballybough Road	72	D1
Ballybrack	60	E4
Ballybrack (Two Rock Mountain)	61	B3
Ballybrew	65	C2
Ballybride	64	D3
Ballybride Road	64	D3
Ballycoolin Road	10	D4
Ballycorus	63	B3
Ballycorus Road	63	A2
Ballycullen Avenue	55	B2
Ballycullen Drive	55	B2
Ballycullen Road	55	C1
Ballydowd Grove	34	E1
Ballydowd Manor	34	E2
Ballyedmonduff (Two Rock Mountain)	61	C2
Ballyedmonduff (Stepaside)	62	E1
Ballyedmonduff Road	62	D1
Ballyfermot	36	D3
Ballyfermot Avenue	36	D3
Ballyfermot Crescent	36	D3
Ballyfermot Drive	36	D3
Ballyfermot Parade	36	D3
Ballyfermot Road (Cherry Orchard)	35	C3
Ballyfermot Road (Ballyfeermot)	36	E3
Ballygall Avenue	24	E1
Ballygall Crescent	24	E2
Ballygall Parade	24	E2
Ballygall Place (off Ballygall Parade)	24	E2 [1]
Ballygall Road	24	E2
Ballygall Road East	24	F2
Ballygall Road West	24	E1
Ballygihen Avenue	60	E1
Ballygihen Villas (off Sandycove Road)	60	E1 [20]
Ballygoran	18	E4
Ballygoran Court	31	C2
Ballygoran View	31	C2
Ballyhoy Avenue	27	A3
Ballymacartle	13	C1
Ballymace Green	46	E4
Ballymacoll	6	D3
Ballymadrough Road	2	F1
Ballymakealy Grove	31	C4
Ballymakealy Lawns	31	C4
Ballyman	66	F1
Ballyman Lane (Carrickgollogan)	63	C4
Ballyman Lane (Ballyman)	66	F1
Ballyman Road	66	F2
Ballymana	54	E4
Ballymanagin Lane (off Newlands Road)	35	A4 [1]
Ballymorris (off Killarney Road)	67	B4 [2]
Ballymorris	67	B4
Ballymoss Parade (off Brewery Road)	58	F2 [5]
Ballymoss Road	58	E2
Ballymount Avenue	45	B2
Ballymount Cottages (off Ballymount Road Lower)	45	B2 [2]
Ballymount Drive	45	B2
Ballymount Road	44	F3
Ballymount Road Lower	45	B2
Ballymount Road Upper	45	A2
Ballymount Square	45	B2
Ballymun	25	A1
Ballymun Main Street	12	D4
Ballymun Road (M50 Junction 4)	12	D4
Ballymun Road (Ballymun)	25	A1
Ballymun Road (Glasnevin)	25	A3
Ballynakelly	42	D4
Ballyneety Road	36	F3
Ballynoe Court	67	B3 [1]
Ballyogan Avenue	58	F4
Ballyogan Close	58	F4
Ballyogan Court	58	F4
Ballyogan Crescent	58	F4
Ballyogan Drive	58	F4
Ballyogan Estate	58	F4
Ballyogan Green	58	F4
Ballyogan Lawn	58	F4
Ballyogan Park (off Ballyogan Drive)	58	F4 [1]
Ballyogan Road	58	F4
Ballyogen Vale	59	A4
Ballyogen Wood	59	A4
Ballyolaf Manor (off Parkvale)	57	C1 [6]
Ballyoulster Park	32	E3
Ballyowen Avenue	34	F1
Ballyowen Court	34	F1
Ballyowen Crescent	34	F1
Ballyowen Drive	34	F1
Ballyowen Green	34	F1
Ballyowen Grove	34	F1
Ballyowen Hall	34	F2
Ballyowen Lane	34	F2
Ballyowen Lawn	34	F1
Ballyowen Road	34	F1
Ballyowen Square	34	F2
Ballyowen View	34	F1
Ballyowen Way	34	F1
Ballyroan Court (off Knocklyon Drive)	56	D1 [3]
Ballyroan Crescent	56	E1
Ballyroan Heights	56	E1
Ballyroan Park	56	D1
Ballyroan Road	56	E1
Ballyshannon Avenue	25	C1
Ballyshannon Road	26	D1
Ballystruan Lane	12	D3
Ballytore Road	46	F3
Ballywaltrim Cottages	67	B4 [1]
Ballywaltrim Heights	67	B3
Ballywaltrim Lane	67	A4
Ballywaltrim Road	67	B4
Ballywilliam Close	67	B4
Balnagowan (off Palmerston Park)	47	B2 [4]
Balrothery Cottages (off Tallaght Road)	55	C1 [5]
Balrothery Estate	45	B4
Balscadden Road	30	E1
Balscott	41	C1
Bancroft Avenue	55	A1
Bancroft Close	55	B1
Bancroft Crescent	45	B4
Bancroft Downs	45	A4
Bancroft Grove	55	B1
Bancroft Park	55	A1
Bancroft Road	55	B1
Bangor Circle	46	E1
Bangor Drive	73	C4
Bangor Road	46	E1
Bankside Cottages	47	B2
Bann Road	24	E3
Bannaville	75	B4
Bannow Road	24	E4
Banshee	51	A2
Bantry Road	25	A3
Bantry Square	22	F1
Banville Avenue	36	D4
Barberstown Lane	1	A4
Bargy Road	72	F1
Barnacoille Park	60	F1
Barnamire	65	A4
Barnamore Crescent	24	D3
Barnamore Grove	24	D3
Barnamore Park	24	D3
Barnaslingan Lane	63	A3
Barneville Green	35	C3
Barneville Walk	35	C4
Barnhall	32	F1
Barnhall Drive	32	F1
Barnhill Avenue	60	E2
Barnhill Cross Road	34	D1
Barnhill Grove (off Barnhill Road)	60	F2 [7]
Barnhill Lawn (off Barnhill Road)	60	E2 [1]
Barnhill Park (off Saval Park Gardens)	60	E2 [3]
Barnhill Road	60	E2
*Barnhill Villas (on Barnhill Road)	60	F2
Barnville Park	35	C4
Barnwell Drive	24	F1
Baroma (off Kimmage Road Lower)	46	E2 [10]
Barrack Bridge	3	A2
Barrack Court	52	F2
*Barrack Lane (off Irishtown Road)	39	A3
Barrett Street (off York Road Dún Laoghaire)	49	C4 [2]
Barrogstown East	18	F4
Barrogstown West	18	E4
Barron Place (off Walsh Road)	25	A3 [4]
Barrow Road	24	E3
Barrow Street	76	F1
Barry Avenue	24	D1
Barry Close (off Barry Drive)	24	D1
Barry Drive	24	D1
Barry Green	24	D1
Barry Park	24	D1
Barry Road	24	D1
Barry's Park	2	D2
Barryscourt Road	26	E1
Barton Avenue	56	F1
Barton Court (off Barton Road East)	57	A1 [3]
Barton Drive	56	F1
Barton Road East	57	B1
Barton Road East Extension	57	A1
Barton Road Extension	57	A1
Barton Road West	56	F1
Bartra Rock Apartments (off Harbour Road)	60	F1 [18]
Basin Grove	74	D1
Basin Lane Flats	74	D1
Basin Street Lower	74	D1
Basin Street Upper	74	D1
*Basin View (off Basin Street Upper)	74	D1
Baskin Cottages	13	C1
Baskin Lane	13	B1
Bass Place	76	D1
Bath Avenue (Malahide)	3	C2
Bath Avenue (Sandymount)	76	F2
Bath Avenue Gardens	76	F2
Bath Avenue Place	76	F2
Bath Lane	71	B2
Bath Place (off Main Street Blackrock)	49	A3 [8]
Bath Street	39	A3
Bawnlea Avenue	54	D2
Bawnlea Close	54	D2
Bawnlea Crescent	54	D2
Bawnlea Drive	54	D2
Bawnlea Green	54	D2

STREET NAME	PAGE/GRID REFERENCE	STREET NAME	PAGE/GRID REFERENCE	STREET NAME	PAGE/GRID REFERENCE	STREET NAME	PAGE/GRID REFERENCE
Bawnogue Cottages	43 C1 [1]	Beaumont Road	25 C2	Beechfield Mews	46 D2 [4]	Belfry Meadows	53 C2
(off Cherrywood Villas)		Beaumont Wood	25 C1 [3]	(off Whitehall Road West)		Belfry Park	53 C2
Bawnogue Road	43 C1	(off Ballyshannon Road)		Beechfield Place	8 E4	Belfry Place	53 C2
Bawnville Avenue	55 A2	Beaupark Downs	49 B4 [15]	Beechfield Rise	8 E4	Belfry Rise	53 C2
Bawnville Close	55 A2	(off Monkstown Valley)		Beechfield Road (Clonee)	8 D4	Belfry Road	53 C2
Bawnville Drive	55 B2	Beaupark Avenue	14 D4	Beechfield Road (Walkinstown)	45 C2	Belfry Square	53 C2
Bawnville Park	55 B2	Beaupark Close	14 D4	Beechfield View	8 E4	Belfry Terrace	53 C2
Bawnville Road	55 A2	Beaupark Cresc	14 D4	Beechfield Way	8 E4	Belfry Walk	53 C2
Baymount Park	27 A4	Beaupark Mews	14 D4	Beechlawn	48 F3	Belfry Way	53 C2
Bayshore Lane	64 E1	Beaupark Place	14 D4	Beechlawn Avenue (Coolock)	26 E1	Belfrymanor	53 C2
Bayside Boulevard North	27 C1	Beaupark Road	14 D4	Beechlawn Avenue (Ballinteer)	57 B1	Belgard Close (off Garrynisk Road)	44 F3 [2]
Bayside Boulevard South	27 C1	Beaupark Row	14 D4	Beechlawn Close	26 E1	Belgard Green	44 E4
Bayside Crescent (off Sarto Park)	27 C1 [1]	Beaupark Street	14 D4	Beechlawn Green	26 E1	Belgard Heights	44 F4
Bayside Park	27 C1	Beaupark Terrace	14 D4	Beechlawn Grove	26 E1	Belgard Road	44 E3
Bayside Square East	27 C1	Beauvale Park	26 D2	Beechlawn Manor	46 F2 [20]	Belgard Square	54 F1
Bayside Square North	27 C1	Beaver Close	72 D2	(off Rathfarnham Road)		Belgard Square East	54 F1
Bayside Square South	27 C1	Beaver Row	47 C1	Beechlawn Mews	46 F2 [21]	Belgard Square North	54 F1
Bayside Square West	27 C1	Beaver Street	72 D2	(off Rathfarnham Road)		Belgard Square South	54 F1
Bayside Walk	27 C1	Beckett Hall	59 B4	Beechmount Drive (Windy Arbour)	47 C3	Belgard Square West	54 F1
Bayswater Terrace	60 F1 [7]	Beckett Way	35 C4	Beechpark	32 E1	Belgrave Avenue	47 B1
(off Breffni Road)		Bective Square	70 F1	Beechpark Avenue	26 E1	Belgrave Place	47 A1 [15]
Baytownpark	6 E1	Bedford Court	46 E1 [5]	Beechpark Close	23 A3 [3]	(off Belgrave Square West)	
Bayview (Loughlinstown)	64 E1	(off Kimmage Road Lower)		(off Beech Park Avenue)		Belgrave Place	49 B4 [10]
Bayview (Bray)	67 C2 [51]	Bedford Lane (off Aston Quay)	71 B4	Beechpark Court	26 E1	(off Seapoint Avenue Monkstown)	
*Bayview (on Seapoint Road)	67 C2	Bedford Row (off Aston Quay)	71 B4	Beechpark Orchard	23 A3	Belgrave Road (Rathmines)	47 A1
Bayview Avenue	72 D1	Beech Drive	57 B1	Beechurst	67 B2	Belgrave Road (Rathmines)	49 B4
Bayview Close	64 E1	Beech Grove (Lucan)	34 E2	Beechview	56 E2 [1]	Belgrave Square (Rathmines)	47 A1
Bayview Court	64 E1	Beech Grove (Blackrock)	48 F2	(off Edmondstown Road)		Belgrave Square (Monkstown)	49 B4
Bayview Crescent	64 E1	Beech Hill	47 C2	Beechwood	14 F1	Belgrave Square East (Rathmines)	47 A1
Bayview Drive	64 E1	Beech Hill Avenue	47 C2	Beechwood Avenue Lower	47 B1	Belgrave Square East (Monkstown)	49 B4
Bayview Glade	64 E1 [12]	Beech Hill Court	47 C1	Beechwood Avenue Upper	47 B1	Belgrave Square North (Rathmines)	47 A1
Bayview Glen	64 E1	Beech Hill Crescent		Beechwood Close (Hartstown)	21 C1	Belgrave Square North (Monkstown)	49 B4
Bayview Green	64 E1	(off Beech Hill Drive)	47 C2 [3]	Beechwood Close (Boghall Road)	67 C4	Belgrave Square South (Rathmines)	47 A1
Bayview Grove	64 E1	Beech Hill Drive	47 C2	Beechwood Court	58 F1	Belgrave Square South (Monkstown)	49 B4
Bayview Lawn	64 E1	Beech Hill Road	47 C2	Beechwood Downs	21 C1	Belgrave Square West (Rathmines)	47 A1
Bayview Rise	64 E1	Beech Hill Terrace	47 C2 [4]	Beechwood Grove	60 D1 [11]	Belgrave Square West (Monkstown)	49 B4
Beach Avenue	39 A3	(off Beech Hill Drive)		(off Beechwood Park)		Belgrave Terrace	49 B4 [11]
Beach Drive	39 A3	Beech Hill Villas	47 C2 [2]	Beechwood House	64 E2 [10]	(off Eaton Place Monkstown)	
Beach Park	15 A1	(off Beech Hill Drive)		Beechwood Lawn	60 D2	Belgrave Terrace (Bray)	68 D2 [10]
Beach Road	39 A3	Beech House (Swords)	1 Inset	Beechwood Lawns	52 F2	Belgrave Villas (Bray)	47 B1 [16]
Beach View	27 C2	Beech House	76 D3	Beechwood Park	47 B1 [7]	(off Belgrave Avenue Rathmines)	
Beacon Court	58 D2	Beech Lawn	57 B1	(off Dunville Avenue Rathmines)		Belgrave Villas (Bray)	68 D2 [9]
*Beacon Hill (off Nerano Road)	60 F2	Beech Lodge	23 A4	Beechwood Park (Dún Laoghaire)	60 D1	Belgree	9 B2
Beaconsfield Court	73 A1	Beech Park (Castleknock)	22 F3	Beechwood Road	47 B1	Belgree Avenue	9 B2
Bealing	9 B2	Beech Park (Lucan)	34 E1	Beggar's Bush Buildings	76 F2	Belgree Close	9 B2
Bealing Avenue	9 B2	Beech Park (Cabinteely)	59 C4	Beggars Bush Court	76 F2	Belgree Court	9 B2
Bealing Close	9 B3	Beech Park Avenue (Castleknock)	23 A3	Belarmine	58 D4	Belgree Drive	9 B2
Bealing Crescent	9 B2	Beech Park Avenue	59 B2	Belarmine Avenue	58 D4	Belgree Green	9 B2
Bealing Grove	9 B2	(Deans Grange)		Belarmine Close	58 D4	Belgree Grove	9 B2
Bealing Mews	9 B2	Beech Park Crescent	23 A3 [1]	Belarmine Court	58 D4	Belgree Heights	9 B2
Bealing View	9 B2	(off Beech Park Avenue)		Belarmine Drive	58 D4	Belgree Lawns	9 B2
Bealing Walk	9 B2	Beech Park Drive	59 B2	Belarmine Grange	58 D4	Belgree Rise	9 B2
Bealing Wood	9 B3	Beech Park Grove	59 B2	Belarmine Heath	58 D4	Belgree Square	9 B2
Bearna Park	58 D3	Beech Park Lawn	23 A3	Belarmine Park	58 D4	Belgree Walk	9 B2
Beatty Grove	32 D2	Beech Park Road	59 B2	Belarmine Place	58 D4	Belgree Woods	9 B2
Beatty Park	32 D3	Beech Road (Fox and Geese)	45 A1	Belarmine Square	58 D4	Belgrove Lawn	36 D2
Beatty's Avenue	76 F3	Beech Road	64 E3	Belarmine Vale	58 D4	Belgrove Park (Vernon Avenue)	26 F4
(off Sandymount Avenue)		Beech Road (Bray)	67 B1	Belarmine Way	58 D4	Belgrove Park (Chapelizod)	36 D2
Beaucourt (off Achill Road)	25 B3 [4]	Beech Row (Newlands Road)	35 A4	Belcamp Avenue	13 B4	Belgrove Road	26 F4
Beaufield	17 C4	Beech Row (off Nangor Road)	44 D1 [3]	Belcamp Crescent	13 B4	*Bella Avenue (off Bella St)	72 D2
Beaufield Ave	17 C4	Beech Walk (off Brookwood)	56 E2 [4]	Belcamp Gardens	13 B4	*Bella Place (off Bella St)	72 D2
Beaufield Close	17 C4	Beechbrook Grove	14 D4 [4]	Belcamp Green	13 B4	Bella Street	71 C2
Beaufield Crescent	17 C4	(off Kilfenora Drive)		Belcamp Grove	13 B4	Belleview Maltings	69 B4
Beaufield Drive	17 C4	Beechcourt	60 D3	Belcamp Lane	13 C4	Belleville	23 C4
Beaufield Gardens	17 C4	Beechdale	7 B3	Belcamp Park	13 A3	Belleville Avenue	47 A2
Beaufield Green	17 C4	Beechdale Avenue	55 B3	Belclare Avenue	11 C4	Bellevue	74 E1
Beaufield Grove	17 C4	Beechdale Close	55 B3 [6]	Belclare Crescent	11 C4	Bellevue Avenue (Merrion)	48 E2
Beaufield Lawn	17 C4	(off Beechdale Avenue)		Belclare Drive	11 C4	Bellevue Avenue (Dalkey)	60 E2
Beaufield Manor	48 E4	Beechdale Court	55 B3	Belclare Green	11 C4	Bellevue Copse	48 E2
Beaufield Mews		Beechdale Crescent	55 B3	Belclare Grove	11 C4	Bellevue Cottages	24 F3 [4]
(off Beaufield Manor)	48 E4 [2]	Beechdale Lawn	55 B3	Belclare Park	11 C4	(off Finglas Road Old)	
Beaufield Park	48 E4	Beechdale Mews	47 B1 [19]	Belclare Terrace	11 C4	Bellevue Court (off Dornden Park)	48 E2 [2]
Beaufort (off Glasthule Road)	60 E1 [19]	(off Palmerston Road)		Belclare View	11 C4	Bellevue Park	48 E2
Beaufort Court	46 F4 [10]	Beechdale Park	55 B3	Belclare Way	11 C4	Bellevue Park Avenue	48 E2
(off Beaufort Downs)		Beechdale Place	55 C3	Belfield Close (off Roebuck Road)	47 C3 [8]	Bellevue Road	60 D2
Beaufort Downs	46 F4	Beechdale Road	55 C3	Belfield Court	48 D2	Bellman's Walk	72 E3
Beaufort Villas	46 F4 [3]	Beechdale Way	55 B3	Belfield Downs	47 C4	Bell's Lane (Swords)	1 C2
(off Willbrook Road)		Beeches Park	60 E1	Belfield Park Apartments	48 E3	Bell's Lane	75 C2
Beaumont	26 D1	Beeches Road	58 D1	Belfry Avenue	53 C2	Belmayne Avenue	14 D3
Beaumont Avenue	47 B4	Beechfield	8 D4	Belfry Close	53 C2	Belmayne Park North	14 D3
Beaumont Close	47 B4 [3]	Beechfield Avenue (Clonee)	8 D4	Belfry Court	53 C2	Belmayne Park South	14 D4
(off Beaumont Avenue)		Beechfield Avenue (Walkinstown)	45 C2	Belfry Crescent	53 C2	Belmont (Stillorgan)	59 A1
Beaumont Cottages	34 D2	Beechfield Close (Clonee)	8 D4	Belfry Dale	53 C2	Belmont (Irishtown)	67 C4
Beaumont Court	25 C1 [2]	Beechfield Close (Walkinstown)	46 D2	Belfry Downs	53 C2	Belmont Avenue	47 C1
(off Ballyshannon Road)		Beechfield Court	8 D4	Belfry Drive	53 C2	*Belmont Court (off Belmont Ave)	47 C1
Beaumont Crescent	26 D2	Beechfield Drive	8 D4	Belfry Gardens	53 C2	Belmont Gardens	47 C1
Beaumont Drive	47 B4	Beechfield Green	8 D4	Belfry Green	53 C2	Belmont Green	58 F1
Beaumont Gardens	48 F4	Beechfield Haven	64 E2 [3]	Belfry Hall	53 C2	Belmont Grove	58 F1
Beaumont Grove	25 C2	Beechfield Heights	8 D4	Belfry Lawn	53 C2	Belmont Lawn	58 F1
Beaumont Hall (off The Park)	25 C2 [7]	Beechfield Lawn	8 E4	Belfry Lodge	53 C2	Belmont Park (Raheny)	27 A2
Beaumont House	46 F2 [25]	Beechfield Manor	64 E2	Belfry Manor	53 C2	Belmont Park	47 C1 [3]
(off Brighton Road)		Beechfield Meadows	8 E4			(off Donnybrook Road)	

STREET NAME	PAGE	GRID
Belmont Place	71	C2
(off Gardiner St Middle)		
Belmont Square	27	A2
*Belmont Terrace	58	F1
(off Stillorgan Road)		
Belmont Villas	47	C1
Belmount Court	25	C4 [18]
(off Philipsburgh Avenue)		
Belton Park Avenue	26	D3
Belton Park Gardens	26	D3
Belton Park Road	26	D3
Belton Park Villas	26	D3
Belton Terrace	67	C2 [44]
Belvedere Court	71	B2
Belvedere Square	71	B1
Belvidere Avenue	71	C1
Belvidere Court	71	B1
Belvidere Place	71	C1
Belvidere Road	71	B1
Ben Edar Road	70	D2
Ben Inagh Park (off Rock Road)	49	A3 [3]
Ben Of Howth	30	D3
Benbulbin Avenue	73	B3
Benbulbin Road	73	B3
Benburb Street	70	E3
Beneavin Court	24	F2
Beneavin Drive	24	F2
Beneavin Park	24	F1
Beneavin Road	24	F2
Bengal Terrace (off Finglas Road)	24	F4 [4]
Benmadigan Road	73	A3
Benson Street	72	F4
Bentley Avenue	67	C4 [3]
Bentley Park	67	C4
Bentley Road	67	C4
Bentley Villas (off George's Place)	49	C4 [17]
Beresford	25	B3
Beresford Avenue	25	B3
Beresford Green	25	B3
Beresford Lane	71	C3
Beresford Lawn	25	B3
Beresford Place	71	C3
Beresford Street	71	A3
Berkeley Avenue	71	A1
Berkeley Place	71	A1
Berkeley Road	71	A1
Berkeley Street	71	A1
Berkeley Terrace	76	F2
Bernard Curtis Court	36	F4
Bernard Curtis House	36	F4 [2]
(off Bluebell Avenue)		
Berryfield	34	D3
Berryfield Crescent	24	D2
Berryfield Drive	24	D2
Berryfield Lane	67	A3
Berryfield Road	24	D2
Berrys Court	73	A2
Bertram Court	74	E2
Berwick Avenue	1	B2
Berwick Court	1	B1
Berwick Crescent	1	B1
Berwick Drive	1	B1
Berwick Grove	1	B1
Berwick Hall	47	A4
Berwick Lawn	1	B1
Berwick Place	1	B1
Berwick Rise	1	B2
Berwick View	1	B1
Berwick Walk	1	B2
Berwick Way	1	B1
Berystede	75	C4
Bessborough Avenue	72	E1
Bessborough Court	75	B4
Bessborough Parade	75	B4
Besser Drive	35	B4
Bethany House (off Gilford Road)	39	B4 [4]
Bethesda Place	71	B2
Bettyglen	27	B2
Bettysford (off Monastery Road)	44	E1 [3]
Bettystown Avenue	26	F3
Beverly Avenue	56	D1
Beverly Court	26	F4
Beverly Crescent	55	C2
Beverly Downs	55	C2
Beverly Drive	56	D2
Beverly Green	55	C2
Beverly Grove	56	D1
Beverly Heights	56	D2
Beverly Lawns	56	D2
Beverly Park	55	C1
Beverly Rise	55	C2
Bewley	34	E2
Bewley Avenue	34	E2
Bewley Drive	34	E2
Bewley Grove	34	E2
Bewley Lawn	34	E2
Bianconi Ave	53	B1
Big Lane	32	D3
Bigger Road	45	C2
Bill Shelly Park	23	C2
Binn Eadair	29	A1
Binn Eadair Court	29	A1
Binn Eadair Crescent	29	A1
Binn Eadair View	29	A1
Binn's Bridge (Royal Canal)	71	B1
Birch Avenue	58	D2
Birch Dale (off Pine Avenue Foxrock)	59	A2 [9]
Birch Dale (off Carriglea Avenue)	59	C1 [12]
Birch Grove	59	C1
Birchdale Close	2	E3
Birchdale Drive	2	E3
Birchdale Park	2	F3
Birchdale Road	2	E3
Birches Road	58	D1
Birchfield Avenue	47	C4
Birchfield Court	47	C4
Birchfield Heights	47	C4
Birchfield Lawn	47	C4
Birchfield Park	47	C4
Birch's Lane	47	C4
Birchview Avenue	45	A4
Birchview Close	45	A4
Birchview Court	45	A4
Birchview Drive	45	A4
Birchview Heights	45	A4
Birchview Lawn	45	A4
Birchview Rise	45	A4
Birchwood Close	44	E4
Birchwood Drive	54	E1
Birchwood Heights	54	E1
Bird Avenue	47	C3
Biscayne	3	C3
Bishop Street	75	A2
Bishops Lane	62	F2
Bishop's Orchard	9	B2
Bishop's Orchard Boulevard	9	B2
Bishop's Orchard House Apartments	9	B2
Bishop's Square	75	A2
Bissett's Loft Apartments	3	B2
Bissett's Strand	3	B2
Black Street	69	C3
Blackberry Lane (Portmarnock)	15	A1
Blackberry Lane (Rathmines)	75	B4
Blackberry Rise	15	A1
Blackburn Square	46	F4 [15]
(off Main Street Rathfarnham)		
Blackcourt Road	22	E1
Blackditch Drive	35	C3
Blackditch Road	35	C3
Blackditch Road	36	D3
Blackglen Court	58	D3
Blackglen Road	57	C3
Blackhall Court	70	E3
Blackhall Green	70	E3
Blackhall Little	5	B1
*Blackhall Parade (Blackhall Street)	70	F3
Blackhall Place	70	E4
Blackhall Place Apartments	70	E3
*Blackhall Square Apartments	70	F3
(King Street North)		
Blackhall Street	70	F4
Blackhall View	70	E3
Blackhall Walk	70	E4
Blackheath Avenue	26	F4
Blackheath Court	26	F4
Blackheath Drive	26	E4
Blackheath Gardens	26	E4
Blackheath Grove	26	E4
Blackheath Park	26	E4
Blackhorse Avenue (Ashtown)	23	C4
Blackhorse Avenue	69	C2
(North Circular Road)		
Blackhorse Grove	70	D2
Blackpitts	74	F2
Blackrock	49	A3
Blackthorn Avenue	58	E2
Blackthorn Close (Portmarnock)	4	D4
Blackthorn Close	58	D2 [7]
(off Spruce Avenue Sandyford)		
Blackthorn Court	58	D2 [4]
(off Moreen Avenue)		
Blackthorn Drive	58	D2
Blackthorn Green	58	D2 [6]
(off Moreen Avenue)		
Blackthorn Grove	58	D2 [3]
(off Moreen Avenue)		
Blackthorn Hall	57	C3
Blackthorn Hill Avenue	52	E2
Blackthorn Hill Close	52	E2
Blackthorn Hill Crescent	52	E2
Blackthorn Hill Drive	52	E2
Blackthorn Hill View	52	E2
Blackthorn Road	58	D2
Blackwater Road	24	E3
Blackwood Close	21	A1
Blackwood Crescent	21	A1
Blackwood Drive	21	A1
Blackwood Lane	3	C4
Blackwood Lawn	21	A1
Blackwood Mews	21	A1
Blackwood Park	21	A1
Blackwood Place	21	A1
Blackwoods	3	B4
Blakeney House (Swords)	2	E2
Blakeney House Mews (Howth)	30	E3
Blake's Court (off Briarwood Lawn)	22	D1 [7]
*Blakes Villas	70	F2
(on Grangegorman Lower)		
Blakesfield	21	C1
Blakestown Cottages	22	D1
Blakestown Drive	22	D1
Blakestown Road (Mulhuddart)	9	A4
Blakestown Road (Hartstown)	22	D1
Blakestown Way	22	D1
Blanchardstown	22	F2
Blanchardstown ByPass	22	F2
Blanchardstown Interchange	23	A2
Blanchardstown Road North	9	B4
Blanchardstown Road South	22	D2
Blanchardstown Roundabout	22	F2
Blarney Park	46	E1
Blasket Square	22	F1
Blessington Court	71	A2
Blessington Lane	71	A2
Blessington Place	71	A2
(off St Joseph's Parade)		
Blessington Road	53	C2
Blessington Street	71	A2
*Blind Quay Apartments	71	A4
(Exchange Street Lower)		
Blizzard Apartments	2	F3 [1]
Blood Stoney Road	72	F4
Bloom Court	74	F3
Bloomfield Avenue (Portobello)	75	A3
Bloomfield Avenue	76	D4
(Morehampton Road)		
Bloomfield Cottages	75	A3
Bloomfield Park (Portobello)	75	A3
Bloomfield Park	76	E4
(Morehampton Road)		
Bluebell	36	E4
Bluebell Avenue	36	E4
Bluebell Road	36	E4
Blundelstown	42	E3
Blunden Drive	13	C4
Blythe Avenue	72	E3
Boardman's Lane (off Cork Street)	74	D2
Boden Dale	56	F1
Boden Heath	56	E1
Boden Heath Apartments	56	E1
Boden Mill	56	E2
Boden Park	56	E1
Boden Wood	46	F4
Boeing Road	12	F4
Boghall Road (Killarney Road)	67	B4
Boghall Road (off Vevay road)	67	C4
Bohammer	13	C2
Boherboy	53	B2
Boherboy Road	53	B2
Bohernabreena Road	55	A3
Bolbrook Avenue	55	B1 [3]
(off Avonbeg Road)		
Bolbrook Close	55	B1 [4]
(off Avonbeg Road)		
Bolbrook Drive	55	B1 [1]
(off Avonbeg Road)		
Bolbrook Grove	55	B1
Bolbrook Park	55	B1
Bolbrook Villas	55	B1
Bolton Green	1	A2
Bolton Street	71	A3
Bond Drive	39	A1
Bond Road	39	A1
Bond Street	74	E1
Bonham Street	70	E4
Boolavogue Road	72	F2
Boot Road	44	D2
Booterstown	48	E2
Booterstown Avenue	48	F3
*Booterstown Grove	48	F2
(off Booterstown Avenue)		
Booterstown Park	48	F3
Boranaraltry	61	B4
Boranaraltry Bridge	61	B4
Boranaraltry Lane	61	C4
Boroimhe Alder	1	C3
Boroimhe Ash	1	C3
Boroimhe Aspen	1	C3
Boroimhe Beech	1	C3
Boroimhe Birches	1	C3
Boroimhe Blackthorn	1	C3
Boroimhe Cedars	1	C3
Boroimhe Cherry	1	C3
Boroimhe Elms	1	C3
Boroimhe Hawthorns	1	C3
Boroimhe Hazel	1	C3
Boroimhe Laurels	1	C3
Boroimhe Maples	1	C3
Boroimhe Oaks	1	C3
Boroimhe Pines	1	C3
Boroimhe Poplars	1	C3
Boroimhe Rowan	1	B3
Boroimhe Willows	1	C3
Botanic Avenue	25	A4
Botanic Hall (Addison Park)	24	F3 [7]
Botanic Mews (off Prospect Avenue)	25	A4 [18]
Botanic Park (off Botanic avenue)	25	A4 [14]
Botanic Road	25	A4
Botanic Square (off Botanic avenue)	25	A4 [17]
Botanic Villas (off Botanic Road)	25	A4 [10]
Bottle Works	39	A3
Boulevard Mount Eustace	9	B2
Boundary Road	39	A1
Bow Bridge (Camac River)	74	D1
*Bow Bridge Court (Bow Bridge)	74	D1
*Bow Bridge Place (Irwin Street)	74	D1
Bow Lane East	75	B1
Bow Lane West	74	D1
Bow Street	70	F4
*Bowbridge House (Mount Brown)	74	D1
Boyd House	14	F4
Boyne Court	74	F4
Boyne Lane	76	D1
Boyne Road	24	E3
Boyne Street	76	D1
*Brabazon Buildings (Cork Street)	74	F2
Brabazon Cottages	67	C2 [16]
Brabazon House	74	E2
Brabazon Place	74	F2
Brabazon Row	74	F2
Brabazon Square	74	F1
Brabazon Street	74	F2
Bracken Drive	4	D4
Bracken Hill	57	C3
Bracken Road	58	D2
Brackenbush Park	60	D4
Brackenbush Road	60	D4
Bracken's Lane	71	C4
Brackenstown Avenue	1	C2
Brackenstown Road	1	C2
Braeburn Terrace	1	Inset
Braemor Avenue	47	A3
Braemor Drive	47	A3
Braemor Grove	47	A3
Braemor Park	47	A3
Braemor Road	47	A3
Braithwaite Street	74	E1
Bramblefield	8	F4
Bramblefield Court	8	F4
Bramblefield Crescent	8	F4
Bramblefield Drive	8	F4
Bramblefield Park	8	F4
Bramblefield View	8	F4
Bramblefield Walk	8	F4
Bramley Avenue	22	E3
Bramley Court	22	E3
Bramley Crescent	22	E3
Bramley Garth	22	E3
Bramley Green	22	E3
Bramley Grove	22	E3
Bramley Heath	22	E3
Bramley Park	22	E3
Bramley Road	22	E3
Bramley View	22	E3
Bramley Walk	22	E3
Bramley Way	22	E3
Brandon Road	36	F4
Brandon Terrace	74	D2

STREET NAME	PAGE/GRID REFERENCE
Bray	68 D1
Bray Commons	67 B2
Bray Head Terrace	67 C3 [20]
Bray Road (Cornelscourt)	59 B2
Bray Road (Shanganagh)	59 C4
Bray Southern Cross Road	67 B4
Breakwater Road North	39 B2
Breakwater Road South	39 B2
Breffni Terrace	60 E1
Breffni Gardens	15 A4 [5]
(off Main Street Baldoyle)	
Breffni Road	60 E1
Bregia Road	24 F4
Brehon Field Road	57 B2
Brehon's Chair	57 A3
Bremen Avenue	39 A3
Bremen Grove	39 A3
Bremen Road	39 A3
Brendan Behan Court	71 C1
Brendan Road	47 C1
Brennans Parade	68 D2 [14]
Brennans Terrace	68 D2 [4]
Brennanstown Avenue	59 C4
Brennanstown Road	59 B4
Brennanstown Square	59 C4
Brennanstown Vale	59 B4
Brewery Road	58 F2
Brian Avenue	25 C4
Brian Boru Avenue	39 C1
Brian Boru Street	39 C1
Brian Road	25 C4
Brian Terrace	25 C4
Briansboro Terrace	74 F3
Briar Walk	4 D4
Briar Wood	68 D3
Briarfield Grove	27 B1
Briarfield Road	27 B2
Briarfield Villas (off Briarfield Grove)	27 B1 [5]
Briarly Court	47 B4 [4]
(off Churchtown Road)	
Briarsfield Walk	27 B1 [4]
(off Greendale Road)	
Briarwood Avenue	22 D1
Briarwood Close	9 A4
Briarwood Gardens	22 D1
Briarwood Green	22 D1
Briarwood Lawn	22 D1
Briarwood Park	22 D1 [1]
(off Briarwood Gardens)	
Briarwood Road	22 D1 [3]
(off Briarwood Lawn)	
Brickfield	67 B3
Brickfield Drive	73 C3
Brickfield Lane (Bray)	67 B3 [8]
Brickfield Lane	74 E2
Bride Close	75 A1
Bride Road	75 A1
Bride Street	75 A1
Brides Glen	63 C2
Bride's Glen Avenue	1 Inset
Brides Glen Park	1 C1
Bride's Glen Park	1 Inset
Bridge Street (Swords)	2 D2
Bridge Street (Ringsend)	39 A3
Bridge Street Lower	70 F4
Bridge Street Upper	74 F1
Bridgefoot Street	70 F4
Bridgeview	35 B3
Bridgewater Quay	69 B4
Bridon	62 F1
Brighton Avenue	26 D4 [1]
(off Charlemont Road Clontarf)	
Brighton Avenue (Rathgar)	46 F2
Brighton Avenue (Monkstown)	49 B4
Brighton Avenue (Carrickmines)	59 A4
Brighton Cottages	59 A3 [1]
(off Brighton Road Foxrock)	
Brighton Court	59 A4
Brighton Gardens	46 F2
Brighton Green	46 F2 [13]
(off Brighton Square)	
Brighton Hall	59 A4
Brighton Lane	49 B4 [22]
(off Monkstown Road)	
Brighton Lodge	
(off Brighton Road Foxrock)	59 A3 [4]
Brighton Place	59 A4
Brighton Road (Terenure)	46 F2
Brighton Road (Foxrock)	59 A3
Brighton Square	46 F2
Brighton Terrace	49 B4 [9]
(off Seapoint Avenue Monkstown)	

STREET NAME	PAGE/GRID REFERENCE
Brighton Terrace	60 E1 [13]
(off Glasthule Road)	
Brighton Vale	49 B3
Britain Place	71 B2
Britain Quay	72 F4
Broadfield Avenue	52 E2
Broadfield Close	52 E2
Broadfield Court	52 E2
Broadfield Heath	52 E2
Broadfield Manor	52 E2
Broadfield Meadows	52 E2
Broadfield Park	52 E2
Broadford Avenue	57 B2
Broadford Close	57 B2
Broadford Crescent	57 B2
Broadford Drive	57 B2
Broadford Hill	57 B2
Broadford Lawn	57 B2
Broadford Park	57 B2
Broadford Rise	57 B2
Broadford Road	57 B2
Broadford Walk	57 B2
Broadmeadow	1 C1
Broadmeadow Mews	3 B2 [7]
Broadstone	70 F2
Broadstone Avenue	71 A2
(off Royal Canal Bank)	
*Broadstone Place	71 A2
(off Royal Canal Bank)	
Broadway Drive	22 E2
Broadway Grove	22 E2
Broadway Park	22 E2
Broadway Road	22 E2
Brockey (Glencullen)	61 C4
Brockey (Glencullen Mountain)	65 A1
Brockey Lane	65 A1
Brodin Row	70 D3
Brompton Court	22 E3
Brompton Green	22 E2
Brompton Grove	22 E3
Brompton Lawn	22 E2
Brook Court	49 B4
Brook House (off Richmond Road)	25 B4 [14]
Brook Wood	67 B2
Brookdale	55 A2
Brookdale Avenue	1 B3
Brookdale Close	1 B2
Brookdale Court	1 B3
Brookdale Drive	1 B2
Brookdale Green	1 B2
Brookdale Grove	1 B2
Brookdale Lawns	1 B2
Brookdale Park	1 B2
Brookdale Road	1 B2
Brookdale Walk	1 B2
Brookdale Way	1 B2
Brookdene	64 E2
Brookfield (Coolock)	26 F2
Brookfield (Lucan)	34 D3
Brookfield (off Anglesea Road	47 C1 [19]
Donnybrook)	
Brookfield (Milltown)	47 B2
Brookfield (Blackrock)	48 F3
Brookfield Avenue (Maynooth)	17 C4
Brookfield Avenue (Blackrock)	49 A4
Brookfield Avenue (Bray)	68 D3 [4]
Brookfield Court	46 E2 [6]
(off Ravensdale Park)	
Brookfield Court	49 A4 [12]
(off Brookfield Place)	
Brookfield Court	54 D1 [1]
(off Brookfield Road Tallaght)	
*Brookfield Court (at Rialto Bridge)	73 C2
Brookfield Estate	46 E2
Brookfield Green	46 E2 [5]
(off Ravensdale Park)	
Brookfield Grove	49 A4 [11]
(off Brookfield Avenue)	
Brookfield Park	17 C4
Brookfield Place	49 A4
Brookfield Road (Tallaght)	54 D1
Brookfield Road (Kilmainham)	73 C1
Brookfield Street	73 C2
Brookfield Terrace	49 A4
Brookhaven Drive	22 E1
Brookhaven Grove	22 E1
Brookhaven Lawn	22 E1
Brookhaven Park	22 E1
Brookhaven Rise	22 E1
Brooklands	48 E1
Brooklawn (Clontarf)	26 D4
Brooklawn (Lucan)	34 D3

STREET NAME	PAGE/GRID REFERENCE
Brooklawn (Palmerston)	35 B1
Brooklawn (Blackrock)	48 F3
Brooklawn Avenue	49 B4 [12]
(off Rockville Drive)	
Brooklawn Wood	49 B4 [13]
(off Stradbrook Road)	
Brookmount Avenue	55 C1
Brookmount Court	46 E4 [2]
(off Butterfield Avenue)	
Brookmount Lawns	55 C1 [1]
(off Tallaght Road)	
Brookpark	34 D3
Brookstone Lane	15 A4 [6]
(off Dublin Street Baldoyle)	
Brookstone Road	15 A4
Brookvale (off Lucan Road)	34 D1 [8]
Brookvale Downs	46 F3
Brookvale Road (Rathfarnham)	46 F3
Brookvale Road (off Eglinton Road)	47 C1 [8]
Brookview Avenue	54 D1
Brookview Close	54 D1
Brookview Court	54 D1
Brookview Crescent	54 D1
Brookview Drive	54 D1
Brookview Gardens	54 D1
Brookview Green	54 D1
Brookview Grove	54 D1
Brookview Lawns	54 D1
Brookview Park	54 D1
Brookview Rise	54 D1
Brookview Terrace	54 D1
Brookview Way	54 D1
Brookville	24 D1
Brookville Crescent	26 E1 [2]
(off Brookville Park)	
Brookville Park (Coolock)	26 E1
Brookville Park (Artane)	26 E2
Brookville Park (Dean's Grange)	59 B1
Brookwood	56 E2
Brookwood Abbey	26 E2 [4]
(off Gracefield Road)	
Brookwood Avenue	26 E2
Brookwood Crescent	26 F2
Brookwood Drive	26 E2
Brookwood Glen	26 F3
Brookwood Grove	26 E2
Brookwood Hall	26 E3
Brookwood Heights	26 F2
Brookwood Lawn	26 F2
Brookwood Meadow	26 E2
Brookwood Park	26 E3
Brookwood Rise	26 F3
Brookwood Road	26 E2
Broombridge Road	24 E4
Broomfield (Malahide)	3 B4
Broomfield (Lucan)	21 B4
Broomfield Court	64 E2
Broomfield Mews	3 B4
Broomhill Close	45 A4
Broomhill Drive	45 A4
Broomhill Road	45 A4
Broomhill Terrace	45 A4
(off Broomhill Road)	
Brown Street North	70 F3
Brown Street South	74 E2
Brownrath	5 B1
Brownsbarn	43 C4
Brownsbarn Court	43 C4
Brownsbarn Garden	43 C4
Brownsbarn Orchard	43 C4
Brownstown (Kilcloon)	5 A2
Brownstown	42 D1
Bruce's Terrace	67 B2 [29]
Brug Chroimlinn	46 D1 [6]
(off St Agnes Road Crumlin)	
Brunswick Place	76 E1
Brunswick Street North	70 F3
Brunswick Villas (Pearse Street)	71 C4
Brusna Cottages	49 A3 [12]
(off Main Street Blackrock)	
Buckingham Street Lower	72 D2
Buckingham Street Upper	72 D2
Buckingham Village	71 C2
Buckleys Lane	33 A1
Bulfin Court	73 A2
Bulfin Gardens	73 B1
Bulfin Road	73 A2
Bull Alley Street	75 A1
Bull Lane (off Main Street)	67 C2 [59]
Bull Wall	40 D1
Bull Wall Cottages	40 D1
Bullock Steps (off Harbour Road)	60 F1 [8]

STREET NAME	PAGE/GRID REFERENCE
Bunbury Gate Avenue	1 Inset
Bunbury Gate Crescent	1 Inset
Bunratty Avenue	26 E1
Bunratty Drive	26 E1
Bunratty Road	26 E1
Bunting Road	45 C1
Burdett Avenue	60 E1
Burg an Ri Glen	34 F3
Burg an Ri Terrace	34 F3
Burgage	13 C3
*Burgage Crescent (Burgage Street)	42 D4
*Burgage Green (Burgage Street)	42 D4
Burgage Street	42 D4
Burgess Lane	70 F4
Burgh Quay	71 C4
Burke Place (off Mount Brown)	74 D1
Burleigh Court	76 D3
Burleigh Mews	76 D3
Burlington Gardens	76 D3
Burlington Mews	76 D3
Burlington Road	76 D3
Burmah Close (off Dalkey Avenue)	60 F2 [22]
Burnell Park Avenue	22 E4
Burnell Park Green	22 E4
Burnell Square	14 D4
Burnside	25 B1
Burren Court	11 C4
*Burris Court (off High Street)	75 A1
Burrow Court (Poppintree)	11 C4
Burrow Court (Portmarnock)	15 A1
Burrow Road (Sutton)	29 B1
Burrow Road (Stepaside)	58 D4
Burrowfield Road	28 D1
Burton Court	58 E2
Burton Hall Avenue	58 E2
Burton Hall Road	58 E2
Burton Road	60 F2
Bushfield Avenue	47 B1 [8]
(off Marlborough Road)	
Bushfield Drive	44 D2
Bushfield Green	44 D2
Bushfield Grove	44 D3
Bushfield Lawns	44 D2
Bushfield Place	47 B1 [17]
(off Bushfield Terrace)	
Bushfield Square	25 C4 [15]
(off Philipsburgh Avenue)	
Bushfield Terrace	47 B1
Bushy Park Gardens	46 F3
Bushy Park House	46 E3
Bushy Park Road	46 F3
Bustyhill	51 B3
Butlerstown	5 C3
Butt Bridge (River Liffey)	71 C4
Buttercup Close	13 C4
Buttercup Drive	13 C4
Buttercup Park	13 C4
Buttercup Square	13 C4
Buttercup Terrace	13 C4
Butterfield Avenue	46 E4
Butterfield Close	46 E4
Butterfield Court	46 F4
Butterfield Crescent	46 E4
Butterfield Drive	46 E4
Butterfield Grove	46 E4
Butterfield Meadow	46 E4 [1]
(off Butterfield Crescent)	
Butterfield Orchard	46 E4
Butterfield Park	46 E4
*Byrne's Cottages (Francis Street)	74 E2
Byrnes Lane (Pearse Sq West)	72 E4
Byrne's Lane (Jervis St)	71 B4
Byrne's Terrace (off Beech Hill Drive)	47 C2 [12]

C

STREET NAME	PAGE/GRID REFERENCE
Cabinteely	59 C4
Cabinteely Avenue	59 C3
Cabinteely Bypass	59 C3
Cabinteely Close	59 C3
Cabinteely Court (off Pottery Road)	59 C3 [2]
Cabinteely Crescent	59 C3
Cabinteely Drive	59 C3
Cabinteely Green	59 C3
Cabinteely Park (off Cabinteely Way)	59 C3 [3]
Cabinteely Way	59 C3
Cabra	69 C1
Cabra Drive	70 D1
Cabra Grove	70 D1
Cabra Park	70 F1
*Cabra Park Mews (Cabra Park)	24 F4

STREET NAME	PAGE/GRID REFERENCE	STREET NAME	PAGE/GRID REFERENCE	STREET NAME	PAGE/GRID REFERENCE	STREET NAME	PAGE/GRID REFERENCE
Cabra Road	70 D1	Cappagh Avenue	24 D1	Carrickhill Road Upper	3 C4	Casino Park	26 D3
Caddell	14 F2	Cappagh Drive	24 D2	Carrickhill Walk	4 D4	Casino Road	25 C4
Cadogan Road	25 C4	Cappagh Green	24 D1	Carrickmines	59 B4	Cassian Court	24 D3
Cairn Brook	63 A1	Cappagh Road (Cappoge)	10 E4	Carrickmines Avenue	59 B4	(off Pelletstown Avenue)2	
Cairn Brook Hall	63 A1	Cappagh Road (Finglas)	24 D1	Carrickmines Chase	59 B4	Castaheany	8 E4
Cairn Brook Manor	63 A1	Cappaghmore Estate	35 A4	Carrickmines Dale	59 B4	Castilla Park	26 F4
Cairn Brook View	63 A1	Cappoge	10 F4	Carrickmines Garth	59 B4	Castle Avenue (Swords)	2 D2
Cairn Brook Way	63 A1	Cappoge Cottages	10 E4	Carrickmines Green	63 A1	Castle Avenue (Clontarf)	26 E4
Cairn Court	12 D4	Captain's Avenue	46 D1	Carrickmines Little	59 A4	Castle Close (Clondalkin)	44 E1
Cairn Hill	59 B2	Captain's Drive	46 D2	Carrickmines Manor	63 A1	Castle Close (Dalkey)	60 F1
Cairnfort	62 E1	Captain's Hill	20 D4	Carrickmines Oaks	59 B4	Castle Court (Clontarf)	26 D4
Cairnwood Avenue	44 E4	Captain's Road	46 D2	Carrickmount Avenue	57 B1	Castle Court	46 F4 [18]
Cairnwood Court	44 E4	Cara Park	13 B3	Carrickmount Drive	57 A1	(off Main Street Rathfarnham)	
Cairnwood Green	44 E4	Caragh Court	25 C4 [12]	Carrig Court	43 B1	*Castle Court (off Cypress Lawn)	46 D4
Caldbeck Way	44 E2	(off Philipsburgh Avenue)		*Carrig Court (Carrigmore Downs)	53 B1	Castle Court (off Whitehall Road)	47 A4 [1]
Calderwood Avenue	25 C3	Caragh Road	69 C1	Carrig Road	11 C4	Rathfarnham)	
Calderwood Grove	25 C3 [3]	Carberry Road	25 C3	Carrigallen Drive	24 E3	Castle Court (Booterstown)	48 F2
(off Calderwood Road)		Carbury Place	49 A3 [20]	Carrigallen Park	24 E3	Castle Court (off Dundrum Castle)	57 C1 [1]
Calderwood Road	25 C3	(off Newtown Avenue Blackrock)		Carrigallen Road	24 E3	Castle Court	58 E4
Caledon Court	72 F2	Carbury Terrace	72 F3	Carrigeen	52 D3	Castle Court (Loughlinstown)	64 E1
Caledon Road	72 F2	Cardiff Castle Road	24 D2	Carriglea	55 B2	Castle Court Apartments	3 B3 [1]
Callaghan Bridge	21 C2	Cardiff Lane	72 E4	Carriglea Avenue (Tallaght)	55 B2	(Malahide)	
Callary Road	48 D3	Cardiffs Bridge	24 D3	Carriglea Avenue	59 C2	Castle Court Apartments	75 A1
Calmount Avenue	45 B2	Cardiffsbridge Avenue	24 D2	(Kill O'The Grange)		Castle Cove (Malahide)	3 A2
Calmount Park	45 B2	Cardiffsbridge Grove	24 D1 [1]	Carriglea Court (Tallaght)	55 B2	Castle Cove	60 F2 [32]
Calmount Road	45 B2	(off Cappagh Road)		Carriglea Court	59 C1 [14]	(off Castle Street Dalkey)	
Camac Close	73 A1	Cardiffsbridge Road	24 D2	(off Carriglea Gardens)		Castle Crescent	44 E1 [4]
Camac Court	73 A1	Card's Lane (Pearse St)	71 C4	Carriglea Downs (Tallaght)	55 B2	(off Monastery Road)	
Camac Park	36 E4	Carleton Road	25 C4	Carriglea Downs	59 C2	Castle Dawson	17 B3
Camaderry Road	68 D3	Carlingford Court	76 E1	(Kill O'The Grange)		Castle Down Croft	2 F2
Camberley Elms	47 B4 [20]	Carlingford Parade	76 E1	Carriglea Drive	55 B2	Castle Down Grove	2 F2
(off Churchtown Road Upper)		Carlingford Road	25 A4	Carriglea Gardens	59 C1	Castle Down Road	2 F2
Camberley Oaks	47 B4 [19]	Carlisle Avenue	47 B1	Carriglea Grove	55 B2	Castle Drive (Swords)	2 D2
(off Churchtown Road Upper)		Carlisle Court	46 F2 [23]	Carriglea Rise	55 B2	Castle Drive (Clondalkin)	44 E1
Cambridge Avenue	39 A3 [7]	(off Terenure Road North)		Carriglea View	55 B2	Castle Drive (Ballyogan Road)	58 E4
(off Pigeon House Road)		Carlisle Street	75 A3	Carriglea Walk	55 B2	Castle Elms	26 E1
Cambridge Court	39 A3 [24]	Carlisle Terrace (Malahide)	3 B3	Carrigmore Avenue	53 B2	Castle Farm	64 E3
(off Cambridge Park)		Carlisle Terrace (off Corrig Road)	60 D1 [17]	Carrigmore Close (Saggart)	53 B2	Castle Farm Wood	64 E3
Cambridge Park	39 A3	*Carlisle Terrace (on Seymour Road)	67 C2	Carrigmore Close (Oldbawn)	54 F3	Castle Gate Apartments	75 A1
Cambridge Road (Ringsend)	39 A3	*Carlisle Terrace (off N C Rd)	70 F1	Carrigmore Court	53 C2	Castle Grove (Swords)	2 D2
Cambridge Road (Rathmines)	47 A1	Carlton Court (Swords)	2 D2	Carrigmore Crescent	53 C1	Castle Grove (Clontarf)	26 E4
*Cambridge Square	39 A3	Carlton Court (Clontarf)	26 D4	Carrigmore Dale	53 B2	Castle Grove (Clondalkin)	44 E1
(off Thorncastle Street)		Carlton Terrace	67 C2 [41]	Carrigmore Downs	53 B1	Castle Lawn	58 E4
Cambridge Street	39 A3 [1]	Carlton Villas (Clontarf)	67 C2 [42]	Carrigmore Drive	54 F2	Castle Lawns (Malahide)	2 F2
(off Cambridge Park)		Carlton Villas	76 F3	Carrigmore Elms	53 B2	Castle Lawns (Tallaght)	45 B4
Cambridge Terrace	49 C4 [24]	(off Sandymount Avenue)		Carrigmore Gardens	53 B1	Castle Market (off Drury Street)	75 B1
(off York Road Dún Laoghaire)		Carmanhall Court	58 E2	Carrigmore Glen	53 B1	Castle Oaks	3 A3 [1]
Cambridge Terrace (Ranelagh)	75 C4	Carmanhall Road	58 E2	Carrigmore Green	53 C2	Castle Park (Swords)	2 D2
Cambridge Villas	47 A1 [16]	Carman's Hall	74 F1	Carrigmore Grove (Saggart)	53 B2	Castle Park (Leixlip)	33 A1
(off Castlewood Park)		Carna Road	35 C3	Carrigmore Grove (Oldbawn)	54 F3	Castle Park (Clondalkin)	44 E1
Camden Avenue	23 C3	Carndonagh Drive	27 B1	Carrigmore Lawns	53 B1	Castle Park (Tallaght)	45 B4
Camden Buildings	75 B2	Carndonagh Lawn	27 B1	Carrigmore Manor	53 B2	Castle Park (Monkstown)	49 C4
Camden Court	75 B3	Carndonagh Park	27 B1	Carrigmore Meadows	53 B2	Castle Park Estate (Tallaght)	55 B1
Camden Lock	76 F1	Carndonagh Road	27 B1	Carrigmore Oak	53 B2	*Castle Place (on Breffni Road)	60 F1
Camden Market	75 B3	Carne Court	8 F4	Carrigmore Park	54 F3	Castle Riada Avenue	34 E2
Camden Place	75 B2	Carnegie Court	2 D1	Carrigmore Place	53 B2	Castle Riada Crescent	34 E2
Camden Row	75 A2	Carnew Street	70 D2	Carrigmore Road	54 F2	Castle Riada Drive	34 E3
Camden Street Lower	75 B2	Carnlough Road	70 D1	Carrigmore Terrace	53 B2	Castle Riada Grove	34 E2
Camden Street Upper	75 B3	Caroline Court	76 E3	Carrigmore View	54 F3	Castle Road (Clontarf)	26 E4
Camden Villas	75 B2	(off Sandymount Road)		Carrigmore Way	53 C2	Castle Road (Lucan)	34 E2
Cameron Square	73 C1	Caroline Row	39 A3 [16]	Carrigwood	55 C2	Castle Rosse	14 F4
Cameron Street	74 E2	(off Irishtown Road)		Carrington	12 E4	Castle Side (off Castlefield Avenue)	55 C1 [7]
Cammock Apartments	73 C1	Carpenterstown	22 D3	Carrow Road	73 A3	Castle Steps (off Castle Street)	75 A1
Camogie Road	69 A3	Carpenterstown Avenue	22 E3	Carton Avenue	18 D2	Castle Street (Dalkey)	60 F2
Campbell Court	30 D2 [16]	Carpenterstown Manor	22 E3	Carton Bridge	18 E3	Castle Street (Bray)	67 C2
(off Main Street Howth)		Carpenterstown Park East	22 E3	Carton Court	17 C4	Castle Street (Cork Hill)	75 A1
Campbell's Court	71 A3	Carpenterstown Road	22 E4	Carton Demesne	18 F2	Castle Terrace (Malahide)	3 B2
Campbell's Lane (off Belvidere Ave)	71 C1	Carraig Close	11 C4	Carton Square	17 C2	*Castle Terrace (off Ulverton Road)	60 F1
Campbell's Row	71 C1	Carraig Glen	59 C4	Carwell Court	2 E2	Castle Terrace (Phibsborough Ave)	70 F1
(off Portland Street N)		Carraig Grennane	60 E4	Carysfort Avenue	49 A4	Castle View (Clondalkin)	44 E1
Campfield Terrace	57 C1	Carraroe Avenue	27 A1	Carysfort Downs	59 A1	Castle View (Carrickmines)	59 A4
Campshire Hall	72 D4	Carrick Court	14 F1	Carysfort Drive (off Carysfort Road)	60 F1 [1]	Castle Village	31 C2
Campshire Mews	72 D4	Carrick Lawn	58 D1 [2]	Carysfort Grove	59 A1	Castle Village Avenue	31 C2
Canal Road	75 B4	(off Kilmacud Road Upper)		Carysfort Hall	49 A4	Castle Village Close	31 C2
Canal Terrace	36 E4	Carrick Terrace	74 D2	Carysfort Park	49 A4	Castle Village Court	31 C2
Canal Turn	35 B4	Carrickaspinkeen	65 A3	Carysfort Road	60 F1	Castle Village Crescent	31 C2
Cannon Mews (off Herbert Road)	39 A4 [29]	Carrickbrack Heath	29 B2	Carysfort Woods	59 A1	Castle Village Drive	31 C2
Cannon Mews East	76 F2	Carrickbrack Hill	29 B2	Casana View	30 E2	Castle Village Green	31 C2
Cannon Mews West	76 F2	Carrickbrack Mews	29 B2	Casement Close (off Barry Road)	24 D1 [2]	Castle Village Lawns	31 C2
Cannon Place (off Herbert Road)	39 A4 [30]	Carrickbrack Park	29 B2	Casement Drive	24 D1	Castle Village Park	31 C2
Cannon Rock Estate	30 E2	Carrickbrack Road (Sutton)	29 B2	Casement Green	24 D1	Castle Village Place	31 C2
Cannon Rock View	30 E2 [1]	Carrickbrack Road	30 D4	Casement Grove	24 D1	Castle Village Rise	31 C2
(Thormanby Road)		(The Summit Howth)		Casement Park	24 D1	Castle Village Walk	31 C2
Cannonbrook	34 D2	Carrickbrennan Lawn	49 C4	Casement Road (Mellows Park)	24 D1	Castle Village Way	31 C2
Cannonbrook Avenue	34 D2	Carrickbrennan Road	49 C4	Casement Road (Finglas South)	24 D2	Castle Village Woods	31 C2
Cannonbrook Court	34 D2	Carrickfoyle Terrace	73 B1	Casement Villas	59 B1	Castle Villas	60 F2
Cannonbrook Lawn	34 D2	Carrickhill Close	4 D4	Cashel Avenue	46 E2	Castlebridge	18 D3
Cannonbrook Park	34 D2	Carrickhill Drive	15 A1	Cashel Road	46 D1	Castlebrook	57 C1
Canon Lillis Avenue	72 E2	Carrickhill Heights	15 A1	Casimir Avenue	46 F1	Castlebyrne Park	49 A4
Canon Mooney Gardens	39 A3 [15]	Carrickhill Rise	4 D4	Casimir Court (off Casimir Avenue)	46 F1 [17]	Castlecurragh Heath	9 A4
(off Cambridge Road)		Carrickhill Road	15 A1	Casimir Road	46 F1	Castlecurragh Park	9 B4
Capel Street	71 A3	Carrickhill Road Middle	15 A1	Casino Drive	3 B2		

STREET NAME	PAGE/GRID REFERENCE
Castlecurragh Vale	9 A4
Castledawson Avenue	48 F3
Castlefarm	1 C1
Castlefield Avenue	55 C1
Castlefield Court (Clonsilla)	21 C2
Castlefield Court (Firhouse)	55 C1
Castlefield Drive	55 C2
Castlefield Green	55 C2
Castlefield Grove	55 C2
Castlefield Lawn	55 C1
Castlefield Manor (Malahide)	3 B3
Castlefield Manor (Firhouse)	55 C1
Castlefield Orchard	55 C1
Castlefield Park (Clonsilla)	21 C2
Castlefield Park (Firhouse)	55 C2
Castlefield Way	55 C2
Castlefield Woods	21 C2
Castleforbes Road	72 F3
Castleforbes Square	72 F3
Castlegate (Monkstown)	59 C1
Castlegate (Shankill)	64 D3
Castlegate Chase	33 C3
Castlegate Close	33 C3
Castlegate Crescent	33 C3
Castlegate Dene	33 C3
Castlegate Drive	33 C3
Castlegate Elms	33 C3
Castlegate Green	33 C3
Castlegate Grove	33 C3
Castlegate Park	33 C3
Castlegate Place	33 C3
Castlegate Square	34 D3
Castlegate Walk	33 C3
Castlegate Way	33 C3
Castlegrange	21 B1
Castlegrange Avenue (Swords)	2 D1
Castlegrange Avenue (Clonsilla)	21 B1
Castlegrange Close (Swords)	2 D1
Castlegrange Close (Clondalkin)	43 B1
Castlegrange Court (Clonsilla)	21 B1
Castlegrange Court (Clondalkin)	43 C1
Castlegrange Dale	21 B1
Castlegrange Drive (Clonsilla)	21 B1
Castlegrange Drive (Clondalkin)	43 B1
Castlegrange Gardens	21 B1
Castlegrange Green (Swords)	2 D1
Castlegrange Green (Clonsilla)	21 B1
Castlegrange Green (Clondalkin)	43 B1
Castlegrange Grove	21 B1
Castlegrange Heights	2 D1
Castlegrange Hill	2 D1
Castlegrange Lawn (Clonsilla)	21 B1
Castlegrange Lawn (Clondalkin)	43 C1
Castlegrange Park	21 B1
Castlegrange Road (Swords)	2 D1
Castlegrange Road (Clondalkin)	43 C1
Castlegrange Row	21 B1
Castlegrange Square (Clonsilla)	21 B1
Castlegrange Square (Clondalkin)	43 C1
Castlegrange Terrace	21 B1
Castlegrange Way	2 D1
Castleheath	3 A3
Castlekevin Road	26 D1
Castleknock	22 F3
Castleknock Avenue	22 F3
Castleknock Brook	22 F3
Castleknock Close	22 F3
Castleknock Court	22 F3 [2]
(off Castleknock Road)	
Castleknock Crescent	22 F3
Castleknock Dale	22 F3
Castleknock Downs	22 E3
Castleknock Drive	22 F3
Castleknock Elms	22 F3
Castleknock Gate	23 B4 [1]
(off Castleknock Road)	
Castleknock Glade	22 F3
Castleknock Grange	22 F3
Castleknock Green	23 A3
Castleknock Grove	22 F3
Castleknock Laurels	22 F3
Castleknock Lodge	23 A4
Castleknock Manor	23 A3 [5]
(off Phoenix Gardens)	
Castleknock Meadows	22 F3
Castleknock Oaks	22 F3
Castleknock Park	23 A3
Castleknock Rise	22 E3
Castleknock Road (Blanchardstown)	22 F3
Castleknock Road (Phoenix Park)	23 A4
Castleknock Vale	22 F3
Castleknock View	22 F3

STREET NAME	PAGE/GRID REFERENCE
Castleknock Walk	22 E3
Castleknock Way	22 F3
Castleknock Wood	22 F3
Castlelands (off Hyde Road)	60 F1 [16]
Castlelands Grove (off Hyde Road)	60 F1 [12]
Castlelyons	42 D4
Castlemoyne	14 D3
Castlepark Court	60 E2 [9]
(off Castlepark Road)	
Castlepark Road	60 E1
Castlerosse Crescent	14 F4
Castlerosse Drive	14 F4
Castlerosse View	14 F4
Castleside Drive	46 F3
Castletimon Avenue	25 C1
Castletimon Drive	25 C1
Castletimon Gardens	25 C1
Castletimon Green	25 C1
Castletimon Park	25 C1
Castletimon Road	25 C1
Castletown	32 F1
Castletown Court	32 D3
Castletown Drive	32 D3
Castletown Grove	32 D3
Castletown Lawn	32 D3
Castletymon Court	45 B4
Castletymon Gardens	45 B4
Castletymon Green	45 B4
Castleview (Dunboyne)	7 B3
Castleview (Artane)	26 E2
Castleview (Clontarf)	26 E4
Castleview (off Dundrum Castle)	57 C1 [7]
Castleview Court	1 Inset
Castleview Avenue	1 Inset
Castleview Close	1 Inset
Castleview Crescent	1 Inset
Castleview Drive	1 Inset
Castleview Green	1 Inset
Castleview Grove	1 Inset
Castleview Heights	1 Inset
Castleview Lawns	1 Inset
Castleview Meadows	1 Inset
Castleview Park (Swords)	1 Inset
Castleview Park (Malahide)	3 A3
Castleview Place	1 Inset
Castleview Rise	1 Inset
Castleview Row	1 Inset
Castleview Walk	1 Inset
Castleview Way	1 Inset
Castlewarden	51 A3
Castlewarden North	51 A3
Castlewood	21 C1
Castlewood Avenue	47 A1
Castlewood Close	47 A1 [24]
(off Castlewood Avenue)	
Castlewood Court	47 B1 [26]
(off Oakley Road)	
Castlewood Park	47 A1
Castlewood Place	47 A1 [6]
(off Church Gardens)	
Castlewood Terrace	47 A1 [5]
(off Castlewood Avenue)	
Cathal Brugha Street	71 B3
Cathedral Lane	75 A2
Cathedral Street	71 B3
Cathedral View Court	75 A2
Cathedral View Walk	75 A2
Catherine Court	72 D1
(off William Street North)	
Catherine Lane	70 F3
Catherine Street (Swift's Alley)	74 F1
*Catherines Close (Catherine Street)	74 F1
Catherine's Well	22 F2 [3]
Cats Ladder (off Torca Road)	60 F2 [5]
Causeway Road	27 B3
Cavalry Row	70 D3
Cavendish Row	71 B2
Caves Strand	3 A2
Ceanchor Road	30 D4
Ceannt Fort (off Mount Brown)	74 D1
Cecil Avenue	26 D4
Cecilia Street (off Temple Bar)	71 B4
Cedar Avenue	45 A3
Cedar Brook	35 C4
Cedar Brook Avenue	35 B3
Cedar Brook Place	35 B3
Cedar Brook Walk	35 B3
Cedar Court (Terenure)	46 F2
Cedar Court (Loughlinstown)	64 D1
Cedar Drive (Dunboyne)	7 B2
Cedar Drive (Palmerstown)	35 B2
Cedar Grove (off Shelerin Road)	21 C2 [2]

STREET NAME	PAGE/GRID REFERENCE
Cedar Hall (off Milltown Road)	47 C1 [16]
Cedar House	76 D3
Cedar Lodge	23 A4
Cedar Lodge Apartments	56 E2
Cedar Park (Leixlip)	19 C4
Cedar Park (Donaghmede)	27 A1
Cedar Square (Swords)	1 B3
Cedar Square (off Linden Grove)	48 F4 [4]
Cedar Walk	27 B2
Cedarhurst Green	23 B3
Cedarhurst Road	23 B3
Cedarmount Road	48 E4
Cedarwood	32 D3
Cedarwood Avenue	24 F1
Cedarwood Close	24 F1
Cedarwood Green	24 F1
Cedarwood Grove	24 F1
Cedarwood Park	24 F1
Cedarwood Rise	24 F1
Cedarwood Road	24 F1
Ceder Park	1 B3
Ceder View	1 B3
Celbridge	32 D3
Celbridge Abbey	31 C4
Celbridge Road (Maynooth)	18 D4
Celbridge Road (Leixlip)	32 F2
Celbridge Road (Lucan)	33 B2
Celestine Avenue	39 A3 [42]
(off Dermot O'Hurley Avenue)	
*Celestine Avenue	39 A3
(off Dermot O'Hurley Ave)	
Celtic Park Avenue	25 C2
Celtic Park Road	25 C2
Cenecle Grove	64 E1
Chalet Gardens	34 E1
Chalfont Avenue	3 B2
Chalfont Park	3 B2
Chalfont Place	3 B2
Chalfont Road	3 A2
*Chamber Court (off Chamber St)	74 F2
Chamber Street	74 F2
*Chamberlain Court	25 C4
(off Richmond Avenue)	
Chamley Gardens	2 F3
Chamley Park	2 F3
Champions Avenue	71 C3
Chancel Mews	24 D4
*Chancery Hall Apartments	70 E4
(Ellis Quay / John Street North)	
Chancery Lane	75 A1
Chancery Place	71 A4
Chancery Street	71 A4
Chandlers Guild Apartments	74 D1
Chandlers Mill	32 D4
Chanel Avenue	26 E2
Chanel Grove	26 E1
Chanel Road	26 E2
*Chapel Avenue (off Bath St)	39 A3
Chapel Crescent	24 D3
Chapel Hill	34 D1
Chapel Lane (Swords)	2 D2
Chapel Lane (Bray)	67 B1
Chapel Lane (Parnell Street)	71 B3
Chapel Road (Kinsaley)	14 D1
Chapel View Apartments	34 D1
Chapelizod	36 E2
Chapelizod Bypass	36 E2
Chapelizod Court	36 E2
Chapelizod Hill Road	36 E2
Chapelizod Road	69 A4
Chaplegate	25 A4
Chaplewood Avenue	9 C1
Chaplewood Crescent	9 C1
Chaplewood View	9 C1
Charlemont	25 C3
Charlemont Avenue (off George's	50 D4 [5]
Place Dún Laoghaire)	
Charlemont Bridge (Grand Canal)	75 B3
Charlemont Court	75 B3
Charlemont Gardens	75 B3
Charlemont Mall	75 B4
Charlemont Parade	72 D1
Charlemont Place	75 C3
Charlemont Road	26 D4
Charlemont Street	75 B3
Charlemont Terrace (off George's	50 D4 [18]
Place Dún Laoghaire)	
Charles Lane	71 C1
Charles Sheils Houses	58 F2
Charles Street Great	71 C2
Charles Street West	71 A4
(off Ormond Quay Upper)	

STREET NAME	PAGE/GRID REFERENCE
Charleston Avenue	47 B1
Charleston Court Flats	47 B1 [9]
(off Charleston Road)	
Charleston Road	47 B1
Charlestown Avenue	11 B4
Charlestown Court	11 B4
Charlestown Drive	11 B4
Charlestown Green	11 B4
Charlestown Mews	11 B4
Charlestown Park	11 B4
Charlestown Place	11 A4
Charlestown Way	11 B4
Charleville	47 B4
Charleville Avenue	72 D1
Charleville Close	47 A1
Charleville Mall	72 D1
Charleville Road (Rathmines)	47 A1
Charleville Road (Phibsborough)	70 E1
Charleville Square	46 E4
*Charleville Terrace	70 E1
(on Charleville Rd)	
Charlotte Quay	76 F1
Charlotte Terrace	60 F2 [18]
(off Victoria Road Dalkey)	
Charlotte Way	75 B3
Charlton Lawn	48 D2
Charnwood (Clonsilla)	21 C2
Charnwood (Bray)	67 C3
Charnwood Avenue	21 C2
Charnwood Court	21 C2
Charnwood Dale	21 C2
Charnwood Gardens	21 C2
Charnwood Green	21 C2
Charnwood Grove	21 C2
Charnwood Heath	21 C2
Charnwood Meadows	21 C2
Charnwood Park	21 C2
Charter House	17 C3 [7]
Chatham Court (on Chatham Street)	75 B1
Chatham Lane (off Chatham Street)	75 B1
Chatham Row	75 B1
Chatham Street	75 B1
*Chaworth Terrace (Hanbury Lane)	74 F1
Cheeverstown Road	54 D1
Chelmsford Avenue	75 C4
Chelmsford Lane	47 B1 [15]
(off Chelmsford Road)	
Chelmsford Road	47 B1
Chelsea Gardens	26 F4
Cheltenham Place	75 B4
Cherbury Court	48 F3
Cherbury Gardens	48 F3
Cherbury Mews	48 F3 [4]
(off Cherbury Court)	
Cherbury Park Avenue	34 D2
Cherbury Park Road	34 D2
Cherries Road	58 D2
Cherrington Close	64 E3
Cherrington Drive	64 E3
Cherrington Road	64 E3
Cherry Avenue (Swords)	1 C3
Cherry Avenue (Carpenterstown)	22 E3
Cherry Court (Terenure)	46 F2
Cherry Court (Loughlinstown)	64 D1 [2]
Cherry Drive	22 E3
Cherry Garth (Swords)	1 C2
Cherry Garth (Stillorgan)	48 E4
Cherry Grove (Swords)	1 B3
Cherry Grove (Crumlin)	45 C2
Cherry House	76 D3
Cherry Lawn	22 E3
Cherry Lawns	33 C2
Cherry Lodge	23 A4
Cherry Orchard Ave	36 D4
Cherry Orchard Avenue	35 C3
Cherry Orchard Court	35 C4
Cherry Orchard Crescent	35 C4
Cherry Orchard Drive	35 C4
Cherry Orchard Green	35 C4
Cherry Orchard Grove	35 C4
Cherry Orchard Parade	35 C4
Cherry Orchard Way	35 C4 [1]
(off Cherry Orchard Drive)	
Cherry Park (Swords)	1 B3
Cherry Park (Carpenterstown)	22 E3
Cherry Tree Drive	67 C3 [1]
Cherry Wood	64 D1
Cherryfield Avenue	45 C2
Cherryfield Avenue Lr	47 B1
Cherryfield Avenue Upr	47 B1
Cherryfield Close	21 C1
Cherryfield Court	21 B1

STREET NAME	PAGE/GRID REFERENCE
Cherryfield Drive	45 C2
Cherryfield Lawn	21 C1
Cherryfield Park	21 C1
Cherryfield Road	45 C2
Cherryfield View	21 B1
Cherryfield Walk	21 C1
Cherryfield Way	46 D4
Cherrymount Crescent	26 D3[1]
(off Casino Park)	
Cherrymount Grove	26 D3[2]
(off Casino Park)	
Cherrymount Park	70 F1
Cherrywood	32 D3
Cherrywood Avenue	44 D1
Cherrywood Crescent	43 C1
Cherrywood Drive	43 C1
Cherrywood Grove	44 D1
Cherrywood Lawn	43 C2
Cherrywood Park (Clondalkin)	43 C2
Cherrywood Park (Loughlinstown)	64 D1
Cherrywood Road	64 D2
Cherrywood Villas	43 C1
Cherrywood Villas (off Tower Road)	44 D1[6]
Chester Downs	60 D1
Chester Road	47 B1
Chester Square	60 E1[23]
(off Albert Road Lower)	
Chesterfield Avenue	23 B4
(Phoenix Park)	
Chesterfield Avenue (Castleknock)	23 B4
Chesterfield Avenue (Phoenix Park)	69 B3
Chesterfield Close	23 B4
Chesterfield Copse	23 B4
Chesterfield Grove	23 B4
Chesterfield Park	23 B3
Chesterfield View	23 B3
Chestnut Court (off Collinswood)	25 C2[1]
Chestnut Grove (Dunboyne)	7 B3
Chestnut Grove (Celbridge)	32 D3
Chestnut Grove (Clondalkin)	44 F3
Chestnut Grove (Ballinteer)	57 B2
Chestnut House (Swords)	1 Inset
Chestnut Park	59 A2[5]
(off Pine Avenue Foxrock)	
Chestnut Road (Clondalkin)	45 A1
Chestnut Road (Mount Merrion)	48 E3
Christchurch Hall	74 F1
Christchurch Place	75 A1
Christchurch Square	75 A1
Church Avenue	14 F2[2]
(off St.Patrick's Avenue)	
Church Avenue (Blanchardstown)	22 F2
Church Avenue (off Ballymun Road)	25 A3[2]
Church Avenue (Drumcondra)	25 B3
Church Avenue (Irishtown)	39 A3
Church Avenue (Rathmines)	47 A1
Church Avenue (Killiney)	60 E4
Church Avenue South	74 D2
(Dolphin's Barn)	
Church Avenue West (Church Street)	70 F4
Church Court (Castleknock)	22 F3
Church Court (East Wall)	72 F2
Church Gardens	47 A1
Church Green	46 F1
Church Grove	55 A2
Church Lands	67 C3
Church Lane (Rathfarnham)	46 F3
Church Lane (College Green)	71 B4
Church Lane South	75 A2
Church Park	46 F1
Church Park Avenue	46 F1
Church Park Court	46 F1
Church Park Drive	46 F1
Church Park Lawn	46 F1
Church Park Way	46 F1
Church Place (off Irvine Terrace)	72 F3
Church Road (Swords)	2 D2
Church Road (Malahide)	3 B3
Church Road (Mulhuddart)	9 A4
Church Road (Finglas)	24 D2
Church Road (Sutton)	29 B1
Church Road (Celbridge)	32 D4
Church Road (Rathcoole)	52 E2
Church Road (Killiney)	60 D3
Church Road (Ballybrack)	60 E4
Church Road (Dalkey)	60 F1
Church Road (Bray)	67 C3
Church Road (East Wall)	72 F2
*Church Row (off Irvine Terrace)	72 F3
Church Street (Finglas)	24 E2
Church Street (Howth)	30 D1
Church Street (Four Courts)	70 F4

STREET NAME	PAGE/GRID REFERENCE
Church Street East	72 F3
Church Street New	70 F4
Church Street Upper	70 F3
Church Terrace (Finglas)	24 E2
Church Terrace (Bray)	67 C2[45]
Church Terrace (off Church Street)	70 F3
Church View	24 D2[7]
(off Church Street Finglas)	
Church View (Drumcondra)	25 B3
Church View	44 D2[1]
(off Oak Way Clondalkin)	
Church Villas	59 C4[2]
(off Brennanstown Road)	
Church Walk	24 D4
Churchfields (Clonskeagh)	47 C2
Churchgate Avenue	39 C1[1]
(off Vernon Avenue)	
Churchill Mews (off Church Road)	60 F1[17]
Churchill Terrace	39 A4[6]
(off Sandymount Avenue)	
Churchlands (off Sandyford Road)	58 D3[1]
Churchtown	47 B4
Churchtown Avenue	47 B3
Churchtown Close	47 B3
Churchtown Drive	47 B3
Churchtown Road	47 B4
Churchtown Road Lower	47 B3
Churchtown Road Upper	47 A4
Churchview Avenue	60 D3
Churchview Drive	60 D3
Churchview Park	60 D3
Churchview Road	60 D3
Churchwell Avenue	14 D3
Churchwell Close	14 D3
Churchwell Drive	14 D4
Churchwell Mews	14 D3
Churchwell Place	14 D4
Churchwell Road	14 D4
Churchwell Square	14 D3
Cian Park	25 B4
Cianlea	1 B1
Cill Cais	54 F2
Cill Eanna	26 F2
Cill Manntan Park	67 C2[9]
Cill Sarain	67 B3
City Quay	72 D4
Citywest Bridge	42 B4
Citywest Avenue	53 C1
Citywest Interchange	42 B4
Citywest Road	53 C1
Claddagh Green	35 C3
Claddagh Road	35 C3
*Claddagh Terrace (on Strand Road)	67 C2
Clanawley Road	26 E3
Clanboy Road	26 E3
Clanbrassil Close	74 F4
Clanbrassil Street Lower	74 F3
Clanbrassil Street Upper	74 F3
Clanbrassil terrace	74 F2
Clancarthy Road	26 D3
Clancy Avenue	24 E1
Clancy Road	24 E1
Clandonagh Road	26 D3
Clane Road	31 B4
Clanfadda Wood	48 F3
Clanhugh Road	26 E3
Clanmahon Road	26 E3
Clanmaurice Road	26 D3
Clanmawr	64 E2
Clanmoyle Road	26 D3
Clanranald Road	26 D3
Clanree Road	26 D3
Clanwilliam Court	76 E2
Clanwilliam Place	76 E2
Clanwilliam Square	76 E1
Clanwilliam Terrace	76 E1
Clare Hall	14 D4
Clare Lane	75 C1
Clare Park Villas (off Achill Road)	25 B3[3]
Clare Road	25 B3
Clare Street	75 C1
Claremont Avenue	25 A3[1]
(off Ballymun Road)	
Claremont Close	24 F4
Claremont Court (Finglas)	24 F4
Claremont Court	39 A4[21]
(off Shelbourne Road)	
Claremont Court	39 A4[36]
(off Claremont Road)	
Claremont Crescent	24 F4
Claremont Drive	24 F2
Claremont Grove	60 E3

STREET NAME	PAGE/GRID REFERENCE
Claremont Lawn	24 F4
Claremont Mews	29 C1
Claremont Park	39 A4
Claremont Road (Sutton)	29 B1
Claremont Road (Sandymount)	39 A4
Claremont Road (Carrickmines)	59 B4
Claremont Road (Killiney)	60 E3
Claremont Terrace	47 C4[7]
(off Main Street Dundrum)	
Claremont Villas (off Adelaide Road)	60 E1[4]
Claremount	64 E3
Claremount Pines	59 B4
Claremount Terrace	68 D2[11]
Clarence Mangan Road	74 F2
Clarence Mangan Square	75 A1
(off John Dillon Street)	
Clarence Place Great	76 E1
Clarence St Great North	72 D2
Clarence Street	49 C4
Clarendon Market	75 B1
(off William Street South)	
Clarendon Row	75 B1
(off King St South)	
Clarendon Street	75 B1
Clareville Court	24 F4[7]
(off Claremont Lawn)	
Clareville Grove	24 F4
Clareville Road	46 F1
Clarinda Manor	60 D1
Clarinda Park East	50 D4
(Dún Laoghaire)	
Clarinda Park North	50 D4
Clarinda Park West	50 D4
Clarion Quay	72 D3
Clarke Terrace	74 D2
Clarke's Bridge (Royal Canal)	72 D1
Clarkeville Terrace	35 C1[3]
(off Lucan Road Palmerston)	
Classon's Bridge	47 B2
Claude Road	25 A4
Clayton Terrace	36 E2[8]
(off St. Laurence Road)	
Clearstream Court	24 E1[4]
Clearwater Apartments	3 C2[2]
Clearwater Court	24 D3[1]
(off Pelletstown Avenue)	
Clearwater Cove	49 C4[31]
(off Dunleary Road)	
Cleggan Avenue	35 C3
Cleggan Park	35 C3
Cleggan Road	35 C3
Clifden Drive	35 C3
Clifden Road	36 D3
Cliff Terrace (off Breffni Road)	60 E1[18]
Clifford's Lane	2 E2
Clifton Avenue	49 C4[11]
(off Monkstown Crescent)	
Clifton Court Apartments	70 E4
Clifton Lane (off Monkstown Road)	49 C4[10]
Clifton Park	64 E2
Clifton Terrace	49 C4[13]
(off Seapoint Avenue)	
Cliftonville Road	25 A4
Clinch's Court	72 D1
*Clipper Court Apartments	70 E4
(off Liffey Street West)	
*Clipper View Apartments	70 F4
(off Liffey Street West)	
Clogher Road	74 D4
Cloghran	1 C4
Cloghran	13 A1
Cloghran Roundabout	1 C4
Cloister Avenue	49 A4
Cloister Close	48 F4
Cloister Court	24 D3
Cloister Gate	49 A4
Cloister Green	49 A4
Cloister Grove	49 A4
Cloister Park	49 A4
Cloister Square	49 A4
Cloister Way	49 A4
Clon Burgh	58 D3
Clonallen	46 E2[11]
(off Kimmage Road Lower)	
Clonard Avenue	57 C2
Clonard Close	57 C2
Clonard Court (off Poddle Close)	46 E2[8]
Clonard Drive	57 C2
Clonard Grove	57 C2
Clonard Lawn	57 C2
Clonard Park	57 C2
Clonard Road (Sandyford)	57 C2

STREET NAME	PAGE/GRID REFERENCE
Clonard Road (Crumlin)	73 B4
Clonasleigh	64 E2[2]
Cloncourt Apartments	8 D3
Clondalkin	44 D1
Clonee	8 D3
Clonee Bridge	8 D3
Clonee Bypass	8 D3
Clonfert Road	46 E1
Clongriffin	14 E4
Clonkeen Court	59 B3
Clonkeen Crescent	59 B2
Clonkeen Drive	59 B2
Clonkeen Grove	59 B2
Clonkeen Lawn (off ClonkeenRoad)	59 B3[5]
Clonkeen Road	59 B2
Clonlara Avenue	43 A4
Clonlara Road (off Pine Road)	39 A3[12]
Clonlara Road (Naas Road)	43 A4
Clonlea	57 C2
Clonlea Wood (off Ballinteer Road)	57 C2[1]
Clonliffe Avenue	72 D1
Clonliffe Gardens	25 B4
Clonliffe Road	25 B4
Clonliffe Square (off Distillery Road)	25 B4[16]
Clonmacnoise Grove	46 E1[4]
(off Clonmacnoise Road)	
Clonmacnoise Road	46 E1
Clonmel Road	25 A2
Clonmel Street	75 B2
Clonmellon Grove	14 D4[3]
(off Ardara Avenue)	
Clonmore Court	25 A3[11]
(off Ballymun Road)	
Clonmore Road (Goatstown)	48 E4
Clonmore Road (Ballybough)	72 D1
Clonmore Terrace	72 D1
*Clonmore Villas (Clonmore Road)	72 D1
Clonrosse Court	26 F1
Clonrosse Drive	26 F1
Clonrosse Park	26 F1
Clonshaugh	13 B3
Clonshaugh Avenue	13 A4
Clonshaugh Close	13 B4
Clonshaugh Court	13 B4[4]
(off Clonshaugh Crescent)	
Clonshaugh Crescent	13 A4
Clonshaugh Drive	13 B4
Clonshaugh Glen	13 B4
Clonshaugh Green	13 B4
Clonshaugh Grove	13 B4
Clonshaugh Heights	13 A4
Clonshaugh Lawns	13 B4
Clonshaugh Meadow	13 A4
Clonshaugh Park	13 B4
Clonshaugh Rise	13 B4[2]
(off Clonshaugh Avenue)	
Clonshaugh Road (Belcamp)	13 A3
Clonshaugh Road (Kilmore)	13 A4
Clonshaugh Walk	13 B4
Clonsilla	21 C2
Clonsilla Close	22 E2
Clonsilla Park	22 E2
Clonsilla Road	22 E2
Clonskeagh	47 C2
Clonskeagh Drive	47 C2[6]
(off Clonskeagh Road)	
Clonskeagh Road	47 C2
Clonskeagh Square	47 C2
(off Clonskeagh Road)7	
Clontarf	39 C1
Clontarf Park	39 C1
Clontarf Road	26 D4
Clonturk Avenue	25 B3[1]
(off Drumcondra Road Upper)	
Clonturk Court	25 B3[6]
(off Church Avenue)	
Clonturk Gardens	25 B4[3]
(off Clonturk Park)	
Clonturk Park	25 B4
Cloonlara Crescent	24 E3
Cloonlara Drive	24 E2
Cloonlara Road	24 E3
Cloonlara Square	23 B3
Cloonmore Avenue	54 E2
Cloonmore Close	54 E2
Cloonmore Crescent	54 D2
Cloonmore Drive	54 D2
Cloonmore Gardens	54 D2
Cloonmore Green	54 D2
Cloonmore Grove	54 D2
Cloonmore Lawn	54 D2
Cloonmore Park	54 D2

STREET NAME	PAGE	GRID
Cloonmore Road	54	D2
*Cloragh Mills Apartments (Edmonstown Park)	56	E2
Cloragh Road	56	E4
Clover Hill	67	A3
Clover Hill Drive	36	D3
Clover Hill Road	36	D4
Cloverhill Road (Clondalkin)	35	A4
Cloverhill Road (Cherry Orchard)	35	B3
Cloyne Road (off Blarney Park)	46	E1 [2]
Cluain Aoibhinn	17	C4
Cluain Mhuire	60	D1
Cluain na Greine Court	64	E3 [4]
Cluain Rí	34	F2
Cluain Shee	58	D3
Club Road	45	A1
Clune Road	24	E1
Cluny Grove	60	D3
Cluny Park	60	E2
Clutterland	42	F1
Clyde Court (off Seafort Avenue)	76	E4
Clyde House (off Serpentine Avenue)	39	A4 [43]
Clyde Lane	76	F4
Clyde Road	76	E4
Cnoc Aoibhean	33	B2
Coast Road (Malahide)	3	C2
Coast Road (Baldoyle)	15	A4
Coates Lane	17	C3 [3]
Coburg	67	B2
Coburg Place	72	D2
*Coghill's Court (off Dame Street)	71	B4
Cois Cairn	67	B1
Cois Coillte	64	D1 [3]
Cois Eala	75	A4
Cois Na hAbhann	54	F2
Cois Sleibhe	67	B4
Coke Lane	70	F4
Coke Ovens Cottages	24	F4
Colbert's Fort (Tallaght)	44	F4
Colbert's Fort (off St James Walk)	74	D2
*Coldbeck Way (off Fonthill Road South)	46	E2
Coldcut Road	35	B2
Coldwater Lakes	53	B2
Coldwell Street	60	D1
Colepark Avenue	36	D3
Colepark Drive	36	D3
Colepark Green	36	D3
Colepark Road	36	D3
Coleraine Street	71	A3
Colganstown	41	B2
Coliemore Road	60	F2
Coliemore Villas (off Coliemore Road)	60	F2 [14]
College Crescent	46	D3
College Drive	46	E3
College Fort	22	F4
College Gate	22	F3
College Green (Maynooth)	17	C4
College Green (Trinity College)	71	B4
College Grove (Castleknock)	22	F4
College Lane (Rathcoole)	52	F1
College Lane (Trinity College)	76	D1
College Manor (off Millmount Avenue)	25	B4 [8]
College Mews (off Clonliffe Road)	25	B4 [11]
College Park (Castleknock)	23	A4
College Park (Kimmage)	46	E3
College Park Avenue	57	C2
College Park Close	57	C2
College Park Court (off College Park Avenue)2	57	C2
College Park Drive (off College Park Avenue)	57	C2 [3]
College Park Grove	57	C2
College Park House	75	C1
College Park Way	57	C2
College Road (Castleknock)	22	F4
College Road (Greenogue Ind Est)	42	E4
College Road (Whitechurch Road)	57	A3
*College Square (at Kimmage Manor)	46	D3
College Street (Baldoyle)	15	A4
College Street (Trinity College)	71	C4
College View (Drumcondra)	25	B3
College View (off Main Street Tallaght)	55	A1 [6]
College Wood	22	F4
Collegeland	42	F4
Collier's Avenue (off Anna Villa)	47	B1 [3]
Colliersland	6	F2
Collindale (off Beaumont Road)	25	C2 [6]

STREET NAME	PAGE	GRID
Collins Avenue	25	C2
Collins Avenue East	26	D3
Collins Avenue Extension	25	A2
Collins Avenue West	25	B2
Collins Bridge	20	F4
Collins Close (off Collins Avenue)	25	C3 [8]
Collins Court (off Collins Avenue)	25	C3 [6]
Collins Court (off Temple Road)	49	A3 [13]
Collins Drive	24	E1
Collins Green	24	E1
Collins Park	26	D3
Collins Place	24	E1
Collins Row (Glasaree Road)	24	E2 [6]
Collinstown Crescent (off Collinstown Road)	35	A3 [3]
Collinstown Grove	35	B3
Collinstown Road	35	A3
Collinswood	25	C2
Colmanstown	51	C2
Colmanstown Lane	51	C2
Colmcille Court	2	D2 [3]
Colthurst Close	34	F2
Colthurst Crescent	34	F2
Colthurst Gardens	34	F2
Colthurst Green	34	F2
Colthurst Mews	34	F2
Colthurst Park	34	F2
Colthurst Rise	34	F2
Colthurst Road	34	F2
Colthurst Way	34	F2
Comeragh Road	36	F4
Comeran Court	74	E2
Common Little	42	D4
Commons (Hazelhatch)	41	C2
Commons (Rathcoole)	52	E1
Commons East	2	D3
Commons Little	42	D4
Commons Lower	41	A1
Commons Road (St. John's Gate)	44	D2
Commons Road (Loughlinstown)	64	E2
Commons Street	72	D3
Compass Court	23	C3
Compass Court Apartments (off Lockkeeper's Walk)	24	D3 [4]
Comyn Place (off Walsh Road)	25	A3 [5]
Con Colbert Road	36	F3
Con Colbert Road	73	A1
Confey	20	D4
Congress Gardens (off Hudson Road)	60	E1 [2]
Congress Hall	7	B3
Congress Park	7	B3 [1]
Connaught Parade (off Connaught Street)	24	F4 [6]
Connaught Place (off Crofton Road)	50	D4 [26]
Connaught Street	24	F4
Connawood	67	B1
Connawood Copse	67	B1
Connawood Crescent	67	B1
Connawood Drive	67	B1
Connawood Green	67	B1
Connawood Grove	67	B1
Connawood Lawn	67	B1
Connawood Walk	67	B1
Connawood Way	67	B1
Connolly Avenue (Malahide)	3	A4
Connolly Avenue (Kilmainham)	73	A2
Connolly Gardens	73	A2
Connolly's Folly	18	E4
Conor Clune Road	23	C4
Conquer Hill Avenue	39	C1
Conquer Hill Road	39	C1
Constellation Road	12	F4
Constitution Hill	71	A3
Convent Avenue (Marino)	25	B4
Convent Avenue (Bray)	68	D2
Convent Close	76	D2
Convent Court (off Coolnevaun Kilmacud)	58	E1 [4]
Convent Lane (Portmarnock)	4	D4
Convent Lane (Maynooth)	17	C3
Convent Lane (Willbrook)	46	F4
Convent Lawns (off Kylemore Road)	36	E3 [4]
Convent Lodge	26	F2
Convent Place	75	C3
Convent Road (Clondalkin)	44	E2
Convent Road (Blackrock)	49	A4
Convent Road (Dún Laoghaire)	50	D4
Convent Road (Dalkey)	60	F2
Convent View (Oldcourt)	67	C3
Convent View (Sidmonton Road Bray)	68	D2 [23]

STREET NAME	PAGE	GRID
Convent View Cottages (off Ratoath Road Cabra)	24	D4 [2]
Convent View Cottages (St. John's Gate)	44	D2
Convent View Crescent (off Ratoath Road Cabra)	24	D4 [3]
Convent Way	24	D4
Conway Court	76	E1
Conyngham Road	69	C4
Cook Street	71	A4
Cooks Road	1	A4
Cookstown	66	E3
Cookstown Court	44	F4
Cookstown Road	44	E4
Cookstown Way	44	E4
Coolamber Court (off Knocklyon Road)	56	D1 [1]
Coolamber Drive	52	F2
Coolamber Park	56	D1
Coolamber Road	52	F2
Coolatree Close	25	C2
Coolatree Park	25	C2
Coolatree Road	25	C2
Cooldrinagh Lane	33	B1
Cooldrinagh Terrace	33	B1
Cooldríona Court	2	D2
Cooleen Avenue	25	C1
Coolevin (Ballybrack)	60	D4
Coolevin Road	75	A2
Cooley Close	36	F4
Cooley Road	73	A4
Coolgariff Road	25	C1
Coolgreena Close	25	C2
Coolgreena Road	25	C1
Coolkill	58	D3
Coolmine	52	F3
Coolmine Boulevard	22	E2
Coolmine Close	22	D2
Coolmine Cottages	9	A4
Coolmine Court	22	E2
Coolmine Green	22	D3
Coolmine Lawn	22	D2
Coolmine Mews (off Coolmine Road)	22	D2 [1]
Coolmine Park	22	E2
Coolmine Road	22	E3
Coolmine Woods	22	E2
Coolnevaun	58	E1
Coolock	26	E1
Coolock Drive	26	E1
Coolock Lane (Santry)	12	F4
Coolock Village	26	E1
Coolock Village Close (off Coolock Village)	26	E1 [3]
Coolrua Drive	25	C1
Coombe Court	74	F1
Coopers Way	70	F3
*Coopers Yard (Smithfield)	70	F3
Coopers Yard Apartments	70	F3
Cope Bridge	20	D3
Cope Street	71	B4
Copeland Avenue	26	D4
Copeland Grove	26	D4
Copper Alley (Eustace Street)	71	A4
Copper Beech Grove	67	B2 [6]
Coppinger	49	A4
Coppinger Close	48	F4
Coppinger Glade	48	F4
Coppinger Row	75	B1
Coppinger Walk	49	A4
Coppinger Wood	48	F4
Corbally	53	C3
Corbally Avenue	53	C2
Corbally Close	53	C2
Corbally Downs	53	C2
Corbally Drive	53	C2
Corbally Glade	53	C2
Corbally Green	53	C2
Corbally Heath	53	C2
Corbally Lawn	53	C2
Corbally Park	53	C2
Corbally Rise	53	C2
Corbally Square	53	C2
Corbally Vale	53	C2
Corbally Way	53	C2
Corbawn Avenue	64	E2
Corbawn Close	64	F2
Corbawn Court	64	F2
Corbawn Dale	64	F2
Corbawn Drive	64	F2
Corbawn Glade	64	E2 [14]
Corbawn Grove	64	F2
Corbawn Lane	64	E2

STREET NAME	PAGE	GRID
Corbawn Lawn	64	E3
Corbawn Wood	64	E2
Corduff	22	F1
Corduff Avenue	22	F1
Corduff Close	22	F1
Corduff Cottages	22	E1
Corduff Crescent	22	F1
Corduff Gardens	22	F1
Corduff Green	22	F1
Corduff Grove	9	B4
Corduff Park	9	B4
Corduff Place	22	F1
Corduff Way	22	F1
Cork Hill (off Dame St)	71	A4
Cork Street	74	E2
Corkagh View	44	D2
Corke Abbey	67	C1
Corke Abbey Avenue	67	B1
Cormac Terrace	46	F2
Corn Exchange Apartments	71	C4
Corn Exchange Place	71	C4
Cornelscourt	59	B3
Cornelscourt Hill Road	59	B3
Cornelstown	6	D2
Cornerpark	42	D3
Cornmarket	74	F1
Corr Castle	29	B1
Corr Castle Apartments (off Howth Road)	29	B1 [3]
Corrbridge Terrace (off Claremont Road)	29	B1 [1]
Corrib Road	46	E2
Corrig Avenue	50	D4
Corrig Close	45	B3
Corrig Hall	57	C3
Corrig Park	50	D4
Corrig Road (Stillorgan)	58	E2
Corrig Road (Dún Laoghaire)	60	D1
Corrig Road (Dalkey)	60	F1
Corrybeg	46	D4
Cosy Lodge (off William's Park)	47	A1 [26]
Coulson Avenue	46	F2
Coultry Avenue	25	B1
Coultry Close	25	A1
Coultry Court	12	D4
Coultry Crescent	12	D4
Coultry Drive	12	D4
Coultry Gardens	12	D4
Coultry Green	12	D4
Coultry Grove	12	E4
Coultry Lawn	12	E4
Coultry Park	12	E4
Coultry Road	12	D4
Coultry Terrace	12	D4
Coultry Way	25	B1
Coundon Court	60	E4
Countess Markievicz House	72	D4
Countybrook Lawns	66	E2
Court House Square	17	C3 [5]
Courthill	7	B2
Courthill Drive	7	B2
Courthouse Square Apartments (off Main Street Tallaght)	55	A1 [13]
Courtlands	59	C3
Courtney Place	72	E1
Courtview	23	C3
Cow Parlour	74	E2
Cowbooter Lane	30	E2
Cowper Downs	47	A1
Cowper Drive	47	B2
Cowper Gardens	47	B2
Cowper Mews (off Cowper Road)	47	A2 [4]
Cowper Road	47	B2
Cowper Street	70	D2
Cowper Village	47	A2
Cows Lane	71	A4
Crag Avenue	35	B4
Crag Crescent	35	B4
Crag Terrace	35	B4
Craigford Avenue	26	E3
Craigford Drive	26	E3
Craiglands (off Ardeevin Road)	60	F2 [26]
Craigmore Gardens (off Temple Road)	49	A3 [5]
Crampton Avenue (off Park Lane)	76	F3
Crampton Court (off Dame St)	71	B4
Crampton Quay	71	B4
Crane Lane (off Dame Street)	71	A4
Crane Street	74	E1
Cranfield Place	39	A3
Cranford Court (off Terenure Road West Kimmage)	46	E2 [12]

STREET NAME	PAGE/GRID REFERENCE
Cranford Court (Stillorgan Road)	48 D2
Cranmer Lane	76 E2
Crannagh (off Milltown Road)	47 C2 9
Crannagh Castle (off Crannagh Road)	46 F3 9
Crannagh Court (off Crannagh Road)	46 F3 10
Crannagh Grove	47 A3
Crannagh Hall	47 A3
Crannagh Park	46 F3
Crannagh Road	46 F3
Crannagh Way (off Crannagh Road)	47 A3 8
Crannogue Close	11 C4
Crannogue Road	11 C4
Crawford Avenue	25 A4
Crawford Terrace (off Kings Avenue)	72 D1
Creighton Street	72 D4
Cremona Road	36 E3
Cremore Avenue	24 F3
Cremore Crescent	24 F3
Cremore Drive	24 F3
Cremore Heights	24 F2
Cremore Lawn	24 F3
Cremore Park	25 A3
Cremore Road	24 F3
Cremore Villas (off Cremore Crescent)	24 F3 5
Cremorne (Terenure Road East)	46 F2
Cremorne (Knocklyon)	56 D1
Crescent Gardens	72 E1
Crescent House (off Marino Crescent)	26 D4 6
Crescent Place	26 D4
Crescent Villas	25 A4
Crestfield Avenue	25 B2
Crestfield Close	25 B2
Crestfield Drive	25 B2
Crestfield Park	25 B2
Crestfield Road	25 B2
Creston	11 B3
Crewhill	17 B1
Crinan Strand	72 D3
Crinken Glen	64 E3
Crinken Lane	64 D4
Crinstown	17 A4
Croaghpatrick Road	24 D4
Crockshane	52 E3
Crodaun Court	31 C2 1
Crodaun Forest Park	32 D2
Crofton Avenue	50 D4
Crofton Mansions (off Crofton Road)	50 D4 28
Crofton Road	50 D4
Crofton Terrace (off Crofton Road)	50 D4 25
Croftwood Crescent	35 C3
Croftwood Drive	35 C3
Croftwood Gardens	35 C3
Croftwood Green	36 D3
Croftwood Grove	35 C3
Croftwood Park	36 D3
Croke Villas	72 D1
Cromcastle Avenue	26 D1
Cromcastle Close (off Cromcastle Green)	26 D1 2
Cromcastle Court (off Kilmore Road)	26 D1 6
Cromcastle Drive	26 D1
Cromcastle Green	26 D1
Cromcastle Park	26 D1
Cromcastle Road	26 D1
Cromlech Close	62 F2
Cromlech Court	11 C4
Cromlech Fields	64 E1
Cromwell's Quarters	74 D1
Cromwellsfort Road	45 C2
Crooksling	53 B4
Crosbie House	75 C4
Cross Avenue (Booterstown)	48 F3
Cross Avenue (Dún Laoghaire)	50 D4
Cross Lane	17 C3
Crosstrees Court (off Main Street Howth)	30 D2 13
Crosthwaite Park East	60 D1
Crosthwaite Park South	60 D1
Crosthwaite Park West	60 D1
Crosthwaite Terrace (off Clarinda Park West)	50 D4 15
Crostick Alley (off Meath St)	74 F1
Crotty Avenue	45 C1
Crow Street (off Dame St)	71 B4
Crown Alley (off Temple Bar)	71 B4
Croydon Gardens	25 C4
Croydon Green	25 C4
Croydon Park Avenue	25 C4
Croydon Terrace (off Griffith Avenue)	25 C3 4
Cruagh Avenue	62 E1
Cruagh Close	62 E1
Cruagh Court	62 E1
Cruagh Green	62 E1
Cruagh Lane	56 E4
Cruagh Rise	62 E1
Cruagh Road	56 E4
Cruagh Wood	62 E1
Cruise Park	9 A2
Cruise Park Avenue	9 A2
Cruise Park Close	9 A2
Cruise Park Court	9 A2
Cruise Park Crescent	9 A2
Cruise Park Drive	9 A2
Cruise Park Hall	9 A2
Cruise Park Rise	9 A2
Cruise Park Square	9 A2
Cruise Park Walk	9 A2
Crumlin	73 A4
*Crumlin Park (off Crumlin Road)	46 D1
Crumlin Road	73 C4
Cuala Grove	68 D3
Cuala Road (Cabra)	24 F4
Cuala Road (Bray)	68 D3
Cuan na Mara (off Harbour Road)	30 D1 13
Cuckoo Lane	71 A3
Cuffe Lane	75 B2
Cuffe Street	75 B2
Cuilenn Park	24 F1
Cul na Greine	54 F2
Cullen's Cottages (off Annaville Avenue)	49 A4 7
Cullen's Wood House	75 C4
*Cullenswood Court (off Cullenswood Park)	47 B1
Cullenswood Gardens	47 B1
Cullenswood Park	47 B1
Cullenswood Road (off Charleston Road)	47 B1 11
*Culmore Park (off Culmore Road)	35 C2 1
Culmore Road	35 C2
*Cumberland Place North (on North Circular Road)	70 F1
Cumberland Road	76 D3
Cumberland Street	49 C4
Cumberland Street North	71 C2
Cumberland Street South	76 D1
Cunningham Drive	60 F2
Cunningham Road	60 F2
Curlew Road	73 A4
Curracloe Drive (off Kilfenora Drive)	27 A1 4
Curragh Hall	9 B3
Curragh Hall Avenue	9 B3
Curragh Hall Close	9 B3
Curragh Hall Court	9 B3
Curragh Hall Crescent	9 B3
Curragh Hall Drive	9 B3
Curragh Hall Gate	9 B3
Curragh Hall Green	9 B3
Curragh Hall Grove	9 B3
Curragh Hall House	9 B3
Curragh Hall Lane	9 B3
Curragh Hall Lodge	9 B3
Curragh Hall Road	9 B3
Curragh Hall View	9 B3
Curragh Hall Way	9 B3
Curragh Hall Wood	9 B3
Curlestown	63 B4
Curzon Street	75 A3
Cushinstown	6 F1
Cushlawn Avenue	54 F2
Cushlawn Close	54 F3
Cushlawn Dale	54 F3
Cushlawn Drive	54 F2
Cushlawn Grove	54 F2
Cushlawn Park	54 F2
Cushlawn Walk	54 F3
Cushlawn Way	54 F3
Custom Hall	71 C3
Custom House Harbour	72 D3
Custom House Quay	71 C3
Custom House Square	72 E3
Cymric Road	39 A3
Cypress Avenue (off Brookwood)	56 D2 2
Cypress Court	64 E1
Cypress Drive	46 D3
Cypress Garth	46 D4
Cypress Grove North	46 D3
Cypress Grove Road	46 D3
Cypress Grove South	46 D3
Cypress House	28 D1
Cypress Lawn	46 D4
Cypress Park	46 D4
Cypress Road	48 E3
Cypress Springs	20 D4 1

D

STREET NAME	PAGE/GRID REFERENCE
*Daisy Market (off Arran Street)	71 A4
Dakota Avenue	12 F4
Dakota Court	25 A4
Dal Riada	3 C4
Dalcassian Downs	24 F4
Dale Close (off Dale Drive)	58 E1 1
Dale Drive	58 E1
Dale Road	58 E1
Dale View	60 E4
Dale View Park (off Madden's Lane)	60 E4 2
Dalepark Road	55 A2
Daletree Avenue	55 B2
Daletree Close	55 C3
Daletree Court	55 C3
Daletree Crescent	55 C2
Daletree Drive	55 C2
Daletree Park	55 C3
Daletree Place	55 C3
Daletree Road	55 C3
Daletree Terrace	55 C3
Daletree View	55 B3
Daleview Road	1 C1
Dalkey	60 F1
Dalkey Avenue	60 F2
Dalkey Court (off Barnhill Road)	60 F2 23
Dalkey Grove (off Dalkey Park)	60 F2 6
Dalkey Park	60 E2
Dalkey Rock	60 F2
*Dalriada Avanue (Dalriada Estate)	55 C3
*Dalriada Close (Dalriada Estate)	55 C3
*Dalriada Square (Dalriada Estate)	55 C3
Dalton Mews	3 B3
Dalymount	70 F1
Damastown Avenue	8 F3
Damastown Close	8 F3
Damastown Court	9 A3
Damastown Drive	8 E3
Damastown Green	8 F3
Damastown Road	8 F3
Damastown Walk	8 E3
Damastown Way	9 A3
Dame Court	75 B1
Dame Lane	71 B4
Dame Street	71 B4
Damer Court	71 A2
Damer House	2 E2
Dane Close	11 C4
Dane Road	11 C4
Danes Court (Dollymount)	27 A4
Danesfort	39 B1
Daneswell Road	25 A4
Danewood Castleknock	23 A3
Dangan	41 A2
Dangan Avenue	46 D2
Dangan Drive	46 D2
Dangan Park	46 D2
Daniel Street	75 A3
Danieli Drive	26 E2
Danieli Road	26 E2
Dara Court	32 D3
Dara Crescent	32 D3
Dargan Court	68 D2 6
Dargan Street	67 B2 10
Dargle Bridge	67 A4
Dargle Court	67 B2 3
Dargle Crescent	67 B2 5
Dargle Drive	57 A1
Dargle Heights	67 B2
Dargle Road (Drumcondra)	25 A4
Dargle Road (Dean's Grange)	59 A1
*Dargle Terrace (on Lower Dargle Road)	67 B2
Dargle Valley	57 A1
Dargle View	57 A1
Dargle Wood	56 D1
Darley Cottages	67 C2 15
Darley Street	74 F4
Darley's Terrace	74 E2
Darling Estate	23 C4
Darndale	13 C4
Dartmouth Lane	75 C4
Dartmouth Place	75 C4
Dartmouth Road	75 C4
Dartmouth Square	75 C3
Dartmouth Square East	75 C3
Dartmouth Square North	75 C3
Dartmouth Square South	75 C4
Dartmouth Square West	75 C4
Dartmouth Terrace	75 C4
Dartry Cottages (off Dartry Road)	47 B3 5
Dartry Park	47 B2
Dartry Road	47 A2
David Park	25 A4
David Road	25 A4
*Davis Court Apartments (off Thomas Davis Street West)	36 F3
Davis Place (off Thomas Davis St Sth)	74 F1
Davitt House	73 A3
Davitt Park	60 D4
Davitt Road (Bray)	67 C2
Davitt Road (Inchicore)	73 B2
Davitt Terrace	73 A3
Dawson Court (Mount Merrion Avenue)	48 F3
*Dawson Court (off Stephen St Lower)	75 B1
Dawson Lane	75 C1
Dawson Street	75 C1
De Bret House (off Stonepark Court)	46 F4 24
De Burgh Road	70 D4
De Courcy Square (off Prospect Avenue)	25 A4 2
De Selby	54 D2
De Selby Close	54 D2
De Selby Court	54 D2
De Selby Crescent	54 D2
De Selby Downs	54 D2
De Selby Drive	54 D2
De Selby Green	54 D2
De Selby Lane	54 D2
De Selby Lawns	54 D2
De Selby Park	53 C2
De Selby Rise	54 F4
De Selby Road	54 D2
De Velara Place	71 B1
*De Vesci Court (off Sloperton)	49 C4
De Vesci Terrace	49 C4
Dean Court	75 A1
Dean Street	75 A2
Dean Swift Green	25 A2
Dean Swift Road	25 A2
Dean Swift Square	74 F1
Deans Court (off Kill Lane)	59 B1 10
Deans Grange	59 B2
Dean's Grange Road	59 B1
Deansrath Avenue	34 F4
Deansrath Crescent	43 C1
Deansrath Green	43 C1
Deansrath Grove	34 F4
Deansrath Lawn	34 F4
Deansrath Park	43 C1
Deansrath Road	43 C1
Deanstown Avenue	24 D2
Deanstown Drive	24 D2
Deanstown Green	24 D2
Deanstown Park	24 D2
Deanstown Road	24 D2
Decies Road	36 E3
Deepdales	67 B4
Deerhaven	8 F4
Deerhaven Avenue	8 F4
Deerhaven Close	8 F4
Deerhaven Crescent	8 F4
Deerhaven Green	8 F4
Deerhaven Park	8 F4
Deerhaven View	8 F4
Deerhaven Walk	8 F4
Deerpark	67 B4
Deerpark Avenue (Castleknock)	23 A4
Deerpark Avenue (Kiltipper)	54 F3
Deerpark Close (Castleknock)	23 A3
Deerpark Close (Kiltipper)	54 F3
Deerpark Downs	54 F3
Deerpark Drive (Castleknock)	23 A3
Deerpark Drive (Kiltipper)	54 F3
Deerpark Green	54 F3
*Deerpark House (off Thomas Davis Street West)	36 F3
Deerpark Lawn	23 B3
Deerpark Lodge	54 F3
Deerpark Place	54 F3
Deerpark Rise	54 F3
Deerpark Road (Castleknock Road)	23 A3
Deerpark Road (Mount Merrion)	48 D4
Deerpark Road (Kiltipper)	54 F3
Deerpark Square	54 F3
Deerpark Terrace	54 F3

STREET NAME	PAGE/GRID REFERENCE	STREET NAME	PAGE/GRID REFERENCE	STREET NAME	PAGE/GRID REFERENCE	STREET NAME	PAGE/GRID REFERENCE
*Deerpark View	54 F3	Dodsboro Cottages	33 B2	Drimnagh Road	45 C1	Dublin Road (Swords)	1 C3
(off Deerpark Way)		Dodsboro Road	33 C2	Drinagh Park	58 F4	Dublin Road (Malahide)	3 A3
Deerpark Walk (Kiltipper)	54 F3	D'Olier Street	71 C4	Drinaghmore	58 F4	Dublin Road (Dunboyne)	7 C3
Deerpark Way	54 F3	Dollymount	27 A4	Drinaghmore Avenue	58 F4	Dublin Road (Maynooth)	18 D3
Del Val Avenue	27 C2	Dollymount Avenue	27 A4	Drinaghmore Close	58 F4	Dublin Road (Donaghmore)	18 F3
Del Val Court	27 C2 [2]	Dollymount Grove	26 F4	Drinaghmore Court	58 F4	Dublin Road (Kilbarrack)	27 C2
Delaford Avenue	55 C1	Dollymount Park	27 A4	Droim na Coille Avenue	34 F2	Dublin Road (Sutton)	29 A1
Delaford Drive	55 C1	Dollymount Rise	27 A4	Droim na Coille Court	34 F2	Dublin Road (Celbridge)	32 D3
Delaford Grove	55 C1	Dolly's Grove	5 C2	Droim na Coille Place	34 F2	Dublin Road (Shankill)	64 E3
Delaford Lawn	55 C1	Dolmen Court	12 D4	Dromard Road	36 F4	Dublin Road (Bray)	67 B1
Delaford Park	55 C1	Dolphin Avenue	74 E3	Dromard Terrace (off Seafort Avenue)	39 A4 [17]	Dublin Street (Swords)	15 A4
Delbrook Manor	57 C2	Dolphin Court	73 C3	Dromawling Road	25 C2	Dublin Street (Baldoyle)	15 A4
Delbrook Park	57 C2	Dolphin House	74 D3	Drombawn Avenue	25 C2	*Duck Lane (Smithfield)	70 F3
Delhurst Avenue	21 B1	*Dolphin Market	74 D3	Dromcarra Avenue	54 E2	Dufferin Avenue	74 F3
Delhurst Close	21 B1	(off Dolphin's Barn St)		Dromcarra Drive	54 E2	Duke Lane Lower	75 C1
Delhurst Mews	21 B1	Dolphin Park	74 D3	Dromcarra Green	54 D2	Duke Lane Upper	75 B1
Delhurst Terrace	21 B1	Dolphin Road	73 C3	Dromcarra Grove	54 E2	Duke Row	72 D2
Delville Road	25 A2	Dolphin's Barn	74 D3	Dromeen Avenue	25 C2	Duke Street	75 B1
Delvin Road (off Annaly Road)	24 F4 [3]	Dolphins Barn Bridge (Grand Canal)	74 D3	Dromheath Avenue	9 B4	Dun Aengus	54 F2
Delwood Close	22 E3	Dolphin's Barn Street	74 D3	Dromheath Drive	9 B4	Dun an Oir	54 F2
Delwood Drive	22 E3	*Dominick Court	71 A2	Dromheath Gardens	9 B4	Dun Emer Drive	57 C1
Delwood Grove	22 E3	(off Dominick Street Upper)		Dromheath Grove	9 B4	Dun Emer Park	57 C1
Delwood Lawn	22 E3	Dominick Lane	71 A3	Dromheath Park	9 B4	Dun Emer Road	57 C1
Delwood Park	22 E3	Dominick Place	71 B3	Dromlee Crescent	25 C2	Dun Gaoithe	58 E3
Delwood Road	22 E3	Dominick Street	50 D4	Dromnanane Park	25 C2 [3]	Dun Laoghaire	50 D4
Delwood Walk	22 E3	*Dominick Street Court	71 A2	(off Dromawling Road)		Dunard Avenue	69 C1
Demesne	26 E3	(Dominick Street Upper)		Dromnanane Road	25 C2 [2]	Dunard Court	69 C1
Denmark Street Great	71 B2	Dominick Street Lower	71 A3	(off Dromawling Road)		Dunard Drive	69 C1
Denville Court	60 D4	Dominick Street Upper	71 A2	Dromore Road	73 A4	Dunard Park	69 C1
Denzille Lane	76 D1	Domville Court (off Santry Villas)	12 E4 [1]	Druid Court	11 C4	Dunard Road	69 C1
*Derby Square (off Werburgh Street)	75 A1	Domville Drive	46 D4	Druid Valley	64 D1	Dunard Walk	69 C1
Dermot O'Hurley Avenue	39 A3	Domville Green	46 D4	Drumahill	58 D1	Dunawley Avenue	44 D1
Derravaragh Road	46 E2	Domville Grove	64 E1 [9]	Drumalee Avenue	70 D2	Dunawley Drive	44 D1
Derry Drive	46 D1	Domville Road	46 D4	Drumalee Court	70 D2	Dunawley Grove	44 D1
Derry Park	46 D1	Donaghmede	14 F4	Drumalee Drive	70 D2	Dunawley Way	44 D1
Derry Road	46 D1	Donaghmede Avenue	27 B1	Drumalee Grove	70 D2	Dunbavin Bridge	51 A4
Derrynane Gardens	39 A3	Donaghmede Drive	27 B1	Drumalee Park	70 D2	Dunbo Hill (off St. Laurence Road)	30 D1 [4]
Derrynane Parade	71 B1	Donaghmede Park	27 B1	Drumalee Road	70 D2	Dunbo Terrace	30 D1 [1]
Derrynane Square	71 B1	Donaghmede Road	27 B1	Drumcairn Avenue	54 E1	(off St. Laurence Road)	
Desmond Avenue (off Cross Avenue)	50 D4 [3]	Donaghmore	18 F3	Drumcairn Drive	54 D1	Dunboy	59 A4
Desmond Cottages	60 F2 [20]	Donard Road	36 F4	Drumcairn Gardens	54 D1	Dunboyne	7 B2
(off Ardbrough Road)		Donnellan Avenue (St Johns Terrace)	73 C1	Drumcairn Green	54 E1	Dunboyne Bridge	7 C3
Desmond Street	75 A3	Donnybrook	47 C1	Drumcairn Parade	54 E1	Dunboyne Road	18 D2
Devenish Road	46 E1	Donnybrook Castle	47 C1 [24]	Drumcairn Park	54 E1	Dunbro Lane	11 C1
Deverell Place	71 C3	(off Stillorgan Road)		Drumcliffe Drive	24 E4	Dunbur Terrace	67 C2 [21]
Devery's Lane	25 A4 [4]	Donnybrook Close	48 D2 [2]	Drumcliffe Road	24 E4	Duncairn Avenue	67 C2
(off Phibsborough Road)		(off Stillorgan Road)		Drumcondra	25 A4	Duncairn Terrace	67 C2
Devitt Villas (off Eden Road Lower)	60 E1 [8]	Donnybrook Court	47 C2	Drumcondra Park	71 C1	Duncarraig	29 B2
Devlin's Place	76 D1	Donnybrook Green	48 D2 [3]	Drumcondra Road Lower	25 B4	Dundaniel Road	26 D1
Devon Close (off Kill Lane)	59 B1 [11]	(off Greenfield Park U.C.D.)		Drumcondra Road Upper	25 B3	Dundela Avenue	60 E1
Devoy Road	73 B2	Donnybrook Manor	47 C1	Drumderg Court	25 C4	Dundela Crescent	60 E1
Dewberry Park	4 D4	Donnybrook Mews	47 C1	Drumfinn Avenue	35 C2	Dundela Haven (off Dundela Park)	60 E1 [24]
Dexter Terrace	75 C4	Donnybrook Road	47 C1	Drumfinn Park	36 D3	Dundela Park	60 E1
Diamond Terrace	67 B2 [15]	Donnycarney	26 D3	Drumfinn Road	36 D2	Dundrum	57 C1
Diamond Valley Apartments	67 B2	Donnycarney Road	26 D3	Drumkeen Manor	60 D3	Dundrum By Pass	57 C1
*Digges Lane (Longford St, Little)	75 B1	Donomore Avenue	54 E2	Drummartin Close	48 D4	Dundrum Gate Apartments	57 C1 [9]
Digges Street Upper	75 B2	Donomore Crescent	54 E2	Drummartin Crescent	58 D1 [1]	(off Ballinteer Road)	
*Dillon Place South	75 A1	Donomore Green	54 E2	(off Drummartin Park)		Dundrum Road	47 C3
(off John Dillon Street)		Donomore Park	54 E2	Drummartin Link Road	58 D1	Dundrum Wood	57 B1
Dillon's Row	17 C2	Donore Avenue	74 E2	Drummartin Park	58 D1	Dunedin Court	59 C1
Dingle Glen	63 A2	Donore Road	74 E2	Drummartin Road	48 D4	Dunedin Drive	59 C1 [8]
Dingle Road	24 E4	Donore Terrace	74 E2	Drummartin Terrace	48 D4	(off St Patrick's Crescent)	
Dispensary Lane	34 D1 [6]	Donovan Lane	74 F3	Drummond Place	75 A4	Dunedin Park	59 C1
(off Main Street Lucan)		Doon Avenue	70 D1	(off Mount Drummond Ave)		Dunedin Terrace	59 C1
Dispensary Lane (Willbrook)	46 F4	Doon Court	11 C4	Drumnigh	14 E3	Dungar Terrace (off Northumberland Avenue Dún Laoghaire)	50 D4 [12]
Distillery House Apartments	36 E2 [14]	Doonamana Road	60 D3	Drumnigh Road	14 E3	Dungriffan Road	30 D2
(off Martin's Row Chapelizod)		Doonanore Park	60 D3	Drumnigh Wood	14 E2	Dungriffan Villas	30 D2 [8]
Distillery Lane	20 D4	Doonsalla Drive	60 D3	*Drury Hall Apartments	75 B1	(off Dungriffan Road)	
Distillery Loft Apartments	25 B4 [15]	Doonsalla Park	60 D3	(Stephen Street Lower)		Dunleary Hill	49 C4
(off Richmond Road)		Doreen House Apartments	24 D4 [8]	Drury Street	75 B1	Dunleary Road	49 C4
Distillery Road	25 B4	(off Nephin Road)		Drynam Avenue	2 E3	Dunluce Road	26 E3
Diswellstown Cottages	22 E4	Doris Street	76 F1	Drynam Close	2 E3	Dunmanus Court (off Kilkieran Road)	24 E4 [4]
Diswellstown Road	22 D3	Dornden Park	48 E2	Drynam Copse	2 E3	Dunmanus Road	24 E4
Dixon Villas	60 E1 [9]	Dorney Court	64 E3	Drynam Court	2 D2	Dunmore Grove	44 F2
(off Adelaide Road)		Dorset Lane	71 B1	Drynam Crescent	2 E3	Dunmore Lawn	44 F3
Doctor's Lane (Maynooth)	17 C3	Dorset Place	71 B1	Drynam Drive	2 E3	Dunmore Park	44 F2
Dodder Avenue	55 B2	Dorset Square	71 B1	Drynam Glen	2 E3	Dunne Street	72 D2
Dodder Bank (off Dundrum Road)	47 B2 [10]	Dorset Street Lower	71 B1	Drynam Green	2 E3	Dunree Park	26 F1
Dodder Court	55 B2	Dorset Street Upper	71 A2	Drynam Grove	2 E3	Dunsandle Court	23 A3
Dodder Crescent	55 B2	Double Lane	17 C3	Drynam Hall	2 E3	Dunsandle Grove	23 A3
Dodder Dale	46 F4	Dowland Road	46 D1	Drynam Mews	2 E3	Dunseverick Road	26 E4
Dodder Green	55 B2	Dowling's Court	72 D4	Drynam Place	2 E4	Dunsink Avenue	24 D2
Dodder Lawn	55 B2	Downpatrick Road	46 E1	Drynam Rise	2 E4	Dunsink Drive	24 D2
Dodder Park Drive (off Dodder Road Lower Rathfarnham)	46 F3 [3]	Downpatrick Road (Crumlin)	73 C4	Drynam Road	2 D2	Dunsink Gardens	24 D2
Dodder Park Grove	46 F3	Dowth Avenue	24 F4	Drynam Square	2 E3	Dunsink Green	24 D2
Dodder Park Road	46 F3	Doyles Lane	27 A4 [6]	Drynam View	2 E3	Dunsink Lane	23 A2
Dodder Road Lower	47 A3	(off Clontarf Road)		Drynam Walk	2 E3	Dunsink Park	24 D2
Dodder Terrace (off Irishtown Road)	39 A3 [18]	Drapier Green	24 F2 [1]	Drynam Way	2 E3	Dunsink Road	24 D2
Dodder Vale (off Orwell Gardens)	47 A3 [13]	(off Drapier Road)		Drysdale Close	55 A2	Dunsoghly	23 C1
Dodder View Cottages	76 F3	Drapier Road	24 F2	Dualla Court	48 E4	Dunsoghly Avenue	23 C1
(off Herbert Road)		Drayton Close (off Monkstown Road)	49 B4 [16]	Dubber Cross	11 B3	Dunsoghly Close	23 C1
		Drimnagh	73 A3	Dublin Airport	12 E1		

STREET NAME	PAGE/GRID REFERENCE	STREET NAME	PAGE/GRID REFERENCE	STREET NAME	PAGE/GRID REFERENCE	STREET NAME	PAGE/GRID REFERENCE
Dunsoghly Court	23 C1	Eaton Wood Green	64 E3	Ellensborough Grove	54 F3	Elton Court	25 C4 [17]
Dunsoghly Drive	23 C1	Eaton Wood Grove	64 E3	Ellensborough Lane	54 F3	(off Philipsburgh Avenue)	
Dunsoghly Green	23 C1	Eaton Wood Square	64 E2	Ellensborough Lawn	54 F3	Elton Court (off Clonrosse Drive)	26 F1 [1]
Dunsoghly Grove	23 C1	Ebenezer Terrace	74 E2	Ellensborough Meadows	54 F3	Elton Court (Leixlip)	32 F1
Dunsoghly Park	23 C1	Eblana Avenue	50 D4	Ellensborough Park	54 F3	Elton Court (Dalkey)	60 E1
Dunstaffnage Hall Apartments	58 F1 [6]	Eblana Villas (off Arbour Hill)	70 E3	Ellensborough Rise	54 F3	Elton Drive (Dunboyne)	7 B2
(off Church Road)		Eblana Villas	76 E1	Ellensborough View	54 F3	Elton Drive (Coolock)	27 A1
Dunville Avenue	47 B1	(Lower Grand Canal Street)		Ellensborough Walk	54 F3	Elton Grove (Dunboyne)	7 B3
Durham Place (off Corrig Road)	60 D1 [18]	Eccles Court	71 B1	Ellensborough Way	54 F3	Elton Park (Coolock)	27 A1
Durham Road	39 B4	Eccles Place	71 B1	Ellesmere (off Brewery Road)	58 F2 [4]	Elton Park (Dalkey)	60 E1
Durrow Road	46 E1	Eccles Street	71 A1	Ellesmere Avenue	70 D1	Elton Walk (off Clonrosse Drive)	27 A1 [1]
Dursey Row	22 F1	Echlin Street	74 E1	Ellis Court	70 E4	Ely Close	55 B3
Dwyer Park	67 C1	Eden Avenue	57 A1	Ellis House Apartments	70 F4	Ely Crescent (off Allenton Road)	55 B3 [1]
		Eden Court	57 A1	Ellis Quay	70 E4	Ely Drive	55 B3
		Eden Crescent	57 A1	Ellis Street	70 E4	Ely Green (off ElyClose)	55 B3 [3]
E		Eden Grove	57 A1	Elm Close	34 E3	Ely Grove (off Ely Drive)	55 B3 [2]
Eagle Hill (off George's Avenue)	49 A3 [15]	Eden Park	60 D1	Elm Court (Lucan)	34 E3	Ely Place	75 C2
Eagle Hill Avenue	46 F2 [4]	Eden Park Avenue	58 D1	Elm Court (Jobstown)	54 D2	Ely Place Upper	75 C2
(off Terenure Road North)		Eden Park Drive	48 D4	Elm Dene	34 E3	Ely View	55 B3
Eagle Park	26 D1	Eden Park Road	58 D1	Elm Drive (Lucan)	34 E3	Embassy Lawn	47 C2
Eagle Terrace	57 C1 [3]	Eden Quay	71 C4	Elm Drive (Jobstown)	54 D2	Emerald Cottages	76 F2
(off Sandyford Road)		Eden Road Lower	60 D1	Elm Green	34 E3	Emerald Place	72 D3
*Eagle Terrace (Dalkey)	60 F2	Eden Road Upper	60 D1	Elm Grove (Lucan)	34 E3	Emerald Square	74 D2
Eagle Valley	66 E4	Eden Terrace (Botanic Ave)	25 A4	Elm Grove	49 A4	Emerald Street	72 E3
Eaglewood Apartments	59 C2 [5]	Eden Terrace (Dún Laoghaire)	60 D1	Elm Grove (Jobstown)	54 D2	Emerald Terrace	74 E2
(off Rochestown Avenue)		Eden Villas (off Coldwell Street)	60 D1 [5]	Elm House	76 D3	Emily Lawless Court	27 C1 [2]
Eaglewood House	59 C2 [7]	Edenbrook Court	56 F1 [5]	Elm House Apartments	54 D2 [1]	(off Bayside Square South)	
(off Rochestown Avenue)		(off Ballyboden Road)		(off Elm Drive)		Emmet Court	73 A2
Eaglewood Mews	59 C2 [8]	Edenbrook Drive	46 E4	Elm Mount Avenue	25 C2	Emmet Crescent	73 A2
(off Rochestown Avenue)		Edenbrook Park	46 E4	Elm Mount Close	26 D2	Emmet Place	70 F4
Earl Place	71 B3	Edenmore	26 F2	Elm Mount Court	26 D3	Emmet Road	73 A1
Earl Street North	71 B3	Edenmore Avenue	26 F1	Elm Mount Crescent	26 D2	Emmet Square	48 F3
Earl Street South	74 F1	Edenmore Crescent	27 A2	Elm Mount Drive	26 D2	Emmet Street	60 D1 [4]
Earls Court (off Terenure Road East)	46 F2 [15]	Edenmore Drive	26 F2	Elm Mount Grove	26 D2	(off Parnell Street Sallynoggin)	
Earls Court (Cabra)	69 C1	Edenmore Gardens	26 F2	Elm Mount Heights	26 D2	Emmet Street (Nth Circular Rd)	71 C1
Earls Court (Dolphins Barn)	74 D3	Edenmore Green	26 F2	Elm Mount Lawn	26 D2	Emmet Street (Harold's Cross)	74 F4
Earlscroft	67 C4	Edenmore Grove	26 F2	Elm Mount Park	26 D2	Emor Street	75 A3
Earlsfort	34 F3	Edenmore Park	26 F2	Elm Mount Rise	26 D2	Emorville Avenue	75 A3
Earlsfort Avenue	34 F3	Edenvale	57 A2	Elm Mount Road	26 D2	Empress Place	72 D2
Earlsfort Close	34 F3	Edenvale Road	47 B1	Elm Mount View	26 D2	Enaville Avenue (off Annesley Place)	72 E1
Earlsfort Court	34 F2	Edenwood	48 D4 [1]	Elm Park (Celbridge)	32 D3	Enaville Road	72 E1
Earlsfort Drive	34 F3	(off Eden Park Drive Goatstown)		Elm Park (Nutley Lane)	48 D1	Engine Alley (off Meath St)	74 F1
Earlsfort Gardens	34 F3	Edgewood (off Richmond Road)	25 B4 [10]	Elm Park Terrace	46 F2	*Engleberg Court	59 C1
Earlsfort Green	34 F3	Edgewood Lawns	22 E1	Elm Road (Donnycarney)	26 D3	(opposite Glandore Park)	
Earlsfort Grove	34 F3	Edmondsbury Court (off Esker Lane)	34 E1 [1]	Elm Road (Fox and Geese)	45 A1	English Row	32 D4
Earlsfort Lane	34 F3	Edmondstown	56 E3	Elm Vale	34 E3	Ennafort Avenue	26 F2
Earlsfort Lawn	34 F2	Edmondstown Green	56 E2	Elm Way (Lucan)	34 E3	Ennafort Court	26 F2
Earlsfort Meadows	34 F2	Edmondstown Road	56 E3	Elm Way (off Grange Wood)	57 A2 [3]	Ennafort Drive	26 F3
Earlsfort Park	34 F2	Edward Court	76 D4	Elm Wood	34 E3	Ennafort Grove	26 F2
Earlsfort Rise	34 F3	Edward Road	68 D3	Elmbrook	34 E2	Ennafort Park	26 F3
Earlsfort Road	34 F2	*Edward Terrace (off Nerano Rd)	60 F2	Elmbrook Crescent	34 E2	Ennafort Road	26 F3
Earlsfort Terrace	75 C3	Edwards Court	56 E2	Elmbrook Lawn	34 E2	Ennel Avenue	26 F2
Earlsfort Vale	34 F3	Edwin Court	60 E2 [5]	Elmbrook Walk	34 E2	Ennel Court	64 E1 [6]
Earlsfort View	34 F3	(off Albert Road Upper)		Elmcastle Close	45 A3	Ennel Drive	26 F2
Earlsfort Way	34 F3	Effra Road	47 A1	Elmcastle Court	45 A3	Ennel Park	26 F2
East Pier (Howth)	30 D1	Eglington Park (Dun Laoghaire)	49 C4 [35]	Elmcastle Drive	45 A3	Ennis Grove (off Londonbridge Road)	39 A3 [19]
East Pier (Dún Laoghaire)	50 E3	Eglington Road	67 C2 [3]	Elmcastle Green	45 A3	Enniskerry	66 D3
East Road	72 F3	Eglinton Court	47 C1	Elmcastle Park	45 A3	Enniskerry Bridge	66 E3
East Wall	72 F1	Eglinton Park (Donnybrook)	47 C1	Elmcastle Walk	45 A3	Enniskerry Demesne	66 E3
East Wall Road (Alexandra Basin)	39 A2	Eglinton Road	47 C1	Elmdale Crescent	35 C3	Enniskerry Road	25 A4 [3]
East Wall Road (Fairview)	72 F1	Eglinton Square	47 C1 [13]	Elmdale Drive	35 C3	(off Phibsborough Road)	
Eastmoreland Court	76 E3	(off Eglinton Road)		Elmdale Park	35 C3	Enniskerry Road (Sandyford)	58 D4
(off Merrion Road)		Eglinton Terrace (Donnybrook)	47 C1	Elmfield (Adjacent Kilgobbin Wood)	58 E4	Erne Place (Lansdowne Park)	76 E1
Eastmoreland Lane	76 E3	Eglinton Terrace (Dundrum)	47 C4	*Elmfield Avenue	14 D4	Erne Place Little	76 D1
(off Gilford Road)		*Eglinton Terrace (Royal Canal Bank)	71 A2	Elmfield Close (off Elmfield Avenue)	14 D4 [2]	Erne Place Lower	72 D4
Eastmoreland Place	76 E3	Eglinton Wood (off Eglinton Road)	47 C1 [22]	Elmfield Court (Clarehall)	14 D4	Erne Street Lower	72 D4
(off Gilford Road)		Eklad Close	13 C4	Elmfield Court (Clondalkin)	44 E1	Erne Street Upper	76 D1
Easton	32 E1	Eklad Park	13 C4	Elmfield Crescent	14 E4	Erne Terrace Front	76 D1
*Easton Drive (Easton)	32 E1	El Greco Apartments	39 A4 [51]	Elmfield Drive	14 E4	Erne Terrace Rere	76 D1
*Easton Green (Easton)	32 E1	(off Serpentine Avenue)		Elmfield Green	14 D4	Errigal Gardens	73 A4
*Easton Mews (Easton)	32 E1	Elbin House (off Serpentine Avenue)	39 A4 [41]	Elmfield Grove	14 D4	Errigal Road	36 F4
Easton Park	19 C4	Elderberry	34 D3	Elmfield Lawn	14 E4	Erris Road	24 D4
Easton Road	19 B4	Elderwood Road	35 B2	Elmfield Park	14 E4	Erris Square	22 F1
*Easton Row (Easton)	32 E1	*Elford Terrace (off Donore Avenue)	74 E2	Elmfield Rise	14 D4	Esker Drive	34 D2
Eastwood (off Kilshane Road)	23 C2 [1]	Elgin Heights	67 A4	Elmfield Vale	14 E4	Esker Glebe	34 D2
Eaton Brae (Orwell Road)	47 A3	Elgin Road	76 E3	Elmfield Walk	14 D4	Esker Lane	34 E2
Eaton Brae (Shankill)	64 E2	Elgin Wood	67 B4	Elmfield Way	14 D4	Esker Lawns	34 D1
Eaton Close	52 F2	*Elizabeth O'Farrell Park	72 D4	Elmgrove	60 D4	Esker Lodge	34 E2
Eaton Court	46 F2 [22]	(Lombard Street East)		Elmgrove Terrace	67 C2 [22]	Esker Lodge Avenue	34 E2
(off Terenure Road North)		Elizabeth Street	25 B4	Elmpark Apartments	48 E2	Esker Lodge Close	34 E2
Eaton Court (Bray)	68 D3 [1]	Elkwood	56 E1	Elmpark Avenue	47 B1	Esker Lodge View	34 E2
Eaton Green	52 F2	Ellenfield Road	25 C2	Elmpark Green	48 E2	Esker Manor	34 E2
Eaton Hall (off Terenure Road North)	46 F2 [18]	Ellensborough	54 F3	Elms	48 F3	Esker Meadow	34 E2
Eaton House	52 F2 [1]	Ellensborough Avenue	54 F3	Elmwood Avenue Lower	47 B1	Esker Meadow Close	34 E2
Eaton Place	49 B4	Ellensborough Close	54 F3	Elmwood Avenue Upper	47 B1	Esker Meadow Court	34 E2
Eaton Road	46 F2	Ellensborough Copse	54 F3	Elmwood Close	21 B1	Esker Meadow Green	34 E2
Eaton Square (Terenure)	46 F2	Ellensborough Court	54 F3	Elmwood Court	1 C1 [1]	Esker Meadow Grove	34 E2
Eaton Square (Monkstown)	49 B4	Ellensborough Crescent	54 F3	Elmwood Drive	1 C1	Esker Meadow Lawn	34 E2
Eaton Terrace	52 F2	Ellensborough Dale	54 F3	Elmwood Park	1 C1	Esker Meadow Rise	34 E2
Eaton Way	52 F2	Ellensborough Downs	54 F3	Elmwood Road	1 C1	Esker Meadow View	34 E2
Eaton Wood Avenue	64 E3	Ellensborough Grange	54 F3	Elner Court	4 D4	Esker Park	34 E2
Eaton Wood Court	64 E3	Ellensborough Green	54 F3	Elton Court (Dunboyne)	7 B3	Esker Pines	34 E1

STREET NAME	PAGE/GRID REFERENCE
Esker Road	34 D2
Esker South	34 D3
Esker Villas	47 A1 [11]
(off Summerville Park)	
Esker Woods	34 E2
Esker Woods Close	34 E2
Esker Woods Court	34 E2
Esker Woods Drive	34 E2
Esker Woods Grove	34 E2
Esker Woods Rise	34 E2
Esker Woods View	34 E2
Esker Woods Walk	34 E2
Esmond Avenue	25 C4
Esmonde Terrace	67 B2 [18]
Esplanade Terrace	68 D2 [3]
Esposito Road	45 C1 [5]
(off John Mc Cormack Avenue)	
Essex Gate (off Essex Quay)	71 A4
Essex Quay	71 A4
Essex Street East	71 A4
Essex Street West (off Fishamble St)	71 A4
Estate Avenue	48 E1
Estate Cottages	76 E2
(Northumberland Rd)	
Estate Cottages	76 F3
(off Sandymount Avenue)	
Estuary Court	2 D1
Estuary Road	2 F2
Estuary Roundabout (Swords)	2 D1
Estuary Row	3 B2
Estuary Walk	2 F2
Eugene Street	74 E2
Eustace Bridge (Grand Canal)	75 C3
Eustace Street	71 B4
*Everton Apartments	56 E1
(Glendoher Road)	
Everton Avenue	70 D2
Evora Crescent	30 D1 [12]
(off Grace O' Malley Road)	
Evora Park	30 D1
Evora Terrace	30 D1 [2]
(off St. Laurence Road)	
Ewington Lane	74 D1
Exchange Court	71 C4
Exchange Street Lower	71 A4
(off Wood Quay)	
Exchange Street Upper	71 A4
(off Lord Edward St)	
Exchequer Street	75 B1
Excise Walk	72 E3
Eyre Court	2 E3

F

STREET NAME	PAGE/GRID REFERENCE
Faber Grove	59 B1 [9]
(off Rory O'Connor Park)	
Fade Street	75 B1
Fagan's Lane	17 C3 [2]
Fair Haven	3 B2 [1]
Fairacre	2 F3
Fairbrook Lawn	46 F4
Fairfield Avenue	72 E2
Fairfield Court	39 A3 [47]
(off Newbridge Avenue)	
Fairfield House (off Harrison Row)	46 F2 [24]
Fairfield Park	47 A2
Fairfield Road	25 A4
Fairgreen	53 A2
Fairgreen Court	67 C2 [50]
Fairgreen Road	67 B2 [11]
Fairgreen Terrace	67 C2 [32]
Fairlawn Park	24 E2
Fairlawn Road	24 E2
Fairlawns (off Saval Park Road)	60 E2 [6]
Fairview Avenue (off Irishtown Road)	39 A3 [49]
Fairview Avenue Lower	25 C4
Fairview Avenue Upper	25 C4
Fairview Close	25 C4
Fairview Court	25 C4 [14]
(off Fairview Avenue Lower)	
Fairview Green	25 C4 [7]
(off Fairview Avenue Upper)	
Fairview Lawn	64 D1
Fairview Passage	25 C4 [10]
(off Fairview Strand)	
Fairview Strand	25 C4
Fairview Terrace	25 C4 [11]
(off Fairview Avenue Lower)	
Fairways	46 E4
Fairway's Avenue	24 F2
Fairway's Green	24 F2
Fairways Grove	24 E2
Fairway's Park	24 F2
Fairy Castle	61 B2
Fairy Grove	12 E3
Fairyhill (Stillorgan)	59 A1
Fairyhill (Oldcourt)	67 B3
Faith Avenue	72 E1
Falcarragh Road	25 B2
Falls Road	64 D2
Farmhill Drive	47 C4
Farmhill Park	47 C4
Farmhill Road	47 C4
Farmleigh	23 A4
Farmleigh Avenue (Castleknock)	23 A4
Farmleigh Avenue (Stillorgan)	58 F1
Farmleigh Close (Castleknock)	23 A4
Farmleigh Close (Stillorgan)	58 F1
Farmleigh Court	23 A4
Farmleigh Park (Castleknock)	23 A4
Farmleigh Park (Stillorgan)	58 F1
Farmleigh View	23 A4
Farmleigh Woods	23 A4
Farney Park	39 A4
Farnham Crescent	24 E2
Farnham Drive	24 E2
Farrenboley Cottages	47 B3
Farrenboley Park	47 B3
Fassaroe	66 F3
Fassaroe	67 A2
Fassaroe Avenue	67 A3
Fassaroe Glen	67 A2
Fassaroe Lane	67 A3
*Father Bidone Court	36 F3
(off St Mary's Avenue West)	
Father Colohan Terrace	67 C2 [11]
Father Kit Court	46 D1 [3]
(off St Agnes RoadCrumlin)	
Father Lemass Court	36 D3
Father Mathew Square	70 F3
Father Matthew Bridge (River Liffey)	70 F4
Father Scully House	71 C2
Fatima Mansions (off James's Walk)	74 D2
Fatima Terrace	67 C2
Faughart Road (off Kells Road)	46 E1 [3]
Faulkner's Terrace	73 C1
Faussagh Avenue	24 E4
Faussagh Road	24 F4
Fawn Lodge	23 A4
Feltrim	3 A4
Feltrim Hall	2 D3
Feltrim Road	2 F4
Fenian Street	76 D1
Fergus Road	46 F2
Ferguson Road	25 A3
Fernbrook	67 B1 [6]
Ferncarrig Avenue	58 D3
Ferncarrig Court	58 D3
Ferncarrig Rise	58 D3
Ferncourt Avenue	55 B3
Ferncourt Close	55 B3
Ferncourt Crescent	55 B3 [5]
(off Ferncourt Avenue)	
Ferncourt Drive	55 B3 [4]
(off Ferncourt Drive)	
Ferncourt Green	55 B3
Ferncourt Park	55 B3
Ferncourt View	55 B3
Ferndale (Hartstown)	21 C1
Ferndale (Tallaght)	55 A2
Ferndale Avenue	24 F2
Ferndale Glen	64 D4
Ferndale Hill	64 D4
Ferndale Road (Glasnevin)	24 F2
Ferndale Road (Shankill)	64 D4
Ferndale Road (Bray)	67 A1
Fernhill Avenue	45 C3
Fernhill Park	45 C3
Fernhill Road	45 C2
Fernleigh	22 D3
Fernleigh Close	22 D3
Fernleigh Court	22 D3
Fernleigh Crescent	22 D3
Fernleigh Dale	22 D3
Fernleigh Dene	22 D4
Fernleigh Drive	22 D3
Fernleigh Grange	22 D4
Fernleigh Green	22 D3
Fernleigh Grove	22 D4
Fernleigh Heath	22 D4
Fernleigh Lawn	22 D3
Fernleigh Park	22 D3
Fernleigh Place	22 D3
Fernleigh Vale	22 D3
Fernleigh View	22 D4
Fernley Court	75 A2
Ferns Road	46 E1
Fernvale Drive	46 D1
Fernwood Avenue	54 E1
Fernwood Close	54 E1
Fernwood Court	54 E1
Fernwood Lawn	54 E1
Fernwood Park	54 E1
Fernwood Way	54 E1
Ferrard Road	46 F2
Ferrycarrig Avenue	13 B4
Ferrycarrig Drive	13 B4
Ferrycarrig Green	13 B4 [3]
(off Ferrycarrig Park)	
Ferrycarrig Park	13 B4
Ferrycarrig Road	13 B4
Ferryman's Crossing	72 E3
Fertullagh Road (off Leix Road)	24 F4 [5]
Fettercairn	44 E4
Fettercairn Road	44 E4
Fey Yerra (off Leopardstown Road)	58 F2 [8]
Fforester	34 E2
Fforester Close	34 E2
Fforester Court	34 E2
Fforester Drive	34 F2
Fforester Lawn	34 E2
Fforester Park	34 E2
Fforester Walk	34 E2
Fforester Way	34 E2
Fforster Crescent	34 E2
Field Avenue (off Balfe Road)	45 C1 [1]
Field's Terrace (off Charleston Road	47 B1 [5]
Fieldview Cottages	49 A4 [6]
(off Annaville Avenue)	
Fiery Lane	62 D4
Findlater Building Apartments	30 D1 [3]
(off Harbour Road)	
Findlater Place	71 B3
Findlater Street	60 E1 [7]
(off Eden Terrace Dún Laoghaire)	
Findlater Street (Nth Circular Rd)	70 D3
Fingal Place	70 E2
Fingal Street	74 E2
Finglas	24 D1
Finglas East	24 E1
Finglas Park	24 E1
Finglas Place	24 E2
Finglas Road	24 E2
Finglas Road Old	24 F3
Finglas Roundabout (M50)	11 A4
Finglas South	24 D2
Finglas Square (off Owenstown	48 D3 [2]
Park Fosters Avenue)	
Finglas West	24 D1
Finglaswood Road	24 D1
Finn Street	70 D3
Finneber Fort	24 E2
Finneber Fort Square	24 E2
Finnscourt	34 D3
Finnsgreen	34 D3
Finnsgrove	34 D3
Finnslawn	34 D3
Finnspark	34 D3
Finnstown Cloisters	34 D3
Finnstown Fairways	34 D3
Finnstown Hall	34 D3
Finnsvale	34 D3
Finnsview	34 D3
Finnswalk	34 D3
Finnswood	34 D3
Finsbury Green	47 B4
Finsbury House (off Herbert Road)	76 F3
Finsbury Park	47 B4
Firgrove	60 E4 [7]
(off Military Road Ballybrack)	
Firhouse	55 C1
Firhouse Road	55 B2
Firhouse Road West	55 A2
First Avenue (Sarsfield Road)	36 F3
First Avenue (Belgard Heights)	44 F4
First Avenue (Seville Place)	72 E3
Fishamble Street	71 A4
Fisherman's Green	3 B2 [6]
Fishermans Wharf (off York Road)	39 A2 [1]
Fitzgerald Park	59 C1 [6]
(off Mounttown Road Lower)	
Fitzgerald Street	75 A4
Fitzgibbon Lane	71 C1
Fitzgibbon Street	71 C1
Fitzmaurice Road (Glasnevin)	24 F2
Fitzmaurice Road (Rathcoole)	52 F2
Fitzpatrick's Cottages	46 F1 [6]
(off Harolds Cross Road)	
Fitzroy Avenue	25 B4
Fitzwilliam Court (Stillorgan Road)	48 E3
Fitzwilliam Court	75 C2
(Fitzwilliam Square)	
Fitzwilliam Court (Leeson Park)	76 D4
Fitzwilliam Lane	76 D2
Fitzwilliam Place	75 C3
Fitzwilliam Place North	70 F3
(Grangegorman)	
Fitzwilliam Point	39 A3 [37]
(off Fitzwilliam Quay)	
Fitzwilliam Quay	39 A3 [36]
(off Fitzwilliam Quay)	
Fitzwilliam Quay	39 A3
Fitzwilliam Square	75 C2
Fitzwilliam Square East	76 D2
Fitzwilliam Square North	76 D2
Fitzwilliam Square South	75 C2
Fitzwilliam Square West	75 C2
Fitzwilliam Street	39 A3 [2]
(off Cambridge Park)	
Fitzwilliam Street Lower	76 D2
Fitzwilliam Street Upper	76 D2
Fitzwilliam Terrace	68 D2 [21]
Fleet Street	71 B4
Fleming Road	25 A3
Fleming's Hall Apartments	76 D3
Fleming's Place	76 D3
Flemingstown Park	47 B4
Flemming House	76 D3
Fleurville	49 A4
Floraville Avenue	44 E1
Floraville Drive	44 E2
Floraville Estate	44 E1
Floraville Lawn	44 E1
Florence Road	67 C2
Florence Street	75 A3
Florence Terrace (Bray)	67 C2 [39]
*Florence Terrace	76 D4
(Leeson Park Avenue)	
Florence Villas (Sandymount)	39 A4
Florence Villas (Bray)	67 C2 [40]
Flower Grove	60 D2
Foley Street	71 C3
Fontenoy Street	71 A2
Fontenoy Terrace	68 D3
Fonthill Abbey (off Fonthill Park)	56 F1 [3]
Fonthill Park	56 F1
Fonthill Road (Clondalkin)	35 A2
Fonthill Road (Rathfarnham)	56 F1
Fonthill Road North	35 A3
Fonthill Road South	44 D2
Forbes Lane	74 E2
Forbes Street	72 E4
Forest Avenue (Swords)	1 B3
Forest Avenue (Kilnamanagh)	45 A3
Forest Boulevard	1 B3
Forest Close	45 A3
Forest Court	1 B2
Forest Crescent	1 B3
Forest Dale	1 B2
Forest Drive (Swords)	1 B3
Forest Drive (Kilnamanagh)	45 A3
Forest Green (Swords)	1 B3
Forest Green (Kilnamanagh)	45 A3
Forest Grove	1 B3
Forest Hills (Swords)	1 C3
Forest Hills (Rathcoole)	52 E2
Forest Lawn	45 A3
Forest Park (Swords)	1 B2
Forest Park (Leixlip)	32 F1
Forest Park (Kilnamanagh)	45 A3
Forest Road	1 B4
Forest View	1 B3
Forest Walk	1 C3
Forest Way	1 C3
Forestfields Road	1 C3
Forestwood Avenue	12 D4
Forestwood Close	12 E4
Forge Court (off Main Street Howth)	30 D2 [15]
Forster Way	2 D2
Fort Ostman	73 C4
Fortescue Lane	75 B4
Fortfield Avenue	46 E3
Fortfield Court (off Fortfield Road)	46 E3 [2]
Fortfield Crescent	46 E3
Fortfield Drive	46 E3
Fortfield Gardens	47 A2
Fortfield Grove	46 E3
Fortfield Park	46 E3

STREET NAME	PAGE/GRID REFERENCE
Fortfield Road (Kimmage)	46 E2
Fortfield Road (Bushy Park)	46 E3
Fortfield Square	46 E3
Fortfield Terrace	47 A2
Forth Road	72 F2
Forthill Court (off Fonthill Road)	56 F1 [6]
Fortlawn Avenue	22 D1
Fortlawn Crescent	22 D1
Fortlawn Drive	22 D1
Fortlawn Park	22 D1
Fortlawns	60 E2
Fortrose Park	46 E4
Fortunestown	53 C1
Fortunestown Close	53 C1
Fortunestown Crescent	53 C1
Fortunestown Lane	53 B1
Fortunestown Road	54 D2
Fortunestown Way	54 D1
Fortview Avenue	39 C1
Fortwilliam	48 E4
Foster Place North	72 D1
Foster Place South (College Green)	71 B4
Foster Terrace	72 D1
Fosterbrook	48 E2
Fosters Avenue	48 D3
Fountain Place	70 F3
Fountain Road	69 C3
*Fountain View Apartments (James's Street)	74 D1
Fourth Avenue (Tallaght)	44 F4
Fourth Avenue (Seville Place)	72 E3
Fownes Street Lower (off Temple Bar)	71 B4
Fownes Street Upper	71 B4
Fox and Geese	45 A1
Fox Hill	55 A4
Foxborough Avenue	34 E3
Foxborough Close	34 F3
Foxborough Court	34 F3
Foxborough Crescent (off Foxborough Road)	34 F3 [2]
Foxborough Downes	34 E3
Foxborough Drive	34 E3
Foxborough Gardens	34 F3
Foxborough Glade	34 F3
Foxborough Glen	34 F3
Foxborough Green	34 F3
Foxborough Grove	34 F3
Foxborough Hall (off Newlands Road)	34 F3 [1]
Foxborough Heights	34 F3
Foxborough Hill	34 E3
Foxborough Lane	34 F3
Foxborough Lawn	34 F3
Foxborough Manor	34 F3
Foxborough Meadows	34 E3
Foxborough Park	34 F3
Foxborough Place	34 F3
Foxborough Rise	34 E3
Foxborough Road	34 E3
Foxborough Row	34 F3
Foxborough Walk	34 F3
Foxborough Way	34 E3
Foxdene Avenue	34 F3
Foxdene Drive	34 F3
Foxdene Gardens	34 F3
Foxdene Green	34 F3
Foxdene Grove	34 F3
Foxdene Park	34 F3
Foxes Grove	64 E3
Foxe's Lane	27 A1
Foxfield	34 D3
Foxfield Avenue	27 B2
Foxfield Crescent	27 B2
Foxfield Drive	27 B2
Foxfield Green	27 B2
Foxfield Grove	27 B2
Foxfield Heights	27 B2
Foxfield Lawn	27 B2
Foxfield Park	27 B2
Foxfield Road	27 B2
Foxfield St John	27 B2
Foxford	34 F2
Foxford Court (off Ballyowen Lane)	34 F2 [2]
Foxhill Avenue	27 A1
Foxhill Close	27 A1
Foxhill Court	27 A1
Foxhill Crescent	27 A1
Foxhill Drive	27 A1
Foxhill Green	14 D4
Foxhill Grove	27 A1
Foxhill Lawn	27 A1
Foxhill Park	27 A1
Foxhill Way	27 A1
Foxpark	34 D3
Foxrock	59 A3
Foxrock Avenue	59 A2
Foxrock Close	59 B2
Foxrock Court	59 A2
Foxrock Crescent	59 B2
Foxrock Green	59 A2
Foxrock Grove	59 B2
Foxrock Manor	58 F2
Foxrock Mount (off Foxrock Park)	59 A2 [4]
Foxrock Park	59 A2
Foxrock Wood	59 B2
Foxwood (Swords)	2 D2
Foxwood (Lucan)	34 D3
Foyle Road	25 C4
Frances Ball House (off Stonepark Court)	46 F4 [23]
Francis Street	74 F1
Frank Sherwin Bridge (River Liffey)	70 D4
Frankfort (off Dundrum Road)	47 B4 [10]
Frankfort Avenue	47 A2
Frankfort Cottages	72 D2
Frankfort Court (off Rathgar Avenue)	46 F2 [8]
Frankfort Flats (off Rathgar Avenue)	46 F2 [9]
Frankfort Mews	47 B4
Frankfort Park	47 B4
Frascati Court (off George's Avenue)	49 A3 [23]
Frascati Hall (off Frascati Road Blackrock)	49 A3 [24]
Frascati Park	49 A3
Frascati Road	49 A3
Frederick Court	71 B2
*Frederick House (Fredrick Street South)	75 C1
Frederick Lane North	71 B2
Frederick Street North	71 B2
Frederick Street South	75 C1
*French Mullen Flats (Charlemont Street)	75 B3
French Park	9 B2
Frenchman's Lane	71 C3
Friar's Walk (off Monastery Park)	44 E1 [5]
Friarsland Avenue (off Larchfield Road)	47 C3 [3]
Friarsland Crescent	47 C3
Friarsland Road	47 C3
Friary Avenue	70 F3
Friary Court	70 F3
Friary Grove	70 F3
Friel Avenue	36 D4
Fumbally Court	75 A2
Fumbally Lane	75 A2
Furry Glen	36 D1
Furry Park Court	26 E3
Furry Park Road	26 E3
Furze Road (Phoenix Park)	36 E1
Furze Road (Sandyford)	58 E2

G

STREET NAME	PAGE/GRID REFERENCE
Gables (off Tonlegee Road)	27 A1 [6]
Gaelic Street	72 E2
Gainsborough	2 F3
Gainsborough Avenue	2 F3
Gainsborough Close	2 F3
Gainsborough Court	2 F3
Gainsborough Crescent	2 F3
Gainsborough Downs	2 F3
Gainsborough Green	2 F3
Gainsborough Lawn	2 F3
Gainsborough Park	2 F3
Gallaun Road	11 C4
Gallery Quay	76 E1
Galloping Green (Stillorgan)	58 F1
Galloping Green (off Belmont)	59 A1 [9]
Gallows Hill	1 C2
Galmoy Road	24 F4
Galtrim Park	67 C2
Galtrim Road	67 C2
Galtymore Close	36 F4
Galtymore Drive	73 B3
Galtymore Park	36 F4
Galtymore Road	73 B3
Gandon Close (off Harolds Cross Road)	46 F1 [9]
Gandon Court (off Main Street Lucan)	34 D1 [16]
Gandon Hall	71 C3
Gandon Mews (off Main Street Lucan)	34 D1 [10]
Garda Terrace (Phoenix Park)	69 C3
Garden Lane	74 F1
Garden Terrace (off Clanbrassil Street Upper)	74 F3
Garden View	75 B4
*Garden View Court (off Francis Street)	74 F1
Gardiner Lane	71 C2
Gardiner Place	71 B2
Gardiner Row	71 B2
Gardiner St Middle	71 C2
Gardiner Street Lower	71 C2
Gardiner Street Upper	71 B1
Garnett Hall	7 A2
Garnett Vale	7 A2
Garnish Square	22 F1
Garrison Mews	64 D1
Garrynisk Close	44 F3
Garrynisk Road	44 F3
Garrynure	47 B2
Garryowen Road	36 E3
Gartan Avenue	25 A4
Gartan Court	2 E1
Gartan Drive	2 E1
Garter Lane	53 B1
Garthy Wood Apartments	56 D1
Garville Avenue Upper	46 F2
Garville Court (off Garville Road)	47 A2 [10]
Garville Drive (off Garville Avenue)	47 A2 [6]
Garville Lane	47 A2
Garville Place (off Garville Avenue)	47 A2 [5]
Garville Road	47 A2
Gas Yard Lane	3 B2
Gateway Apartments	25 A1 [5]
Gateway Avenue	25 A1
Gateway Court	25 A1
Gateway Crescent	25 A1
Gateway Gardens	25 A1
Gateway Mews	25 A1
Gateway Place	25 A1
Gateway View	25 A1
Gaybrook Lawns	3 A3
Gazelle Avenue	9 B2
Gazelle Lane	9 B2
Gazelle Mews	9 B2
Gazelle Terrace	9 B2
Gazelle Walk	9 B2
Geoffrey Keating Road	74 F2
*George Reynolds Flats (off Oliver Plunkett Avenue)	39 A3
George's Avenue (Blackrock)	49 A3
Georges Court	72 D4
Georges Dock	72 D3
George's Dock	72 D3
George's Hill	71 A3
George's Lane	70 F3
George's Place (off George's Avenue)	49 A3 [6]
George's Place (Dún Laoghaire)	50 D4
George's Place (Temple Street)	71 B1
George's Quay	71 C4
*Georges Quay House (Georges Quay)	71 C4
Georges Road (off Mckee Avenue)	24 E1 [1]
George's Street Lower	50 D4
George's Street Upper	50 D4
Georgian Hamlet	15 A4
Georgian Village	23 A4
Gerald Street	76 F1
Geraldine Court	17 C3 [4]
Geraldine Street	71 A1
Geraldstown Woods Apartments	12 D4
Gertrude Terrace	67 B2 [25]
Gilbert Road	74 F3
Gilford Avenue	39 B4
Gilford Court (off Gilford Road)	39 A4 [10]
Gilford Drive	39 A4
Gilford Park	39 A4
Gilford Pines (off Gilford Road)	39 A4 [46]
Gilford Place	72 D2
Gilford Road	39 A4
Gilford Terrace (off Gilford Road)	39 B4 [1]
Giltspur Heights	67 B4
Giltspur Lane	67 B4
Giltspur Wood	67 B3
Glandore Park	59 C1
Glandore Road	25 C3
Glasanaon Court	24 E2
Glasanaon Park	24 E2
Glasanaon Road	24 E2
Glasaree Court	24 E2
Glasaree Road	24 E2
Glasilawn Avenue	24 F2
Glasilawn Road	24 F2
Glaslyn	26 D4
Glasmeen Road	24 F2
Glasmore Park	1 C1
Glasnamana Place (off Glasnamana Road)	24 F2 [2]
Glasnamana Road	24 F2
Glasnevin	24 F3
Glasnevin Avenue	24 F1
Glasnevin Court	24 E3
Glasnevin Downs	24 F3
Glasnevin Drive	25 A1
Glasnevin Hill	25 A3
Glasnevin North	24 F1
Glasnevin Oaks (off Finglas Road Old)	24 F3 [3]
Glasnevin Park	24 F1
Glasnevin Woods	24 E3
Glasson Court	47 B3
Glasthule Buildings (off Glasthule Road)	60 E1 [11]
Glasthule Road	60 E1
Gleann na Rí	63 C1
Gleann na Smol (Monkstown)	49 B4
Gleann na Smól (Tallaght)	54 F2
Glebe (Airport)	13 B1
Glebe (Newcastle)	41 C3
Glebe (Rathcoole)	52 D3
Glebe Hall	59 C1
Glebe View (off Church Street Finglas)	24 E2 [7]
Gledswood Avenue	47 C3
Gledswood Close	47 C3
Gledswood Drive (off Bird Avenue)	47 C3 [5]
Gledswood Park	47 C3
Glen Avenue	59 B3
Glen Close	59 B3
Glen Dale	59 B3
Glen Drive	59 B3
Glen Druid	64 E1
Glen Ellan Avenue	1 C1
Glen Ellan Close	1 C1
Glen Ellan Court	1 C1
Glen Ellan Crescent	1 C1
Glen Ellan Drive	1 C1
Glen Ellan Gardens	1 C1
Glen Ellan Green	1 C1
Glen Ellan Grove	1 C1
Glen Ellan Park	1 C1
Glen Ellan Pines	1 C1
Glen Ellan Walk	1 C1
Glen Garth	59 B3
Glen Grove	59 B3
Glen Lawn Drive	59 B3
Glen na Smol	67 C4
Glen Terrace (off Link Road)	60 E1 [10]
Glen Walk	59 B3
Glenaan Road	25 B2
Glenabbey Road	48 E4
Glenacre	62 E4
Glenageary Avenue	60 D2
Glenageary Court	60 D2
Glenageary Hall	60 E2
Glenageary Lodge	60 D2
Glenageary Park	60 D2
Glenageary Road Lower (Dun Laoghaire)	50 D4
Glenageary Road Lower (Sallynoggin)	60 D1
Glenageary Road Upper	60 D1
Glenageary Woods	60 D1
Glenalbyn Road	58 F1
Glenalua Heights	60 E3
Glenalua Road	60 E3
Glenalua Terrace	60 E3
Glenamuck Cottages	63 A2
Glenamuck North	62 E1
Glenamuck Road (Brighton Road)	59 B4
Glenamuck Road (Golden Ball)	62 F2
Glenamuck Road (Carrickmines)	63 A1
Glenann (off Willbrook Road)	46 F4 [4]
Glenanne	46 E2
Glenard Avenue (Bray)	67 C2
Glenard Avenue (Cabra)	70 D1
Glenard Hall (off Roebuck Downs)	47 C3 [7]
Glenarm Avenue	25 B4
Glenarriff Road	23 C3
Glenart Avenue	48 F4
Glenaulin	36 D2

STREET NAME	PAGE/GRID REFERENCE
Glenaulin Drive	36 D2
Glenaulin Green	35 C2 [2]
(off Oakcourt Avenue)	
Glenaulin Park	36 D2
Glenaulin Road	35 C2
Glenavon Court (off Griffith Avenue)	25 A3 [18]
Glenavon Park	64 D1
Glenavy Park	46 E2
Glenayle Road	26 F1
Glenayr Road	46 F2
Glenbeigh Park	69 C1
Glenbeigh Road	70 D2
Glenbourne Avenue	58 F4
Glenbourne Close	58 F4
Glenbourne Crescent	58 F4
Glenbourne Drive	58 F4
Glenbourne Green	58 F4
Glenbourne Grove	58 F4
Glenbourne Park	58 F4
Glenbourne Road	58 F4
Glenbourne View	58 F4
Glenbourne Walk	58 F4
Glenbourne Way	58 F4
Glenbower Park	47 B4 [1]
(off Churchtown Road)	
Glenbrae	64 E2
Glenbrian Hall (off Howth Road)	26 D4 [8]
Glenbrook (Enniskerry)	66 E3
Glenbrook (Bray)	67 B3 [6]
Glenbrook Park	46 F4
Glenbrook Road	23 C3
Glenburgh Terrace	67 B2 [2]
Glencairn	58 E3
Glencairn Avenue	58 E3
Glencairn Chase	58 E3
Glencairn Close	58 E3
Glencairn Copse	58 E4
Glencairn Court	58 E4
Glencairn Crescent	58 E4
Glencairn Dale	58 E3
Glencairn Drive	58 E3
Glencairn Garth (off Glencairn Road)	58 E3 [1]
Glencairn Glade	58 E4
Glencairn Glen	58 F4
Glencairn Green	58 E3
Glencairn Grove	58 E4
Glencairn Heath	58 E3
Glencairn Heights	58 E3
Glencairn Lawn	58 E3
Glencairn Oaks	58 E4
Glencairn Park	58 E3
Glencairn Place	58 E4
Glencairn Rise	58 E3
Glencairn Road	58 E3
Glencairn Thicket	58 F3
Glencairn View	58 E3
Glencairn Walk	58 E3
Glencairn Way	58 E3
Glencar Road	69 C2
Glencarr Court	64 E1 [8]
Glencarr Lawn	64 E1
Glencarraig	29 B1
Glencarrig Court	55 B2
Glencarrig Drive	55 B2
Glencarrig Green	55 B2
Glencarthy Court Apartments	26 D3
Glencloy Road	25 B2
Glencorp Road	25 C2
Glencourt Estate	67 C3
Glencullen	62 E4
Glencullen Bridge	65 B1
Glendale	20 D4
Glendale Drive	67 C3
Glendale Meadows	20 E4
Glendale Park	46 D3
Glendalough Road	25 A4 [6]
(off Hollybank Road)	
Glendhu Park	23 C3
Glendhu Road	23 C3
Glendinning Lane	75 B1
(off Wicklow Street)	
Glendoher Avenue	56 F1
Glendoher Close	56 F1
Glendoher Drive	56 F1
Glendoher Park	56 E1
Glendoher Road	56 E1
Glendoo Close	45 B3
Glendown Avenue	46 D3
Glendown Close	46 D3
Glendown Court	46 D3
Glendown Crescent	46 D3
Glendown Drive	46 D3
Glendown Green	46 D3
Glendown Grove	46 D3
Glendown Lawn	46 D3
Glendown Park	46 D3
Glendown Road	46 D3
Glendun Road	25 B2
Glenealy Downs	8 F4
Glenealy Road	74 D4
Gleneaston	19 B4
Gleneaston Avenue	19 B4
Gleneaston Close	19 B4
Gleneaston Crescent	19 B4
Gleneaston Drive	19 B4
Gleneaston Gardens	19 B4
Gleneaston Green	19 B4
Gleneaston Grove	19 B4
Gleneaston Lawns	19 B4
Gleneaston Manor	19 B4
Gleneaston Park	19 B4
Gleneaston Rise	19 B4
Gleneaston Square	19 B4
Gleneaston View	19 B4
Gleneaston Way	19 B4
Gleneaston Woods	19 B4
Glenesk Court (off Claremont Road)	39 A4 [32]
Glenfarne Road	26 F1
Glenfield Avenue	35 A2
Glenfield Close	35 A2
Glenfield Drive	35 A2
Glenfield Grove	35 A2
Glenfield Park	35 A2
Glengara Close	60 D1 [15]
(off Glenageary Road Lower)	
Glengara Park	60 D1
Glengariff Parade	71 A1
Glengarriff Crescent	71 B1
Glengarriff Parade	71 B1
Glenhill Avenue	24 E2
Glenhill Court	24 E2
Glenhill Drive	24 E2
Glenhill Grove	24 E2
Glenhill Road	24 E2
Glenhill Villas (off Glenhill Drive)	24 E2 [2]
Glenlucan	67 B2
Glenlyon Crescent	55 C2
Glenlyon Grove	55 C2
Glenlyon Park	55 C2
Glenmalure Park	73 C2
Glenmalure Square	47 B2
*Glenmalure Villas	74 D2
(off St Jame's Walk)	
Glenmaroon Park	35 C2
Glenmaroon Road	35 C2
Glenmore	8 E1
Glenmore Court	56 F2
Glenmore Park	56 F2
Glenmore Road	69 C1
Glenmurry Park	45 C3
Glenomena Grove	48 E2
Glenomena Park	48 E2
Glenpark Close	35 B1
Glenpark Drive	35 B1
Glenpark Road	35 B1
Glenshane Close	54 D1
Glenshane Crescent	54 D1
Glenshane Dale	54 D1 [5]
(off Glenshane Lawns)	
Glenshane Drive	54 D1
Glenshane Gardens	54 D1
Glenshane Green	54 D1
Glenshane Grove	54 D1
Glenshane Lawns	54 D1
Glenshane Park	54 D1
Glenshane Place	54 D1 [6]
(off Glenshane Lawns)	
Glenshesk Road	25 C2
Glenside Villas	35 C1 [2]
(off Lucan Road Palmerston)	
Glenthorn	67 B4
Glenties Drive	24 D2
Glenties Park	24 D2
Glentow Road	25 B2
Glentworth Park	27 A1 [2]
(off Slademore Avenue)	
Glenvale	34 E3
Glenvar Park	48 F3
Glenvara Park	55 C2
Glenview (Rochestown Avenue)	60 D3
Glenview (Enniskerry)	66 D3
Glenview Drive	55 B1
Glenview Lawns	55 B1
Glenview Park	55 B1
Glenville Avenue	22 E2
Glenville Court	22 E3
Glenville Drive	22 E3
Glenville Garth	22 E3
Glenville Green	22 E2
Glenville Grove	22 E2
Glenville Lawn	22 E2
Glenville Road	22 E3
Glenville Terrace	47 C4 [8]
(off Main Street Dundrum)	
Glenville Way	22 E2
*Glenwood (Laragcon Lucan)	33 C1
Glenwood (Bray)	67 B2
Glenwood Road	26 F1
Glin Avenue	13 B4
Glin Close (off Glin Drive)	13 B4 [6]
Glin Court (off Glin Crescent)	13 B4 [7]
Glin Crescent	13 B4
Glin Drive	13 B4
Glin Grove	13 B4
Glin Park	13 B4
Glin Road	13 B4
Glitspur Brook	67 C3
Gloucester Diamond	71 C2
Gloucester Lane (off Sean McDermott Street Lower)	71 C2
Gloucester Place	71 C2
Gloucester Place Lower	71 C2
Gloucester Place Lower	71 C2
Gloucester Place Upper	71 C2
Gloucester Street South	72 D4
Glovers Alley	75 B1
Glovers Court (off York Street)	75 B1
Goatstown Avenue	47 C4
Goatstown Road	47 C4
Gobán Saor	58 E4
Godfrey Place	70 D2
(off Oxmanstown Road)	
Gofton Hall (off Mckee Avenue)	24 E1 [2]
Golden Ball	62 F2
Golden Lane	75 A1
Goldenbridge Avenue	73 B2
Goldenbridge Gardens	73 A2
Goldenbridge Terrace	73 A2
Goldenbridge Walk (Tyrconnell Road)	36 F4
Goldenbridge Walk (Goldenbridge)	73 A2
Goldsmith Hall Apartments	72 D4
Goldsmith Street	71 A1
Goldsmith Terrace	67 C2 [25]
Goldstone Court Apartments	74 D4
Golf Links Road (Portmarnock)	15 A2
Gordon Avenue	59 A3
Gordon Place	75 B3
Gordon Street	76 F1
Gorsefield Court (off McAuley Road)	26 F2 [1]
Gort na Mona Drive	59 B3
Gortbeg Avenue	24 E3
Gortbeg Drive	24 E3
Gortbeg Park	24 E3
Gortbeg Road	24 E3
Gortmore Avenue	24 E2
Gortmore Drive	24 E2
Gortmore Park	24 E3
Gortmore Road	24 E3
Gosworth Park	60 E1
Gowrie Park	60 D1
Grace O'Malley Drive	30 D2
Grace O'Malley Road	30 D2
Grace Park Avenue	25 B4
Grace Park Court	25 C2
Grace Park Gardens	25 B4
Grace Park Heights	25 C3
Grace Park Lawns	25 C2 [9]
(off Grace Park Heights)	
Grace Park Manor	25 B3
Grace Park Meadows	25 C3
Grace Park Road	25 C3
Grace Park Terrace	25 C3
Gracefield Avenue	26 F2
Gracefield Road	26 E2
Grafton Street	75 B1
Graham Court	71 B2
Graham's Row	71 A2
Graigue Court	11 C4
Granby Lane	71 A2
Granby Place	71 B3
Granby Row	71 A2
*Grand Canal Bank (on James Walk)	74 D2
*Grand Canal Court	73 C3
(Herberton Bridge)	
Grand Canal Docks	76 F1
Grand Canal Place	74 E1
Grand Canal Plaza	76 E1
Grand Canal Quay	76 E1
Grand Canal Street Lower	76 E1
Grand Canal Street Upper	76 E2
Grand Canal View Apartments	73 B2
Grand Parade	75 C3
Grange (Meath)	6 E4
Grange (Malahide)	14 E1
Grange Abbey Crescent	14 E4
Grange Abbey Drive	14 E4
Grange Abbey Grove	14 E4
Grange Abbey Road	14 E4
Grange Avenue	14 F4
Grange Brook	56 F2
Grange Close (Kilbarrack)	27 C1
Grange Close (Pottery Road)	59 C3
Grange Cottages (off Brewery Road)	58 F1 [3]
Grange Court	57 A1
Grange Crescent	59 B2
Grange Downs	57 A1
Grange Drive	27 C1
Grange Grove	59 B1 [2]
(off Dean's Grange Road)	
Grange Hall	57 B3
Grange Hall Apartments	27 A2
Grange Lodge Avenue	14 D4
Grange Lodge Court	14 D4
Grange Manor	34 D3
Grange Manor Avenue	57 A1
Grange Manor Close	57 A1
Grange Manor Drive	57 A1
Grange Manor Grove	57 A1
Grange Manor Road	57 A1
Grange Parade	27 C1
Grange Park (Baldoyle)	14 F4
Grange Park (Willbrook)	56 F1
Grange Park (Cornelscourt)	59 B2
Grange Park Avenue	27 A2
Grange Park Close	27 B2
Grange Park Crescent	27 B2
Grange Park Drive	27 A2
Grange Park Green	27 B2
Grange Park Grove	27 A2
Grange Park Rise	27 B1
Grange Park Road	27 A2
Grange Park View	27 B1
Grange Park Walk	27 A2
Grange Rise	14 F4
Grange Road (Baldoyle)	14 F4
Grange Road (Rathfarnham)	46 F4
Grange Road (The Priory)	56 F1
Grange Road (Marley Park)	57 A2
Grange Terrace	59 B1 [6]
(off Dean's Grange Road)	
Grange View Close	43 B1
Grange View Court	43 B1
Grange View Green	43 B1
Grange View Grove	43 B1
Grange View Lawn	43 B1
Grange View Park	43 B1
Grange View Road	43 B1
Grange View Walk	43 B1
Grange View Way	43 B1
Grange View Wood	43 B1
Grange Way	27 C1
Grange Wood (Ballinteer)	57 A2
Grangebrook Avenue	56 F2
Grangebrook Close	56 F2
Grangebrook Park	56 F2
Grangebrook Vale	56 F2
Grangefield	57 B3
Grangegorman Lower	70 F3
Grangegorman Upper	70 F2
*Grangegorman Villas	70 F2
(Grangegorman Upper)	
Grangemore	14 E4
Grangemore Avenue	14 D4
Grangemore Court	14 D4
Grangemore Crescent	14 D4
Grangemore Drive	14 E4
Grangemore Grove	14 E4
Grangemore Lawn	14 E4
Grangemore Park	14 E4
Grangemore Rise	14 D4
Grangemore Road	14 D4
Grangewood	59 C1
Granite Hall (off Rosmeen Gardens)	60 D1 [7]
Granite Place (off Gilford Road)	76 F4
Granite Terrace	36 F3 [11]
(off Inchicore Terrace South)	

STREET NAME	PAGE/GRID REFERENCE	STREET NAME	PAGE/GRID REFERENCE	STREET NAME	PAGE/GRID REFERENCE	STREET NAME	PAGE/GRID REFERENCE
Granitefield	59 C3	Greenlea Avenue	46 E2	Grosvenor Terrace	49 C4[9]	Hampton Court	36 F3[16]
Granitefield Manor	59 C3	Greenlea Drive	46 E2	(off The Hill Dún Laoghaire)		(off Tyrconnell Road)	
Granitefield Mews	59 C3	Greenlea Grove	46 E2	Grosvenor Terrace	60 F2[17]	Hampton Court	76 E4
Grantham Place	75 B3	Greenlea Park	46 E3	(off Sorrento Road)		Hampton Crescent	48 E3
Grantham Street	75 A3	Greenlea Place (off The Laurels)	46 F2[12]	Grosvenor Villas (Rathmines)	47 A1	Hampton Green (Cabra)	69 B1
Grants Avenue (Greenogue Ind Est)	42 E4	Greenlea Road	46 E2	*Grosvenor Villas (off Sorrento Rd)	60 F2	Hampton Park	48 E3
Grants Court (Greenogue Ind Est)	42 E4	Greenmount Avenue	74 F4	Grotto Avenue	48 F2	Hampton Square	69 C1
Grants Cresents (Greenogue Ind Est)	42 E4	Greenmount Court	74 F4	Grotto Place	48 F2	Hampton Wood	11 C4
Grants Drive (Greenogue Ind Est)	42 E4	Greenmount Lane	74 F4	Grove Avenue (Malahide)	3 C3	Hampton Wood Avenue	11 B4
Grants Hill (Greenogue Ind Est)	42 E4	Greenmount Lawns	46 F2	Grove Avenue (Finglas)	24 E1	Hampton Wood Court	11 C4
Grants Lane (Greenogue Ind Est)	42 F4	Greenmount Lodge	62 F2	Grove Avenue (Mount Merrion)	48 F4	Hampton Wood Crescent	11 B4
Grants Park (Greenogue Ind Est)	42 E4	Greenmount Road	46 F2	Grove Avenue (Harold's Cross)	75 A4	Hampton Wood Drive	11 C4
Grants Place (Greenogue Ind Est)	42 E4	Greenmount Square	74 F4	Grove Court (Brackenstown Road)	1 A2[1]	Hampton Wood Green	11 B4
Grants Rise (Greenogue Ind Est)	42 E4	Greenoge	42 F4	Grove Court	22 D1	Hampton Wood Lawn	11 C4
Grants Road (Greenogue Ind Est)	42 E4	Greenogue Drive	52 F2	Grove Court	36 F4[4]	Hampton Wood Park	11 B4
Grants Row (Greenogue Ind Est)	42 E4	Greenore Court	76 E1	(off Naas Road Bluebell)		Hampton Wood Road	11 B4
Grant's Row	76 D1	Greenore Terrace	76 E1	Grove Court Apartments	22 D1	Hampton Wood Square	11 C4
Grants View (Greenogue Ind Est)	42 E4	Greenpark Road	33 C2	Grove House Apartments	59 A3	Hampton Wood Way	11 C4
Grants Way (Greenogue Ind Est)	42 E4	Greenridge Court	22 E1	Grove House Gardens	48 F4[5]	Hamwood	6 F3
Granville Close	60 D3	Greentrees Drive	45 C2	(off Stillorgan Grove)		Hanbury Court	74 F1
Granville Crescent	60 D3[2]	Greentrees Park	45 C2	Grove Lane	13 C4	*Hanbury Hall (Hanbury Lane)	74 F1
(off WoodleyRoad)		Greentrees Road	45 C2	Grove Lawn (Stillorgan)	48 F4	Hanbury Lane (off Main Street Lucan)	34 D1[3]
Granville Park	59 A1	Greenview	14 E2	Grove Lawns (Malahide)	3 C3	Hanbury Lane (The Coombe)	74 F1
Granville Road (Deans Grange)	59 A2	Greenville Avenue	74 F3	Grove Paddock	48 F4	*Hanbury Mews (Hanbury Lane)	74 F1
Granville Road (Cabinteely)	59 C3	Greenville Parade (Blackpitts)	74 F3	Grove Park (Coolock)	13 C4	Hanlon's Lane	61 B1
Grattan Bridge (River Liffey)	71 A4	Greenville Place	74 F3	Grove Park (Rathmines)	75 B4	Hanna Square	35 A1
Grattan Court (Celbridge)	31 C4	Greenville Road	49 B4	Grove Park Avenue	24 F1	Hannaville Park	46 F2
Grattan Court (off Mount Street)	76 E1	Greenville Terrace	74 F3	Grove Park Crescent	24 F1	Hanover Lane	75 A1
Grattan Court East	76 E1	Greenwood	13 C1	Grove Park Drive	24 F1	Hanover Quay	72 F4
Grattan Crescent	36 F3	Greenwood Avenue	14 D4	Grove Park Road	24 F1	Hanover Square	75 A1
Grattan Hall	14 E4	Greenwood Close	14 D4	Grove Road (Malahide)	3 C3	Hanover Street East	72 D4
Grattan Lodge	14 E4	Greenwood Court	14 D4	Grove Road (Blanchardstown)	22 D2	Hanover Street West	74 F1
Grattan Parade	25 A4	Greenwood Drive	14 D4	Grove Road (Finglas)	24 E1	Hansfield	8 E4
Grattan Place	76 E1	*Greenwood Lawn	14 D4	Grove Road (Rathmines)	75 A4	Hansted Close	34 D4
Grattan Street	76 E1	(on Greenwood Drive)		Grove Wood (Finglas)	24 E1	Hansted Crescent	34 D4
*Gravel Walk Church Apartments	70 E4	Greenwood Park	14 D4	Grove Wood (Foxrock)	59 A3	Hansted Dale	34 D4
(off Hendrick Street)		Greenwood Walk	14 D4	Grovedale	63 B2	Hansted Drive	34 D4
Gray Square	74 F1	Greenwood Way	14 D4	Guild Street	72 E3	Hansted Park	34 D4
Gray Street (off Meath St)	74 F1	Grenville Lane	71 B2	Guilford Terrace	64 E3[1]	Hansted Place	34 D4
Great Western Avenue	70 F1	Grenville Street	71 B2	Gulistan Cottages	47 A1	Hansted Road	34 D4
Great Western Square	70 F1	Greygates (off Sycamore Crescent)	48 E4[1]	Gulistan Place	47 A1	Hansted Way	34 D4
Great Western Villas	70 F1	Grey's Lane	30 D2	Gulistan Terrace	47 A1	Harbour Court	71 C4
Greeg Court	71 B3	Greythorn Park	60 D1	Gunny Hill	55 C3	Harbour Crescent	60 F1
Greek Street	71 A4	Griannan Fidh	58 D3	Gurteen Avenue	36 D3	Harbour Master Place	72 D3
Green Acre Court	56 D1	Griffeen	34 E3	Gurteen Park	36 D3	Harbour Road (Howth)	30 D1
Green Court View Apartments	71 A3	Griffeen Avenue	34 D3	Gurteen Road	36 D2	Harbour Road (Dún Laoghaire)	50 D4
Green Isle Court	44 D2[2]	Griffeen Glen Avenue	34 E3			Harbour Road (Dalkey)	60 F1
(off Bushfield Lawns)		Griffeen Glen Boulevard	34 E3			Harbour Square	50 D4
Green Lane (Leixlip)	19 C4	Griffeen Glen Chase	34 E3	**H**		Harbour Terrace (off Harbour Road)	49 C4[8]
Green Lane (Celbridge)	31 A2	Griffeen Glen Close	34 E3			Harbour View	30 D1[6]
Green Lane (Rathcoole)	52 E2	Griffeen Glen Court	34 E3	Hacketsland	64 E1	(off St. Laurence Road)	
Green Park (Rathgar)	47 B3	Griffeen Glen Court Yard	34 E3	Haddington Lawns	60 E2	Harbour View (Dún Laoghaire)	50 D4
Green Park Road	67 B2	Griffeen Glen Crescent	34 E3	Haddington Park	60 E2	Harcourt Green	75 B3
Green Road (Blackrock)	48 F3	Griffeen Glen Dene	34 E3	Haddington Place	76 E2	Harcourt Hall	75 B3
Green Street	71 A3	Griffeen Glen Drive	34 E3	Haddington Road	76 E2	Harcourt Lane	75 B3
Green Street East	72 F4	Griffeen Glen Green	34 E3	Haddington Terrace	50 D4[7]	Harcourt Lodge	73 B2
Green Street Little	71 A3	Griffeen Glen Grove	34 E3	(off Adelaide Street)		Harcourt Place	75 B3
Greencastle Avenue	26 E1	Griffeen Glen Lawn	34 E3	*Haddington Way East	76 F2	Harcourt Road	75 B3
Greencastle Crescent	26 E1	Griffeen Glen Park	34 E3	(Canon Mews East)		Harcourt Street	75 B2
Greencastle Drive	13 B4	Griffeen Glen Road	34 E3	*Haddington Way West		Harcourt Terrace	75 C3
Greencastle Parade	26 F1	Griffeen Glen Vale	34 E3	(Canon mews West)	76 F2	*Harcourt Villas	47 C3
Greencastle Park	13 B4	Griffeen Glen View	34 E3	Haddon Court (off Haddon Road)	39 B1[2]	(off Dundrum Rd/Mulvey Pk)	
Greencastle Road	13 B4	Griffeen Glen Way	34 E3	Haddon Park	26 D4[5]	Hardebeck Avenue	45 C1
Greendale Avenue	27 C2	Griffeen Glen Wood	34 D3	(Seaview Avenue North)		Hardiman Road	25 A3
Greendale Court	27 B2[2]	Griffeen Road	34 E3	Haddon Road	26 E4	Hardwicke Arch (off Hardwicke St)	71 B2
(off Greendale Road)		Griffeen Way	34 E2	Hadleigh Court	23 A3	Hardwicke Lane	71 B2
Greendale Road	27 B2	Griffin Rath Hall	18 D4	Hadleigh Green (off Auburn Avenue)	23 A3[2]	Hardwicke Place	71 B2
Greenfield Close	17 C4	Griffin Rath Manor	18 D4	Hadleigh Park	23 A3	Hardwicke Street	71 B2
Greenfield Crescent	48 D2	Griffin Rath Road	18 D4	Hagan's Court	76 D2	*Hardwicke Street Flats	71 B2
Greenfield Drive	18 D4	Griffith Avenue	25 B3	Haigh Terrace	50 D4	(Hardwicke Street)	
Greenfield Manor	48 D2[4]	Griffith Bridge (Grand Canal)	73 B2	Hainault Drive	59 B3	Harelawn Avenue	35 A3
(off Greenfield Park U.C.D.)		Griffith Close	24 F2	Hainault Grove	59 B3	Harelawn Crescent	35 A3
Greenfield Park (Stillorgan Road)	48 D2	Griffith Court	25 C4	Hainault Lawn	59 B3	Harelawn Drive	35 A2
Greenfield Park (Ballycullen Road)	55 C2	Griffith Crescent	24 F2	Hainault Park	59 A3	Harelawn Green	35 A3
Greenfield Place	75 A4	Griffith Downs	25 B3	Hainault Road	59 A3	Harelawn Grove	35 A2
(off Mount Drummond Ave)		Griffith Drive	24 F2	Halfpenny or Liffey Bridge	71 B4	Harelawn Park	35 A2
Greenfield Road (Sutton)	29 B1	Griffith Hall	25 C3	(River Liffey)		Harlech Crescent	48 D3
Greenfield Road (Mount Merrion)	48 E4	Griffith Heights	24 F2	Halliday Road	70 E3	Harlech Downs	47 C3
Greenfort Avenue	35 A2	Griffith Lawns	25 A3	Halliday Square	70 D3	Harlech Grove	48 D3
Greenfort Close	35 A2	Griffith Parade	24 F2	Hallscourt	67 C2	Harlech Villas (off Harlech Downs)	47 C3[4]
Greenfort Crescent	35 A2	Griffith Road	24 F2	Halston Street	71 A3	Harmac Court	46 F2
Greenfort Drive	35 A2	Griffith Square	74 F3	Hamilton Court (Dunboyne)	7 B3[2]	Harman Street	74 E2
Greenfort Gardens	35 A2	Grosvenor Avenue	68 D3[3]	Hamilton Court	71 A4	Harmoney Court	72 E1
Greenfort Lawns	35 A2	Grosvenor Court (Clontarf)	26 E4	(off Strand St Little)		Harmonstown Road	26 F2
Greenfort Park	35 A2	Grosvenor Court (Templeville Road)	46 D3	Hamilton Hall	7 B3	Harmony Avenue (off Eglinton Road)	47 C1[5]
Greenfort Walk	35 A2	Grosvenor Lane	47 A1	*Hamilton House (Wellington Lane)	76 E4	Harmony Court (off Eglinton Road)	47 C1[20]
Greenhills	45 B3	Grosvenor Lodge	47 A1	Hamilton Street	74 E3	Harmony Row	76 D1
Greenhills Court	55 A1	Grosvenor Park	47 A1[7]	Hammond Lane	70 F4	Harold Bridge Court	74 F4
Greenhills Road	45 A4	(off Leinster Road)		Hammond Street	74 F4	*Harold Crescent (off Eden Rd Lower)	60 E4
Greenisle Road	42 C3	Grosvenor Place	47 A1	Hampstead Avenue	25 A2	Harold Road	70 E3
Greenlands	58 D2	Grosvenor Road	47 A1	Hampstead Court	25 A2	Harold Ville Avenue	74 D2
Greenlawns (off Macroom Avenue)	13 B4[1]	Grosvenor Square	47 A1	Hampstead Park	25 A3	Harold's Cross	74 F4
				Hampton Court (Clontarf)	26 F4		

STREET NAME	PAGE/GRID REFERENCE		STREET NAME	PAGE/GRID REFERENCE		STREET NAME	PAGE/GRID REFERENCE		STREET NAME	PAGE/GRID REFERENCE	
Harold's Cross Cottages	74	F4	Hazelcroft Road	24	E2	Hermitage Downs	57	A1	Hillside Drive	47	A3
Harold's Cross Road	74	F4	Hazeldene	47	C1	Hermitage Drive	56	F1	Hillside Park	56	E1
Harold's Grange Road	57	B3	Hazeldine Apartments	67	C4	Hermitage Garden	34	F1	Hillside Terrace	30	D2 [7]
Harrington Court	75	B3	Hazelgrove	54	D2	Hermitage Green	34	F1	(Thormanby Road)		
Harrington Street	75	A3	Hazelgrove Court	54	E2	Hermitage Grove	56	F1	Hilltop Lawn	64	D3
Harrison Row	46	F2	Hazelhatch	41	B1	Hermitage Lawn	56	F1	Hilltown	1	B3
Harristown	5	A2	Hazelhatch Park	32	D4	Hermitage Manor	34	F1	Hilltown Close	1	C2
Harry Street	75	B1	Hazelhatch Road	41	C3	Hermitage Park (Lucan)	34	F1	Hilltown Court	1	C2
Hartstown Road	21	C1	Hazelwood (Santry Avenue)	12	E4	Hermitage Park (Grange Road)	56	F1	Hilltown Crescent	1	A2
Harty Avenue	45	C1	Hazelwood (Shankill)	64	E2	Hermitage Place	34	F1	Hilltown Green	1	C2
Harty Court (off Harty Avenue)	45	C1 [8]	Hazelwood (Bray)	67	B2	Hermitage Road	34	F1	Hilltown Grove	1	C2
Harty Court (off Daniel Street)	75	A2	Hazelwood Avenue	21	C1	Hermitage Valley	34	F1	Hilltown Lawn	1	C2
Harty Place	75	A2	Hazelwood Bank	44	D2	Hermitage View	56	F1	Hilltown Park	1	C2
Harvard	48	D3	Hazelwood Close	44	D2	Hermitage Way	34	F1	Hilltown Road	1	C2
Hastings Street	76	F1	Hazelwood Court (Hartstown)	21	C1	Heronford Lane	63	C2	Hilltown Way	1	C2
Hastings Terrace	60	E1 [12]	Hazelwood Court (Beaumont)	26	D1	Heskin Court	48	E2	Hillview	52	E2
(off Glasthule Road)			Hazelwood Crescent (Hartstown)	21	C1	Heuston Square	73	A1	Hillview Cottages (off Hillview Drive)	59	C2 [1]
Hatch Lane	75	C3	Hazelwood Crescent (Clondalkin)	44	D2	Hewardine Terrace	72	D2	Hillview Court	57	B1 [6]
Hatch Place	75	C3	Hazelwood Crescent (Bray)	67	B2	(off Killarney Street)			(off Beech Lawn Avenue)		
Hatch Street Lower	75	C3	Hazelwood Drive	26	D2	Heytesbury Court	76	E3	Hillview Drive	59	C2
Hatch Street Upper	75	B3	Hazelwood Green	21	C1	(off Merrion Road)			Hillview Glade	57	B1 [5]
Hatter's Lane	74	F4	Hazelwood Grove	26	E1	Heytesbury Lane	76	E4	(off Beech Lawn Avenue)		
Havelock Place	76	F2	Hazelwood House	75	B4	Heytesbury Street	75	A3	Hillview Grove	57	B1
Havelock Square	76	F2	Hazelwood Lane	44	D2	Hibernian Avenue	72	E2	Hillview Lawn	59	C2
Havelock Terrace	39	A3 [17]	Hazelwood Park	26	D1	Hibernian Road	72	E4	Hilton Gardens	57	C2
(off O'Connell Gardens)			Hazelwood View	44	D2	Hibernian Terrace	36	E2 [3]	Hoey Close	14	D4
Haven View	3	B2 [2]	Hazlebury Park	8	E4	(off Chapelizod Road)			Hoey Court	14	D4
Haverty Road	25	C4	Headford Grove	47	B4	High Park	25	C2	Hoey Place	14	D4
Hawkins Street	71	C4	Healthfield Road	46	F2	High Street	55	A1 [2]	*Hoeys Court (off Werburgh Street)	75	A1
Hawkridge	33	B2	Healy Street	71	C2	(off Old Blessington Road)			Hogan Avenue	76	E1
Hawthorn Avenue	72	E2	(off Rutland Place North)			High Street (Christ Church)	75	A1	Hogan House (off Stonepark Court)	46	F4 [25]
Hawthorn Drive (off Acorn Road)	57	B1 [2]	Heaney Avenue	35	C4	Highdownhill	51	C1	Hogan Place	76	D1
Hawthorn Lawn	22	F3	Heany Avenue (off Coliemore Road)	60	F2 [19]	Highfield Avenue (Dundrum)	57	A2	Hogan Square	76	E1
Hawthorn Lodge (Castleknock Road)	22	F3	Heath Square (off Mckee Avenue)	24	E1 [3]	Highfield Close	1	C2	Holles Place	76	D1
Hawthorn Lodge (Farmleigh)	23	A4	Heather Close	57	A2	Highfield Court	47	A2 [3]	Holles Row	76	D1
Hawthorn Manor	59	A1 [4]	Heather Drive	57	A2	(off Highfield Road)			Holles Street	76	D1
(off Newtown Park)			Heather Gardens	4	D4	Highfield Crescent	1	C2	Holly Avenue	58	D1
Hawthorn Park	1	C2	Heather Grove (Palmerston)	35	B2	Highfield Downs	1	C2	Holly Court	64	D1
Hawthorn Road (Clondalkin)	44	F1	Heather Grove (Ballinteer)	57	B2	Highfield Drive	57	A2	Holly Park	64	E2
Hawthorn Road (Bray)	67	B1	Heather Lawn	57	A2	Highfield Green	1	C2	Holly Park Avenue	59	A1
Hawthorn Terrace	72	E2	Heather Park	57	B2	Highfield Grove	47	A2	Holly Road (Donnycarney)	26	D3
Hawthorn View	32	D2	Heather Road (Ballinteer)	57	A2	Highfield Lawn	1	C2	Holly Road (Fox and Geese)	44	F1
Hawthorns Road	58	D2	Heather Road (Burton Hall)	58	E2	Highfield Manor	47	A2	Holly Tree Square	11	C4
Hayden Square (off Owenstown	48	D3 [3]	Heather View Avenue	54	F2	Highfield Park (Celbridge Road)	33	A1	Holly Tree Terrace	11	C4
Park Fosters Avenue)			Heather View Close	54	F2	Highfield Park (Churchtown)	47	B3	Hollybank Avenue Lower	47	B1
Hayden's Lane	34	D3	Heather View Drive	54	F2	Highfield Road	47	A2	Hollybank Avenue Upper	47	B1
Haydens Park	34	D3	Heather View Lawn	54	F2	Highland Avenue	59	B3	Hollybank Road	25	A4
Haydens Park Avenue	34	D3	Heather View Park	54	F2	Highland Grove	59	B3	Hollybrook	59	A3
Haydens Park Close	34	D3	Heather View Road	54	F2	Highland Lawn	59	B3	Hollybrook Court	26	D4 [3]
Haydens Park Dale	34	D3	Heather Walk	4	D4	Highland View	59	B3	(off Hollybrook Road)		
Haydens Park Drive	34	D3	Heatherwood	67	B4	Highridge Green	58	E1	Hollybrook Court Drive	26	D4 [2]
Haydens Park Glade	34	D3	Heathfield (off Monkstown Road)	49	B4 [17]	Highthorn Park	59	C1	(off Hollybrook Road)		
Haydens Park Green	34	D3	Heidelberg	48	D3	Highthorn Woods	59	C1 [10]	Hollybrook Grove	26	D4
Haydens Park Grove	34	D3	*Heatley Villas (on Pearse Road)	59	C2	(off Highthorn Park)			Hollybrook Manor	26	D4
Haydens Park Lawn	34	D3	Hempenstal Terrace	39	B4 [5]	Hill Cottages (off Killiney Hill Road)	60	E3 [1]	Hollybrook Mews (off Howth Road)	26	D4 [11]
Haydens Park View	34	D3	(off Durham Road)			Hill Court	14	F1	Hollybrook Park (Clontarf)	26	D4
Haydens Park Walk	34	D3	Hendrick Place	70	E4	Hill Crest	3	C4	Hollybrook Park (Irishtown)	67	C4
Haydens Park Way	34	D3	Hendrick Street	70	F4	Hill Drive	3	B3	Hollybrook Road	26	D4
Haymarket	70	F4	Henley Court (off Henley Villas)	47	B4 [8]	Hill Street	71	B2	Hollybrook Wood	26	D4
Haymarket House	70	F4	Henley Park	47	B4	Hill View	57	B1	Hollybrooke (off Bluebell Avenue)	36	E4 [4]
Haymarket Way	70	F4	Henley Villas	47	B4	Hillbrook Woods	22	D1	Hollyrood Apartments	39	A4 [47]
*Hayworth Close	21	B1	Henrietta Lane	71	A2	Hillcourt	47	A2	(off Hollyrood Park)		
Hayworth Court	21	B1	Henrietta Place	71	A3	Hillcourt Park	60	D2	Hollystown	9	B1
Hayworth Drive	21	B1	Henrietta Street	71	A3	Hillcourt Road	60	D2	Hollystown Park	9	B1
Hayworth Mews	21	A1	Henry Place	71	B3	Hillcrest (Malahide)	3	A2 [1]	Hollyville Lawn	35	C1
Hayworth Place	21	A1	Henry Road	36	D4	Hillcrest (Lucan)	34	D2	Hollywell	11	C4
Hayworth Rise	21	A1	Henry Street	71	B3	Hillcrest (off Templeogue Road)	46	D4 [1]	Hollywell Avenue	2	E3
Hayworth Terrace	21	A1	Herbert Avenue	48	E1	Hillcrest (Rathgar)	47	A2	(in Hollywell Estate)		
Hazel Avenue	58	D1	Herbert Cottages (off Merrion Road)	76	F3	Hillcrest Avenue	33	C2	Hollywell Close	2	E3
Hazel Court (off Strand Road)	14	F2 [7]	Herbert Court (off Hollyrood Park)	39	A4 [48]	Hillcrest Close	33	C2	(in Hollywell Estate)		
Hazel Grove	14	F2	Herbert Crescent (off Herbert Road)	22	F2 [1]	Hillcrest Court (off Griffith Avenue)	25	A3 [19]	Hollywell Court	2	D3
Hazel Lane	26	F4	Herbert House	76	E1	Hillcrest Court	34	D2	(in Hollywell Estate)		
Hazel Lawn (Blanchardstown)	22	E2	Herbert Lane	76	D2	Hillcrest Downs	58	D3	*Hollywell Crescent North	2	D3
Hazel Lawn (off Carriglea	59	C2 [4]	Herbert Park (Oldcourt)	67	B3	Hillcrest Drive	33	C2	(in Hollywell Estate)		
Avenue Kill O'The Grange)			Herbert Park (Ballsbridge)	76	F4	Hillcrest Green	33	C2	*Hollywell Crescent South	2	D3
Hazel Park	46	E2 [2]	Herbert Park Lane	76	F4	Hillcrest Grove	34	D2	(in Hollywell Estate)		
(off Kimmage Road Lower)			Herbert Park Mews	47	C1	Hillcrest Heights	33	C2	*Hollywell Dale	2	D3
Hazel Road	26	D3	*Herbert Place (off Bath St)	39	A3	Hillcrest Lawns	33	C2	(in Hollywell Estate)		
Hazel Villas	58	D1	Herbert Place (Baggot Street Lower)	76	D2	Hillcrest Manor			*Hollywell Dene	2	D3
Hazelbrook (Malahide)	14	E1	Herbert Road (Blanchardstown)	22	F2	(off Templeogue Road)	46	D4 [2]	(in Hollywell Estate)		
Hazelbrook (Tymon North)	45	B4	Herbert Road (Sandymount)	39	A4	Hillcrest Park (Glasnevin)	24	F2	Hollywell Gardens	2	D3
Hazelbrook (Kilmacud)	58	D1	Herbert Road (Oldcourt)	67	B3	Hillcrest Park (Lucan)	33	C2	(in Hollywell Estate)		
Hazelbrook Apartments	46	E2 [7]	Herbert Street	76	D2	Hillcrest Road (Lucan)	34	D2	*Hollywell Green	2	D3
(off Hazelbrook Court)			Herbert View	67	B2 [26]	Hillcrest Road (Sandyford)	58	D3	(in Hollywell Estate)		
Hazelbrook Court	46	E2	Herberton Bridge (Grand Canal)	73	C3	Hillcrest View	33	C2	Hollywell Grove	2	E3
Hazelbrook Drive	46	E2	Herberton Drive	74	D3	Hillcrest Walk	33	C2	(in Hollywell Estate)		
Hazelbrook Road	46	E2	Herberton Park	73	C2	Hillcrest Way	33	C2	Hollywell Heath	2	D3
Hazelbury Green	8	E4	Herberton Road	73	C2	Hillsbrook Avenue	46	D2	(in Hollywell Estate)		
Hazelbury Park	8	E4	Hermitage Avenue	56	F1	Hillsbrook Crescent	46	D2	*Hollywell Heights	2	D3
Hazelcroft Gardens	24	E2	Hermitage Close	56	F1	Hillsbrook Drive	46	D2	(in Hollywell Estate)		
Hazelcroft Green	24	E2	Hermitage Court	57	A1	Hillsbrook Grove	46	D2	*Hollywell Lawn	2	D3
Hazelcroft Park	24	E2	Hermitage Crescent	34	F1	Hillside	60	E2	(in Hollywell Estate)		

STREET NAME	PAGE/GRID REFERENCE
*Hollywell Manor (in Hollywell Estate)	2 D3
*Hollywell Meadows (in Hollywell Estate)	2 D3
*Hollywell Mews (in Hollywell Estate)	2 D3
Hollywell Place (in Hollywell Estate)	2 D3
Hollywell Rise (in Hollywell Estate)	2 D3
Hollywell Road (in Hollywell Estate)	2 D3
*Hollywell Row (in Hollywell Estate)	2 D3
Hollywell Square (in Hollywell Estate)	2 E3
Hollywell View (in Hollywell Estate)	2 E3
*Hollywell Villas (in Hollywell Estate)	2 D3
Hollywell Walk (in Hollywell Estate)	2 D3
Hollywell Wood (in Hollywell Estate)	2 D3
Hollywood Drive	48 D4
Hollywood Park	48 D4
*Holme's Cottages (on Church Avenue Rathmines)	47 A1
Holmston Avenue	60 D1
Holmwood	59 B4
Holycross Avenue (off Clonliffe Road)	25 B4 [5]
*Holycross Cottages (off Holycross Avenue)	25 B4
Holyrood Park	39 A4
Holywell	58 D1
Holywell Avenue	27 B1
Holywell Crescent	27 B1
Holywell Road	27 B1
Home Farm Park	25 B3
Home Farm Road	25 A3
Home Villas	47 C1
Homelawn Avenue	55 B1
Homelawn Drive	55 B1
Homelawn Gardens	55 B1
Homelawn Road	55 A1
Homelawn Villas	55 A1
Homelee (off Serpentine Park)	39 A4 [11]
Homeleigh	22 D4
Homeville (off Ballycullen Road)	55 C1 [4]
Homeville Court (off Ballycullen Road)	55 C1 [3]
Honey Park (off Sallynoggin Road)	60 D2 [1]
Hope Avenue	72 E1
Hope Street (off Gordon Street)	76 F1
Hopkins Square (off Owenstown Park Fosters Avenue)	48 D3 [1]
Horan Hall (off Belgard Square West)	54 F1 [5]
Horse Fair	72 E4
Horton Court	46 F2
Hospital Lane	69 B4
Hotel Yard	71 B3
Houghton Terrace	70 E3
Howard Street (off Gordon Street)	76 F1
Howth	30 D2
Howth Harbour	30 D1
Howth House Apartments (off Harbour Road)	30 D1 [10]
Howth Junction Cottages (off Kilbarrack Road)	27 B1 [1]
Howth Lodge Apartments	29 C1
Howth Peninsula Apartments (off Harbour Road)	30 D1 [14]
Howth Road (Marino)	26 D4
Howth Road (Killester)	26 E3
Howth Road (St Anns Park)	26 F3
Howth Road (Raheny)	27 B2
Howth Road (Sutton)	29 B1
Howth Road (Howth)	29 C1
Howth Road Apartments	26 E3
Howth Terrace (off St. Laurence Road)	30 D1 [5]
Howth View Park	27 B1
Huband Bridge (Grand Canal)	76 E2
Huband Road	36 F4
Hudson Road	60 E1
Hughes Road East	45 C1
Hughes Road North	45 C1
Hughes Road South	45 C1
Hume Ave	36 D4
Hume Avenue	35 C4
Hume Street	75 C2
Hunters Avenue	55 C3
Hunters Court	55 C3
Hunters Crescent	55 C3
Hunters Green	55 C3
Hunters Grove	55 C3
Hunters Hall	55 C3
Hunters Hill	55 C3
Hunters Lane	55 C3
Hunters Meadow	55 C3
Hunters Parade	55 C3
Hunters Place	55 C3
Hunters Road	55 C3
Hunter's Row (off Seapark Road)	26 F4 [2]
Hunters Run	8 E4
Hunters Run The Close	8 E4
Hunters Run The Drive	8 F4
Hunters Run The Glade	8 E4
Hunters Run The Grove	8 E4
Hunters Run The Park	8 E4
Hunters Run The Rise	8 F4
Hunters Run The View	8 F4
Hunters Run The Way	8 F4
Hunters Walk	55 C3
Hunters Way	55 C3
Huntstown Avenue	21 C1
Huntstown Close	8 F4
Huntstown Court	8 F4
Huntstown Drive	8 F4
Huntstown Glen	8 F4
Huntstown Green	8 F4
Huntstown Grove	8 F4
Huntstown Lawn	22 D1
Huntstown Park	8 F4
Huntstown Rise	9 A4
Huntstown Road	21 C1
Huntstown Way	9 A4
Huntstown Wood	8 F4
Hutchinson's Strand	2 E1
Huttonread	51 C4
Huxley Court	74 E2
Huxley Crescent	74 E2
Hyacinth Street	72 E2
Hybreasal	73 B2
Hybreasal Apartments	73 B2
Hyde Park (Templeogue)	46 E3
Hyde Park (Dalkey)	60 E1
Hyde Park Avenue	48 F3
Hyde Park Gardens	48 F3
Hyde Road	60 F1
Hyde Square (off Owenstown Park Fosters Avenue)	48 D3 [4]
*Hyde Square (Kilmainham)	73 B2
Hynestown	42 D2

I

STREET NAME	PAGE/GRID REFERENCE
Idrone Avenue	56 D1
Idrone Close	56 D1
Idrone Drive	56 D1
Idrone Mews (off Idrone Terrace)	49 A3 [11]
Idrone Park	56 D1
Idrone Terrace	49 A3
Imaal Road	70 E1
Inagh Court	64 E1
Inagh Road	36 D3
Inbhir Ide	3 A2
Inbhir Ide Close	3 A2
Inbhir Ide Drive	3 A2
Inchicore	73 A1
Inchicore Road	73 A1
Inchicore Square (off Inchicore Terrace South)	36 F3 [13]
Inchicore Terrace North (off Inchicore Terrace South)	36 F3 [3]
Inchicore Terrace South	36 F3
Infirmary Road	69 C3
Inglewood Close	21 C2
Inglewood Crescent	21 C2
Inglewood Drive	21 C2
Inglewood Road	21 C2
Ingram Road	74 F3
Inis Fáil	54 F2
Inis Thiar	54 F2
Inishowen	12 F3
*Inkerman Cottages (off Amiens Street)	72 D2
Innisfallen Parade	71 B1
Innishmaan Road	25 B2
Innishmore Terrace (St Mary's Road)	46 D1
Innismore	46 D1
*Inns Court (on Winetavern Street)	75 A1
Inns Quay	70 F4
Inver Road	24 E4
Invermore Grove (off Carraroe Avenue)	27 A1 [3]
Inverness Road	25 C4
Iona Avenue	25 A4
Iona Crescent	25 A4
Iona Drive	25 A4
Iona Park	25 A4
Iona Road	25 A4
Iona Villas	25 A4
Iris Grove	48 E3
Irishtown (Ringsend)	39 A3
Irishtown (Bray)	67 C4
Irishtown Road	39 A3
Irvine Cottages	72 F3
Irvine Terrace	72 F3
Irwin Court	73 C1
Irwin Street	73 C1
Island Key	72 F2
Island Street	70 E4
Island View (Malahide)	3 C3
Island View (Kilbarrack)	27 C2
Island View Apartments (off Harbour Road)	30 D1 [9]
Island View Court Apartments	27 C2
Island Villa	76 E1
Islandbridge	69 B4
Islandbridge Court	69 B4
Islington Avenue	50 E4
Isolda Road	39 A3
Isolde Gardens (off Martin's Row Chapelizod)	36 E2 [6]
Isolde House Apartments (off Martin's Row Chapelizod)	36 E2 [13]
Ivar Street	70 E3
Iveagh Buildings	75 A2
Iveagh Court	75 B3
Iveagh Gardens	73 A4
Iveleary Road	25 B2
Iveragh Court (off Seafort Avenue)	76 F3
Iveragh Road	25 B2
Ivy Cottages	75 C4
Ivy Court (off Ballyshannon Road)	25 C1 [1]
Ivy Terrace	74 E2

J

STREET NAME	PAGE/GRID REFERENCE
Jackson's Bridge	17 A3
James Connolly Park	35 A4
James Connolly Square	67 C2 [5]
James Everett Park	67 B2
James Joyce Bridge (River Liffey)	70 F4
James Joyce Court (off Ferguson Road)	25 A3 [21]
James Joyce Court (off Sutton Downs)	27 C1 [5]
James Joyce St	71 C3
James Larkin Road	27 B2
James McCormack Gardens (off Burrowfield Road)	29 A1 [1]
James Plunkett House	36 F3
James's Place East	76 D2
James's Street	74 D1
James's Street East	76 D2
James's Street North	72 E1
James's Terrace	3 B2
James's Terrace Upper	3 B2 [11]
James's Walk	74 D2
Jamestown	62 F1
Jamestown Avenue	36 F4
Jamestown Cottages	62 E1
Jamestown Court	36 F4
Jamestown Road (Poppintree)	11 B4
Jamestown Road (Finglas)	24 E1
Jamestown Road (Inchicore)	36 F4
Jamestown Road (Grand Canal)	36 E4
*Jane-Ville (off Tivoli Road)	50 D4
Jerome Connor Place	69 C3
Jervis Lane Lower	71 A4
Jervis Lane Upper	71 A3
Jervis Street	71 A3
Jobstown	54 D2
Jobstown Road	54 D2
Jobstown Village Square (off Jobstown Road)	54 D1 [2]
John Dillon Street	75 A1
John F Kennedy Avenue	45 A1
John F Kennedy Drive	45 A1
John F Kennedy Park	36 D4
John F Kennedy Road	36 D4
John Field Road	75 A1
John MacCormack Avenue	45 C1
John McCormack Bridge (Tolka River)	72 F1
John Street North (off Ellis Quay)	70 E4
John Street South	74 F2
John Street West	74 F1
Johns Court (Christchurch)	74 F1
John's Court (Dolphins Barn Street)	74 E2
John's Lane East	75 A1
John's Lane West	74 F1
Johnsbridge	34 D3
Johnsbridge Avenue	34 D3
Johnsbridge Close	34 D3
Johnsbridge Green	34 D3
Johnsbridge Grove	34 D3
Johnsbridge Meadows	34 D3
Johnsbridge Park	34 D3
Johnsbridge Walk	34 D3
Johnson Place	75 B1
Johnson's Court	75 B1
Johnstown	51 C4
Johnstown Avenue	59 C2
Johnstown Court	59 C2
Johnstown Gardens (off Glasanon Road)5	24 E2
Johnstown Grove	59 C3
Johnstown House (off Johnstown Park)	24 F2 [3]
Johnstown Lane	59 C3
Johnstown Park (Glasnevin)	24 F2
Johnstown Park (Cornelscourt)	59 C3
Johnstown Road (Rathcoole)	52 E2
Johnstown Road (Cornelscourt)	59 C3
Jones Terrace	68 D2 [18]
Jones's Road	71 C1
Jordanstown	42 F4
Jordanstown Avenue (Greenogue Ind Est)	42 F4
Jordanstown Drive (Greenogue Ind Est)	42 F4
Jordanstown Road (Greenogue Ind Est)	42 F4
Josephine Avenue	71 B1
Joy Street (off Gordon Street)	76 F1
Joyce Avenue	59 A3
Joyce Hall	59 B4
Joyce Way	35 C4
Jugback Close	1 C1
Jugback Court	1 C1
Jugback Crescent	1 C1
Jugback Green	1 Inset
Jugback Lane	1 C1
Juliet Square	35 B1

K

STREET NAME	PAGE/GRID REFERENCE
Kavanagh Avenue	36 D4
Keadeen Avenue	45 B2
Kearneystown Lower	41 A3
Kearn's Place	73 B1
Keatingspark	52 D2
*Keegan's Cottages (off Merrion Rd)	48 E1
Keeloges	42 D3
Keeper Road	73 C3
Kells Road	46 E1
Kelly's Avenue	50 D4
Kelly's Lane (Maynooth)	17 C3 [1]
Kelly's Lane (Phibsborough)	71 A1
Kelly's Row	71 B1
Kelly's Square	71 B1
Kellystown Lane	19 A3
Kellystown Road	57 B4
Kelston Avenue	59 A2
Kelston Drive	59 A2
Kelston Hall (off Kelston Drive)	59 A2 [11]
Kelston Park	59 A2
Kelston View	59 A2
Kelvin Close	4 D4
Kempton	23 C3
Kempton Avenue	23 C3
Kempton Court	23 C3
Kempton Green	23 C3
Kempton Grove	23 C3
Kempton Heath	23 C3
Kempton Lawn	23 C3
Kempton Park	23 C3
Kempton Rise	23 C3
Kempton View	23 C3
Kempton Way	23 C3
Kenah Court	60 E3
Kengar Mews (off Rathgar Avenue)	46 F1 [14]
Kenilworth Lane	46 F1

STREET NAME	PAGE/GRID REFERENCE	STREET NAME	PAGE/GRID REFERENCE	STREET NAME	PAGE/GRID REFERENCE	STREET NAME	PAGE/GRID REFERENCE
Kenilworth Manor (off Harolds Cross Road)	46 F1 [11]	Kilcronan Lawns	34 E4	Killinarden	54 E3	Kiltalown Hill	54 D2
Kenilworth Park	46 F1	Kilcronan View	34 E4	Killinarden Estate	54 E2	Kiltalown Park	54 D2
Kenilworth Road	47 A1	Kilcroney Lane	67 A4	Killinarden Heights	54 E2	Kiltalown Road	54 D2
Kenilworth Square	46 F1	Kilcross Avenue	58 D3	Killinarden Road	54 E3	Kiltalown View	54 D2
Kenilworth Square East	47 A1	Kilcross Close	58 D3	Killiney	60 E3	Kiltalown Walk	54 D2
Kenilworth Square North	46 F1	Kilcross Court	57 C3	Killiney Avenue	60 E4	Kiltalown Way	54 D2
Kenilworth Square South	46 F1	Kilcross Crescent	57 C3	Killiney Court	64 E1 [1]	Kilteel Road	52 E2
Kenilworth Square West	46 F1	Kilcross Drive	57 C3	Killiney Gate	60 E4	Kilteragh Drive	59 A3
Kenmare Parade	71 B1	Kilcross Grove	57 C3	Killiney Grove	60 E2	Kilteragh Pines (off Westminster Road)	59 A3 [2]
Kennedy Court (off Pembroke Street)	39 A3 [31]	Kilcross Lawn	58 D3	Killiney Heath	60 E4	Kilteragh Road	59 A3
Kennedy Park	67 C3 [5]	Kilcross Park	57 C3	Killiney Hill Road	60 E3	Kilternan	62 F2
Kennelsfort Green	35 B2	Kilcross Road	58 D3	Killiney Hill Road	64 E1	Kiltiernan Bridge	62 F3
Kennelsfort Road Lower	35 C1	Kilcross Square	57 C3	Killiney Oaks	64 E1 [2]	Kiltipper	54 F3
Kennelsfort Road Upper	35 C2	Kilcross Way	57 C3	Killiney Road	60 E2	Kiltipper Avenue	55 A2
Kennilworth Lodge (off Harolds Cross Road)	46 F1 [19]	Kildare Bridge	18 D2	Killiney Terrace (off Breffni Road)	60 E1 [15]	Kiltipper Close	55 A2
Kennington Close	45 C4	Kildare Park	46 D1	Killiney Towers (off Killiney Road)	60 E2 [2]	Kiltipper Drive	55 A2
Kennington Crescent	45 C4	Kildare Place	75 C1	Killiney View	60 E1	Kiltipper Gate	54 F3
Kennington Lawn	45 C4	Kildare Road	46 D1	Killininny Cottages	55 B2	Kiltipper Rise	54 F3
Kennington Road	45 C3	Kildare Street	75 C1	Killininny Court Apartments (off Kilakee Grove)	55 B2 [2]	Kiltipper Road	55 A3
*Kent Terrace (on Barnhill Road)	60 F2	Kildonan Avenue	24 D1	Killininny Road	55 B2	Kiltipper View	54 F3
Kentfield	64 E2	Kildonan Court	24 D1	Kilmactalway	42 F3	Kiltipper Way	54 F2
Kerlogue Road	39 A3	Kildonan Drive	24 D1	Kilmacud	58 E1	Kiltuck Park	64 E4 [1]
Kerrygold House (off Harolds Cross Road)	46 F1 [18]	Kildonan Road	24 D1	Kilmacud Avenue	58 E1	Kilvere	46 E4
Kerrymount Avenue	59 A4	Kildress House	76 D2	Kilmacud Park	58 E1	Kilvere Park	46 D4
Kerrymount Close (off Kerrymount Rise)	59 B3 [1]	Kilfenora Drive	27 A1	Kilmacud Road Upper	58 E1	Kilwogan Manor	31 C2
Kerrymount Green	59 B3	Kilfenora Road	46 E1	Kilmahuddrick Avenue	43 B1	Kilworth Road	36 F4
Kerrymount Mall	59 B3	Kilgarran	66 D3	Kilmahuddrick Close	43 B1	Kimmage	46 D2
Kerrymount Rise	59 B3	Kilgarron Park	66 D3	Kilmahuddrick Court	43 B1	Kimmage Court (off Kimmage Road Lower)	46 E2 [3]
Kettles Drive	2 E4	Kilgobbin Grove	58 E4	Kilmahuddrick Crescent	43 B1	Kimmage Grove	46 E2
Kettles Lane	2 E4	Kilgobbin Heights	58 E4	Kilmahuddrick Drive	43 B1	Kimmage Manor Way	46 D2
Kettles Place	2 E4	Kilgobbin Lane	58 D4	Kilmahuddrick Green	43 B1	Kimmage Road Lower	46 F1
Kevin Barry Flats (off Church Street Upper)	70 F3	Kilgobbin Lawn	58 E4	Kilmahuddrick Grove	43 B1	Kimmage Road West	46 D2
*Kevin Street Cross (on New Bride Street)	75 A2	Kilgobbin Road	58 E3	Kilmahuddrick Lawn	43 B1	Kinahan Street	70 D3
Kevin Street Lower	75 A2	Kilgobbin Wood	58 E4	Kilmahuddrick Place	43 B1	Kincora Avenue	26 E4
Kevin Street Upper	75 A2	Kilgraigue	5 B3	Kilmahuddrick Road	43 B1	Kincora Court	39 C1
Kew Park	33 C1	Kilgrastor Court	67 B3 [5]	Kilmahuddrick Walk	43 B1	Kincora Drive	26 E4
Kew Park Avenue	33 B2	Kilkieran Court (off Kilkieran Road)	24 E4 [1]	Kilmahuddrick Way	43 B1	Kincora Grove	26 E4
Kew Park Crescent	33 B1	Kilkieran Road	24 E4	Kilmainham	73 B1	Kincora Park	26 E4
Kickham Road	73 B2	Kill Abbey	59 B1	Kilmainham Bank	73 A1	Kincora Road	26 E4
Kilakee Close	45 B3	Kill Avenue	59 C1	Kilmainham Lane	73 C1	Kincora Walk	26 F4 [3]
Kilakee Drive	45 B3	Kill Lane	59 B2	Kilmainham Orchard	73 B1	King Edward Court	67 C2 [53]
Kilbarrack	27 C1	Kill O' the Grange	59 C1	Kilmainham Square (South Circular/Inchicore Road)	73 B1	King Edward Lawn	67 C2
Kilbarrack Avenue	27 C2	Killadoon Park	31 C4	Kilmalin	65 C3	King Edward Park	67 B2
Kilbarrack Gardens	27 C2	Killakee Avenue	55 B2	Kilmantain Place	67 C2 [10]	King Edward Road	67 B2
Kilbarrack Grove	27 C2	Killakee Court	55 B2	Kilmartin Avenue	54 D1	King Street North	70 F3
Kilbarrack Parade	27 B1	Killakee Gardens	55 B2	Kilmartin Crescent	44 D4	King Street South	75 B1
Kilbarrack Road	27 B1	Killakee Green	55 B2	Kilmartin Drive	54 D1	King William's Rampart	24 D2
Kilbarrack Way	27 B1	Killakee Grove	55 B2	Kilmartin Gardens	54 D1	Kingram Place	75 C3
Kilbarron Avenue	26 D1	Killakee Lawns	55 B2	Kilmartin Green	54 D1	King's Avenue	72 D1
Kilbarron Court (off Kilbarron Park)	26 D1 [1]	Killakee Park	55 B2	Kilmartin Park	54 D1	King's Court	70 E2
Kilbarron Drive	26 D1	Killakee Rise	55 B2	Kilmashogue Bridge	56 F3	*Kings Court Apartments (Brunswick Street North)	70 F3
Kilbarron Park	26 D1	Killakee Road	56 D4	Kilmashogue Close	45 B3	King's Hall	36 E2
Kilbarron Road	26 D1	Killakee View	55 B2	Kilmashogue Drive	45 B3	Kings Inns	71 A3
Kilbegnet Close (off Castle Street Dalkey)	60 F2 [24]	Killakee Walk	55 B2	Kilmashogue Grove	45 B3	King's Inn's Court	71 A2
Kilbogget Grove	59 C4	Killakee Way	55 B2	Kilmashogue Lane	56 F3	King's Inns Street	71 A3
Kilbogget Villas (off Bray Road)	59 C4 [1]	Killala Road	24 E4	Kilmore	26 D1	Kingsbury	17 C4
Kilbride Grove	67 B3	Killan Court	72 F3	Kilmore Avenue (Coolock)	26 E1	Kingsland Parade	75 A4
Kilbride Lane	67 B3	Killan Road	72 F3	Kilmore Avenue (Killiney)	60 E4	Kingsland Park Avenue	75 A3
Kilbride Road (Killester)	26 E3	Killarney Avenue	72 D2	Kilmore Close	26 E1	*Kingsmill Court Apartments (Yarnhall Street)	71 A3
Kilbrina	7 B2	Killarney Court	67 B3 [4]	Kilmore Court (off Kilmore Road)	26 D1 [5]	Kingsmill Road	67 C2
Kilcarbery Ave	43 C2	Killarney Court (on Killarney Avenue)	72 D2	Kilmore Crescent	26 E1	Kingston	57 B3
Kilcarbery Close	43 C2	Killarney Glen	67 B2	Kilmore Drive	26 E1	Kingston Avenue	57 B3
Kilcarbery Court	43 C2	Killarney Heights	67 B3	Kilmore Place Apartments	26 D1	Kingston Close	57 B3
Kilcarbery Lawn	43 C2	Killarney Lane	67 B3	Kilmore Road	26 D1	Kingston Court	56 F2
Kilcarrig Avenue	44 E4	Killarney Parade	71 B1	Kilmorony Close	27 A1	Kingston Crescent	57 B3
Kilcarrig Close	54 E1	Killarney Park	67 B3	Kilnamanagh	45 A3	Kingston Drive	57 C3
Kilcarrig Crescent	44 E4	Killarney Road	67 B3	Kilnamanagh Court	45 C1	Kingston Green	57 B3
Kilcarrig Green	44 E4	Killarney Street	72 D2	Kilnamanagh Estate	45 A3	Kingston Grove	57 B3
Kilclare Avenue	54 E2	Killarney Villas	67 C2 [48]	Kilnamanagh Road	45 C1	Kingston Hall	57 B3
Kilclare Crescent	54 E2	Killary Grove	27 B1	Kilrock Road	30 E2	Kingston Heights	57 C3
Kilclare Drive	54 E2	Killeany	5 A4	Kilronan Court (off Howth Road)	26 D4 [7]	Kingston Lawn	57 B3
Kilclare Gardens	54 E2	Killeck	1 A2	Kilshane	10 E2	Kingston Lodge (off Clonliffe Road)	25 B4 [4]
Kilcloon	5 A2	Killeck Lane	1 A3	Kilshane Avenue	10 D2	Kingston Park	57 B3
Kilcloon Lawns	5 A2	Killeen	2 F3	Kilshane Cross	10 F2	Kingston Rise	57 B3
Kilcock Maynooth Leixlip ByPass	32 E1	Killeen Avenue	2 F3	Kilshane Drive	10 E3	Kingston View	57 B3
Kilcock Road	17 C3	Killeen Court	2 F3	Kilshane Park	10 D2	Kingston Walk	57 B3
Kilcock-Maynooth-Leixlip Bypass	33 A1	Killeen Crescent	2 F3	Kilshane Road (North Road)	10 E3	Kingswood	43 C3
Kilcolman Court (off Glenageary Road Upper)	60 E2 [4]	Killeen Mews	3 B3	Kilshane Road (Rathoath Road)	23 C2	Kingswood Avenue (Citywest)	43 C4
Kilcronan Avenue	34 E4	Killeen Park	2 F3	Kilshane View	10 D2	Kingswood Avenue (Kilnamanagh)	44 F3
Kilcronan Close	34 E4	Killeen Road (Bluebell)	36 D4	Kilshane Way	10 D3	Kingswood Castle	45 A2
Kilcronan Court	34 E4	Killeen Road (Fox and Geese)	45 A1	Kiltalown	54 D3	Kingswood Drive (Citywest)	43 C4
Kilcronan Crescent	34 E4	Killeen Road (Rathmines)	47 B1	Kiltalown Avenue	54 D2	Kingswood Drive (Kilnamanagh)	44 F3
Kilcronan Grove	34 E4	Killeen Terrace	3 B2	Kiltalown Close	54 D2	Kingswood Heights	44 F3
Killegar	65 C1	Kiltalown Cottages	54 F4	Kingswood Interchange	42 C3
*Killery Terrace (on Upper Dargle Road)	67 B2	Kiltalown Court	54 D2	Kingswood Road	43 C4
Killester	26 E3	Kiltalown Crescent	54 D2	Kingswood View	44 F3
Killester Avenue	26 E3	Kiltalown Drive	54 D2	Kinsaley	14 D1
Killester Court (off Killester Park)	26 E3 [4]	Kiltalown Green	54 D2		
Killester Park (off Killester Park)	26 E3 [5]	Kiltalown Grove	54 D2		
Killester Park	26 E3	Kiltalown Heights	54 D2		

STREET NAME	PAGE/GRID REFERENCE
Kinsaley Bridge	14 D1
Kinsaley Lane	3 A4
Kinsealy Court	2 E3
Kinsealy Downs	2 E3
Kinsealy Lane	14 D1
Kinvara Avenue	24 D4
Kinvara Drive	23 C4
Kinvara Grove	23 C4
Kinvara Park	24 D4
Kinvara Road	23 C4
Kippure Avenue	45 B3
Kippure Park	24 D3
Kirkfield (off Clonsilla Road)	22 D2 [2]
Kirkpatrick Avenue	22 D3
Kirkpatrick Drive	22 D3
Kirkwood	39 A4
Kirwan Street	70 E3
Kirwan Street Cottages	70 E2
Kitestown Road	30 E3
Knapton Court	49 C4 [21]
(off York Road Dún Laoghaire)	
Knapton Lawn (off Knapton Road)	49 C4 [22]
Knapton Road	49 C4
Knapton Terrace (off Knapton Road)	49 C4 [27]
*Knapton Villas (on Knapton Road)	49 C4
Knights Bridge	26 E4 [4]
(off Castle Avenue Clontarf)	
Knights Wood	12 F4
Knock Riada	36 D2
Knockaire	56 D1
Knockandinny	52 E4
Knockaulin	20 D4
Knockcullen	56 D1
Knockcullen Drive	56 D1
Knockcullen Lawn	56 D1
Knockcullen Park	56 D1
Knockcullen Rise	56 D1
Knockdara	3 C3
Knockfield Manor	55 C1
Knocklyon	56 D1
Knocklyon Avenue	55 C1
Knocklyon Close	56 D1
Knocklyon Court	56 D1
Knocklyon Drive	56 D1
Knocklyon Gate Apartments	55 C2 [3]
(off Knocklyon Hill)	
Knocklyon Green	56 D1
Knocklyon Grove	56 D1
Knocklyon Heights	55 C1
Knocklyon Mews	55 C1 [2]
(off Knocklyon Avenue)	
Knocklyon Park	55 C1
Knocklyon Road	55 C1
Knockmaree Apartments	36 E2
Knockmaroon Hill	36 D1
Knockmaroon Road	36 D1
Knockmeenagh Lane	44 E2
Knockmeenagh Road	44 E2
Knockmitten Close	44 F1 [1]
(off Knockmitten Lane)	
Knockmitten Lane	45 A1
Knockmitten Lane North	44 F1 [2]
(off Knockmitten Lane)	
Knockmore Avenue	54 E2
Knockmore Crescent	54 E2
Knockmore Drive	54 E2
Knockmore Gardens	54 E2
Knockmore Green	54 E2
Knockmore Grove	54 E2
Knockmore Park	54 E2
Knock-na-Cree Grove	60 F2
Knock-na-Cree Park	60 F2
Knock-na-Cree Road	60 F2
Knocknagow (off Stradbrook Road)	49 B4 [23]
Knocknarea Avenue	73 B4
Knocknarea Road	73 A4
*Knocknarrow Terrace	73 C1
(Kilmainham Lane)	
Knocknashee	48 D4
Knocksedan Bridge	1 A2
Knocksedan Drive	1 A2
Knocksedan Wood	1 A2
Knocksink Bridge	66 E3
Knocksinna	59 A2
Knocksinna Court	59 A2 [2]
(off Granville Road)	
Knocksinna Crescent	59 A2
Knocksinna Grove	59 A2 [1]
(off Knocksinna Park)	
Knocksinna Park	59 A2
Knowth Court	11 C4
Kyber Road	36 F2
Kyle-Clare Road (off Pine Road)	39 A3 [13]
Kylemore Avenue	36 D3
Kylemore Drive	36 D3
Kylemore Park North	36 D4
Kylemore Park South	36 D4
Kylemore Park West	36 D4
Kylemore Road (Ballyfermot)	36 D2
Kylemore Road (Grand Canal)	36 E4
Kylemore Way	36 E4

L

STREET NAME	PAGE/GRID REFERENCE
La Rochelle Apartments	74 F1
La Touche Court	36 F4 [3]
(off Bluebell Avenue)	
La Touche Court (Ballinteer)	57 A2
La Touche Drive	36 E4
La Touche Road	36 F4
La Vallee	67 A3
La Vista Avenue	29 B2
Labre Park	36 E4
Laburnum Road	47 C2
Laburnum Walk	35 B2
Lad Lane	76 D2
Lad Lane Apartments	76 D3
Lad Lane Upper	76 D3
Lady's Lane	73 B1
Lady's Well Road	9 A4
Lagan Road	24 E3
Lake Drive	53 C1
Lakelands Avenue	58 D1
Lakelands Close	58 D1
Lakelands Crescent	58 E1
Lakelands Drive	58 E1
Lakelands Grove	58 D1
Lakelands Lawn	58 D1
Lakelands Park	46 E3
Lakelands Place	58 D1
Lakelands Road	58 E1
Lakeshore Drive	2 D3
Lakeview Drive	2 D3
Lally Road	36 E3
Lamb Alley	74 F1
Lambay Close	64 E1
Lambay Court	3 C3
Lambay Drive	64 E1
Lambay Road	25 A3
Lambourn Park (Clonsilla)	21 C2
Lambourne Avenue	21 C2
Lambourne Court	21 C2
Lambourne Drive	21 C2
Lambourne Road	21 C2
Lambourne Village	26 E4 [3]
(off Kincora Grove)	
Lambourne Wood	59 C4
Lamb's Brook	58 D3
Lamb's Court (off James Street)	74 D1
Landen Road	36 E3
Landore	47 A3 [9]
(off Orwell Road Rathgar)	
Landscape Avenue	47 A3
Landscape Crescent	47 A4
Landscape Gardens	47 B4
Landscape Park	47 A4
Landscape Road	47 A3
Landsdown Valley Place	45 C1
Landsdowne Valley	45 C1 [6]
(off Slieve Bloom Park)	
*Landsdowne Valley Apartments	45 C1
(Landsdowne Valley)	
Landsdowne Valley Park	36 F4 [5]
(off Davitt Road)	
Lanesborough Avenue	11 B4
Lanesborough Court	11 B4
Lanesborough Drive	11 B4
Lanesborough Gardens	11 B4
Lanesborough Grove	11 B4
Lanesborough Mews	11 B4
Lanesborough Park	11 B4
Lanesborough Road	11 B4
Lanesborough Square	11 B4
Lanesborough Terrace	11 B4
Lanesborough View	11 B4
Lanesville	59 B1
Lanesville Terrace	59 B1
Lanewood Mews	76 E3
(off Wellington Road)	
Langrishe Place	71 C2
Lanndale Lawns	54 E1
*Lansdowne Court	76 F3
(Lansdowne Park)	
Lansdowne Crescent	76 F2
Lansdowne Gardens	76 F3
(off Sandymount Avenue)	
Lansdowne Hall	39 A3 [25]
(off Sandymount Road)	
Lansdowne Lane	76 F2
Lansdowne Park (Templeogue)	56 D1
Lansdowne Park (Ballsbridge)	76 F2
Lansdowne Road	76 F3
Lansdowne Square	39 A4 [24]
(off Herbert Road)	
Lansdowne Terrace	76 F2
Lansdowne Village	39 A3
Lansdowne Villas	76 F2
Lansdowne Woods	76 F3
(off Merrion Road)	
Lapwing Apartments	48 E3
Laracor Gardens (off Ardara Avenue)	27 A1 [5]
Laragh	60 E4
Laragh Close	27 A1
Laragh Flats (off Grace Park Court)	25 C2 [5]
Laragh Grove	27 A1
Laraghbryan East	17 B2
Laraghbryan West	17 A2
Laraghon	34 D1
Larch Drive (off Brookwood)	56 E2 [3]
Larch Grove	21 C2
Larch Grove	47 B1
Larch Hill	12 F4
Larch House (Swords)	1 Inset
Larchfield	7 C3
Larchfield	47 C4
Larchfield Park	47 C4
Larchfield Road	47 C4
Larkfield	34 F2
Larkfield Avenue (Liffey Valley)	34 F2
Larkfield Avenue (Harold's Cross)	46 F1
Larkfield Close	34 F2
Larkfield Court	34 F2
Larkfield Gardens	46 F1
Larkfield Green	34 F2
Larkfield Grove (Liffey Valley)	34 F2
Larkfield Grove (Harold's Cross)	46 F1
Larkfield Mews	32 D3
Larkfield Park	46 F1
Larkfield Place	34 F2
Larkfield Rise	34 F2
Larkfield Square	34 F2
Larkfield View	34 F2
Larkfield Way	34 F2
Larkhill Road	25 B2
Larrisa Court	46 E1 [7]
(off Kimmage Road Lower)	
Latchford	21 B1
Latchford Close	21 B1
Latchford Court	21 B1
Latchford Green	21 B1
Latchford Park	21 B1
Latchford Row	21 B1
Latchford Square	21 B1
Latchford Terrace	21 B1
Latouche Bridge (Grand Canal)	75 B4
Latouka Apartments	34 F1 [1]
(off Ballyowen Lane)	
Lauderdale Estate	67 C3
Lauderdale Terrace (Bray)	67 C3 [16]
*Lauderdale Terrace	75 A2
(on New Row South)	
Lauder's Lane	29 A1
Laundry Lane	16 F1
Laurel Avenue (Dundrum)	57 B1
Laurel Avenue (Ballybrack)	64 E1
Laurel Bank	59 C1
Laurel Court	22 E3
Laurel Drive	57 B1
Laurel Hill	60 D1 [6]
(off Glenageary Road Upper)	
Laurel Lodge Road	22 F3
Laurel Park	44 E1
Laurel Place	46 F2
Laurel Road	57 B1
Laurelton (Rathbeale Road)	1 C1
Laurelton (Terenure)	46 F3
Laurence Brook	36 E2
Laurence Court	46 F1
Laurence Place East	72 E3
Laurleen	58 F1
Lavarna Grove	46 E2
Lavarna Road	46 E2
Laverna Avenue	22 E3
Laverna Dale	22 E3
Laverna Grove	22 E3
Laverna Way	22 E3
Laverty Court	75 C2
Lavery Avenue	35 C4
Lavista Avenue	26 E3
Lawnswood Park	58 F1
Lawrence Grove	26 D4
Lawrence's Avenue	18 D4
Lawson Spinney	3 A3
Lawson Terrace	60 E1 [14]
(off Sandycove Road)	
Lazer Lane	72 E4
Le Bas Terrace	46 F1 [2]
(off Leinster Road West)	
Le Brett Terrace	46 F3 [7]
(off Main Street Rathfarnham)	
Le Brocquy Avenue	36 D4
Le Fanu Drive (off Clover Hill Road)	36 D3 [1]
Le Fanu Road	36 D3
Le Vere Terrace	74 F4
Lea Crescent	39 B4
Lea Road	39 B4
Leahy's Terrace	39 A3
Lealand Avenue	43 C1
Lealand Close	43 C1
Lealand Crescent	43 C1
Lealand Drive	43 C1
Lealand Gardens	43 C1
Lealand Grove	43 C1
Lealand Road	43 C1
Lealand Walk	43 C1
Leamount	59 C4
Leda Mews (off Waterloo Road)	76 E3
Ledwidge Crescent	67 B1
Lee Road	24 E3
Leeson Close	75 C3
Leeson Court	76 D4
Leeson Lane	75 C2
Leeson Mews	75 C4
Leeson Park	75 C4
Leeson Park Avenue	76 D4
Leeson Place	75 C3
Leeson Street Lower	75 C2
Leeson Street Upper	76 D4
Leeson Village	76 D4
Leeson Walk	75 C4
Lehaunstown Road	63 C1
Leicester Avenue	47 A1
Leighlin Road	46 E1
Lein Gardens	26 F2
Lein Park	26 F2
Lein Road	26 F2
Leinster Avenue	72 E1
Leinster Cottages	17 C3 [6]
Leinster Court	18 D3 [3]
Leinster Lane	75 C1
Leinster Lodge Apartments	18 D3 [1]
Leinster Market	71 C4
Leinster Park (Maynooth)	18 D3
Leinster Park (Harold's Cross)	46 F1
Leinster Place	46 F1
Leinster Road	47 A1
Leinster Road West	46 F1
Leinster Square (Leinster Road)	47 A1 [2]
Leinster Street	17 C3
Leinster Street East	72 E1
Leinster Street North	24 F4
Leinster Street South	75 C1
Leinster Terrace (off Nangor Road)	44 D1 [2]
Leitrim Place	76 E2
Leix Road	70 D1
Leixlip	33 B1
Leixlip Bridge	33 A1
Leixlip Gate	32 E1
Leixlip Park	32 F1
Leixlip Road	33 B1
Lemon Street	75 B1
Lennox Place	75 A3
Lennox Street	75 B3
Lennox Terrace	75 B3
Lentisk Lawn	27 A1
Leo Avenue	71 B1
Leo Street	71 B1
Leonard's Court	74 F3
Leopardstown	58 F3
Leopardstown Abbey	58 F4
Leopardstown Avenue	58 F2
Leopardstown Court	58 F2 [1]
(off Brewery Road)	
Leopardstown Drive	58 F2
Leopardstown Gardens	58 F2
Leopardstown Grove	58 F2
Leopardstown Heights	58 E3

STREET NAME	PAGE/GRID REFERENCE
Leopardstown Lawn (off Leopardstown Drive)	58 F2 [2]
Leopardstown Oaks	58 F2
Leopardstown Park	58 F2
Leopardstown Rise	58 E3
Leopardstown Road (Leopardstown)	58 D3
Leopardstown Road (Stillorgan Road)	58 F2
Leopardstown Valley	58 F4
Leslie Avenue	60 F1
Leslie's Buildings	70 F1
Leukos Road (off Pine Road)	39 A3 [11]
Levmoss Estate	58 F3
*Liberty Court (Corporation Street)	71 C3
*Liberty Court (Clanbrassil Terrace)	74 F2
Liberty House	71 C2
Liberty Lane	75 B2
*Liberty Square (off Hanbury Lane)	74 F1
Library Road (Dún Laoghaire)	50 D4
Library Road (Shankill)	64 E2
Library Square	52 F2
Library View Villas	71 A1
Liffey Ave	34 F2
Liffey Close	34 F2
Liffey Court	34 F2
Liffey Crescent	34 F2
Liffey Dale	34 F2
Liffey Downs	34 F2
Liffey Drive	34 F2
Liffey Gardens	34 F2
Liffey Glen	34 F2
Liffey Green	34 F2
Liffey Grove	34 F2
Liffey Hall (off Liffey Crescent)	34 F2 [1]
Liffey Junction	24 E4
Liffey Lawn	34 F2
Liffey Park	34 F2
Liffey Place	34 F2
Liffey Road	34 F2
Liffey Row	34 F2
Liffey Street Lower	71 B4
Liffey Street South	36 F3
Liffey Street Upper	71 B3
Liffey Street West	70 E4
Liffey Terrace (off St. Laurence Road)	36 E2 [7]
Liffey Vale	34 F2
Liffey Valley Park	34 F2
Liffey View	34 F2
Liffey View Apartments	33 A1 [2]
Liffey Villas	34 F2
Liffey Walk	34 F2
Liffey Way	34 F2
Liffey Wood	34 F2
Lighthouse Apartments	72 F1
Lilys Way	21 A1
Lime Street	72 E4
Limekiln Avenue	45 B3
Limekiln Close	45 C3
Limekiln Drive	45 C3
Limekiln Green	45 B3
Limekiln Grove	45 C2
Limekiln Lane (Kimmage)	45 C2
Limekiln Lane (Harold's Cross)	74 F4
Limekiln Park	45 C2
Limekiln Road	45 C3
Limelawn Court	22 D2
Limelawn Glade	22 D2
Limelawn Green	22 D2
Limelawn Hill	22 D2
Limelawn Park	22 D2
Limelawn Wood	22 D2
Limes Road	58 D2
Limetree Avenue	4 D4
Limewood Avenue	26 F1
Limewood Park	26 F1
Limewood Road	27 A1
Lincoln Hall (Swords)	1 Inset
Lincoln House	70 F4
Lincoln Lane	70 F4
Lincoln Place	76 D1
Linden Court	48 F4
Linden Grove	48 F4
Linden Lea Park	58 F1
Linden Square	48 F4
Lindenvale (off Proby Square)	49 A4 [4]
Lindisfarne Avenue	43 C1
Lindisfarne Drive	43 C1
Lindisfarne Green	43 C1
Lindisfarne Grove	43 C1
Lindisfarne Lawns	43 C1
Lindisfarne Park	34 F4
Lindisfarne Vale	43 C1
Lindisfarne Walk	43 C1
Lindsay Grove (off Prospect Road)	25 A4 [15]
Lindsay Road	25 A4
Linenhall Parade	71 A3
Linenhall Street (off King Street North)	71 A3
Linenhall Terrace	71 A3
Link Road (off Monkstown Crescent)	49 C4
Link Road (Glasthule)	60 E1
Linnbhlá	12 D4
Linnetfields	21 A1
Linnetfields Avenue	8 E4
Linnetfields Close	8 E4
Linnetfields Court	21 A1
Linnetfields Drive	8 E4
Linnetfields Park	21 A1
Linnetfields Rise	8 E4
Linnetfields Square	8 E4
Linnetfields View	8 D4
Linnetfields Walk	21 A1
Lios na Sidhe	54 F2
Lioscian	1 B1
Lisalea (off Frascati Park Blackrock)	49 A3 [22]
Lisburn Street	71 A3
Liscannor Road	24 E4
Liscanor (off Harbour Road)	60 F1 [9]
Liscarne Court	35 A3
Liscarne Dale (off Collinstown Road)	35 A3 [2]
Liscarne Gardens	35 A3
Lisle Road	46 D1
Lismeen Grove (off Beechpark Avenue)	26 E1 [1]
Lismore	18 E4
Lismore Road	46 E1
Lissadel Avenue	73 B4
Lissadel Court	73 A4
Lissadel Crescent	2 F2
Lissadel Drive	73 A4
Lissadel Green	73 A3
Lissadel Grove	2 F2
Lissadel Park	2 F2
Lissadel Road	73 A4
Lissadel Wood	2 F2
Lissane Apartments	22 E1
Lissen Hall	2 E1
Lissen Hall Drive	2 E1
Lissenfield	75 B4
Lissenhall Avenue	2 D1
Lissenhall Bridge	2 E1
Lissenhall Court	2 D1
Lissenhall Drive	2 D1
Lissenhall Park	2 D1
Little Britain Street	71 A3
Little Fitzwilliam Place	76 D2
Little Meadow (off Pottery Road)	59 C3 [1]
Little Orchard (off Pottery Road)	59 C3 [5]
Littlepace	8 E4
Littlepace Close	8 E4
Littlepace Court	8 E4
Littlepace Crescent	8 E4
Littlepace Drive	8 E4
Littlepace Gallops	8 E4
Littlepace Meadow	8 E4
Littlepace Park	8 E4
Littlepace Road	8 E4
Littlepace View	8 E4
Littlepace Walk	8 E4
Littlepace Way	8 E4
Littlepace Woods	8 E4
Littlewood	58 D4
Litton Lane	71 B4
Llewellyn Close	57 A1
Llewellyn Court	57 A1
Llewellyn Grove	57 A1
Llewellyn Lawn	57 A1
Llewellyn Park	57 A1
Llewellyn Way	57 A1
Llex House	76 D3
Lock Road	34 D3
Lockkeeper's Walk	24 D3
Loftus Hall (off Belgard Square West)	54 F1 [9]
Loftus Lane	71 A3
Loftus Square (off Main Street Rathfarnham)	46 F4 [14]
Lohunda Close	22 D2
Lohunda Court	22 D2
Lohunda Crescent	21 C2
Lohunda Dale	22 D2
Lohunda Downs	22 D2
Lohunda Drive	22 D2
Lohunda Grove	22 D2
Lohunda Park	21 C2
Lohunda Road	22 D2
Lombard Court (Lombard Street East)	72 D4
Lombard Court (Clanbrassil Street)	74 F3
Lombard Street East	72 D4
Lombard Street West	75 A3
Lomond Avenue	25 C4
Londonbridge Drive (off Londonbridge Road)	39 A3 [20]
Londonbridge Road	39 A3
*Long Lane (off Mountjoy Street)	71 A2
Long Lane (New Bride Street)	75 A2
Long Lane Close (off Long Lane)	75 A2
Long Meadow Apartments	69 C4
Long Mile Road	45 B1
Longdale Terrace	25 A1
Longdale Way	25 A1
Longford Lane	75 B1
Longford Place	49 C4
Longford Street Great	75 A1
Longford Street Little	75 B1
Longford Terrace	49 C4
Longlands	2 D2
Longmeadow	59 C3
Longmeadow Grove	59 C3
Long's Place	74 E1
Longwood Avenue	75 A3
Longwood Park	46 F4
Looceville Court (off St Agnes Road Crumlin)	46 D1 [7]
Lorcan Avenue	25 C1
Lorcan Crescent	25 C1
Lorcan Drive	25 B1
Lorcan Green	25 C1
Lorcan Grove	25 C1
Lorcan O'Toole Court (off Lorcan O'Toole Park)	46 D2 [2]
Lorcan O'Toole Park	46 D2
Lorcan Park	25 C1
Lorcan Road	25 B1
Lorcan Villas	25 C1
Lord Edward Court	75 A1
Lord Edward Street	75 A1
Lordello Road	64 D3
Lords Walk	69 B2
Loreto Abbey	47 A4
Loreto Avenue (Nutgrove Avenue)	47 A4
Loreto Avenue (Dalkey)	60 F1
Loreto Court	47 A4
Loreto Crescent	47 A4
Loreto Grange	67 C3
Loreto Park	47 A4
Loreto Road	74 E2
Loreto Row	47 A4
Loreto Terrace	46 F4
Loretto Avenue	67 C2 [34]
Loretto Terrace	67 C2 [35]
Loretto Villas	67 C2 [54]
Lorne Terrace (off Almeida Avenue)	73 C2
Losset Hall (off Belgard Square West)	54 F1 [6]
Lotts	71 B4
Lough Conn Avenue	36 D2
Lough Conn Drive	36 D2
Lough Conn Road	36 D2
Lough Conn Terrace	36 D2
Lough Derg Road	27 A2
Lough na Mona	19 C4
Loughlinstown	64 D1
Loughlinstown Drive	64 D1
Loughlinstown Park	64 D1
Loughlinstown Wood	64 D1
Loughmorne House (off Terenure Road West)	46 F2 [27]
Loughoreen Hills	30 D3
Loughsallagh Bridge	7 C3
Loughtown Lower	41 C1
Loughtown Upper	42 D1
Louis Lane (off Leinster Road)	47 A1 [23]
Louisa Vally	19 C4
Lourdes House	71 C2
Lourdes Road	74 D2
Louvain	48 D3
Louvain Glade	48 D3
Lower Lucan Road (Lucan)	34 D1
Lower Road (Strawberry Beds)	35 B1
Lower Road (Shankill)	64 E3
Luby Road	73 B1
Lucan	34 D2
Lucan Bridge	34 D1
Lucan Bypass	34 D2
Lucan Heights	34 E1
Lucan Newlands Road (Esker)	34 D2
Lucan Newlands Road (Ronanstown)	35 A4
Lucan Road (Lucan)	34 D1
Lucan Road (Palmerstown)	35 C1
Lucan Road (near Qaurryvale)	35 A1
Lucan Road (Chapelizod)	36 D2
Lucan-Newlands Road	34 F3
Ludford Drive	57 B1
Ludford Park	57 B1
Ludford Road	57 B2
Lugg	52 F4
Lugmore	54 D3
Lugmore Lane	53 C3
Lugnaquilla Avenue	45 B3
Luke Street	71 C4
Lullymore Terrace	74 E3
Lurgan Street	71 A3
Lutterell Hall	7 A2
Luttrell Park	22 D3
Luttrell Park Close	22 D3
Luttrell Park Court	22 D3
Luttrell Park Crescent	22 E3
Luttrell Park Drive	22 E3
Luttrell Park Green	22 E3
Luttrell Park Grove	22 D3
Luttrell Park Heath (off Carpenterstown Road)	22 E3 [2]
Luttrell Park Lawn	22 D3
Luttrell Park View	22 D3
Luttrellstown Avenue	22 E4
Luttrellstown Chase	22 D4
Luttrellstown Close	22 E4
Luttrellstown Court	22 D4
Luttrellstown Dale	22 D4
Luttrellstown Drive	22 D4
Luttrellstown Glade	22 D4
Luttrellstown Green	22 D4
Luttrellstown Grove	22 D4
Luttrellstown Heath	22 D4
Luttrellstown Heights	22 D4
Luttrellstown Lawn	22 D4
Luttrellstown Oaks	22 D4
Luttrellstown Park	22 D4
Luttrellstown Place	22 D4
Luttrellstown Rise	22 D3
Luttrellstown Thicket	22 D4
Luttrellstown View	22 E4
Luttrellstown Walk	22 D4
Luttrellstown Way	22 D4
Luttrellstown Wood	22 E4
Lymewood Mews	12 E4
Lynches Lane	34 E4
Lynch's Lane (off Ballyfermot Road)	36 E3 [2]
Lynch's Place	71 A1
Lyndon Gate (off Blackhorse Avenue)	24 D4 [4]
Lynton Court (off Sandymount Avenue)	39 A4 [12]
Lynwood	57 C1
Lyons	41 A4
Lyons Avenue	42 D4
*Lyons Avenue North (off Newcastle Boulevard)	42 D4
*Lyons Avenue South (off Newcastle Boulevard)	42 D4
*Lyons Lane (off Newcastle Boulevard)	42 D4
Lyons Road	41 B4
*Lyons Street (off Newcastle Boulevard)	42 D4
*Lyre House (off Thomas Davis Street West)	36 F3
Lyreen Court	17 C3
Lyreen Park	18 D2

M

STREET NAME	PAGE/GRID REFERENCE
M1 Junction 1 (M50/M1)	13 A3
M1 Junction 2 (Dublin Airport)	13 A1
M1 Junction 3 (Swords)	2 E3
M4 Junction 5 (Leixlip)	33 B1
M4 Junction 6 (Celbridge)	32 D1
M4 Junction 7 (Maynooth)	17 C1
M50 Junction 1 (Dublin Port)	39 A1

STREET NAME	PAGE/GRID REFERENCE
M50 Junction 10 (Ballymount)	45 A3
M50 Junction 11 (N81 Tallagh)	45 C4
M50 Junction 12 (Firhouse)	55 C2
M50 Junction 13 (Dundrum)	57 C3
M50 Junction 14	58 E3
(N31 Dun Laoghaire)	
M50 Junction 15 (Carrickmines)	59 A4
M50 Junction 16 (Cherrywood)	63 C2
M50 Junction 17 (M50/M11)	64 D3
M50 Junction 2 (Santry)	12 C1
M50 Junction 3 (M1/M50)	12 F3
M50 Junction 4 (Ballymun)	12 D3
M50 Junction 5 (N2/M50 Finglas)	11 A4
M50 Junction 6	22 F2
(N3/M50 Blanchardstown)	
M50 Junction 7 (N4/M50)	35 B1
M50 Junction 9 (N7/M50 Red Cow)	44 F1
Ma Tuire Apartments	48 D4
Mabbot House	71 C3
Mabbot Lane	71 C3
Mabel Street	25 B4
Mac Mahon Bridge (Grand Canal)	76 E1
*Mac Ulliam Avenue (Mac Ulliam)	53 C1
*Mac Ulliam Close (Mac Ulliam)	53 C1
*Mac Ulliam Court (Mac Ulliam)	53 C1
*Mac Ulliam Crescent (Mac Ulliam)	53 C1
*Mac Ulliam Dale (Mac Ulliam)	53 C1
*Mac Ulliam Drive (Mac Ulliam)	53 C1
*Mac Ulliam Gardens (Mac Ulliam)	53 C1
*Mac Ulliam Green (Mac Ulliam)	53 C1
*Mac Ulliam Lane (Mac Ulliam)	53 C1
*Mac Ulliam Lawns (Mac Ulliam)	53 C1
*Mac Ulliam Mews (Mac Ulliam)	53 C1
*Mac Ulliam Parade (Mac Ulliam)	53 C1
*Mac Ulliam Road (Mac Ulliam)	53 C1
*Mac Ulliam Walk (Mac Ulliam)	53 C1
*Mac Ulliam Way (Mac Ulliam)	53 C1
Macken Street	76 E1
Macken Villa	76 E1
Mackies Place	75 C2
Mackintosh Park	59 C2
Macroom Avenue	13 B4
Macroom Road	13 B4
Madden Road	74 F2
*Madden's Court (off Thomas Street)	74 E2
Madden's Lane	60 E4
Madison Road	73 C2
Magdalen Terrace	39 A3 [39]
(off Oliver Plunkett Avenue)	
Magennis Place	72 D4
Magennis Square	72 D4
Magenta Crescent	25 B1
Magenta Hall	25 B1
Magenta Place (off Eden Road Upper)	60 D1 [8]
Magna Avenue	53 C2
Magna Drive	53 C2
*Maher's Terrace	47 C4
(on Main Street Dundrum)	
Maidens Row	36 E2 [2]
(off Martin's Row Chapelizod)	
Main Road (Tallaght)	55 A1
Main Street (Swords)	2 D2
Main Street (Malahide)	3 B2
Main Street (Dunboyne)	7 B2
Main Street (Clongriffin)	14 E4
Main Street (Baldoyle)	15 A4
Main Street (Maynooth)	17 C3
Main Street (Blanchardstown)	22 E2
Main Street (Finglas)	24 E2
Main Street (Raheny)	27 A2
Main Street (Howth)	30 D3
Main Street (Celbridge)	32 D3
Main Street (Leixlip)	33 A1
Main Street (Lucan)	34 D1
Main Street (Newcastle)	42 D4
Main Street (Clondalkin)	44 E1
Main Street (Rathfarnham)	46 F4
Main Street (Dundrum)	47 C4
Main Street (Blackrock)	49 A3
Main Street (Rathcoole)	52 F2
Main Street (Tallaght)	55 A1
Main Street (Bray)	67 C2
Maitland Street	67 B2
Malachi Place	72 E2
Malachi Road	70 E3
Malahide	3 B2
Malahide Demesne	3 A3
Malahide Road (Swords)	2 E1
Malahide Road (Darndale)	13 C4
Malahide Road (Balgriffin)	14 D3
Malahide Road (Marino)	26 D4
Malahide Road (Artane)	26 E2
Malahide Road (Coolock)	26 F1
Malahide Roundabout (Swords)	2 D2
Mallin Avenue	74 D2
Malone Gardens	76 F2
Malpas Court	75 A2
Malpas Place (off Malpas Street)	75 A2
Malpas Street (off New Street)	75 A2
Malpas Terrace	75 A2
Manders Terrace	75 C4
Mander's Terrace	75 C4
Mangerton Road	36 F4
Mannix Road	25 A4
Manor Avenue	46 E3
Manor Close	57 A2
Manor Court	17 C3
Manor Crescent	21 B1
Manor Drive	14 D4
Manor Green	57 A2
Manor Grove	46 D2
*Manor Hall	73 C1
(Adjacent Cromwells Quarter)	
*Manor Hall Apartments	74 D1
(Mount Brown)	
Manor Heath	57 A1
Manor Mews (off Norseman Place)	70 E3
Manor Park (Palmerston)	35 C2
Manor Park (Ballinteer)	57 A2
Manor Place (Clonsilla)	21 A1
Manor Place (Stoneybatter)	70 E3
Manor Rise	57 A2
Manor Road	35 C2
Manor Square	21 A1
Manor Street	70 E3
Manor Villas	46 F1 [4]
(off Mount Argus Grove)	
Manorfields	21 B1
Mantua Park	2 D1
Maolbuille Road	25 A2
Mapas Avenue	60 E2
Mapas Road	60 E2
Maple Avenue (Carpenterstown)	22 E3
*Maple Avenue (off Blackthorn Drive)	58 D2
Maple Close	22 E3
Maple Drive (Dunboyne)	7 B2
Maple Drive (Carpenterstown)	22 E3
Maple Drive (off The Cloisters)	46 F2 [6]
Maple Glen	22 E3
Maple Green	22 E3
Maple Grove (Carpenterstown)	22 E3
Maple Grove (Rathcoole)	52 F2
Maple Grove (Bray)	67 B2
Maple House	76 D3
Maple Lawn	22 E3
Maple Lodge	23 A4
Maple Manor	59 C3
Maple Road	47 C2
Maples Road	58 D2
Maplewood Avenue	54 E1
Maplewood Close	54 E1
Maplewood Court	54 E1
Maplewood Drive	54 E1
Maplewood Green	54 E1
Maplewood Lawn	54 E1
Maplewood Park	54 E1
Maplewood Road	54 E1
Maplewood Way	54 E1
Maquay Bridge (Grand Canal)	76 E2
Maretimo Gardens East	49 A3
Maretimo Gardens West	49 A3 [4]
(off Newtown Avenue Blackrock)	
Maretimo Place	49 A3 [17]
(off Newtown Avenue Blackrock)	
Maretimo Road	49 A3 [2]
(off Newtown Avenue Blackrock)	
Maretimo Terrace	49 A3 [16]
(off Newtown Avenue Blackrock)	
Maretimo Villas	49 A3 [18]
(off Temple Road)	
Marewood Crescent	24 F1
Marewood Drive	11 C4
Marewood Grove	24 F1
Margaret Place	76 F2
Marguerite Road	25 A4
Marian Court	14 F4
Marian Crescent	46 E4
Marian Drive	46 E4
Marian Grove	46 E4
Marian Park (Baldoyle)	27 C1
Marian Park (Templeogue)	46 E4
Marian Park (Blackrock)	59 A1
Marian Road	46 E4
Marianella	47 A2
Mariavilla	17 C2
Marie Villas	67 C2 [55]
Marigold Avenue	13 C4
Marigold Court	13 C4
Marigold Crescent	13 C4
Marigold Drive	13 C4
Marigold Grove	13 C4
Marigold Park	13 C4
Marina House Apartments	49 C4 [32]
(off Clarence Street Dún Laoghaire)	
Marina Village	3 B2
Marine Avenue	60 E1
Marine Court (off Crofton Road)	50 D4 [17]
Marine Court (Dalkey)	60 E1
Marine Cove (off Baldoyle Road)	28 D1 [4]
Marine Drive	39 A4
Marine Parade	60 E1
Marine Road	50 D4
Marine Terrace	50 D4 [9]
(off Park Road Dún Laoghaire)	
Marine Terrace (Bray)	68 D2 [17]
Marine View	48 F3
Marine Villas (off Harbour Road)	30 D1 [7]
Mariners Court (off Kilbarrack Road)	27 C2 [1]
Mariners Cove	30 E2
Mariner's Port	72 E3
Marino	25 C4
Marino Avenue	26 D4
Marino Avenue East	60 E4
Marino Avenue West	60 E4
Marino Court	25 C4 [13]
(off Fairview Avenue Lower)	
Marino Crescent	25 C4
Marino Green	25 C4
Marino Mart (off Haverty Road)	25 C4 [9]
Marino Park	25 C4
Marino Park Avenue	25 C4
Marino Villa (off Casino Park)	26 D3 [3]
Marion Villas	74 E2
Mark Street	72 D4
Market House	67 C2
Market Square (Bray)	67 C2 [49]
Market Square (Smithfield)	70 F3
Market Square Apartments	71 A3
Market Street South	74 E1
Mark's Alley West	74 F1
Mark's Lane	72 D4
Marlay View	57 B2
Marlborough Court (off Sharavogue)	60 E2 [8]
Marlborough Court	70 D2
(Blackhorse Avenue)	
Marlborough Court	71 C3
(Marlborough Street)	
Marlborough Lane	47 B1 [25]
(off Marlborough Road)	
Marlborough Mews	70 D2
Marlborough Park	60 D1 [9]
(off Adelaide Road)	
Marlborough Place	71 C3
Marlborough Road (Donnybrook)	47 B1
Marlborough Road (Glenageary)	60 E1
Marlborough Road (Nth Circular Rd)	70 D2
Marlborough Street	71 C3
Marlborough Terrace	68 D2 [16]
Marley Avenue	57 A1
Marley Close	57 A1
Marley Court North	57 A1
Marley Court South	57 A1
Marley Drive	57 A1
Marley Grove	57 A1
Marley Lawn	57 A1
Marley Rise	57 A1
Marley Villas	57 A1 [1]
(off Marley Walk)	
Marley Walk	57 A1
Marlfield	59 C3
Marlfield Close	54 F3
Marlfield Court	54 F3
Marlfield Crescent	54 F3
Marlfield Green	54 F3
Marlfield Grove	54 F3
Marlfield Lawn	54 F3
Marlfield Mall	54 F3
Marlfield Place	54 F3
Marmion Court Flats	70 F3
Marne Villas	70 F2
Marrowbone Lane	74 E2
Marrowbone Lane Close	74 E1
(off Marrowbone Lane)	
Marrowbone Lane Flats	74 E1
Marshal Court Apartments	74 E1
Marshal's Lane	74 E1
*Marshalsea Court	70 E4
(off Bridgefoot Street)	70 F4
Marshalsea Court (Merchants Quay)	
*Marshalsea Lane	70 E4
(off Bridgefoot Street)	
Marsham Court	58 E1
Mart Lane	59 B3
Martello Avenue	50 D4 [14]
(off Summerhill Road)	
Martello Court	4 D4
Martello Mews	48 E1
Martello Terrace	29 B3 [2]
(off Shielmartin Road)	
Martello Terrace	48 F3 [1]
(off Seafort Parade Booterstown)	
Martello Terrace (off Windsor	50 E4 [2]
Terrace Dún Laoghaire)	
Martello Terrace (Bray)	67 C1 [1]
Martello View (off Strand Road)	39 B4 [1]
Martello Wood (off Strand Road)	39 B4 [6]
Martin Grove	24 D4
Martin Savage Park	23 C3
Martin Street	75 A3
Martin White Chalets	39 A4 [9]
(off Herbert Road)	
Martin's Row	36 E2
*Martin's Terrace	72 D4
(off Hanover Street East)	
Mary Street	71 A3
Mary Street Little	71 A4
Maryfield Avenue (off Ardlea Road)	26 E2 [1]
Maryfield Crescent	26 E2
Maryfield Drive	26 D2
Maryland	64 E2 [5]
Marymount	12 F2
Mary's Abbey	71 A4
Mary's Lane	71 A4
Maryville Road	26 F3
Mask Avenue	26 E2
Mask Crescent	26 E2
Mask Drive	26 E2
Mask Green	26 E2
Mask Road	26 E2
Mather Road North	48 E3
Mather Road South	48 D3
Matt Talbot Court	71 C2
Maunsell Place	71 A2
Maxwell Court (off Maxwell Road)	47 A1 [18]
Maxwell Lane	47 A2
Maxwell Road	47 A1
Maxwell Street	74 E2
May Lane	70 F4
May Park	26 D3
*May Street (off Fitzroy Avenue)	25 B4
Mayberry Park	45 A4
Mayberry Road	44 F4
Mayeston Boulevard	11 B3
Mayeston Close	11 B3
Mayeston Court	11 B4
Mayeston Crescent	11 B4
Mayeston Downs	11 C4
Mayeston Drive	11 B3
Mayeston Lawn	11 B3
Mayeston Rise	11 B4
Mayeston Square	11 B4
Mayeston Walk	11 C4
Mayfair	3 C2
Mayfield	47 A2
Mayfield Park	35 B4
Mayfield Road (Terenure)	46 F2
Mayfield Road (Kilmainham)	73 C2
Mayfield Terrace (Ballinteer)	57 C2
Mayfield Terrace (Bray)	67 C3 [17]
Mayne Bridge	14 F3
Maynetown	14 F3
Maynooth	18 D2
Maynooth Park	18 D4
Maynooth Road (Dunboyne)	7 A3
Maynooth Road (Celbridge)	31 C1
Mayola Court	47 B4
Mayor Square	72 E3
Mayor Street Lower	72 D3
Mayor Street Upper	72 F3
Mayville Terrace (off Leslie Avenue)	60 F1 [11]
Maywood Avenue	27 B2
Maywood Close	27 B2
Maywood Crescent	27 B3
Maywood Drive	27 B2
Maywood Grove	27 B2
Maywood Lawn	27 B3
Maywood Park	27 B2
Maywood Road	27 B2

STREET NAME	PAGE/GRID REFERENCE		STREET NAME	PAGE/GRID REFERENCE		STREET NAME	PAGE/GRID REFERENCE		STREET NAME	PAGE/GRID REFERENCE	
Mc Cartney Bridge (Grand Canal)	76	D3	Melrose Park (Swords)	2	E3	Milesian Grove	2	E2	*Minstrel Court	58	F2
Mc Kenny Bridge (Grand Canal)	76	E2	Melrose Park (Clondalkin)	43	C1	Milesian Lawn	2	E2	(Charles Sheil's Houses)		
McAuley Avenue	26	F2	Melrose Park The Avenue	2	E3	Milestown	19	C1	Misery Hill	72	E4
McAuley Drive	26	F2	Melrose Park The Close	2	E3	Milford	3	A2	Mitchelstown	10	D2
McAuley Park	26	F2	Melrose Park The Crescent	2	E3	Military Road (Phoenix Park)	36	F2	Moat Lane	1	A2
McAuley Road	26	F2	Melrose Park The Drive	2	E3	Military Road (Killiney)	60	E4	Moatfield Avenue	26	F1
McCabe Villas	48	E3	Melrose Park The Green	2	E3	Military Road (Kilmainham)	73	C1	Moatfield Park	26	F1
McCarthy Terrace (on James Walk)	74	D2	Melrose Park The Grove	2	E3	Military Road (Rathmines)	75	B4	Moatfield Road	26	F1
McCreadies Lane	3	A3	Melrose Park The Heights	2	E3	Mill Bank (off Lower Lucan Road)	34	D1 [15]	Moatview Avenue	13	B4
McDowell Avenue	74	D1	Melrose Park The Lawn	2	E3	Mill Bridge (Swords)	2	D2	Moatview Court	13	B4
McGrane Court (off Sandyford Road)	57	C1 [5]	Melrose Park The Park	2	E3	Mill Brook Apartments	35	C1	Moatview Drive	13	B4
McKee Avenue	24	E1	Melrose Park The Rise	2	E3	Mill Court Avenue	43	C1	Moatview Gardens	13	B4
McKee Park	69	C1	Melrose Park The Villa	2	E3	Mill Court Drive	43	C1	Moatview Terrace	13	B4 [5]
McKee Road	24	E1	Melrose Park The Walk	2	E3	Mill Field (Enniskerry)	66	E3	(off Moatview Avenue)		
McKelvey Avenue	11	A4	Melrose Road	34	F4	Mill House	62	F3	Mobhi Court	25	A3 [16]
McKelvey Road	11	A4	Melville Close	11	B4	Mill Lane (off Ashtown Road)	23	B3 [1]	(off St. Mobhi Boithirin)		
McMahon Street	75	A3	Melville Court	11	B4	Mill Lane (Leixlip)	33	A1	Mobhi Road	25	A3
McMorrough Road	46	F2 [14]	Melville Cove	11	B4	Mill Lane (Palmerstown)	35	C1	Moeran Road	45	C1
(off Terenure Road North)			Melville Crescent	11	B4	Mill Lane (Loughlinstown)	64	E2	Moira Road (off Oxmanstown Road)	70	D3
Meade's Terrace	76	D1	Melville Drive	11	B4	Mill Lane (Newmarket)	74	F2	Moland House	71	C3
Meadow Avenue (off Meadow Grove)	57	B1 [1]	Melville Green	11	B4	Mill Park	44	D1	Moland Place	71	C3
Meadow Close (Dundrum)	57	A1	Melville Grove	11	B4	Mill Road (Blanchardstown)	22	F2	Molesworth Close	1	A2
Meadow Close (Newtown Park Ave)	59	A1	Melville Lawn	11	B4	Mill Road (Saggart)	53	A2	Molesworth Place	75	C1
Meadow Copse	21	C1	Melville Park	11	B4	Mill Street (off Cross Avenue	50	D4 [19]	Molesworth Street	75	C1
Meadow Court (off Wyattville Road)	60	D4 [2]	Melville Rise	11	B4	Dún Laoghaire)			Mollison Avenue	14	D4
Meadow Dale (off Meadow Green)	21	C1 [1]	Melville Square	11	B4	Mill Street (The Coombe)	74	F2	Molyneux Yard	74	F1
Meadow Downs	21	C1	Melville Terrace	11	B4	Millar's Hall (Bridgefoot Street)	74	F1	Monalea Grove	55	C1
Meadow Drive	21	C1	Melville View	11	B4	Millar's Hall (Cork Street)	74	E2	Monalea Park	55	C1
Meadow Green	21	C1	Melville Way	11	B4	Millbank	14	F2	Monalea Wood	55	C1
Meadow Grove	57	A1	Melvin Road	46	F2	Millbourne Avenue	25	A4	Monaloe Avenue	59	C3
Meadow Mount	57	A1	Memorial Court	69	B4	Millbrook Avenue	27	A1	Monaloe Court	59	B3 [6]
Meadow Park	57	A1	Memorial Road	71	C3	Millbrook Court	73	C1	(off Clonkeen Road)		
Meadow Park Avenue	47	A4	(Custom House Quay)			Millbrook Drive	27	A1	Monaloe Crescent	59	B3 [4]
Meadow Vale	59	B2	Memorial Road (Inchicore Road)	73	A1	Millbrook Grove	27	A1	(off Clonkeen Road)		
Meadow View (Dunboyne)	7	B2	Mercer House	75	B2	Millbrook Lawns	55	A1	Monaloe Drive	59	C3
Meadow View (Nutgrove Avenue)	57	A1	Mercer Street Lower	75	B1	Millbrook Road	27	A1	Monaloe Park	59	C3
Meadow Villas (off Meadow Grove)	57	A1 [2]	Mercer Street Upper	75	B2	Millbrook Terrace	73	B1	Monaloe Park Road	59	C3
Meadow Way	21	C1	Merchamp	26	F4	Millbrook Village	47	C1 [17]	Monaloe Way	59	C3
Meadowbank	46	F3	Merchants Arch (off Temple Bar)	71	B4	(off Milltown Road)			Monasterboice Road	46	D1
Meadowbrook	17	C4	Merchant's Court	70	F4	Millennium Bridge (River Liffey)	71	B4	Monastery	66	E3
Meadowbrook Avenue (Maynooth)	17	C4	*Merchant's Hall (Merchants Quay)	70	F4	Millers Wood	67	B3	Monastery Crescent	44	E1
Meadowbrook Avenue (Sutton)	28	D1	Merchant's House	70	F4	Millfarm	7	C2	Monastery Drive	44	E1
Meadowbrook Close	17	C4	Merchant's Quay	70	F4	Millfield (Portmarnock)	14	F2	Monastery Gate	44	F1
Meadowbrook Court	17	C4	Merchant's Road	39	A1	Millgate Drive	45	C3	Monastery Gate Avenue	44	F1
Meadowbrook Crescent	17	C4	Merchant's Square	72	F3	Millmount Avenue	25	A4	Monastery Gate Close	44	F1
Meadowbrook Drive	17	C4	Meretimo Villas	68	D3 [2]	Millmount Grove	47	B3	Monastery Gate Copse	44	F1
Meadowbrook Lawn	28	D1	Merlyn Drive	48	D1	Millmount Place	25	B4	Monastery Gate Green	44	F1
Meadowbrook Lawns	17	C4	Merlyn Park	48	D1	*Millmount Terrace (Drumcondra)	25	B4	Monastery Gate Lawn	44	F1
Meadowbrook Park	28	D1	Merlyn Road	48	D1	Millmount Villas	25	A4 [1]	Monastery Gate Villas	44	F1
Meadowbrook Road	17	C4	Merrion	48	E1	(off Millmount Avenue)			Monastery Grove	66	E2
Meadowfield	58	E4	Merrion Close	76	D1	Millrace Avenue	53	A2	Monastery Heath	44	E1
Meadowlands	59	C1	Merrion Court (Ailesbury Road)	48	E1 [1]	Millrace Court	53	A2	Monastery Heath Avenue	44	E1
Meadowlands Avenue	59	C1	Merrion Crescent	48	E2 [3]	Millrace Crescent	53	A2	Monastery Heath Court	44	E1
Meadowlands Court	59	C1 [17]	(off Trimleston Road)			Millrace Green	53	A2	Monastery Heath Green	44	E1
(off Meadowlands Avenue)			Merrion Gates (off Strand Road)	48	E1 [2]	Millrace Park	53	A2	Monastery Heath Square	44	E1
Meadowlands Mews	59	C1 [18]	Merrion Grove	48	E3	Millrace Road	23	B3	Monastery Heights	44	E1 [2]
(off Meadowlands Avenue)			Merrion Hall	48	E4	Millrace Walk	53	A2	(off Monastery Road)		
Meadowview Grove	33	C2	Merrion Park	48	E3	Millrose Estate (off Canal Terrace)	36	E4 [2]	Monastery Park	44	E1
Meakstown Cottages	11	B3	Merrion Place	75	C2	Millstead	22	F2	Monastery Rise	44	E1
Meath Market	74	F1	Merrion Road	39	A4	Millstream	14	F2	Monastery Road	44	E1
Meath Place (Bray)	67	C2	Merrion Row	75	C2	Millstream Road	33	C2	Monastery Walk	44	E1
Meath Place (Meath Street)	74	F1	Merrion Square East	76	D2	Milltown (Peamount)	42	F2	Monck Place	70	F1
Meath Road	68	D2	Merrion Square North	76	D1	Milltown (Clonskeagh)	47	C2	Monks Hill	66	E2
Meath Square	74	F1	Merrion Square South	76	D2	Milltown Avenue	47	B2	Monks Meadow	4	D4
Meath Street	74	F1	Merrion Square West	76	D1	Milltown Bridge Road	47	C2	Monksfield	44	F1
*Meath Terrace (on Meath Place)	74	F1	Merrion Strand	48	E1	*Milltown Collonade	47	B2	Monksfield Court	44	F1
*Meathville Terrace (on Long Lane)	75	A2	Merrion Street Lower	76	D1	(on Milltown Road)			Monksfield Downs	44	F1
Meenan Square (off Owenstown	48	D3 [5]	Merrion Street Upper	75	C2	Milltown Drive	47	A3	Monksfield Grove	44	F1
Park Fosters Avenue)			Merrion View Avenue	48	D1 [1]	Milltown Grove	47	B2 [6]	Monksfield Heights	44	F1
Meetinghouse Lane	71	A4	(off Ailesbury Road)			(off Dundrum Road)			Monksfield Lawn	44	F1
Méile an Rí Crescent	34	F3	Merrion Village	48	E1	Milltown Grove (Churchtown)	47	A3	Monksfield Meadows	44	F1
Méile an Rí Drive	34	F3	Merry Bush (off Tritonville Avenue)	39	A4 [34]	Milltown Hill (off Milltown Road)	47	B2 [7]	Monksfield Walk	44	F1
Méile an Rí Green	34	F3	Merrycourt	8	E2	Milltown Park	47	B1	Monkstown	49	B4
Méile an Rí Park	34	F3	Merton Avenue	74	F3	Milltown Path	47	B2	Monkstown Avenue	59	B1
Méile an Rí Road	34	F3	*Merton Crescent	47	B2	Milltown Road	47	B2	Monkstown Crescent	49	C4
Méile an Rí View	34	F3	(off Milltown Avenue)			Milltown Terrace	47	B3 [4]	Monkstown Farm	59	C1
Mellifont Avenue	50	D4	Merton Drive	47	B1	(off Dundrum Road)			Monkstown Gate	49	C4 [29]
Mellowes Avenue	24	D1	Merton Park	74	F3	Millview (off Ninth Lock Road)	44	E1 [7]	(off The Hill Dún Laoghaire)		
Mellowes Court (off Mellowes Road)	24	D2 [3]	Merton Road	47	B2	Millview Close	3	A3	Monkstown Grove	59	C1
Mellowes Crescent	24	D2 [4]	Merton Walk	47	B2	Millview Cottages	73	A2	Monkstown Road	49	B4
(off Mellowes Road)			Merville Avenue (Fairview)	25	C4	Millview Court	3	A2	Monkstown Square	59	B1 [12]
Mellowes Park	24	D1	Merville Avenue (Stillorgan)	58	F1	Millview Lawns	3	A3	(off Monkstown Avenue)		
Mellowes Road	24	D1	Merville Road	58	F1	Millview Road	3	A3	Monkstown Valley	49	B4
Mellows Bridge (River Liffey)	70	F4	Mespil Estate	76	D3	Millwood Court	27	A1	Montague Court	75	B2
Melrose Avenue (Fairview)	25	C4	Mespil Lodge	76	D3	Millwood Park	27	A1	Montague Lane	75	B2
Melrose Avenue (Clondalkin)	43	C1	Mespil Road	76	D3	Millwood Villas	27	A1	Montague Place	75	B2
Melrose Court	25	C4 [16]	Metropolitan Apartments	73	A1	Milton Hall	1	C2	Montague Street	75	B2
(off Philipsburgh Avenue)			Michael Collins Park	35	A4	Milton Terrace (Swords)	2	D2	Monte Vella (off Barnhill Road)	60	D2 [9]
Melrose Crescent	43	C1	Middle Third	26	E3	Milton Terrace (Bray)	67	C2 [13]	Montebello Terrace	68	D2 [2]
Melrose Green	43	C1	Middle Third Terrace	26	E3	Milward Terrace	68	D2 [13]	Montini Road	27	C1
Melrose Grove	43	C1	Milesian Avenue	2	E2	Mine Hill Lane	63	B3	Montpelier Court	70	D3
Melrose Lawn	34	F4	Milesian Court	2	E2	Minnow Brook	46	F2	Montpelier Drive	70	D3

STREET NAME	PAGE/GRID REFERENCE
Montpelier Gardens	70 D3
Montpelier Hill	70 D3
Montpelier Manor	49 B4 [2]
(off Monkstown Road)	
*Montpelier Mews	70 D3
(Montpellier Hill)	
Montpelier Parade	49 B4
Montpelier Park	70 D3
Montpelier Place	49 B4 [1]
(off Monkstown Road)	
Montpelier Square	70 D3
Montpelier View	54 D2
Montpelier Walk	54 D2 [2]
(off Kiltalown Road)	
Montrose Avenue	26 D2
Montrose Close	26 D2
Montrose Court	26 D2
Montrose Crescent	26 D1
Montrose Drive	26 D1
Montrose Grove	26 D2
Montrose Park	26 D2
Moore Lane	71 B3
Moore Street	71 B3
Moorefield	60 E4
Moore's Cottages	59 A1 [3]
(off Annaville Avenue)	
Mooretown	1 B1
Mooretown Avenue	1 C1
Mooretown Grove	1 C1
Mooretown Park	1 C1
Moorfield	35 A4
Moorfield Avenue	35 A4
Moorfield Close	35 A4 [2]
(off Moorefield Drive)	
Moorfield Drive	35 A4
Moorfield Green	35 A4
Moorfield Grove	35 A4
Moorfield Lawns	35 A4
Moorfield Parade	35 A4
Moorfield Walk	35 A4
Moracrete Cottages	73 C4
Moran's Cottages	47 B1 [12]
(off Charleston Road)	
Moreen Avenue	58 D2
Moreen Close	58 D2
Moreen Lawn(off Moreen Avenue)	58 D2 [2]
Moreen Park	58 D2
Moreen Road	58 D2
Moreen Walk	58 D2
Morehampton Lane	76 E4
Morehampton Mews	76 E4
(off Sandymount Avenue)	
Morehampton Road	76 E4
Morehampton Square	76 E4
(off Serpentine Park)	
Morehampton Terrace	47 C1
Morgan Place	70 F4
Morgans Place	23 A3
Moritz House	55 B2
Morning Star Avenue	70 F3
Morning Star Road	74 D2
Mornington Avenue	50 E4 [1]
(off Sandycove Point)	
Mornington Grove	26 E2
Mornington Park	26 E2
Mornington Road	47 B1
Morrogh Terrace	25 C3 [2]
(off Philipsburgh Avenue)	
Morrow House	14 F4
Moss Street	71 C4
Mount Albany	59 A1
Mount Albion Road	57 B1 [3]
Mount Albion Road (Dundrum)	57 B1
Mount Alton	55 C1
Mount Alton Court	56 D1
Mount Andrew	34 F2
Mount Andrew Avenue	34 F2
Mount Andrew Close	34 F1
Mount Andrew Court	34 F1
Mount Andrew Crescent	34 F1
Mount Andrew Dale	34 F2
Mount Andrew Grove	34 F1
Mount Andrew Place	34 F1
Mount Andrew Rise	34 F1
Mount Anthony Estate	47 A1 [22]
(off Ardee Road)	
Mount Anville Lawn	48 D4
Mount Anville Park	48 D4
Mount Anville Road	48 D4
Mount Anville Wood	48 D4
Mount Argus Avenue	46 F1
Mount Argus Close	46 F1
Mount Argus Court	46 F1
Mount Argus Crescent	46 F1
Mount Argus Green	46 F1
Mount Argus Grove	46 F1
Mount Argus Park	46 F1
Mount Argus Road	46 F1
Mount Argus Square	46 F1 [15]
(Mount Argus Avenue)	
Mount Argus Terrace	46 F1
Mount Argus View	46 F1
Mount Argus Way	46 F1
Mount Auburn	60 E3 [2]
(off Killiney Hill Road)	
Mount Bellew Crescent	34 F2
Mount Bellew Green	34 F2
Mount Bellew Rise	34 E2
Mount Bellew Way	34 E2
Mount Brown	73 C1
Mount Carmel	71 A3
Mount Carmel Avenue	47 C4
Mount Carmel Park	55 C1
Mount Carmel Road	47 C4
Mount Dillon Court	26 E2
Mount Drinan Avenue	2 E3
Mount Drinan Crescent	2 E3
Mount Drinan Grove	2 E3
Mount Drinan Lawn	2 E3
Mount Drinan Park	2 E3
Mount Drinan Walk	2 E3
Mount Drummond Avenue	74 F4
Mount Drummond Court	74 F4
Mount Drummond Square	75 A4
Mount Eagle Court	58 E3
Mount Eagle Drive	58 E3
Mount Eagle Green	58 E3
Mount Eagle Grove	58 E3
Mount Eagle Lawn	58 E3
Mount Eagle Park	58 E3
Mount Eagle Rise	58 D3
Mount Eagle View	58 E3
Mount Eagle Way	58 E3
Mount Eden Road	47 C1
Mount Eustace	9 B2
Mount Eustace Avenue	9 B2
Mount Eustace Close	9 A2
Mount Eustace Drive	9 B2
Mount Eustace Green	9 B2
Mount Eustace Grove	9 A2
Mount Eustace Park	9 B2
Mount Eustace Rise	9 B2
Mount Eustace Walk	9 B2
Mount Gandon (off Lucan Road)	34 D1 [9]
Mount Garrett	9 B2
Mount Harold Terrace	46 F1 [1]
(off Leinster Road)	
Mount Hybla Court	23 A4
Mount Hybla House	23 A4
Mount Merrion	48 E4
Mount Merrion Avenue	48 F3
Mount Norris Villas	68 D2 [19]
Mount Olive Grove	27 B1
Mount Olive Park	27 B1
Mount Olive Road	27 B1
Mount Prospect Avenue	26 F4
Mount Prospect Drive	26 F4
Mount Prospect Grove	26 F4
Mount Prospect House	27 A4 [4]
(off Clontarf Road)	
Mount Prospect Lawn	26 F4
Mount Prospect Park	26 F4
Mount Salus Road	60 F2
Mount Sandford (off Milltown Road)	47 C1 [14]
Mount St. Annes	47 B2
Mount Street Crescent	76 E2
Mount Street Lower	76 D1
Mount Street Upper	76 D2
Mount Symon Avenue	21 C2
Mount Symon Close	21 C2
Mount Symon Crescent	21 B2
Mount Symon Dale	21 B2
Mount Symon Drive	21 C2
Mount Symon Estate	21 B2
Mount Symon Green	21 B2
Mount Symon Lawn	21 C2
Mount Symon Park	21 C2
Mount Symon Rise	21 B2
Mount Talbot	44 F1
Mount Tallant Avenue	46 F2
Mount Temple Road	70 F3
Mount Venus Road	56 D4
Mount View Road	22 D2
Mount Wood	59 C1
Mountain Park	55 A1
Mountain View (Jobstown)	54 D2
Mountain View (Shankill)	64 E3
Mountain View Apartments	67 C3 [11]
Mountain View Avenue	46 F1 [3]
(off Shamrock Villas)	
Mountain View Cottages	22 D4
(Castleknock)	
Mountain View Cottages	47 B1 [13]
(off Mountain View Road)	
Mountain View Court	46 F1 [16]
(off Shamrock Villas)	
Mountain View Court	71 C2
Mountain View Drive	57 A1
Mountain View Park (Churchtown)	47 A4
Mountain View Road (Ranelagh)	47 B1
Mountain View Road	60 E4 [5]
(off Church Road Ballybrack)	
Mountain Villa (off Dale View)	60 E4 [3]
Mountainview Drive	67 C4
Mountbrook (off Seamount)	48 E3 [2]
Mountdown Avenue	45 C3
Mountdown Drive	45 C3
Mountdown Park	45 C3
Mountdown Road	45 C3
Mountfield	3 B3
Mountgorry Wood Apartments	2 E2
Mountjoy Parade	71 C1
Mountjoy Place	71 C2
Mountjoy Square	71 C2
Mountjoy Square Apartments	71 B2
(Mountjoy Square West)	
Mountjoy Square Apartments	71 C2
(Mountjoy Square South)	
Mountjoy Square East	71 C2
Mountjoy Square North	71 C2
Mountjoy Square South	71 C2
Mountjoy Square West	71 B2
Mountjoy Street	71 A2
Mountjoy Street Middle	71 A2
Mountpleasant Avenue Lower	75 B4
Mountpleasant Avenue Upper	75 B4
Mountpleasant Parade	75 B4
Mountpleasant Place	75 C4
Mountpleasant Square	75 B4
Mountpleasant Terrace	75 B4
*Mountpleasant Terrace Upper	75 C4
(Mountpleasant Villas)	
*Mountpleasant Terrace Upper	75 C4
(off Mountpleasant Place)	
Mountpleasant Villas (Bray)	67 B2 [13]
Mountpleasant Villas	75 C4
Mountsandel	59 B4
Mountshannon Road	73 C2
Mounttown Cottages	49 C4 [26]
(off Mounttown Road)	
Mounttown Park	59 C1 [3]
(off Mounttown Lower)	
Mounttown Road Lower	59 C1
Mounttown Road Upper	49 C4
Mourne Road (Drimnagh)	36 F4
Mourne Road (Brickfields Park)	73 A3
Moy Elta Road	72 E2
Moy Glas Avenue	34 E3
Moy Glas Chase	34 E3
Moy Glas Close	34 E3
Moy Glas Court	34 E3
Moy Glas Dale	34 E3
Moy Glas Dene	34 E3
Moy Glas Drive	34 E3
Moy Glas Glen	34 E3
Moy Glas Green	34 E3
Moy Glas Grove	34 E3
Moy Glas Lawn	34 E3
Moy Glas Park	34 E3
Moy Glas Road	34 E3
Moy Glas Vale	34 E3
Moy Glas View	34 E3
Moy Glas Way	34 E3
Moy Glas Wood	34 E3
Moyclare Avenue	28 D1
Moyclare Close	28 D1
Moyclare Drive	28 D1
Moyclare Gardens	28 D1 [6]
(off Moyclare Road)	
Moyclare Park	28 D1
Moyclare Road	28 D1
Moycullen Road	35 C3
Moygaddy	18 D1
Moyglare	17 A1
Moyglare Abbey	17 B2
Moyglare Hall	17 C2
Moyglare Meadows	17 C2
Moyglare Road	17 C2
Moyglare Village	17 C2
Moyle Crescent	44 E1
Moyle Road	24 E3
Moyne	14 F3
Moyne Court (off Moyne Road)	47 B1 [22]
Moyne Park	14 F3
Moyne Road (Balgriffin)	14 E3
Moyne Road (Ranelagh)	47 B1
Moynihan Court	55 B1 [6]
(off Avonmore Road)	
Moyville	56 E2
Moyville Lawns	56 E1
Muckross Avenue	46 D2
Muckross Crescent	46 D2
Muckross Drive	46 D2 [1]
(off Muckross Avenue)	
Muckross Green	46 D2
Muckross Grove	46 D2
Muckross Parade	71 B1
Muckross Park	46 D2
Muirfield Drive	36 F4 [1]
(off Naas Road Bluebell)	
Mulally's Lane	52 F2
Mulberry Crescent	22 F4
Mulberry Drive	22 F4
Mulberry Park	22 F4
Muldowney Court	3 C3
Mulgrave Street	50 D4
Mulgrave Terrace	50 D4
Mulhuddart	9 A4
Mulhuddart Bridge	9 A4
Mulhuddart Wood	9 A4
Mullauns	42 D1
Mullen Bridge	18 D3
Mullinastill Road	64 D2
Mullingar Terrace	36 E2 [10]
(off Martin's Row Chapelizod)	
Mulroy Road	24 E4
Mulvey Park	47 C3
Munster Street	24 F4
Munster Terrace (off Breffni Road)	60 E1 [16]
Murphy's Lane	63 B4
Murphystown Road	58 E3
Murragh	14 F2
Murray's Cottages	36 F3 [4]
(off Sarsfield Road)	
Murtagh Road	70 E3
Muskerry Road	36 E3
Mutton Lane	56 E4
Myra Cottages	73 A1
Myra Manor	3 A4
Myrtle Avenue	60 D1 [3]
(off Royal Terrace East)	
Myrtle Grove (Stillorgan)	58 F1
Myrtle Grove (Bray)	67 B1 [3]
Myrtle Park	60 D1
Myrtle Square	14 F4
Myrtle Street	71 A2

N

STREET NAME	PAGE/GRID REFERENCE
N2 Junction 1 (M50/N2 Finglas)	11 A4
N2/M2 Junction 2 (Saint Margaret's)	10 D1
N4 Junction 1 (N4/M50)	35 B1
N4 Junction 2 (Liffey Valley)	35 A1
N4 Junction 3 (Lucan)	34 E1
N4 Junction 4 (Newcastle)	34 D2
N4 Junction 4a (Dodsboro)	33 C2
N7 Junction 1 (M50/N7 Red Cow)	44 F2
N7 Junction 1A (Newlands Cross)	44 E2
N7 Junction 2 (Kingswood)	43 C3
N7 Junction 3 (Citywest)	34 B4
N7 Junction 4 (Rathcoole)	52 F1
N7 Junction 5 (Athgoe)	51 B3
Naas Road (Kingswood)	43 C4
Naas Road (Walkinstown)	45 A1
Naas Road (Rathcoole)	52 F1
Naas Road (Saggart)	53 B1
Nagle Court	18 D2
Nangor Crescent	44 D1 [5]
(off Cherrywood Villas)	
Nangor Place	43 C1 [2]
(off Cherrywood Villas)	
Nangor Road (Grange Castle)	43 A2
Nangor Road (Clondalkin)	44 D1
Nangor Road (Fox and Geese)	44 F1
Nanikin Avenue	27 A3
Nash Street	36 F3
Nashville Park	30 E2
Nashville Road	30 D2

STREET NAME	PAGE/GRID REFERENCE
Nassau Street	75 C1
Naul Road (Brackenstown Road)	1 A3
Naul Road (Cloghran)	1 C4
Navan Road (Dunboyne)	7 B2
Navan Road (Clonee)	8 E3
Navan Road (Mulhuddart)	8 F4
Navan Road (Blanchardstown)	22 E1
Navan Road (Castleknock)	23 A3
Navan Road (Cabra)	69 C1
Neagh Road	46 E2
Neilstown Avenue	35 A3
Neilstown Cottages	35 A4 [3]
(off Neilstown Road)	
Neilstown Crescent	35 A3
Neilstown Drive	35 A3
Neilstown Gardens	35 A3
Neilstown Park	35 A3
Neilstown Road	35 A3
Neilstown Village Court	35 A3 [1]
(off Neilstown Road)	
Nelson Street	71 A1
Nephin Road	24 D4
Neptune Terrace (off Breffni Road)	60 E1 [17]
Nerano Road	60 Inset
Nerney's Court	71 B2
Nethercross Court	2 D1
Neville Road	47 A2
Nevinstown Lane	1 C3
New Bancroft Hall	55 A1 [11]
(off Main Street Tallaght)	
New Bancroft Place	55 A1 [9]
(off Main Street Tallaght)	
New Bancroft Square	55 A1 [12]
(off Main Street Tallaght)	
New Bawn Drive	55 A2
New Bawn Park	55 A2
New Bride Street	75 A2
New Bridge	32 F2
New Brighton Terrace	67 C2 [47]
New Cornelscourt (off Bray Road)	59 B3 [7]
New Grange Road	59 A1
New Grove Estate	14 E4
New Ireland Court	73 C2
New Ireland Road	73 C2
New Lucan Road	35 B1
New Nangor Road	43 C1
New Park Lodge	59 A2 [3]
(off Knocksinna Park)	
New Park Road	59 A1
New Rathmore Terrace	67 B2 [23]
New Ravenswell Row	67 B2 [20]
New River Road	23 A2
New Road (Swords)	2 D2 [5]
New Road (Howth)	30 E3
New Road (Inchicore)	36 F3
New Road (Clondalkin)	44 E2
New Row	36 E2 [12]
(off Martin's Row Chapelizod)	
New Row Place	75 A2
New Row South	74 F2
New Row Square	74 F2
New Street	3 B2
New Street Garden's (off New Street)	75 A2
New Street North (off Church Street)	70 F3
New Street South	75 A2
New Vale	64 E3
New Vale Cottages	64 D3
New Vale Crescent	64 E3
New Wapping Street	72 F3
Newbridge Avenue (Irishtown)	39 A3
Newbridge Drive	39 A3
Newbrook Avenue	27 B1
Newbrook Road	27 B1
Newbury Avenue	13 A4
Newbury Drive	13 A4
Newbury Grove	13 A4
Newbury Lawns	13 B4
Newbury Park	13 A4
Newbury Terrace	13 A4 [1]
(off Newbury Avenue)	
Newcastle	41 C4
Newcastle Boulevard	42 D4
Newcastle Demesne	41 B4
Newcastle Farm	41 B4
Newcastle Lyons	42 D4
Newcastle Manor	42 D4
Newcastle Road (Lucan)	34 D2
Newcastle Road (Rathcoole)	52 E1
Newcomen Avenue	72 D1
Newcomen Bridge (Royal Canal)	72 D2
Newcomen Court	72 D1
Newcourt (Swords)	2 D1
Newcourt (Bray)	68 D4
Newcourt Avenue	68 D3
Newcourt Mews	2 D1
Newcourt Road	68 D3
Newcourt Villas	67 C3 [8]
Newgrange Road	24 F4
Newgrove Avenue	39 B4
Newhall Court	54 D2
Newington Terrace	47 A1 [27]
(off Castlewood Avenue)	
Newlands Avenue	44 E2
Newlands Court	26 D2 [1]
Newlands Drive	44 E2
Newlands Manor	44 D3
Newlands Manor Court	44 D3
Newlands Manor Drive	44 D3
Newlands Manor Fairway	44 D3
Newlands Manor Green	44 D3
Newlands Manor Park	44 D3
Newlands Park	44 E2
Newlands Road (Ronanstown)	34 F3
Newlands Road (Clondalkin)	44 E2
Newman Place	18 D3
Newmarket	74 F2
Newmarket Street	74 F2
Newpark	59 A2
Newport Street	74 E1
Newtown (Dunboyne)	7 A3
Newtown (Rathfarnham)	56 E3
Newtown (Glencullen)	62 E3
Newtown (Tinnehinch)	66 E4
Newtown Avenue (Coolock)	26 F1
Newtown Avenue (Blackrock)	49 A3
Newtown Bridge	7 A2
Newtown Close	13 C4
Newtown Cottages (St. Margaret's)	11 A1
Newtown Cottages (Coolock)	26 F1
Newtown Court (Coolock)	13 C4
Newtown Court (Maynooth)	17 B4
Newtown Court	47 A3 [5]
(off Eaton Brae Rathgar)	
Newtown Drive	26 F1
Newtown Glendale	20 D4
Newtown Grove	17 C3
Newtown Hall	17 B3
Newtown House	47 A3 [12]
(off Eaton Brae Rathgar)	
Newtown Lower	51 C4
Newtown Park (Leixlip)	20 D4
Newtown Park (Coolock)	26 F1
Newtown Park (Tallaght)	55 B1
Newtown Park (Blackrock)	59 A1
Newtown Park Court	59 A1 [8]
(off Mount Albany)	
Newtown Road (Coolock)	13 C4
Newtown Road (Maynooth)	17 B4
Newtown Road (Celbridge)	32 D4
Newtown Upper	52 D4
Newtown Villas (off Braemor Road)	47 A3 [4]
Newtown Villas	49 A3 [1]
(off Newtown Avenue Blackrock)	
Newtown Way	13 C4
Newtownpark Avenue	49 A4
Newtownpark House	59 A1 [11]
(off Mount Albany)	
Newtownsmith	50 E4
Niall Street	70 D3
Nicholas Avenue	70 F3
Nicholas Street	75 A1
Ninth Lock Road	44 D1
No2 Nth. Road Extension	39 B1
Noel Purcell Park	75 B1
Nore Road	24 E3
Norfolk Road	24 F4
Norseman Court	70 E3
(off Norseman Place)	
Norseman Place	70 E3
North Avenue	48 E3
North Bull Island	27 B4
North Circular Road (Phoenix Park)	70 D2
North Circular Road	71 C1
(Phibsborough)	
North Clarence Street Flats	72 D2
North Great George's Street	71 B2
North Quay Extension	39 A2
North Road (Phoenix Park Ashtown)	23 B4
North Road (Finglas)	24 D1
North Road	69 B1
(Phoenix Park North Circular)	
North Strand Road	72 E1
North Street	2 D1
North Wall	72 E3
North Wall Quay	72 E4
Northbrook Avenue (Ranelagh)	75 C4
Northbrook Avenue Lower	72 E1
Northbrook Avenue Upper	72 E1
Northbrook Lane	75 C4
Northbrook Road	75 C4
Northbrook Terrace	72 E1
*Northbrook Villas (on Northbrook	75 C4
Road Ranelagh)	
Northcote Avenue	49 C4
Northcote Place	49 C4 [23]
(off North Cote Avenue)	
Northcote Terrace	49 C4 [20]
(off North Cote Avenue)	
Northern Close	13 B3
Northern Cross Route (Poppintree)	11 B3
Northern Cross Route(Abbotstown)	23 A2
Northland Drive (off Tolka Estate)	24 F3 [2]
Northland Grove (off Tolka Estate)	24 F3 [1]
Northumberland Avenue	50 D4
Northumberland Park	50 D4 [11]
(off Northumberland Avenue	
Dún Laoghaire)	
Northumberland Place	50 D4 [10]
(off Northumberland Avenue	
Dún Laoghaire)	
Northumberland Place	76 E2
(Grand Canal St. Upr.)	
Northumberland Road	76 E2
Northumberland Square	71 C3
Northway Estate	11 A4
Northwood	12 E4
Norton's Avenue	70 F1
Norwood	64 E1
Norwood Park (off Sandford Road)	47 C1 [7]
Nottingham Street	72 E1
Novara Avenue	67 C2
Novara Mews	67 C2 [57]
Novara Park	67 C2 [7]
Novara Terrace	67 C2 [27]
Nugent Road	47 A4
Nunciature Road (Phoenix Park)	23 C4
Nun's Lane	26 E3
Nuns Walk	26 E3
Nurney Lawn	14 D4
Nutgrove Avenue	47 B4 [14]
(off Nutgrove Avenue)	
Nutgrove Avenue	47 A4
Nutgrove Court	47 A4 [2]
(off Nutgrove Avenue)	
Nutgrove Crescent	57 A1
Nutgrove Park (Clonskeagh)	47 C2
Nutgrove Way	57 A1
Nutley Avenue	48 D1
Nutley Lane	48 D2
Nutley Park	48 D2
Nutley Road	48 D1
Nutley Square	48 D2 [1]
(off Greenfield Park U.C.D.	

O

STREET NAME	PAGE/GRID REFERENCE
O'Neill's Park	18 D3
Oak Apple Green	47 A2
Oak Avenue	12 F4
Oak Close	44 F1
Oak Court	12 F4
Oak Crescent	12 F4
Oak Dene	60 E3
Oak Downs	44 D2
Oak Drive (Santry)	12 F4
Oak Drive (Fox and Geese)	44 F1
Oak Glen Park	67 C4
Oak Glen View	67 C4
Oak Green	12 F4
Oak Grove	12 F4
Oak Hall	3 B3
Oak House (Swords)	1 Inset
Oak House	76 D3
Oak Lawn (Santry)	12 F4
Oak Lawn (Castleknock)	22 F3
Oak Lodge	23 A4
Oak Rise (Santry)	12 F4
Oak Rise (Clondalkin)	44 D2
Oak Road (Donnycarney)	26 D3
Oak Road (Fox and Geese)	44 F1
Oak View	12 E4
Oak Way	44 D2
Oakbury Court	39 A4 [44]
(off Serpentine Avenue)	
Oakcourt Avenue	35 C2
Oakcourt Close	35 C2
Oakcourt Drive	35 C2
Oakcourt Grove	35 C2
Oakcourt Lawn	35 C2
Oakcourt Park	35 C2
Oakdale Close	55 B3
Oakdale Crescent	55 B3
Oakdale Drive (Firhouse)	55 B3
Oakdale Drive (Sallynoggin)	59 C2
Oakdale Grove	55 B3
Oakdale Park	55 B3
Oakdale Road	55 B3
Oakdown Road	47 A4
Oakfield Place	75 A3
Oaklands Avenue	2 D2
Oaklands Court	39 A4 [38]
(off Claremont Road)	
Oaklands Crescent	47 A2
Oaklands Drive (Sandymount)	39 A4
Oaklands Drive (Rathgar)	47 A2
Oaklands Park (Swords)	2 D2
Oaklands Park (Sandymount)	39 A4
Oaklands Terrace	46 F2
Oaklawn	19 C4
Oaklawn Close	19 C4
Oaklawn West	19 C4
Oakleigh	31 C4
Oakleigh Court	3 A3 [3]
Oakley Court (off Oakley Road)	47 B1 [10]
Oakley Grove	49 A4
Oakley Park (Clontarf)	26 F4
Oakley Park (off Oakley Road)	47 B1 [23]
Oakley Park (Blackrock)	49 A4
Oakley Road	47 B1
Oakley Square (off Oakley Road)	47 B1 [20]
Oakpark Avenue	25 C1
Oakpark Close	25 C1
Oakpark Drive	25 C1
Oakpark Grove	25 C1
Oakton Court (off Oakton Park)	60 E4 [1]
Oakton Drive	60 D4
Oakton Green (off Oakton Park)	60 D4 [3]
Oakton Park	60 D4
Oaktree Avenue	22 E3
Oaktree Drive	22 E3
Oaktree Green	22 E3
Oaktree Grove	22 E3
Oaktree Lawn	22 E3
Oaktree Road	58 F1
Oakview Avenue	21 C1
Oakview Close	21 C1
Oakview Court	21 C1
Oakview Drive	21 C1
Oakview Grove (off Oakview Avenue)	21 C1 [2]
Oakview Lawn	21 C1
Oakview Park	21 C1
Oakview Rise	21 C1
Oakview Walk	21 C1
Oakview Way	21 C1
Oakwood (off Tivoli Road)	49 C4 [7]
Oakwood Apartments	27 B3 [3]
(off The Glen Raheny)	
Oakwood Avenue (Swords)	1 C2
Oakwood Avenue (Glasnevin)	24 E1
Oakwood Close	24 E1
Oakwood Grove Estate	35 A4
Oakwood Park	24 E1
Oakwood Road	24 E1
Oatfield Avenue	35 B3
Oatfield Close	35 B3
*Oatfield Crescent (off Oatfield Drive)	35 B2
Oatfield Drive	35 B3
Oatfield Grove	35 B3
Oatfield Lawn	35 B3
Oatfield Park	35 B3
Obelisk Avenue (off Obelisk Grove)	59 A1 [12]
Obelisk Court (Malahide)	3 C2 [3]
Obelisk Court (Stillorgan)	59 A1
Obelisk Grove	59 A1
Obelisk Lane	18 E4
Obelisk Rise	59 A1
Obelisk Walk	59 A1
Oblate Drive (off Nash Street)	36 F3 [14]
O'Brien Road	45 C1
O'Brien's Place North	25 A3 [13]
(off Joyce Road)	
Observatory Court	75 B4
Observatory Lane	47 A1 [14]
(off Rathmines Road Lower)	
O'Byrne Road	67 C3
O'Byrne Villas	67 C3 [9]
O'Carolan Road	74 F2
O'Casey Avenue	35 C4

STREET NAME	PAGE/GRID REFERENCE	STREET NAME	PAGE/GRID REFERENCE	STREET NAME	PAGE/GRID REFERENCE	STREET NAME	PAGE/GRID REFERENCE
O'Connell Avenue	71 A1	Oldbridge Close	34 E3	Orby Avenue	58 E3	Orwell Mews	47 A2 [8]
O'Connell Bridge (River Liffey)	71 B4	Oldbridge Court	34 E3	Orby Close	58 F3	(off Orwell Road Rathgar)	
O'Connell Gardens	39 A3	Oldbridge Glen	34 E3	Orby Court	58 F3	Orwell Park (Templeogue)	45 C4
O'Connell Street	71 B3	Oldbridge Green	34 E3	Orby Lawn	58 E3	Orwell Park (Rathgar)	47 A3
O'Curry Avenue (off O'Curry Road)	74 F2	Oldbridge Grove	34 E3	Orby Park	58 F3	Orwell Park Avenue	46 D3
O'Curry Road	74 F2	Oldbridge Park	34 E3	Orby View	58 E3	Orwell Park Close	46 D3
O'Daly Road	25 A3	Oldbridge View	34 E3	Orby Village	58 E3	Orwell Park Crescent	46 D3
Odd Lamp Road	36 F1	Oldbridge Walk	34 E3	Orby Way	58 E3	Orwell Park Dale	45 C4
O'Devaney Gardens	70 D3	Oldbridge Way	34 E3	Orchard Avenue (Clonsilla)	21 C2	Orwell Park Drive	46 D3
O'Donnell Gardens	60 D1 [1]	Oldcarton	18 F1	Orchard Avenue (Citywest)	53 B1	Orwell Park Glade	45 C3
(off Eden Road Lower)		Oldcastle Avenue	29 B2	Orchard Close	22 D2	Orwell Park Glen	46 D3
O'Donoghue Street	36 F3	Oldcastle Drive	43 B1	Orchard Cottages	59 A1 [1]	Orwell Park Green	46 D3
O'Donovan Road	74 F3	Oldcastlepark	43 B1	(off Newtown Park)		Orwell Park Grove	45 C3
O'Donovan Rossa Bridge	71 A4	Oldcastlepark Close	43 B1	Orchard Court	22 E2	Orwell Park Heights	45 C3
(River Liffey)		Oldcastlepark Green	43 B1	Orchard Green	22 D2	Orwell Park Lawns	45 C3
O'Dwyer Road (off O'Brien Road)	45 C1 [4]	Oldcastlepark Grove	43 B1	Orchard Grove (Blanchardstown)	22 E2	Orwell Park Rise	45 C4
Offaly Bridge	18 E1	Oldcastlepark Lawn	43 B1	Orchard Grove (Newcastle)	42 D4	Orwell Park View	45 C4
Offaly Road	24 F4	Oldcastlepark View	43 B1	Orchard Lane (Clondalkin)	44 E1	Orwell Park Way	46 D3
Offington Avenue	29 B2	Oldchurch Avenue	43 C1	Orchard Lane (Blackrock)	59 A1	Orwell Road	47 A2
Offington Court	29 B2	Oldchurch Close	43 C1	Orchard Lane (Ranelagh)	75 C4	Orwell Walk	47 A3
Offington Drive	29 B2	Oldchurch Court	43 C1	Orchard Lawns	35 C3	Orwell Woods	47 A2
Offington Lawn	29 B2	Oldchurch Crescent	43 C1	Orchard Lodge	44 E1	*Osborne Terrace (Northbrook Road)	75 C4
Offington Manor Apartments	29 B1 [4]	Oldchurch Drive	43 C1	Orchard Road (Ballybough)	25 B4	Oscar Square	74 F2
(off Howth Road)		Oldchurch Grove	43 C1	Orchard Road (Raheny)	27 B2	Oscar Traynor Road (Kilmore)	13 A3
Offington Park	29 B1	Oldchurch Lawn	43 C1	Orchard Road South	47 B2	Oscar Traynor Road (Coolock)	26 E1
Ogham	60 D3	Oldchurch Park	43 C1	Orchard Square	47 C3	O'Shea's Cottages	59 C3 [4]
O'Hanlon's Lane	3 B2	Oldchurch Way	43 C1	Orchard Terrace (Bray)	67 C3 [19]	(off Bray Road Cabinteely)	
O'Hara Avenue	75 A4	Oldcourt	67 B3	*Orchard Terrace	70 F2	Osprey Avenue	45 C3
O'Hogan Road (off O'Hogan Road)	36 E3 [1]	Oldcourt Avenue (Bohernabreena)	55 B2	(Grangegorman Upper)		Osprey Court	64 E3 [3]
O'Hogan Road	36 E3	Oldcourt Avenue (Boghall Road)	67 B3	*Orchard View	70 F2	Osprey Drive	45 C3
Oisin Court (off Claremont Road)	39 A4 [35]	Oldcourt Close	55 B2	(Grangegorman Upper)		Osprey Lawn	45 C3
Olaf Hall (off Balally Hill)	58 D2 [8]	Oldcourt Cottages	55 B3	Orchardstown Avenue	46 E4	Osprey Park	45 C3
*Olaf House Apartments	70 F4	Oldcourt Drive	67 B3	Orchardstown Drive	46 E4	Osprey Road	45 C3
(Ushers Quay)		Oldcourt Farm	55 B2	Orchardstown Park	46 E4	Ossory Road	72 E2
Olaf Road	70 E3	Oldcourt Grove	67 B4	Orchardstown Villas	56 E1	Ostman Place	70 E3
Olcovar	64 E3	Oldcourt Lawn (off Oldcourt Avenue)	55 B2 [1]	Orchardton (off Willow Bank Drive)	56 E1 [1]	O'Sullivan Avenue	72 D1
Old Bawn Avenue	55 A2	Oldcourt Lodge	55 B2	Ordnance Survey Road	36 E1	Oswald Road	39 A3
Old Bawn Bridge	55 A2	Oldcourt Manor	55 B3	O'Reilly Avenue	73 C1	Otranto Place	60 E1
Old Bawn Close	55 A2	Oldcourt Park	67 B3	O'Reilly's Cottages	74 F4	Otterbrook (off Willbrook Road)	46 F4 [16]
Old Bawn Court (off Old Bawn Road)	55 A1 [5]	Oldcourt Road	55 B3	Oriel Hall	72 D3	Oulart	1 C3
Old Bawn Drive	55 A2	Oldcourt Terrace	67 C3 [15]	Oriel Street Lower	72 E2	Oulton Road	26 E4
Old Bawn Park	55 A2	Oldcourt View	55 B2	Oriel Street Upper	72 D3	Ounavarra	33 C1
Old Bawn Road	55 A1	Oldfarm	22 E3	Orlagh Avenue	56 D2	Our Lady's Close	74 E2
Old Bawn Terrace	55 A2	Oldfield Hall	57 C3	Orlagh Close	56 D2	(off Our Lady's Road)	
Old Bawn Way	55 A2	Oldtower Crescent	35 A2	Orlagh Court	56 D2	Our Lady's Road	74 E2
Old Belgard Road	44 F4	Oldtown Avenue	25 A1	Orlagh Crescent	56 D2	Outer Ring Road	43 B2
Old Blessington Road	55 A1	Oldtown Cottages	31 C3	Orlagh Downs	56 D2	Outfarm Lane	22 E3
Old Brazil Way	1 A2	Oldtown Mill	31 C3	Orlagh Grange	56 D2	Outlands	1 B1
Old Bridge Road	46 D4	Oldtown Mill Road	31 C3	Orlagh Green	56 D2	Overend Way	57 C1
Old Brighton Terrace	67 C2 [46]	Oldtown Park (off Shanliss Road)	25 A1 [3]	Orlagh Grove	56 D2	Ovoca Road	75 A3
Old Cabra Road	70 D1	Oldtown Road	25 A1	Orlagh Lawn	56 D2	Owendoher Haven	56 E1
Old Camac Bridge (Camac River)	73 B1	O'Leary Road	73 B2	Orlagh Lodge	56 D2	Owendoher Lodge	56 E1
Old Carrickbrack Road	30 D4	Olivemount Grove	47 C3 [2]	Orlagh Meadows	56 D2	Owendore Avenue	46 F4
Old Connaught	67 A1	(off Olivemount Road)		Orlagh Park	56 D2	Owendore Crescent	46 F4
Old Connaught Avenue	67 B1	Olivemount Road	47 C3	Orlagh Pines	56 D2	Owen's Avenue	73 C1
Old Connaught Grove	67 B2	Olivemount Terrace	47 C3 [6]	Orlagh Rise	56 D2	Owensilla	24 F1
Old Connaught View	67 B2	(off Olivemount Road)		Orlagh View	56 D2	Owenstown Park	48 D3
Old Corduff Road	22 E1	Oliver Bond House Flats	70 F4	Orlagh Way	56 D2	Oxford Lane	75 C4
Old Cornmill Road	33 C2	Oliver Bond Street	70 F4	Orlagh Wood	56 D2	Oxford Road	47 B1
Old County Glen	73 C4	Oliver Plunkett Avenue (Ringsend)	39 A3	Ormeau Drive	60 F1 [2]	Oxford Terrace	72 E2
Old County Road	73 B4	Oliver Plunkett Avenue	59 C1	(off Carysfort Road)		(on Hawthorn Terrace)	
Old Dublin Road (Stillorgan)	48 E4	(Dún Laoghaire)		Ormeau Street	76 F1	Oxmantown Lane	70 F4
Old Dunleary	49 C4	Oliver Plunkett Road	59 C1	Ormond Avenue	1 B1	Oxmantown Road	70 D2
Old Estuary Mill	2 F2	Oliver Plunkett Square	59 C1 [1]	Ormond Close	1 B1		
Old Fairgreen	7 B2	(off Oliver Plunkett Road)		Ormond Crescent	1 B1	**P**	
Old Fort Road	1 A2	Oliver Plunkett Terrace	59 C1 [5]	Ormond Drive	1 B1		
Old Greenfield	17 C4	(off Oliver Plunkett Road)		Ormond Grove	1 B1	Pace Avenue	8 E4
Old Hill	20 D4	Oliver Plunkett Villas	59 B1 [3]	Ormond Lawn	1 B1	Pace Crescent	8 E4
Old Kilmainham	73 C1	(off Oliver Plunkett Avenue)		Ormond Market	71 A4	Pace Road	8 E4
Old Kilmainham Village	74 D1	Olney Crescent	46 F2	(off Ormond Quay Upper)		Pace View	8 E4
Old Mill Court	74 F2	Olney Grove (off Olney Crescent)	46 F2 [17]	Ormond Place	71 A4	Pacelli Avenue	27 C1
Old Mountpleasant	75 C4	Omni Park	25 B1	Ormond Quay Lower	71 B4	Pairc Gleann Trasna	55 A3
Old Naas Road (Bluebell)	36 E4	O'Moore Road	36 E3	Ormond Quay Upper	71 A4	Páirc Mhuire	53 A2
Old Naas Road (Brownsbarn)	43 C4	O'Neachtain Road	25 A3 [14]	Ormond Road	25 B4	Páirc View	53 A2
Old Naas Road Cottages	36 E4 [1]	(off Ferguson Road)		Ormond Road South	47 B1	Pakenham (off Sloperton)	49 C4 [28]
(off Old Naas Road)		O'Neill's Buildings	75 A2	Ormond Square	71 A4	Pakenham Bridge	21 A2
Old Navan Road	22 F2	Ongar Chase Estate	21 A1	Ormond Street	74 F2	Pakenham Road	49 C4
Old Quarry (Kilshane)	10 D2	Ongar Green	21 A1	*Ormond Terrace	60 F2	Palace Street (off Dame Street)	71 B4
Old Quarry (Dalkey)	60 F2	Ongar Park Estate	21 B1	(off Sorrento Road)		Palmer Park	56 F2
Old Quay	29 B2	Ongar Road	21 B2	Ormond View	1 B1	Palmers Avenue	35 B2
Old Quay Mews	29 B2	Ongar Village	21 A1	Ormond Way	1 B1	Palmers Close	35 B2
Old Quay Terrace	29 B2	Ongar-Hartstown Relief Road	21 C2	O'Rourke Park	59 C2	Palmers Copse	35 B2
Old Rathmichael	64 D3	Ontario Terrace	75 B4	Orpen	58 F1	Palmers Court	35 B2
Old Rathmore Terrace	67 B2 [22]	Onward Close	3 C4	Orpen Close	48 F4	Palmers Crescent	35 B2
Old Ravenswell Row	67 B2 [29]	Onward Walk	3 C4	Orpen Dale (off Stillorgan Grove)	48 F4 [2]	Palmers Drive	35 B2
Old Rectory (off Chapel Hill)	34 D1 [11]	Ophaly Court	47 C4	Orpen Green	58 F1	Palmers Glade	35 B2
Old Rectory Park	47 C4	O'Rahilly House Flats	39 A3 [28]	Orpen Hill	58 F1	Palmers Grove	35 B2
Old Road	14 E2	(off Thorncastle Street)		Orpen Rise	58 F1	Palmers Lawn	35 B2
Old Street	3 B2	O'Rahilly Parade	71 B3	Orr's Terrace	74 F4	Palmers Park	35 B2
Old Yellow Walls Road	3 A2	Oranmore Road	35 C3	Orwell Bank (off Orwell Park)	47 A3 [7]	Palmers Road	35 B2
Oldbawn	55 A2	Oratory Mews Court	50 D4 [24]	Orwell Court (off Braemor Road)	47 A3 [3]	Palmers Walk	35 B2
Oldbridge	34 E3	(off Library Road)		Orwell Gardens	47 A3	Palmerston	35 C1

STREET NAME	PAGE/GRID REFERENCE
Palmerston Close (off Windsor Road)	47 B1 [21]
Palmerston Court	47 A1
Palmerston Gardens	47 B2
Palmerston Grove (off Milltown Road)	47 C2 [5]
Palmerston Lane	47 B2
Palmerston Park (Rathgar)	47 B2
Palmerston Place	71 A2
Palmerston Road	47 B1
Palmerston Villas	47 A1
Palmerstown Avenue	35 C2
Palmerstown Close	35 B2
Palmerstown Court	35 C2
Palmerstown Drive	35 C2
Palmerstown Green	35 B2
Palmerstown Heights	35 B2
Palmerstown Lawn	35 B2
Palmerstown Manor	35 B2
Palmerstown Park (Kennelsfort Road)	35 B2
Palmerstown Woods	35 B4
Paradise Place	71 A2
Park Avenue (Brackenstown Road)	1 B2
Park Avenue (Castleknock)	22 F3
Park Avenue (Sandymount)	39 B4
Park Avenue (Willbrook)	56 F1
Park Avenue (Deans Grange)	59 A1
Park Avenue West	70 D3
Park Boulevard	9 B2
Park Close (Sallynoggin)	60 D2
Park Court (off Park Lane Sandymount)	39 A4 [16]
Park Court Apartments (off Peck's Lane)	23 A3 [4]
Park Crescent (Kimmage)	46 D2
Park Crescent (Blackhorse Avenue)	69 A1
Park Crescent House (off Blackhorse Avenue)	24 D4 [6]
Park Drive (Ranelagh)	47 B1
Park Drive (Cabinteely)	59 B3
Park Drive Avenue	22 F3
Park Drive Close	22 F3
Park Drive Court	22 F3
Park Drive Crescent	22 F3
Park Drive Green	22 F3
Park Drive Grove	22 F3
Park Drive Lawn	22 F3
Park Lane (off Martin's Row Chapelizod)	36 E2 [1]
Park Lane (Sandymount)	39 A4
Park Lane (off Park Road Dún Laoghaire)	50 D4 [21]
Park Lawn	27 A4
Park Lodge	22 F3
Park Manor	22 E3
Park Place	69 B4
*Park Road (off Navan Road)	23 C3
Park Road (Dún Laoghaire)	50 D4
Park Road (Sallynoggin)	60 D2
Park Spring's (off Nephin Road)	24 D4 [5]
Park Street (off First Avenue)	36 F3 [1]
*Park Street (off Hanover St West)	74 F1
Park Terrace (Coombe)	74 F1
Park View (Portmarnock)	15 A1
Park View (Clonsilla)	22 D2
Park View (Castleknock)	23 B4
Park View (Mount Prospect Lawns off Kincora Court)	26 F4 [1]
Park View (off Orwell Road Rathgar)	47 A3 [10]
Park View (Enniskerry Road)	58 D4
Park View (Cabra)	69 C1
Park View House	9 B2
Park View Lawns	44 D2
Park View Manor	9 B2
Park Villas (Castleknock)	23 A3
Park Villas (off Stillorgan Grove)	48 F4 [3]
Park West Avenue	35 C4
Park West Road	36 D4
Parker Hill (off Rathmines Road Lower)	47 A1 [12]
Parker House	14 F4
Parkgate Place (off Parkgate Street)	70 D4
Parkgate Street	70 D4
Parkhill Avenue	44 F3
Parkhill Close	45 A3
Parkhill Court	44 F3
Parkhill Drive	44 F3
Parkhill Green	44 F3
Parkhill Heights (off Greenhills Road Kilnamanagh)	45 A3 [1]
Parkhill Lawn	44 F3
Parkhill Rise	44 F3
Parkhill Road	44 F3
Parkhill Way	45 A3
Parkhill West	44 F4
Parklands (Santry)	12 E4
Parklands (Maynooth)	18 D3
Parklands (Castleknock)	22 F3
Parklands Avenue	55 B2
Parklands Close	18 D3
Parklands Court (Maynooth)	18 D3
Parklands Court (Scholarstown Link Road)	55 B2
Parklands Crescent	18 D3
Parklands Drive	55 B2
Parklands Grove	18 D3
Parklands Lawns	18 D3
Parklands Lodge	18 D3
Parklands Rise	18 D3
Parklands Road	55 B2
Parklands Square	18 D3
Parklands View	55 B2
Parklands Way	18 D3
Parkmore	23 A3
Parkmore Drive	46 E2
Parknasilla Avenue	64 D2
Parknasilla Close	64 D2
Parknasilla Lane	64 D2
Parknasilla Rise	64 D2
Parknasillog	65 C2
Parkside View (off Nephin Road)	24 D4 [7]
Parkvale (Sutton)	28 D1
Parkvale (Dundrum)	57 C1
Parkview (Swords)	1 B2
*Parkview (Robswall)	3 C3
Parkview (Ashtown)	23 C3
Parkview (off Greenhills Road Kilnamanagh)	45 A3 [2]
Parkview Avenue (Harold's Cross)	46 F1
Parkview (off Harolds Cross Road)	46 F1 [8]
Parkview Court (Blackhorse Avenue)	69 B1
Parkview Place (off Bridge Street)	39 A3 [14]
Parkview Terrace	67 B2 [16]
Parkwood Avenue	55 A2
Parkwood Grove	55 A2
Parkwood Lawn	55 A2
Parkwood Road	55 A2
Parliament Street	71 A4
Parnell Avenue	74 F4
Parnell Bridge (Grand Canal)	74 E3
Parnell Cottages	3 B3
Parnell Court	74 F4
Parnell Drive	9 A4
Parnell Green	9 A4
Parnell Hall	74 E4
Parnell Lane	9 A4
Parnell Place	71 B2
Parnell Road (Bray)	67 C2
Parnell Road (Harold's Cross)	74 E3
Parnell Square East	71 B2
Parnell Square North	71 B2
Parnell Square West	71 B2
Parnell Street (Sallynoggin)	60 D1
Parnell Street (O'Connell Street)	71 B3
Parochial Avenue (off Main Street Baldoyle)	15 A4 [2]
Parslickstown Avenue	9 A4
Parslickstown Close	9 A4
Parslickstown Court	9 A4
Parslickstown Drive	9 A4
Parslickstown Gardens	9 A3
Parslickstown Green	9 A4
Parson Court	17 C3
Parson Lodge	17 C3
Parson Street	17 C3
*Parson's Court (Opposite Newcastle Manor)	42 D4
Parsons Hall	17 B3
Partridge Terrace (off Nash Street)	36 F3 [5]
Pass If You Can	11 A1
Patrician Park (off Kill Avenue)	59 C1 [2]
Patrician Villas	48 F4
Patrick Doyle Road	47 B2
Patrick Street (Dún Laoghaire)	50 D4
Patrick Street (Kevin Street Upper)	75 A1
Patrick's Row (off George's Avenue)	49 A3 [14]
*Patricks Terrace	71 A2
Patrickswell Court (off Patrickswell Place)	24 D2 [8]
Patrickswell Place	24 D2
Paul Street	70 F3
Pavillion Gate	59 A4
Pea Field	48 F3
Peamount	42 D2
Peamount Road (Newcastle)	42 D3
Peamount Road (Peamount)	42 E2
Pear Tree Field (off Carysfort Downs)	58 F1 [5]
Pearse Avenue	60 D2
Pearse Brothers Park	56 F1
Pearse Close (off Pearse Street Sallynoggin)	60 D2 [3]
Pearse Drive	60 D2
Pearse Gardens	59 C2
Pearse Green	60 D2
Pearse Grove	76 E1
Pearse House	72 D4
Pearse Park	60 D2
Pearse Road (Sallynoggin)	60 D2
Pearse Road (Bray)	67 B2 [12]
Pearse Square (Bray)	67 B2
Pearse Square (Pearse Street)	76 E1
Pearse Street (Sallynoggin)	60 D2
Pearse Street (Westland Row)	71 C4
Pearse Villas	60 D2
Pebble Hill	18 D2
Pebble Hill Lodge	18 D2
Peck's Lane	23 A3
Pelletstown Avenue	23 C3
Pemberton	67 A3
Pembroke Cottages (Ringsend)	39 A2
Pembroke Cottages (off Donnybrook Mews)	47 C1 [2]
Pembroke Cottages (off Main Street Dundrum)	47 C4 [5]
Pembroke Cottages (off Rosemount Terrace Booterstown)	48 F3 [2]
*Pembroke Court (off Pembroke Road)	76 F3
Pembroke Gardens	76 E3
Pembroke Lane (Lower Baggot Street)	76 D2
Pembroke Lane (Pembroke Road)	76 E3
Pembroke Park	76 E4
Pembroke Place (Pembroke St Upr)	75 C3
Pembroke Place (off Sandymount Avenue)	76 F4
Pembroke Road	76 E3
Pembroke Row	76 D2
Pembroke Square	76 E1
Pembroke Street	39 A3
Pembroke Street Lower	75 C2
Pembroke Street Upper	75 C2
Pembroke Terrace (off Main Street Dundrum)	47 C4 [6]
Penrose Street	76 F1
*Percy Close (off Haddington Road)	76 E2
Percy French Road (off Balfe Avenue)	45 C1 [3]
Percy Lane	76 E2
Percy Place	76 E2
Peter Place	75 B3
Peter Row	75 A2
Peter Street	75 A2
Peter's Court	71 A1
Peterson's Court	72 D4
Petrie Road	74 F3
Peyton	52 F4
Pheasant Run	8 F4
Pheasant Run The Drive	8 F4
Pheasant Run The Green	8 F4
Pheasant Run The Grove	8 F4
Pheasant Run The Park	8 F4
Phelan Avenue	24 D3
Phibblestown Avenue	21 A1
Phibblestown House Apartments	21 B1
Phibsborough	71 A1
Phibsborough Avenue	70 F1
Phibsborough Place	71 A2
Phibsborough Road	71 A1
Philipsburgh Avenue	25 C4
Philipsburgh Terrace	25 C4
Philomena Terrace (off Oliver Plunkett Avenue)	39 A3 [41]
Phoenix Avenue	23 A3
Phoenix Court (Castleknock)	23 A3
Phoenix Court (North Circular Road)	70 D2
Phoenix Court (Arbour Hill)	70 D3
Phoenix Court Apartments	69 C3
Phoenix Drive	23 A3
Phoenix Gardens	23 A3
*Phoenix House (Leinster Street South)	75 C1
Phoenix Manor	70 D2
Phoenix Park	69 A2
Phoenix Park Way	23 B3
Phoenix Place	23 A3
Phoenix Street (off First Avenue)	36 F3 [2]
Phoenix Street North	70 F4
*Phoenix Street West (off Phoenix Street North)	70 F4
Phoenix Terrace	48 F3
Phoenix View	74 D1
Phrompstown	66 F1
Pickford's Terrace	72 F3
Pig Lane	71 C2
Pigeon House Road (Ringsend)	39 A2
Pike Bridge	18 F3
*Pile's Terrace (Sandwith St Upper)	76 D1
Pilot View (off Harbour Road)	60 F1 [14]
Pim Street	74 E1
Pimlico	74 F1
Pimlico Cottages	74 E1
Pine Avenue	59 A2
Pine Copse Road	57 B1
Pine Court (Portmarnock)	15 A1
Pine Court (Deans Grange)	59 A1
Pine Grove (off Firhouse Road)	56 D1 [7]
Pine Grove Park	1 C1
Pine Grove Road	1 C1
Pine Haven	48 F3
Pine Hurst	24 E4
Pine Lawn (Tallaght)	55 A2
Pine Lawn (Deans Grange)	59 A1
Pine Road	39 A3
Pine Valley Avenue	57 B2
Pine Valley Drive	57 B3
Pine Valley Grove	57 B3
Pine Valley Park	57 B3
Pine Valley Way	57 B3
Pinebrook Avenue	26 D2
Pinebrook Close	21 C1
Pinebrook Crescent	26 D2
Pinebrook Downs	21 C1
Pinebrook Drive	26 D2
Pinebrook Glen	21 C1
Pinebrook Grove	26 E2
Pinebrook Heights	21 C1
Pinebrook Lawn	21 C1
Pinebrook Rise	26 D2
Pinebrook Road	26 D2
Pinebrook Vale	21 C1
Pinebrook View	21 C1
Pinebrook Way	21 C1
Pinecroft	62 F1
Pinetree Crescent (off Parkhill Road)	44 F4 [1]
Pinetree Grove (off Parkhill Road)	44 F3 [1]
Pineview Avenue	55 A2
Pineview Drive	55 A2
Pineview Grove	55 A2
Pineview Lawn	55 A2
Pineview Park	55 A2
Pineview Rise	55 A2
Pineview Road	55 A2
Pinewood	60 D4
Pinewood Avenue	24 F1
Pinewood Close	67 C4
Pinewood Court	8 F4
Pinewood Crescent	24 F1
Pinewood Drive	24 F1
Pinewood Green	24 F1
Pinewood Grove (off Pinewood Drive)	25 A1 [1]
Pinewood Park	56 E1
Pinewood Villas	24 F1
Pinewoods	44 D2
Pinnockhill Roundabout	1 C3
Pipe Hill	1 C2
Pleasants Lane	75 B2
Pleasants Place	75 B2
Pleasants Street	75 A2
Pluckstown	51 A2
Plums Road	58 D1
Plunket Hall	2 E2
Plunkett Avenue (Finglas)	24 D1
Plunkett Avenue (Foxrock)	59 A3
Plunkett Crescent	11 A4
Plunkett Drive	24 D1
Plunkett Green	24 D1
Plunkett Grove	24 D1
Plunkett Hall	7 A2
Plunkett Road	24 D1
Poddle Close	46 E1
Poddle Green (off Poddle Park)	46 E1 [6]
Poddle Park	46 E2
Polo Road	69 A2
Poolbeg Quay	39 A3
Poolbeg Street	71 C4
Poole Street	74 F2

STREET NAME	PAGE/GRID REFERENCE
Poplar Row	72 E1
Poplar Row Flats	72 E1
Poppintree	11 C4
Poppintree Lane	11 C4
Poppintree Parade	11 C4
Poppintree Park Lane West	11 C4
Poppintree Terrace	11 C4
Port Tunnel (Santry Entrance)	25 C1
Port Tunnel (East Wall Entrance)	71 C1
Port View House	39 A2
Porters Avenue	22 D2
Porters Gate	21 B2
Porters Gate Avenue	21 C2
Porters Gate Close	21 B2
Porters Gate Court	21 B2
Porters Gate Drive	21 B2
Porters Gate Green	21 B2
Porters Gate Grove	21 B2
Porters Gate Heights	21 C2
Porters Gate Lawn	21 B2
Porters Gate Rise	21 C2
Porters Gate View	21 B2
Porters Gate Way	21 B2
Porters Road	22 D2
Portersfield Apartments	22 D2
Porterstown	5 A3
Porterstown Road	22 D2
Portland Close	72 D2
Portland Court (off Portland Place)	71 C1
*Portland Lock (off Portland Place)	71 C1
Portland Lock Apartments	71 C1
Portland Place	71 B1
Portland Row	72 D2
Portland Square	71 C1
Portland Street North	71 C1
Portland Street West	74 E1
Portmahon Drive	73 C2
Portmarnock	15 A1
Portmarnock Avenue	4 D4
Portmarnock Crescent	15 A1
Portmarnock Drive	4 D4
Portmarnock Grove	4 D4
Portmarnock Park	4 D4
Portmarnock Rise	15 A1
Portmarnock Walk	4 D4
*Portobello Dock (Lennox Street)	75 B3
Portobello Harbour	75 B3
Portobello Harbour Apartments	75 A4
Portobello Place	75 B3
Portobello Road	75 A4
Portside Court	72 E1
Pottery Road	59 C2
Pound Hill	17 C1
Pound Lane	17 C3
Pound Park	17 C3
Pound Street	33 A1
Power's Court	76 E2
Power's Square (off John Dillon Street)	75 A1
Prebend Street	70 F3
Premier Square	24 E2
Preston Street	72 D2
*Price's Lane (Aston Quay)	71 B4
Price's Place (Ranelagh)	75 B4
Priestfield Cottages	74 E3
Priestfield Drive	74 E3
Primeside Park	10 D3
Primrose Avenue	71 A2
Primrose Gate	32 E4
Primrose Grove	13 C4
Primrose Hill (Celbridge)	32 D4
Primrose Hill (off Tivoli Road)	49 C4 [25]
Primrose Lane	34 D1
Primrose Street (off Wellington Street Upper)	71 A2
Prince Arthur Terrace (Leinster Road)	47 A1 [3]
Prince Edward Terrace Lower (off Carysfort Avenue Blackrock)	49 A4 [2]
Prince Edward Terrace Upper (off Carysfort Avenue Blackrock)	49 A4 [3]
Prince of Wales Terrace (off Sandymount Avenue)	39 A4 [7]
Prince of Wales Terrace (Bray)	67 C2 [26]
Prince's Street North	71 B3
Prince's Street South	72 D4
Princeton	48 D3
Prior Hall	74 D1
Priorswood Road	13 C4
Priory Avenue	48 F4
Priory Chase	31 C4
Priory Close	31 C4
Priory Court (Celbridge)	31 C4
Priory Court (off Grange Road)	57 A2 [1]
Priory Crescent	31 C4
Priory Drive (Celbridge)	31 C4
Priory Drive (Stillorgan)	48 F4
Priory East	24 D4
Priory Green	31 C4
Priory Grove (Celbridge)	31 C4
Priory Grove (Stillorgan)	48 F4
Priory Hall (Donaghmede)	14 E4
Priory Hall (Kimmage)	46 D2
Priory Hall (Stillorgan)	48 F4
Priory Lodge	31 C4
Priory North	24 D3
Priory Road	46 F1
Priory Square	31 C4
Priory View	31 C3
Priory Walk (Celbridge)	31 C4
Priory Walk (Kimmage)	46 D2
Priory Way (Celbridge)	31 C3
Priory Way (Kimmage)	46 D2
Priory West	24 D4
Proby Garden	49 A4
Proby Hall	60 E2
Proby Park	60 E2
Proby Square	49 A4
Proby's Lane	71 B3
Promenade Road	39 A1
Prospect Avenue (Finglas Road)	25 A4
Prospect Avenue (Stocking Lane)	56 E2
Prospect Court (off Prospect Avenue)	25 A4 [19]
Prospect Drive	56 E2
Prospect Glen	56 E2
Prospect Grove	56 E2
Prospect Heath	56 E2
Prospect Heights	56 E2
Prospect Lane (off Milltown Road)	47 C2 [1]
Prospect Lawn	59 B3
Prospect Lodge (off Knocklyon Road)	55 C1 [6]
Prospect Meadows	56 E2
Prospect Road	25 A4
Prospect Square (off Prospect Avenue)	25 A4 [5]
Prospect Terrace (off Marine Drive Sandymount)	39 B3 [1]
Prospect Terrace (Kilmainham)	73 B1
Prospect View	56 E2
Prospect Way	25 A4
Protestant Row	75 B2
Proud's Lane	75 B2
Provost Row	70 E3
Prussia Street	70 E2
Pucks Castle Lane	63 C3
Purcell Lane (off Main Street Bray)	67 C2 [60]
Purley Park	3 C4
Purser Gardens (off Summerville Park)	47 A1 [10]
Putland Road	67 C3
Putland Villas	67 C3 [14]
Pyro Villas	74 E2

Q

STREET NAME	PAGE/GRID REFERENCE
Quarry Cottages (off Killester Avenue Middle)	26 E3 [3]
Quarry Drive	45 C2
Quarry Road (Cabra)	24 E4
Quarry Road (Ferndale Road)	64 D4
Quarryfield Court	44 E2
Quarryvale	35 A1
Quarryvale Park	35 A2
Quartiere Bloom	71 B4
Queen's Park	49 B4
Queen's Road	50 D4
Queen's Street	70 F4
Quinn Avenue	74 D1
Quinn's Lane	75 C2
Quinn's Road	64 E3
Quinsborough	51 A4
Quinsborough Road	67 C2

R

STREET NAME	PAGE/GRID REFERENCE
Radcliff Hall (off St. John's Road East)	39 B4 [9]
Radcliffe (off Binn Eadair View)	29 A1 [3]
Radharc na hAbhann	55 A2
Radlett Grove	4 D4
Rafter's Avenue	73 A4
Rafter's Lane	73 A4
Rafter's Road	73 A4
Raglan Hall Apartments (off Seafort Avenue)	76 E4
Raglan House (off Serpentine Avenue)	39 A4 [42]
Raglan Lane	76 E4
Raglan Road	76 E4
Raheen Avenue	54 E1
Raheen Close	54 E1
Raheen Court	54 E1
Raheen Crescent	54 E1
Raheen Drive (Ballyfermot)	36 D3
Raheen Drive (Tallaght)	54 E1
Raheen Green	54 E1
Raheen Park (Ballyfermot)	36 D3
Raheen Park (Tallaght)	54 E1
Raheen Park (Bray)	68 D3
Raheen Road	54 E1
Raheny	27 A2
Raheny Park	27 A3
Raheny Road	27 A1
Railpark	18 E3
Railway Avenue (Malahide)	3 B2
Railway Avenue (Baldoyle)	28 D1
Railway Avenue (Inchicore)	36 F3
Railway Close	14 F4
Railway Cottages (off Serpentine Park)	39 A4 [8]
Railway Court	3 B2 [3]
Railway Mews	14 F4
Railway Road	14 F4
Railway Road (off Castle Street Dalkey)	60 F2 [2]
Railway Street	71 C2
Railway Terrace (off Macken St)	76 E1
Rainsford Avenue	74 E1
Rainsford Lane (off Military Road Ballybrack)	60 E4 [6]
Rainsford Street	74 E1
Ralahine	60 D4
Raleigh Square	73 B4
Ralph Square	33 A1 [1]
Ramillies Road	36 E3
Ramleh Close	47 C2
Ramleh Park	47 C2
Ramor Park	22 E2
Ranelagh	75 C4
Ranelagh Avenue	75 C4
Ranelagh Road	75 C4
Raphoe Road	46 D1
Rath Geal	43 C1
Rathbeale Court	1 C1 [2]
Rathbeale Crescent	1 C1
Rathbeale Rise	1 C2
Rathbeale Road	1 C1
Rathborne Avenue	23 C3
Rathborne Close	23 C3
Rathborne Drive	23 C3
Rathborne Place	23 C3
Rathborne Way	23 C3
Rathbourne Court (off Rathbourne Avenue)	23 C3 [1]
Rathclaren	67 B3 [2]
Rathcoole Interchange (N7)	52 F1
Rathcoole Park	52 F2
Rathcreedan	52 D1
Rathdown Avenue	46 F3
*Rathdown Court (off Corrib Road)	46 F2 [10]
Rathdown Crescent	46 F3
Rathdown Drive	46 E3
Rathdown Grove (off Sandyford Road)	58 D2 [9]
Rathdown Park	46 F3
Rathdown Road	70 F1
Rathdown Square	70 E2
Rathdown Terrace (off Sandyford Road)	58 D2 [5]
Rathdown Villas	46 F3
Rathdrum Road	74 D4
Rathe Lawns	52 E2
Rathfarnham	46 F3
Rathfarnham Mill (off Main Street Rathfarnham)	46 F4 [12]
Rathfarnham Park	46 F3
Rathfarnham Road	46 F3
Rathfarnham Wood	46 F4
Rathgar	47 A2
Rathgar Avenue	46 F2
Rathgar Court (off Rathgar Road)	47 A1 [28]
Rathgar Park (off Terenure Road East)	46 F2 [16]
Rathgar Park (off Orwell Road Rathgar)	47 A2 [7]
Rathgar Place	47 A1
Rathgar Road	47 A1
Rathgar Villas (off Rathgar Avenue)	46 F2 [11]
Rathingle Road	1 B3
Rathland Drive (off Ravensdale Drive)	46 E2 [4]
Rathland Road	46 E2
Rathlin Road	25 A3
Rathlyon Grove	55 C2
Rathlyon Park	55 C2
Rathmichael	63 C3
Rathmichael Dales	64 D3
Rathmichael Haven	64 D3
Rathmichael Hill	63 C2
Rathmichael Lane	63 C2
Rathmichael Manor	64 D2
Rathmichael Park	64 E2
Rathmichael Road	63 C2
Rathmichael Woods	64 E2
Rathmines	75 A4
Rathmines Avenue	47 A1
Rathmines Avenue Court (off Rathmines Road Upper)	47 A1 [25]
Rathmines Close	47 A1
Rathmines Park (off Rathmines Road Upper)	47 A1 [1]
Rathmines Road Lower	75 B4
Rathmines Road Upper	47 A1
Rathmintan Close	54 D2
Rathmintan Court	54 D2
Rathmintan Crescent	54 D2
Rathmintan Drive	54 D2
Rathmore	14 F2
Rathmore Avenue	9 B2
Rathmore Avenue	58 D1
Rathmore Crescent	9 B2
Rathmore Drive	9 B2
Rathmore Grove	9 B2
Rathmore Park	27 A2
Rathmore Villas	46 F2
Rathsallagh Avenue	64 E2
Rathsallagh Bridge	64 E2
Rathsallagh Drive	64 E2
Rathsallagh Grove	64 E2
Rathsallagh Park	64 E2
Rathvale Avenue	26 F1
Rathvale Drive	26 F1
Rathvale Grove	26 F1
Rathvale Park	26 F1
Rathvilly Drive	24 D2
Rathvilly Park	24 D2
Ratoath Avenue	24 D2
Ratoath Drive	23 C1
Ratoath Estate	24 D3
Ratoath Road (Hollystown)	9 B1
Ratoath Road (Finglas)	23 C2
Ratoath Road (Cabra)	24 E4
Ratra Park	23 C4
Ratra Road	23 C4
Ravens Court (off Cardiff Castle Road)	24 D2 [1]
Ravens Rock Road	58 E2
*Ravensdale Drive (off Ravensdale Park)	46 E2
Ravensdale Park	46 E2
Ravensdale Road	72 F2
Ravenswell Road	67 C2
Ravenswood	3 A3 [2]
Ravenswood Avenue	21 B1
Ravenswood Crescent	21 B1
Ravenswood Drive	21 B1
Ravenswood Estate	21 B1
Ravenswood Green	21 B1
Ravenswood Lawn	21 B1
Ravenswood Rise	21 B1
Ravenswood Road	21 B1
Ravenswood View	21 B1
Raverty Villas	67 B1 [1]
Rawson Court	76 E2
Raymond Street	74 F3
Rectory Slopes	67 B3
Rectory Way	67 A3
*Red Arches Avenue (Red Arches Estate)	14 F4
*Red Arches Close (Red Arches Estate)	14 F4
*Red Arches Drive (Red Arches Estate)	14 F4
*Red Arches Park (Red Arches Estate)	14 F4

STREET NAME	PAGE	GRID
Red Arches Road	14	F4
Red Brick Terrace	59	A1 [2]
(off Annaville Avenue)		
Red Cow Cottages	35	C1 [4]
(off Lucan Road Palmerston)		
Red Cow Interchange	44	F1
Red Cow Lane	70	F3
Redberry	34	D3
Redesdale Crescent	48	D4
Redesdale Road	48	D4
Redfern Avenue	3	C4
Redgap	52	E3
Redmond's Court	27	B1 [3]
(off Kilbarrack Road)		
Redmond's Hill	75	B2
Redwood	9	B1
Redwood Avenue	45	A4
Redwood Close	45	A4
Redwood Court (Tallaght)	44	F4
Redwood Court (Churchtown)	47	A3
Redwood Drive	44	F4
Redwood Grove	48	F3
Redwood Heights	45	A4
Redwood Lawn	44	F4
Redwood Park	45	A4
Redwood Rise	45	A4
Redwood View	45	A4
Redwood Walk	44	F4
Regal Park	69	B1
Reginald Square	74	F1
Reginald Street	74	F1
Rehoboth Avenue	74	E3
Rehoboth Place	74	D3
Reilly's Avenue	74	D3
Renoir Apartments	39	A4 [50]
(off Serpentine Avenue)		
Reuben Avenue	74	D2
Reuben Square Apartments	74	D3
(Reuben Street)		
Reuben Street	74	D2
Reuben Walk	74	D2
*Rhodaville (off Mountpleasant Ave)	75	B4
Riachville (off Collinswood)	25	C2 [10]
Rialto Buildings	74	D2
Rialto Cottages	73	C2
Rialto Drive	73	C3
*Rialto Park (off Rialto Street)	74	D2
Rialto Street	74	D2
Ribh Avenue	26	F2
Ribh Road	26	F2
Richelieu Park	48	E1
Richmond	59	A1
*Richmond Apartments	70	F3
Richmond Avenue (Fairview)	25	B4
Richmond Avenue (Monkstown)	49	C4
Richmond Avenue South	47	B2
Richmond Cottages (Summerhill)	72	D1
Richmond Cottages North	72	D1
Richmond Court (Marino)	25	C4
Richmond Court (Milltown)	47	B2
Richmond Crescent	72	D1
Richmond Estate	25	C4
Richmond Green	49	C4 [12]
(off Carrickbrennan Road)		
Richmond Grove	49	C4
Richmond Hall	25	B4 [13]
(off Richmond Road)		
Richmond Hill (Monkstown)	49	C4
Richmond Hill (Rathmines)	75	B4
Richmond House	25	B4 [12]
(off Richmond Road)		
Richmond Lane	71	C1
Richmond Lodge	25	B4
*Richmond Manor (Richmond Hill)	75	B4
Richmond Mews	75	B4
Richmond Parade	72	D1
Richmond Park (Monkstown)	49	B4
Richmond Park (Herbert Road)	67	A4
Richmond Place (Rathmines)	75	B4
Richmond Place South	75	B3
(Sth Richmond St)		
Richmond Road	25	B4
Richmond Row	75	B3
Richmond Street North	72	D1
Richmond Street South	75	B3
Richmond Terrace	68	D2 [12]
Richmond Villas	75	B3
Richview	47	C2
Richview Park	47	B2
Richview Villas	47	C2 [11]
(off Whitethorn Road)		
Riddlesford	67	C4
Ridge Hall	64	E1
Ridge Hill	64	E1
Ridgewood Avenue	1	B3
Ridgewood Close	1	B3
Ridgewood Court	1	B3
Ridgewood Green	1	B3
Ridgewood Grove	1	B3
Ridgewood Park	1	B3
Ridgewood Place	1	B3
Ridgewood Square	1	B3
Rinawade Avenue	32	E1
Rinawade Close	32	E1
Rinawade Crescent	32	E1
Rinawade Downs	32	E1
Rinawade Glade	32	E1
Rinawade Green	32	E1
Rinawade Grove	32	E1
Rinawade Lawns	32	E1
Rinawade Park	32	F1
Rinawade Rise	32	E1
Rinawade Vale	32	E1
Rinawade View	32	E1
Ring Street (off Ring Terrace)	36	F3 [12]
Ring Terrace	36	F3
Ringsend	39	A3
Ringsend Park	39	A2
Ringsend Road	76	F1
Rinn na Mara (off Clontarf Road)	27	A4 [3]
Ripley Court	67	B3
Ripley Hills	67	B3
River Close	64	E1 [23]
River Court	7	B3
*River Court Apartments	73	A1
(off Emmet Road)		
River Drive	24	D3
River Forest	20	D4
River Forest View (Leixlip)	19	C3
River Gardens (off Glasnevin Hill)	25	A3 [15]
River Lane (Loughlinstown)	64	E2 [1]
River Lane (Bray)	67	B2
River Lane Grove	64	E2 [13]
River Lawns	31	C4
River Mall	2	D2
River Road (Blanchardstown)	22	F2
River Road (Ashtown)	23	C3
River Road Cottages	23	A2
River Valley Avenue	1	C2
River Valley Close	1	B2
River Valley Court	1	B2
River Valley Drive	1	C2
River Valley Grove	1	C3
River Valley Heights	1	C2
River Valley Lawn	1	C2
River Valley Park	1	C2
River Valley Rise	1	C3
River Valley Road	1	C2
River Valley View	1	B2
River Valley Way	1	B2
River View	31	C4
Riverbank (Braemor Road)	47	A3
Riverbank	57	C1 [10]
(off Overend Way Dundrum)		
Riverbank Hall	24	F3
Riverdale	20	D4
Riverpark Apartments	69	C4
Riverpark View (off Village Heights)	9	A4 [3]
Riverrun Apartments	74	D1
Riversdale (Palmerston)	35	C1
Riversdale	57	C1 [11]
(off Overend Way Dundrum)		
Riversdale Avenue (Palmerston)	35	C1
Riversdale Avenue (Clondalkin)	44	E1
Riversdale Avenue (Terenure)	46	F3
Riversdale Court	35	C1
Riversdale Crescent	44	E1
Riversdale Drive	44	E1
Riversdale Green	35	B4
Riversdale Grove (Palmerston)	35	B1
Riversdale Grove	46	E2 [1]
(off Kimmage Road Lower)		
Riversdale Park (Palmerston)	35	C1
Riversdale Park (Clondalkin)	44	E1
Riversdale Road	44	E1
Riversdale View (off Boden Wood)	46	F4 [26]
Riverside (off Mulhuddart Bridge)	9	A4 [4]
Riverside (off Watery Lane)	44	E1 [6]
Riverside	46	E2 [9]
(off Poddle Park Kimmage)		
Riverside Avenue	13	A4
Riverside Cottages	46	E4
Riverside Crescent	13	A4
Riverside Drive (Coolock)	13	B4
Riverside Drive (Palmerston)	35	C1
Riverside Drive (Rathfarnham)	47	A3
Riverside Grove	13	A4
Riverside Park	13	A4
Riverside Road	13	A4
Riverside Walk	47	C1 [21]
(off Clonskeagh Road)		
Riverston Abbey	24	D4
Riverstown Gardens	24	D3 [5]
(off Ashington Gardens)		
Rivervale	23	C3
Rivervale Apartments	67	B2 [27]
Riverview (Palmerston)	35	C1
Riverview (Oldbawn)	55	A2
*Riverview (Grand Canal Docks)	76	E1
Riverview Apartments	32	D4
Riverview Court	36	E2 [11]
(off Lucan Road Chapelizod)		
Riverwood Chase	22	D3
Riverwood Close	22	D3
Riverwood Copse	22	D3
Riverwood Court	22	D3
Riverwood Crescent	22	D3
Riverwood Dale	22	D3
Riverwood Dene	22	D3
Riverwood Drive	22	D3
Riverwood Gardens	22	D3
Riverwood Glebe	22	D3
Riverwood Glen	22	D3
Riverwood Green	22	D3
Riverwood Grove	22	D3
Riverwood Hall	22	D3
Riverwood Heath	22	D3
Riverwood Lawn	22	D3
Riverwood Park	22	D3
Riverwood Place	22	D3
Riverwood Road	22	D3
Riverwood Terrace	22	D3
Riverwood Vale	22	D3
Riverwood View	22	D3
Riverwood Way	22	D3
Robert Emmet Bridge (Grand Canal)	74	F4
Robert Emmett Close	70	E4
Robert Place (off Mabel Street)	25	B4 [7]
Robert Street	25	B4 [6]
(Jones's Road off Mabel Street)		
Robert Street	74	E1
Robin Villas	35	C1
Robinhood Park	45	B1
Robinhood Road	45	A1
Robinsons Court	74	F2
Robswall	3	C3
Robswall Path	4	D3
Robswall Walk	4	D3
Rochestown Avenue	59	C2
Rochestown House	59	C2 [9]
(off Rochestown Avenue)		
Rochestown House Apartments	59	C2 [6]
(off Rochestown Avenue)		
Rochestown Park	60	D2
Rochfort Avenue	34	F2
Rochfort Close	34	F2
Rochfort Crescent	34	F3
Rochfort Downs	34	F2
Rochfort Green	34	F2
Rochfort Park	34	F2
Rochfort Way	34	F2
Rock Bridge	32	D4
Rock Hall	49	A3
Rock Hill	49	A3
*Rock Lane (Baggot Street Lower)	76	D2
Rock Lodge	60	E3
Rock Road	49	A3
Rockbrae Hall	57	C3
Rockbrook	56	E4
Rockfield (Maynooth)	18	D4
Rockfield (Lucan)	34	D3
Rockfield (Dundrum)	57	C1
Rockfield Avenue (Maynooth)	18	D4
Rockfield Avenue (Kimmage)	46	D2
Rockfield Close	22	D3
Rockfield Drive (Coolmine)	22	D3
Rockfield Drive (Clondalkin)	44	D2
Rockfield Drive (Kimmage)	46	D2
Rockfield Gardens	18	D3
Rockfield Green	18	D3
Rockfield Lodge	18	D4
Rockfield Manor	18	D4
Rockfield Park (Maynooth)	18	D4
Rockfield Park (Coolmine)	22	D2
Rockfield Rise	18	D3
Rockfield Square	18	D3
Rockfield Walk	18	D3
Rockford Manor	59	B1
Rockford Park	59	B1
Rockford Terrace (off Rowan Park)	49	B4 [14]
Rockfort Avenue	60	F2
Rockingham Avenue	19	C4
Rockingham Green	19	C4
Rockingham Grove	19	C4
Rockingham Park	19	C4
Rockingham Terrace	2	D2
Rocklands (off Harbour Road)	60	F1 [6]
Rockmeade Court	46	D1 [5]
(off Windmill Road Crumlin)		
Rockstown	30	E2
Rockview	57	C3
Rockville	62	F2
Rockville Crescent	49	B4
Rockville Drive (Monkstown)	49	B4
Rockville Drive (Carrickmines)	63	A1
Rockville Estate (off Rockville Road)	49	A4 [9]
Rockville Park	49	B4
Rockville Road	49	A4
Rockwell Cove Apartments	49	A3 [9]
(off Idrone Terrace)		
Rockwood	34	D3
Rocwood	58	F2
Roe Lane	70	E4
Roebuck Avenue	48	E3
Roebuck Castle	48	D3
Roebuck Crescent (off Roebuck Road)	47	C3 [10]
Roebuck Downs	47	C3
Roebuck Drive	46	D2
Roebuck Hill	48	D3
Roebuck Lawn	47	C3 [9]
(off Beechmount Drive)		
Roebuck Park	47	C4
Roebuck Road	48	D3
Roger Casement Park	67	B2
Roger's Lane	75	C2
Roland Court (off Rathgar Road)	47	A1 [20]
Rollins Court (off Rollins Villas)	60	D1 [12]
Rollins Villas	60	D1
Ronanstown	35	A4
Roncalli Road	27	C1
Rookwood View	56	E2
Roosevelt Cottages	24	D4 [1]
(off Nephin Road)		
Rooske Road	7	B3
Ropewalk Place (off Cambridge Park)	39	A3 [30]
Rory O'Connor Park	59	B1
Rory O'More Bridge (River Liffey)	70	E4
Ros Mór View	56	D2
Rosary Gardens East	50	D4 [2]
(off Library Road)		
Rosary Gardens West	49	C4 [1]
(off Library Road)		
Rosary Road	74	D2
Rosary Terrace (Ringsend)	39	A3
*Rosary Terrace (off Library Road)	50	D4
Rosbeg Court	27	C2
Rosberry	34	E3
Rosberry Avenue	34	E3
Rosberry Court	34	E3
Rosberry Lane	34	E3
Rosberry Park	34	E3
Rosberry Place	34	E3
Rose Park	59	C1
Rose Vale Court	22	D1 [6]
(off Briarwood Lawn)		
Roseacre	58	E3
Rosebank	55	A2
Rosebank Court (off Nangor Road)	35	B4 [2]
Rosebank Hall (off Nangor Road)	35	A4 [5]
Rosebank Place (off Nangor Road)	35	A4 [4]
Rosebank View (off Nangor Road)	35	B4 [1]
Rosedale (Dunboyne)	7	B2
Rosedale (Clonsilla)	21	B1
*Rosedale Apartments	36	F3
(off Tyrconnell Road)		
Rosedale Close	21	B1
Rosedale Crescent	21	B1
Rosedale Terrace	74	F3
(Lower Clanbrassil St)		
Roseglen Avenue	27	B2
Roseglen Manor	27	B2 [3]
(off Roseglen Avenue)		
Roseglen Road	27	B2
Rosehaven	22	E3 [1]
(off Carpenterstown Park East)		
Rosehill (off Carysfort Avenue)	59	A1 [5]
Roselawn	34	E1
Roselawn Avenue	22	E2

STREET NAME	PAGE/GRID REFERENCE
Roselawn Close	22 F2
Roselawn Court	22 F2
Roselawn Crescent	22 E2
Roselawn Drive (Blanchardstown)	22 E2
Roselawn Drive (Oldcourt)	67 C3
Roselawn Glade	22 E2
Roselawn Grove	22 E2
Roselawn Park	67 C3 [2]
Roselawn Road	22 E2
Roselawn View	22 E2
Roselawn Walk	22 E2
Roselawn Way	22 F2
Rosemount (off Charlemont)	25 C3 [10]
Rosemount	26 D3
(Malahide Road Donnycarney)	
Rosemount (Churchtown)	47 C4
Rosemount Avenue	26 E2
Rosemount Court (Dundrum)	47 C4
Rosemount Court (Booterstown)	48 F3
Rosemount Court (Inchicore Road)	73 B1
Rosemount Crescent	47 C3
(Roebuck Road)	
Rosemount Glade	47 C4
Rosemount Hall	47 C4
Rosemount Park	47 C4
Rosemount Park Drive	10 D4
Rosemount Park Road	10 D4
Rosemount Road	70 F1
Rosemount Terrace	47 B4 [11]
(off Dundrum Road)	
Rosemount Terrace (Booterstown)	48 E3
Rosemount Terrace (Arbour Hill)	70 E3
Rosevale Court	26 F3
Rosevale Mansions	26 F3
Roseville Court	67 B1 [7]
Roseville Terrace	47 C4 [4]
(off Dundrum Road)	
Rosewood Grove	34 F3
Rosmeen Gardens	50 D4
Rosmeen Park	60 D1
Ross Cottages	3 B2 [8]
Ross Road	75 A1
Ross Street	70 D2
Ross View	35 C1
Rossaveal Court (off Drumfinn Road)	36 D2 [1]
Rossberry Terrace	34 E4
Rossecourt Avenue	34 F3
Rossecourt Green	34 F3
Rossecourt Grove	34 F3
Rossecourt Heights	34 F3
Rossecourt Lane	34 F3
Rossecourt Rise	34 F3
Rossecourt Square	34 F3
Rossecourt Terrace	34 F3
Rossecourt Way	34 F3
Rossfield Avenue	54 D1
Rossfield Close	54 D1 [4]
(off Glenshane Crescent)	
Rossfield Court	54 D1 [3]
(off Rossfield Gardens)	
Rossfield Crescent	54 D1
Rossfield Drive	54 D1
Rossfield Gardens	54 D1
Rossfield Green	54 D1
Rossfield Grove	54 D1
Rossfield Park	54 D1
Rossfield Way	54 D1
Rosslyn	67 C2 [37]
Rosslyn Court	67 C2
Rosslyn Grove	67 C2 [4]
Rossmeen Park (off Sumerhill Road)	50 E4
Rossmore Avenue (Ballyfermot)	36 D3
Rossmore Avenue (Templeogue)	45 C4
Rossmore Close	46 D4
Rossmore Crescent	46 D4
Rossmore Drive (Ballyfermot)	36 D2
Rossmore Drive (Templeogue)	45 C4
Rossmore Grove	45 C4
Rossmore Lawns	46 D4
Rossmore Park	46 D4
Rossmore Road (Ballyfermot)	36 D2
Rossmore Road (Templeogue)	46 D4
Rostrevor Court	76 E1
Rostrevor Road	47 A3
Rostrevor Terrace (Orwell Road)	47 A2
Rostrevor Terrace	76 E1
(Lower Grand Canal Street)	
Rothe Abbey	73 B2
Rowan Avenue	58 D2
Rowan Close	32 D3
Rowan Grove	67 B2
Rowan Hall (off Milltown Road)	47 C1 [15]
Rowan Hamilton Court	24 E4 [3]
(off Dunmanus Road)	
Rowan House	76 D3
Rowan Park	49 B4
Rowan Park Avenue	49 B4
Rowanbyrn	59 B1
Rowans Road	58 D2
Rowlagh Avenue	35 A3
Rowlagh Crescent	35 A3
Rowlagh Gardens	35 A3
Rowlagh Green	35 A3
Rowlagh Park	35 A3
Rowserstown Lane	73 B1
Royal Canal Avenue	23 C3
Royal Canal Bank (Phibsborough)	25 A4
Royal Canal Bank (Phibsborough)	71 A1
Royal Canal Terrace	70 F2
Royal Hibernian Way	75 C1
Royal Marine Terrace	67 C2 [12]
Royal Oak	12 F4
Royal Terrace East	60 D1
Royal Terrace Lane	60 D1 [10]
(off Royal Terrace West)	
Royal Terrace North	60 D1 [2]
(off Royal Terrace East)	
Royal Terrace West	60 D1
Royse Road	25 A4
Royston	46 D2
Royston Village	46 D2
Ruben Square	73 D3
Ruby Hall	59 C2
Rugby Road	47 B1
Rugby Villas (off Oxford Road)	47 B1 [6]
Rushbrook	22 E2
Rushbrook Avenue	45 C3
Rushbrook Court	45 C4
Rushbrook Crescent	45 C3
Rushbrook Drive	45 C3
Rushbrook Grove	45 C3
Rushbrook Park	45 C3
Rushbrook Road	45 C3
Rushbrook View	45 C3
Rushbrook Way	45 C4
Rusheeney	21 B1
Rusheeney Avenue	21 B1
Rusheeney Close	21 B1
Rusheeney Court	21 B1
Rusheeney Crescent	8 F4
Rusheeney Green	21 C1
Rusheeney Grove	21 B1
Rusheeney Manor	21 B1
Rusheeney Park	21 B1
Rusheeney View	21 C1
Rusheeney Way	21 B1
Rus-in-Urbe Terrace	60 D1 [19]
(off Glenageary Road Lower)	
Russel Street Bridge (Royal Canal)	71 C1
Russell Avenue (Fortunestown Way)	54 D1
Russell Avenue (Jones's Road)	71 C1
Russell Avenue East	72 E2
Russell Close	54 D2
Russell Court	54 D2
*Russell Court Apartments	71 A3
(Little Britain Street)	
Russell Crescent	54 D1
Russell Downs	54 D1
Russell Drive	54 D2
Russell Green	54 D2
Russell Grove	54 D1
Russell House	2 E2
Russell Lane	54 D1
Russell Lawns	54 D2
Russell Meadows	54 D1
Russell Place	54 D1
Russell Rise	54 D1
Russell Street	71 C1
Russell View	54 D2
Russell Walk	54 D1
Russell's Mews	2 E3
Russell's Place	2 E3
Russell's Terrace	2 E4
Rutland Avenue (Clogher Road)	46 E1
Rutland Avenue (Crumlin Road)	74 D4
Rutland Cottages	71 C2
Rutland Court	71 C2
Rutland Grove	46 F1
Rutland Place North	71 C2
Rutland Place West	71 B2
Rutland Street Lower	71 C2
Rutledge Terrace	74 E3
Ryan's Cottages	46 F1 [7]
(off Harolds Cross Road)	
Ryder's Row	71 A3
Rye Bridge	33 A1
Rye River Avenue	20 D4
Rye River Close	20 D4
Rye River Court	20 D4
Rye River Crescent	20 D4
Rye River Gardens	20 D4
Rye River Grove	20 D4
Rye River Mall	20 D4
Rye River Park	20 D4
Ryecroft	67 C3
Ryemont Abbey	20 D4
Ryevale Lawns	20 D4
Rynville Manor	67 B4

S

STREET NAME	PAGE/GRID REFERENCE
Sackville Avenue	72 D1
Sackville Court Apartments	71 B2
Sackville Gardens	72 D1
Sackville Place	71 B3
Saddlers Avenue	9 A4
Saddlers Close	9 A4
Saddlers Court	75 B4
Saddlers Crescent	9 A4
Saddlers Drive	9 A4
Saddlers Glade	9 A4
Saddlers Grove	9 A4
Saddlers Lawn	9 A4
Sadleir Hall	7 A2
Saggart	53 B2
Saggart Abbey	53 C2
Saggart Lakes	53 B1
Saint Canice's Court	23 C1
Saint Canice's Square	24 E2
Saint Pappin's Street	12 D4
Saintdoolaghs	14 D3
Saintsbury Avenue	60 E4
Salamanca	48 D4
Salem Court (off Maxwell Road)	47 A1 [17]
Salestown	6 D4
Sallowood View	12 E4
Sallowood Walk	12 E4
Sally Park	55 C1
Sally Park Close	55 C1
Sallyglen Road	60 D2
Sallymount Avenue	47 B1
Sallymount Gardens	47 B1 [1]
(off Sallymount Avenue)	
Sallymount Terrace	47 B1 [14]
(off Sallymount Avenue)	
Sallynoggin	60 D2
Sallynoggin Park	59 C2
Sallynoggin Road	59 C2
Salmon Pool Apartments	69 A4
Salthill	49 C4
*Salthill Place (off Crofton Road)	50 D4
Saltzburg	48 D4
Sampson's Lane	71 B3
Samuel Beckett Bridge	72 E4
Sanderling Apartments	48 E3
Sandford Avenue (Donnybrook)	47 C1
Sandford Avenue (Donore Avenue)	74 E3
Sandford Close	47 B1
Sandford Gardens	47 C1 [10]
(off Sandford Avenue)	
Sandford Gardens	74 F3
Sandford Lodge	47 B1
Sandford Park (Sandford Gardens)	74 F3
Sandford Road	47 B1
Sandford Row	47 B1
Sandford Terrace	47 B1
Sandford Wood	1 C1
Sandon Cove	26 E4
Sandwith Street Lower	72 D4
Sandwith Street Upper	76 D1
Sandycove Avenue East	60 E1
Sandycove Avenue North	50 E4
Sandycove Avenue West	60 E1
Sandycove Lane East	60 E1
Sandycove Point	50 E4
Sandycove Road	60 E1
Sandyford	58 D2
Sandyford Downs	58 D3
Sandyford Hall	58 E3
Sandyford Hall Avenue	58 E3
Sandyford Hall Close	58 E4
Sandyford Hall Court	58 E3
Sandyford Hall Crescent	58 E3
Sandyford Hall Drive	58 E4
Sandyford Hall Green	58 E3
Sandyford Hall Grove	58 E4
Sandyford Hall Lawn	58 E3
Sandyford Hall Park	58 E3
Sandyford Hall Place	58 E3
Sandyford Hall Rise	58 E3
Sandyford Hall View	58 E4
Sandyford Hall Walk	58 E4
Sandyford Park	58 D3
Sandyford Road	57 C1
Sandyford View	57 C1
Sandyford Village	58 D3
Sandyhill Avenue	24 F1
Sandyhill Court	11 C4
Sandyhill Gardens	24 F1
Sandyhill Terrace	11 C4
Sandyhill Way	11 C4
Sandymount	39 A4
Sandymount Avenue	39 A4
Sandymount Castle	39 A4 [5]
(off Gilford Road)	
Sandymount Castle Drive	39 A4 [3]
(off Gilford Road)	
Sandymount Castle Park	39 B4 [2]
(off Gilford Road)	
Sandymount Castle Road	39 A4 [2]
(off Gilford Road)	
Sandymount Court	39 A3 [26]
(off Beach Road)	
Sandymount Green	39 A4 [1]
(off Gilford Road)	
Sandymount Road	39 A3
Sans Souci Park	48 F3
Sans Souci wood	67 C3
Santa Sabina Manor	29 B2
Santry	25 B1
Santry Avenue	12 E4
Santry Close	12 F4
Santry Court	12 F4
Santry Cross (Ballymun)	12 D4
Santry Cross	12 E4
Santry Villas	12 E4
Sarah Bridge (River Liffey)	69 B4
Sarah Curran Avenue	56 F1
Sarah Curran Road	56 F1 [1]
(off Sarah Curran Avenue)	
Sarah Place	69 B4
Saran Wood	67 B4
Sarney	6 E2
Sarsfield Court	34 D1 [1]
(off Main Street Lucan)	
Sarsfield Court (Inchicore)	36 F3
Sarsfield Park	34 D1
Sarsfield Quay	70 E4
Sarsfield Road	36 F3
Sarsfield Street (Sallynoggin)	60 D1
Sarsfield Street (Phibsborough)	71 A1
Sarsfield Terrace	34 D1 [1]
(off Main Street Lucan)	
Sarto Lawn	27 C1
Sarto Park	27 C1
Sarto Rise	27 C1
Sarto Road	27 C2
Saul Road	46 E1
Saval Grove	60 E2
Saval Park Crescent	60 E2
Saval Park Gardens	60 E2
Saval Park Road	60 E2
Scariff House	22 F1
Scholarstown Park	56 D2
Scholarstown Road	56 D2
School Avenue	26 E2
School Street	74 E1
Schoolhouse Court	25 B1
Schoolhouse Lane (Santry)	25 B1
Schoolhouse Lane (Kildare Street)	75 C1
Schoolhouse Lane West	75 A1
(off High Street)	
Schoolhouse Mews	25 B1 [2]
(off Schoolhouse Lane)	
Schools Road	67 B4
Scotchstone Bridge	2 D1
Scott Park	67 C3
Scribblestown	23 C3
Scribblestown Avenue	23 C3
Scribblestown Close	23 C3
Scribblestown Grove	23 C3
Scribblestown Park	24 D3
Scribblestown Place	23 C3
Scribblestown Road	23 B3
Scribblestown Road	24 D3
Sea Road	3 A2
Seabank Court (Malahide)	3 C2 [1]
Seabank Court (off Marine Parade)	60 E1 [21]

STREET NAME	PAGE	GRID
Seabrook Manor	14	E2
Seabury	48	E1
Seabury Avenue	2	F2
Seabury Close	2	F2
Seabury Court	2	F2
Seabury Crescent	2	F2
Seabury Dale	2	F2
Seabury Downs	2	F2
Seabury Drive	3	A2
Seabury Gardens	2	F2
Seabury Glen	2	F2
Seabury Green	2	F2
Seabury Grove	2	F2
Seabury Heights	2	F2
Seabury Lane	2	F2
Seabury Lawns	2	F2
Seabury Meadows	2	F2
Seabury Orchard	2	F2
Seabury Parade	2	F2
Seabury Park	2	F2
Seabury Place	2	F2
Seabury Road	2	F2
Seabury Vale	2	F2
Seabury View	2	F2
Seabury Walk	2	F2
Seabury Wood	2	F2
Seacliff Avenue	27	C1
Seacliff Drive	27	C1
Seacliff Road	27	C1
Seacourt	26	F4
Seacrest	67	C3
Seafield (off Baldoyle Road)	28	D1 [2]
Seafield (Shankill)	64	F2
Seafield Avenue (Clontarf)	26	F4
Seafield Avenue (Monkstown)	49	B4
Seafield Close	48	E3
Seafield Court (Malahide)	3	B2
Seafield Court (Loughlinstown)	64	E1
Seafield Crescent	48	E3
*Seafield Downs	26	F4
(off Kincora Road Clontarf)		
Seafield Drive	48	E2
Seafield Grove (off St. Gabriel's Road)	27	A4 [1]
Seafield Park (off Seafield Road)	48	E2 [1]
Seafield Road (Booterstown)	48	E2
Seafield Road (Killiney)	60	E4
Seafield Road (Ballybrack)	64	E1
Seafield Road East	26	F4
Seafield Road West	26	E4
Seafield Terrace	60	F2 [15]
(off Coliemore Road)		
Seafort Avenue	39	A4
Seafort Cottages	39	A4 [18]
(off Seafort Avenue)		
Seafort Gardens	39	A3 [10]
(off Sandymount Road)		
Seafort Parade	48	F3
Seafort Terrace (off Seafort Avenue)	39	A4 [19]
Seafort Villas (off Seafort Avenue)	39	A4 [20]
Seagrange Avenue	14	F4
Seagrange Drive	27	C1
Seagrange Road	27	C1
Seagrave	14	F2
Seagrave Close	11	B4
Seagrave Court	11	B4
Seagrave Drive	11	B4
Seagrave Terrace	11	B4
Seagrave Way	11	B4
Seamount	3	C3
Seamount	48	E3
Seamount Drive	3	C3
Seamount Grove	3	C3
Seamount Heights	3	C3
Seamount Park	3	C3
Seamount Road	3	C3
Seamount View	2	E2
Seamus Ennis Road	24	E1
Sean Heuston Bridge (River Liffey)	70	D4
Sean MacDermott Street Lower	71	C2
Sean MacDermott Street Upper	71	C3
Sean Moore Road	39	A3
Sean O'Casey Avenue	71	C2
Sean O'Casey Bridge (River Liffey)	72	D4
Sean Tracey House	72	D2
Seapark (Malahide)	3	C3
Seapark (Dollymount)	26	F4
Seapark Drive	26	F4
Seapark Hill	3	C3
Seapark Road	26	F4
Seapoint Avenue	15	A4 [1]
(off College Street Baldoyle)		
Seapoint Avenue (Blackrock)	49	B3
Seapoint Court	15	A4 [7]
(off College Street Baldoyle)		
Seapoint Court (Bray)	67	C1
Seapoint Road	67	C2
Seapoint Terrace	39	A3 [4]
(off Strand Street Ringsend)		
Seapoint Terrace (off Belgrave Road)	49	B3 [4]
Seapoint Terrace (Bray)	67	C2 [24]
Seapoint Villas	67	C2 [20]
Seascout Den	40	D1
Seatown Park	2	D1
Seatown Park The Avenue	2	D1
Seatown Park The Court	2	D1
Seatown Park The Crescent	2	D1
Seatown Park The Drive	2	D1
Seatown Park The Green	2	D1
Seatown Park The Grove	2	D1
Seatown Road	2	D1
Seatown Roundabout (Swords)	2	D1
Seatown Terrace	2	D2
Seatown Villas	2	D1
Seatown Walk	2	D2
Seatown West	2	D1
Seaview Avenue East	72	F2
Seaview Avenue North	26	D4
Seaview Cottages	63	C4
Seaview Lawn	64	E2
Seaview Park	64	E2
Seaview Terrace	30	D2 [2]
(off Main Street Howth)		
Seaview Terrace (Donnybrook)	48	D1
Seaview Terrace	49	C4 [15]
(off Clarence Street Dún Laoghaire)		
Seaview Wood	64	E2
Second Avenue (Tallaght)	44	F4
Second Avenue (Seville Place)	72	E3
Sefton	59	C2
Sefton Green	59	C2
Sefton Hall (off Kelston Avenue)	59	A2 [12]
*Selskar Terrace (Old Mountpleasant)	75	C4
Serpentine Avenue	39	A4
Serpentine Park	39	A4
Serpentine Road	39	A4
Serpentine Terrace	39	A4
Seskin View Avenue	55	A2
Seskin View Drive	55	A2
Seskin View Park	55	A2
Seskin View Road	55	A2
Setanta Place	75	C1
Seven Houses	60	D1 [13]
(off Glenageary Road Lower)		
Seven Oaks (Whitehall)	25	B3
Seven Oaks (Inchicore)	36	F3
Seventh Lock Cottages	36	D4
Seventh Lock Place	36	D4
Seville Place	72	D2
Seville Terrace	72	D2
Seymour Road	67	C2
Shackleton	8	F4
Shakelton	8	F4
Shaldon Grange	62	F2
Shalimar Apartments	44	F3 [3]
Shamrock Cottages	72	D2
Shamrock Hill Mews	47	C1 [23]
(off Stillorgan Road)		
Shamrock Place	72	D2
Shamrock Street	71	A2
Shamrock Terrace	72	D2
Shamrock Villas	46	F1
Shanagarry (off Milltown Road)	47	B2 [9]
Shanard Avenue	25	A1
Shanard Road	25	A1
Shanboley Road	25	C1
Shancastle Avenue	35	A2
Shancastle Close	35	A2
Shancastle Crescent	35	A2
Shancastle Drive	35	A2
Shancastle Lawns	35	A2
Shancastle Park	35	A2
Shandon Crescent	24	F4
Shandon Drive	24	F4
Shandon Gardens	24	F4
Shandon Green	24	F4 [8]
(off Shandon Crescent)		
Shandon Mill (off Shandon Park)	24	F4 [9]
Shandon Park (Phibsborough)	24	F4
Shandon Park (Monkstown)	49	B4
Shandon Road	24	F4
Shangan Avenue	25	B1
Shangan Court	25	A1
Shangan Crescent	25	A1
Shangan Drive	25	B1
Shangan Gardens	25	B1
Shangan Green	25	B1
Shangan Hall Apartments	25	A1 [4]
(off Shangan Road)		
Shangan Park	25	B1
Shangan Road	25	A1
Shanganagh Cliffs	64	E2
Shanganagh Grove	64	E3
Shanganagh Road	64	E1
Shanganagh Terrace	60	E4
Shanganagh Vale	60	D4
Shanganagh Wood	64	E2 [8]
Shanglas Road	25	C1
Shanid Road	46	F2
Shankill	64	E3
Shankill View	67	C2 [38]
Shanliss Avenue	25	B1
Shanliss Drive	25	B1
Shanliss Gardens (off Shanliss Road)	25	A1 [2]
Shanliss Grove	25	B1
Shanliss Park	25	B1
Shanliss Road	25	A1
Shanliss Walk	25	B1
Shanliss Way	25	B1
Shannon Terrace	73	C1
Shanowen Avenue	25	A1
Shanowen Crescent	25	B1
Shanowen Drive	25	B1
Shanowen Grove	25	A1
Shanowen Hall	25	B2
Shanowen Park	25	A1
Shanowen Road	25	B1
Shanowen Square	25	B1
Shanowen Square	25	B2
Shanrath Road	25	B1
Shantalla Avenue	25	C1
Shantalla Drive	25	C2
Shantalla Park	25	C2
Shantalla Road	25	C1
Shanvarna Road	25	B1
Sharavogue	60	E2
Shaw Court Apartments	75	B3
Shaw Street	71	C4
Shaw's Lane	76	F2
Shea's Court	70	E2
Shea's Lane	70	E2
Sheelin Avenue	64	E1
Sheelin Drive	64	E1
Sheelin Grove	64	E1 [7]
Sheelin Hill	64	E1 [13]
Sheelin Walk	64	E1 [14]
Sheephill Avenue	9	C4
Sheephill Green	9	C4
Sheephill Park	9	C4
Sheepmoor Avenue	22	D1
Sheepmoor Close	22	D1
Sheepmoor Crescent	22	D1
Sheepmoor Gardens	22	D1
Sheepmoor Green	22	D1
Sheepmoor Grove	22	D1
Sheepmoor Lawn	22	D1
Sheepmoor Way	22	D1
Shelbourne Avenue	76	F3
(off Gilford Road)		
Shelbourne Lane	76	F3
(off Gilford Road)		
Shelbourne Park Mews	76	F1
Shelbourne Place	76	F2
Shelbourne Road	76	F2
Shelbourne Village	76	F1
Shelerin Road	21	C2
Shellys Banks Road	39	B3
Shelmalier Road	72	F2
Shelmartin Avenue	25	C4
Shelmartin Terrace	25	C4 [2]
(off Shelmartin Avenue)		
Shelton Drive	46	D2
Shelton Gardens	46	D2
Shelton Grove	46	D2
Shelton Park	46	D2
Sherborne	47	A2
Sheridan Court	71	B2
Sheridan Place	71	B2
Sheriff Street Lower	72	D3
Sheriff Street Upper	72	F3
Sherkin Court	25	B3
Sherkin Gardens	25	B3
Sherrard Avenue	71	B1
*Sherrard Court (off Portland Place)	71	B1
Sherrard Street Lower	71	C1
Sherrard Street Upper	71	B1
Sherrards Court	71	B1
Shielmartin Drive	29	B3
Shielmartin Park	29	B3 [1]
(off Shielmartin Road)		
Shielmartin Road	29	B3
Shinkeen Bridge	32	E2
Ship Street Great	75	A1
Ship Street Little	75	A1
Shrewsbury	39	A4
Shrewsbury Hall	64	E3
Shrewsbury House	59	C4
Shrewsbury Lawn	59	C4
Shrewsbury Lodge	59	C3
Shrewsbury Park	48	D1
Shrewsbury Road(Ailesbury Road)	48	D1
Shrewsbury Road (Shankill)	64	E3
Shrewsbury Woods	59	C4
Sibthorpe Lane	76	D4
Sidbury Court	68	D2 [5]
Sidmonton Avenue	67	C2
Sidmonton Court	68	D3 [5]
Sidmonton Gardens	67	C2 [36]
Sidmonton Gardens	67	C2
Sidmonton Park	68	D2
Sidmonton Place	67	C2 [6]
Sidmonton Road	67	C2
Sidmonton Square	67	C2 [1]
Sigurd Road	70	E3
Silchester Court	60	D1
Silchester Crescent	60	D1
Silchester Park	60	D1
Silchester Road	60	D1
Silchester Wood (off Adelaide Road)	60	D1 [16]
Silken Vale	17	C3
Silleachain Lane	20	D4
Silloge Avenue	25	A1
Silloge Crescent	25	A1
Silloge Gardens	25	A1
Silloge Road	25	A1
Silver Birches (Dunboyne)	7	B2
Silver Birches (Dundrum)	47	C4
Silver Birches Close	7	B2
Silver Birches Crescent	7	B2
Silver Pines (off Brewery Road)	58	F2 [3]
Silverberry	34	D3
Silverdale	34	D3
Silverpine	67	B3
Silverwood	34	D3
Silverwood Drive	46	E4
Silverwood Road	46	E4
Simmon's Place	71	C2
(off Thompson's Cottages)		
Simmonscourt Avenue	48	D1 [2]
(off Simmonscourt Road)		
Simmonscourt Castle	48	D1
Simmonscourt Road	39	A4
Simmonscourt Square	48	D1 [5]
(off Simmonscourt Road)		
Simmonscourt Terrace	47	C1 [18]
(off Beaver Row)		
Simmonscourt View	48	D1 [3]
(off Simmonscourt Road)		
Simmonstown	41	A1
Simmonstown Manor	32	D4
Simmonstown Park	32	D4
Simons Ridge	57	C3
Simpsons Lane (off Bath Street)	39	A3 [32]
Sion Hill Avenue	46	F1
Sion Hill Court (off Sion Hill Road)	25	C3 [5]
Sion Hill Road	25	C3
*Sion House	36	F3
(off Thomas Davis Street West)		
Sion Road	60	D2
Sionhill	48	F3
Sir Ivor Mall	58	F2 [7]
(off Leopardstown Road)		
Sir John Rogerson's Quay	72	E4
Sitric Place (off Sitric Road)	70	E3
Sitric Road	70	E3
Skeagh	41	A3
Skelligs Court	22	F1
Skelly's Lane	26	D2
Skreen Road	69	B1
Slade	53	A3
Slade Castle Avenue	53	A2
Slade Castle Close	53	A2
Slade Castle Heights	53	A2
Slade Castle View	53	A2
Slade Road	53	A2
Slade Row	70	D3
Slademore Avenue	26	F1
Slademore Close	26	F1
Slademore Court	13	C4

Street Name	Page	Grid
Slademore Drive	26	F1
Slane Road	73	C4
Slaney Close	24	E3
Slaney Road	24	E3
Slate Cabin Lane	57	C3
Slemish Road	69	B1
Slí an Chanáil	19	C4
Slieve Rua Drive	58	D1
Slievebloom Park	45	C1
Slievebloom Road	45	C1
Slievemore Road	73	A4
Slievenamon Road	73	B3
Sloan Terrace	68	D2 [8]
Sloperton	49	C4
Smithfield	70	F4
Smithfield Gate Apartments	70	F3
*Smithfield Market Square Apartments (Smithfield)		
*Smithfield Terrace (Smithfield)	70	F4
Smith's Cottages	47	B1 [18]
(off Bushfield Terrace)		
Smith's Lane	46	F1 [13]
(off Harolds Cross Road)		
Smith's Villas	49	C4 [3]
(off York Road Dún Laoghaire)		
Smyth Gardens	49	C4 [34]
(off York Road Dún Laoghaire)		
Snowdrop Walk	13	C4
Snugborough	14	E3
Snugborough Road	22	F1
Snugborough Road Extention	22	D2
Somerset Street	76	F1
Somerton	59	C2
Somerton Mews	59	C2
Somerton Road	22	E4
Somerville Avenue	45	C1
Somerville Court	46	D1 [8]
(off St Agnes RoadCrumlin)		
Somerville Drive	46	D1
Somerville Park	45	C1 [7]
(off Somerville Avenue)		
Sommerville	47	C4
Sonesta	3	A2
Sophie Baret Residence	48	D4 [2]
(off Lower Kilmacud Road)		
Sorbonne	48	D4
Sorrel Dale	22	D2
Sorrel Drive	21	C2
Sorrel Heath	21	C2
Sorrel Park	21	C2
Sorrell Hall	57	C3
Sorrento Close (off Sorrento Road)	60	F2 [25]
Sorrento Court (off Sorrento Road)	60	F2 [29]
Sorrento Drive (off Sorrento Road)	60	F2 [12]
Sorrento Heights (off Sorrento Road)	60	F2 [30]
Sorrento Lawn (off Sorrento Road)	60	F2 [13]
Sorrento Mews (off Sorrento Road)	60	F2 [28]
*Sorrento Park (on Sorrento Rd)	60	F2
Sorrento Road	60	F2
Sorrento Terrace	60	Inset
South Avenue	48	E4
South Bank (Swords)	1	C1
South Bank	2	D1
South Bank Road	39	B3
South Circular Road (Islandbridge)	69	B4
South Circular Road (Kilmainham)	73	C2
South Circular Road (Dolphin's Barn)	74	D3
South Circular Road (Portobello)	74	E3
South City Market (on South Great Georges Street)	75	B1
South Dock Place	76	F1
South Dock Road	76	F1
South Dock Street	76	F1
South Esplanade	68	D2
South Great George's Street	75	B1
South Hill (Howth)	29	C3
South Hill (Milltown)	47	B2
South Hill Avenue	48	F3
South Hill Park	48	E3
South Lotts Road	76	F1
South Park (Cornelscourt)	59	B3
South Park Drive	59	B2
South Richmond View	75	B3
South Winds	60	F1 [4]
(off Ulverton Road Dalkey)		
South Wood Park	48	F3
Southdene	49	B4 [18]
(off Monkstown Valley)		
Southern Cross Avenue	73	A2
Southern Cross Route	57	B3
Southmede	57	C1
Southview Terrace	74	D1
Spa Road (Inchicore)	36	F3
Spa Road (Phoenix Park)	69	B2
Spafield Terrace	39	A4 [13]
(off Sandymount Avenue)		
Spawell Cottages	45	C4 [1]
(off Tallaght Road)		
Spawell Roundabout	46	D4
Spencer Dock (North Wall)	72	E3
Spencer Dock	72	E3
Spencer Dock (Guild Street)	72	E3
Spencer Place (off Spencer Street N)	72	E1
Spencer Row	71	C3
Spencer Street North	72	E1
Spencer Street South	75	A3
Spencer Terrace (off Cork Street)	74	E2
Spencer Villas	60	E1
Spences Terrace	74	E2
Sperrin Road	73	A3
Spiddal Park	35	C3
Spiddal Road	35	C3
Spire View	24	D4
Spire View	70	F1
Spire View Lane	47	A1
Spitalfields	74	F1
Spring Garden Lane	71	C4
Spring Garden Street	72	D1
Springbank Cottages	53	A2
Springdale Court Apartments	26	F2
Springdale Road	26	F2
Springfield (Tallaght)	54	F1
Springfield (Cabra)	69	B1
Springfield Avenue	46	E4
Springfield Close	31	C4
Springfield Crescent	46	E4
Springfield Drive	46	E4
Springfield Lane	63	A1
Springfield Park (Templeogue)	46	E4
Springfield Park (Deans Grange)	59	A2
Springfield Road	46	E3
Springhill Avenue	59	A1
Springhill Cottages	59	B1 [5]
(off Brookville Park)		
Springhill Park (Deans Grange)	59	B1
Springhill Park (Dalkey)	60	E2
Springlawn	22	E2
Springlawn Close	22	E2
Springlawn Court	22	E2
Springlawn Drive	22	E2
Springlawn Heights	22	E2
Springlawn Park	22	E2
Springlawn Road	22	E2
Springmount Apartments	24	D2
Springvale	56	E2
Springvale Hall	57	C3
Spruce Avenue	58	D2
St Agnes Park	46	D1
St Agnes Road	46	D1
St Agnes Terrace (off Dodder Road Lower Rathfarnham)	46	F3 [2]
St Agnes Terrace	46	D1 [4]
(off St Agnes RoadCrumlin)		
*St Agnes Terrace (on St Agnes Rd)	46	D1
St Aidan's Drive	48	D4
St Aidan's Halting Site	54	D1
St Aidan's Park	25	C4 [6]
(off St Aidan's Park Road)		
St Aidan's Park Avenue	25	C4
St Aidan's Park Road	25	C4
St Aidan's Terrace	67	C2 [23]
St Alban's Park	48	E1
St Alphonsus Avenue	25	A4 [11]
(off St. Joseph's Avenue)		
St Alphonsus Road	25	A4
St Andrews	34	F2
St Andrews Court	34	D1 [17]
(off Main Street Lucan)		
St Andrews Drive	34	F2
St Andrews Fairway	34	F2
St Andrews Green	34	F2
St Andrew's Grove	3	B3
St Andrews Park	1	C1
St Andrews Wood	34	F2
St Anne's Court	27	A3 [2]
(off All Saint's Park)		
St Anne's (Kimmage)	46	E2
St Anne's (Ranelagh)	75	C4
St Anne's Avenue	27	A3
St Anne's Drive	27	A3
St Anne's Park	64	E3
St Anne's Road North	25	A4
St Anne's Square	14	F2 [6]
(off St. Marnock's Avenue)		
St Anne's Square	49	A3 [7]
(off Frascati Road Blackrock)		
St Anne's Terrace (Raheny)	27	A3
St Anne's Terrace (Rathcoole)	52	E2
St Anne's Terrace (Ranelagh)	75	C4
St Anns Close	49	A3 [26]
St Ann's Square Lower	14	F2 [5]
(off St. Marnock's Avenue)		
St Anthony's Avenue	44	E2
St Anthony's Crescent	45	C2
St Aongus Court	45	B4
St Aongus Crescent	45	B4
St Aongus Green	45	B4
St Aongus Grove	45	B4
St Aongus Lawn	45	B4
St Aongus Park	45	B4
St Aongus Road	45	B4
St Assam's Avenue	27	A2
St Assam's Drive	27	A2
St Assam's Park	27	A2
St Assam's Road East	27	B2
St Assam's Road West	27	A2
St Attracta Road	24	F4
St Aubyn's Court	64	E1 [5]
St Augustine's Park	59	A1
St Begnet's Villas	60	E1
St Benedicts Gardens	71	B1
St Berach's Place	27	B1 [6]
(Swan's Nest Avenue)		
St Brendan's Avenue	26	E2
St Brendan's Cottages	39	A3 [6]
(off Irishtown Road)		
St Brendan's Crescent	45	B2
St Brendan's Drive	26	E2
St Brendan's Park	26	F2
St Brendan's Road	25	A4 [12]
(off St Anne's Road North)		
St Brendan's Terrace (Coolock)	26	E1
St Brendan's Terrace	49	C4 [19]
(off North Cote Avenue)		
St Brendan's Terrace (Rockbrook)	56	E4
St Bridget's Avenue (North Strand)	72	E1
St Bridget's Drive	45	B2
St Bridget's Flats	47	C2 [8]
(off Embassy Lawn)		
St Brigid's Green	26	E2
St Brigid's Grove	26	E2
St Brigid's Avenue	14	F2 [4]
(off St. Marnock's Avenue)		
St Brigid's Church Road	58	F1
St Brigid's Cottages	22	F2
(Blanchardstown)		
St Brigid's Cottages (Clondalkin)	44	F2
St Brigid's Cottages (North Strand)	72	E1
St Brigid's Court (off Killester Park)	26	E3 [2]
St Brigid's Crescent	26	E2
St Brigid's Drive (off Killester Park)	26	E3 [1]
St Brigid's Drive (Clondalkin)	44	E2
St Brigid's Lawn	26	E2
St Brigid's Park (Blanchardstown)	22	F2
St Brigid's Park (St Brigid's Road)	44	E2 [1]
St Brigid's Park (Cornelscourt)	59	B3
St Brigid's Road (Artane)	26	E2
St Brigid's Road (Clondalkin)	44	E2
St Brigid's Road Lower	25	A4
St Brigid's Road Upper	25	A4
St Brigid's Terrace	67	C2 [33]
St Broc's Cottages	47	C1 [1]
(off Victoria Avenue)		
St Canice's Park	24	F2
St Canice's Road	25	A2
St Catherines Grove	43	C1 [3]
(off St. Cutberth's Road)		
St Catherine's Park	60	E1
St Catherine's Road	60	E1
St Catherine's Terrace	29	A1 [2]
(off Sutton Cross)		
St Catherine's View	20	E4
St Catheryn's Court	39	B4 [7]
(off Durham Road)		
St Clair's Lawn	67	B3
St Clair's Terrace	67	B3 [3]
*St Clare's Avenue	74	F4
(off Harolds Cross Road)		
St Clement's Road	25	A4 [13]
(off St Anne's Road North)		
St Colmcille's Way	55	C2
St Columbanus Avenue	47	B3
St Columbanus Place	47	B3 [1]
(off St. Columbanus Road)		
St Columbanus Road	47	B3
St Columbas Heights	1	C2
St Columbas Rise	1	C2
St Columba's Road	45	B2
St Columba's Road Lower	25	A4
St Columba's Road Upper	25	A4
St Columcille's Crescent	2	D2 [1]
St Columcille's Drive	2	D2
St Columcille's Terrace	67	C2 [18]
St Columcills Park	2	D2
St Conleth's Road	45	C2
St Cronan's Cottages	1	C2
St Cronan's Avenue	1	B1
St Cronan's Close	1	B2
St Cronan's Cottages	1	C2
St Cronan's Court	1	B1
St Cronan's Grove	1	C1
St Cronan's Lawn	1	B1
*St Cronan's Road	67	C2 [8]
St Cronan's View	1	B2
St Cronan's Way	1	C2
St Cuthbert's Road	43	B1
St David's	26	D2
St David's Court	26	E4 [5]
(off Castle Avenue Clontarf)		
St David's Park	26	D2
St David's Terrace	25	A3 [3]
(off Glasnevin Hill)		
St Davids Wood	26	D2
St Declan's Road	25	C4
St Declan's Terrace	25	C4 [5]
(off St Declan's Road)		
St Domhnach's Well Street	28	D1 [3]
(off Baldoyle Road)		
St Dominic's Avenue	55	A1
St Dominic's Court	55	A1 [4]
(off St Dominic's Terrace)		
St Dominic's Road	55	A1
St Dominic's Terrace	55	A1
St Donagh's Crescent	27	B1
St Donagh's Park	27	B1
St Donagh's Road	27	B1
St Edmunds	35	A1
St Eithne Road	24	F4
St Elizabeth's Court	70	E1
St Enda's Drive	56	F1
St Enda's Park	56	F1
St Enda's Road	46	F2
St Finbarr's Court	24	E4 [2]
(off Kilkieran Road)		
St Finbarr's Close	45	B3
St Finbarr's Road	24	E4
St Finian's Grove	34	D2
St Finian's Avenue	34	D2
St Finian's Close	34	D2
St Finian's Crescent	34	D2
St Fintan Road	24	F4
St Fintan Terrace	24	F4
St Fintan's Crescent	29	B3
St Fintan's Grove	29	B3
St Fintan's Park (Sutton)	29	B2
St Fintan's Park (Deans Grange)	59	A1
St Fintan's Road	29	B3
St Fintan's Terrace	35	C1 [1]
(off Lucan Road Palmerston)		
St Fintan's Villas	59	B1
St Gabriel's	59	C3
St Gabriel's Court	27	A4 [2]
(off St. Gabriel's Road)		
St Gabriel's Road	26	F4
St Gall Gardens North	47	B3 [2]
(off St. Columbanus Road)		
St Gall Gardens South	47	B [33]
(off St. Columbanus Road)		
St Gatien Road	56	F1 [2]
(off Whitechurch Road)		
St George's Avenue (Clonliffe Road)	25	B4
St George's Avenue (Killiney)	60	E3
St George's Villas	36	F3 [18]
(off Inchicore Terrace South)		
St Gerard's Road	45	C2
St Helena's Court	24	E2 [3]
(off St Helena's Drive)		
St Helena's Drive	24	E2
St Helena's Road	24	E2
St Helen's (off Marine Parade)	60	E1 [22]
St Helen's Road	48	E2
St Helen's Terrace	73	A2
St Helen's Villas (off St Helen's Road)	48	F2 [1]
St Helen's Wood	48	E3
St Helier's Copse	48	F4 [1]
(off Coppinger Wood)		
St Ignatius Avenue	71	B1
St Ignatius Road	71	B1

STREET NAME	PAGE/GRID REFERENCE
St Ita's Road (off Botanic Avenue)	25 A3 [6]
St Ives	3 B2
St James Avenue (Clonliffe Road)	72 D1
St James Court	39 A4 [49]
(off Serpentine Avenue)	
*St James Place (Sandymount Road)	39 A3
St James Terrace	39 A3 [23]
(off Sandymount Road)	
St James's	26 D4
St James's Place	36 F3 [17]
(off Tyrconnell Road)	
St James's Road	45 B2
St Jarlath Road	24 F4
St John's Court (Donnycarney)	26 D3
St John's	48 E1
St John's Avenue (Clondalkin)	44 D2
*St Johns Close	59 C1
(opposite Glandore Park)	
St John's Close	44 D2
St John's Court	25 B1
St John's Court (Beaumont)	26 D1
St John's Court (Clondalkin)	44 D2
St John's Crescent	44 D2
St John's Drive	44 D2
St John's Gate	44 D2
St John's Green	44 D2
St John's Grove	44 D2
*St John's Lane (off Strand Road)	48 E1
St John's Lawn	44 D2
St John's Park (Dún Laoghaire)	49 C4
St John's Park East	44 D2
St Johns Park West	44 D2
St John's Road	44 D2
St John's Road East	48 E1
St John's Road West (Clondalkin)	44 D2
*St Johns Terrace	73 C1
(Donnellan Avenue)	
St John's Wood	26 E4 [2]
(off Castle Avenue Clontarf)	
St John's Wood (Clondalkin)	44 D2
St John's Wood West	44 D2
St Joseph Street (off Leo Street)	71 B1
St Joseph's	23 C2
St Joseph's Avenue	25 B4 [2]
(off Clonliffe Road)	
St Joseph's Avenue (Drumcondra)	25 A4
St Joseph's Cottages	23 C4 [3]
(off Blackhorse Avenue)	
St Joseph's Grove	47 C4 [9]
(off Rosemount Park)	
St Joseph's Parade	71 A1
St Joseph's Road (Walkinstown)	45 C2
St Joseph's Square	39 C1 [2]
(off Vernon Avenue)	
St Joseph's Terrace	25 C4 [4]
(off Philipsburgh Avenue)	
*St Joseph's Terrace	39 A3
(off Pembroke Street)	
*St Joseph's Terrace	50 D4
(on Tivoli Road)	
St Joseph's Terrace	71 C1
(North Circular Road)	
St Joseph's Villas (Summerhill)	72 D1
St Judes Apartments	31 C3 [3]
St Kevin's Court	47 A2
St Kevin's Gardens	47 A2
St Kevin's Park (Rathgar)	47 A2
St Kevin's Park (Stillorgan)	58 D1
St Kevin's Road	75 A4
St Kevin's Square	67 C2
St Kevin's Terrace (Bray)	67 C2 [14]
St Kevin's Villas	60 D1
St Killian's Avenue	45 B2
St Killians Crescent	67 B4
St Killian's Park (off Watery Lane)	44 E1 [1]
St Laurence Court	36 E3
St Laurence Grove	36 E2 [4]
(off St. Laurence Road)	
St Laurence Park	48 F4
St Laurence Road	36 E2
St Laurence Terrace	36 E2 [9]
(off Lucan Road Chapelizod)	
St Laurence's Terrace (Bray)	67 C2 [17]
St Lawrence Building Apartments	30 D1 [16]
(off Harbour Road)	
St Lawrence Glen	36 E3 [3]
(off St Lawrence Road)	
St Lawrence O'Toole Avenue	14 F2 [1]
(off St.Patrick's Avenue)	
St Lawrence Quay (off Harbour Road)	30 D1 [8]
St Lawrence Road (Clontarf)	26 D4
St Lawrence Road (Howth)	30 D1
St Lawrence's Court	26 D4
St Lawrence's Terrace	30 D2 [1]
(off Grace O'Malley Road)	
St Loman's Road	34 F2
St Luke's Court	26 D1 [3]
(off Cromcastle Green)	
St Luke's Crescent	47 B2 [3]
(off Dundrum Road)	
St Maelruans Park	55 A1 [1]
(off Old Bawn Road)	
St Malachy's Drive	45 C2
St Malachy's Road	25 A3 [7]
(off Botanic Avenue)	
St Margaret's Close	60 E1 [30]
(off Castlepark Road)	
St Margaret's (North Road)	11 B1
St Margaret's (Booterstown)	48 F3
St Margaret's Avenue (Malahide)	3 B3
St Margaret's Avenue (Kilbarrack)	27 C2
*St Margaret's Avenue North	71 C1
(Richmond Lane)	
St Margaret's Court	11 A4 [1]
(off Saint Margaret's Road)	
St Margaret's Halting Site	11 C4
St Margaret's Park	3 B3
St Margaret's Road (Malahide)	3 B3
St Margaret's Road (Poppintree)	11 C4
St Margaret's Road (Finglas)	11 A4
St Margaret's Road (Ballymun)	12 D4
St Mark's Avenue	35 A2
St Mark's Crescent	35 A3
St Mark's Drive	35 A3
St Mark's Gardens	35 A3
St Mark's Green	35 A3
St Mark's Grove	35 A3
St Marnock's Avenue	14 F2
St Martin's Drive	46 E2
St Martin's Park	46 E1
St Mary's Avenue (Rathfarnham)	46 F4
St Mary's Avenue West	36 F3
*St Mary's Court (on Church Road)	72 F2
St Mary's Crescent	45 C1
St Mary's Drive	45 C1
St Mary's Park (Leixlip)	20 D4
St Mary's Park (Finglas)	23 C2
St Mary's Park (Crumlin)	45 C1
St Mary's Place	30 D2 [4]
(off Main Street Howth)	
St Mary's Road	30 D2 [3]
(off Main Street Howth)	
St Mary's Road (Crumlin)	46 D1
St Mary's Street	49 C4 [5]
(off North Cote Avenue)	
St Marys Terrace (Bray)	68 D2 [20]
St Mary's Terrace (Dunboyne)	7 B2 [1]
St Mary's Terrace	36 E2 [5]
(off Martin's Row Chapelizod)	
*St Mary's Terrace (Bath Street)	39 A3
St Mary's Terrace	46 F4 [5]
(off Grange Road Rathfarnham)	
St Mary's Terrace (Boghall Road)	67 C4 [6]
St Mathias Wood	60 D4
St Mel's Avenue	45 B3
St Michael's Estate	73 A2
St Michael's House	47 C4
St Michael's Road	25 A3 [8]
(off Botanic Avenue)	
St Michael's Terrace	49 C4 [18]
(off York Road Dún Laoghaire)	
*St Mobhi Avenue (on St. Mobhi Road)	25 A3
St Mobhi Boithirin	25 A3
St Mobhi Drive	25 A3
St Mobhi Grove (off Botanic Road)	25 A3 [10]
St Mobhi Road	25 A3
St Mochtas Avenue	22 D3
St Mochtas Chase	22 D2
St Mochtas Close	22 D3
St Mochtas Drive	22 D3
St Mochtas Green	22 D3
St Mochtas Grove	22 D3
St Mochtas Lawn	22 D2
St Mochtas Road	22 D3
St Mochtas Vale	22 D3
St Mura's Terrace	72 F2
St Nathy's House	47 B4 [5]
(off Churchtown Road)	
St Nathy's Villas	47 B4 [17]
(off Nutgrove Avenue)	
St Nessan's Apartments	30 E2 [3]
(Thormanby Road)	
St Nessan's Close	30 D2 [9]
(off Tuckett's Lane)	
St Nessans Court	30 D2 [12]
(off Main Street Howth)	
St Nessan's Terrace	30 D2 [5]
(off Tuckett's Lane)	
St Oliver's Park	35 B3
St Pappin's Green	24 F2
St Pappin's Road	25 A2
St Patrick's Avenue (Portmarnock)	14 F2
St Patrick's Avenue	44 D1 [1]
(St Patrick's Park)	
St Patrick's Avenue	60 F2 [1]
(off Castle Street Dalkey)	
St Patrick's Avenue (Fairview)	72 E1
St Patrick's Close	59 C1
(off St Patrick's Crescent)9	
St Patrick's Cottages	46 F4
St Patrick's Crescent (Rathcoole)	52 E2
St Patrick's Crescent	59 C1
(Kill O'The Grange)	
St Patrick's Parade	25 A4
St Patrick's Park (Dunboyne)	7 B2
St Patrick's Park	22 E2
(Blanchardstown)	
St Patrick's Park (Celbridge)	31 C3
St Patrick's Park (Celbridge)	32 D3
St Patrick's Park (Clondalkin)	44 D1
St Patrick's Park (Stepaside)	58 E4
*St Patrick's Place	25 A4
(off Royal Canal Bank)	
St Patrick's Road (Drumcondra)	25 A4
St Patrick's Road (Clondalkin)	35 A4
St Patrick's Road (Walkinstown)	45 C2
St Patrick's Road	60 F2
(off Castle Street Dalkey)8	
St Patrick's Square	25 A4
(off Castle Street Dalkey)	
St Patrick's Square	60 F2 [4]
St Patrick's Square (Bray)	67 C1 [1]
*St Patrick's Terrace	25 B4
(off Fitzroy Avenue)	
St Patrick's Terrace	36 F3 [9]
(off Inchicore Terrace South)	
St Patrick's Terrace	59 C1 [7]
(off Oliver Plunkett Road)	
*St Patrick's Terrace (Russell Street)	71 C1
St Patrick's Villas	39 A3 [3]
(off Thorncastle Street)	
St Paul's Terrace (off Adelaide Road)	60 E1 [5]
St Peter's Avenue	70 F1
St Peter's Close	71 A1
St Peter's Crescent	45 C2
St Peter's Drive	45 C2
St Peter's Park	7 B2
St Peter's Road (Phibsborough)	24 F4
St Peter's Road (Walkinstown)	45 C2
St Peter's Road (Bray)	67 B1
St Peter's Square	71 A1
St Peter's Terrace (Howth)	30 D2
St Peter's Terrace (off St. Peter's	45 C2 [1]
Drive Walkinstown)	
St Peter's Terrace	60 E1 [6]
(off Adelaide Road)	
St Peter's Terrace (Bray)	67 B1 [2]
St Philomenas	9 C4
St Philomena's Court	9 C4
St Philomena's Park	9 C3
St Philomena's Road	60 E1
(off Dalcassian Downs)	
St Raphaels Avenue	31 C4
St Ronan's Avenue	35 A3
St Ronan's Close	35 A3
St Ronan's Crescent	35 A3
St Ronan's Drive	35 A3
St Ronan's Gardens	35 A3
St Ronan's Green	35 A3
St Ronan's Grove	35 A3
St Ronan's Park	35 A3
St Ronan's Way	35 A3
*St Samson Court	14 D3
St Samson Square	14 D3
St Sylvester Villas	3 B3
St Teresa's Place	25 A4 [9]
(off Prospect Avenue)	
St Teresa's Road	25 A4 [8]
(off Botanic Road Glasnevin)	
St Teresa's Road (Crumlin)	46 D2
St Thomas Mead	48 E3
St Thomas's Road	48 E3
(Mount Merrion)	
St Vincent Street North	71 A1
St Vincent Street West	73 A2
St Vincent's Cottages	23 C4 [2]
(off Blackhorse Avenue)	
St Vincent's Court	25 C3 [7]
(off Collins Avenue)	
St Vincent's Court	26 D3
St Vincent's Park	49 A4
St Werburghs	2 E2
St Wolstan's Abbey	32 E2
St Wolston's Abbey	32 D4
St. Agatha Court (off William St N)	72 D2
St. Alban's Road	74 F3
St. Andrew Street	75 B1
St. Andrew's Lane	75 B1
(off Exchequer Street)	
St. Anne's Road South	74 E3
St. Anns Court	71 B2
St. Anthony Crescent	74 D2
St. Anthony's Place	71 B2
St. Anthony's Place	71 B2
(off Temple Street North)	
St. Anthony's Road	74 D2
St. Audoen's House Flats	70 F4
St. Audoen's Terrace	75 A1
(off High Street)	
St. Augustine Street	70 F4
St. Barnabas Gardens	72 E2
St. Bricin's Park	70 D3
St. Catherine's Avenue	74 E3
St. Catherine's Lane West	74 F1
St. Catherines West	74 E3
St. David's Terrace	70 D2
(Blackhorse Avenue)	
St. Francis Square	75 A1
St. Jame's Wood (Suir Road)	73 B2
St. Jame's Wood	73 B2
St. James's Avenue (James's Street)	74 D1
St. James's Court Apartments	74 E1
St. James's Terrace (Dolphin's Barn)	74 D3
St. James's Walk	74 D2
St. John Street	74 F2
St. John's Avenue (The Coombe)	74 F2
St. John's Cottages	73 C1
St. John's Road West (Islandbridge)	69 C4
St. John's Terrace (Mount Brown)	73 C1
St. John's Well Way	73 C1
St. Joseph's Court	70 E2
St. Joseph's Court	70 E2
St. Joseph's Mansions	72 D2
St. Joseph's Place	70 E2
St. Joseph's Place (Prussia Street)	70 E2
St. Joseph's Place	71 B2
(Dorset Street Lower)	
St. Joseph's Road (Aughrim Street)	70 E2
St. Joseph's Terrace	71 A2
*St. Joseph's Terrace	74 D3
(off Dolphin's Barn)	
St. Kevin's Avenue (off Blackpitts)	74 F2
St. Kevins Church Apartments	75 A3
St. Kevin's Cottages	75 A3
St. Kevin's Parade	75 A3
*St. Kevin's Terrace (New Bride Street)	75 A2
*St. Laurence O'Toole Court	72 D3
(off Oriel Street Upper)	
St. Laurence Place (Western Way)	71 A2
St. Laurence Place East	72 E3
(Lower Sheriff Street)	
St. Luke's Avenue	74 F2
St. Luke's Gate	74 F2
St. Maignenn's Terrace	73 C1
St. Margaret's Avenue	74 F1
(off Pimlico)	
St. Margaret's Terrace	74 E2
St. Mary's Ave North	71 A2
(Mountjoy Street)	
St. Mary's Lane	76 E2
St. Mary's Mansions	71 C2
St. Mary's Place North	71 A2
St. Mary's Road North (East Wall)	72 E2
St. Mary's Road South (Ballsbridge)	76 E3
St. Mary's Terrace (Arbour Hill)	70 E3
St. Mary's Terrace (Mountjoy Street)	71 A2
St. Michael's Close (off High Street)	75 A1
St. Michael's Hill (off High Street)	75 A1
St. Michael's Place	71 A2
St. Michael's Terrace (Blackpitts)	74 F2
St. Michan's House Flats	71 A4
St. Michans Park	71 A3
St. Michan's Place	71 A4
(off Chancery Street)	
St. Nicholas Street	71 A4
St. Nicholas Place	75 A1
St. Patrick's Close	75 A2
(Kevin Street Upper)	
St. Patrick's Court	74 F3

STREET NAME	PAGE/GRID REFERENCE	STREET NAME	PAGE/GRID REFERENCE	STREET NAME	PAGE/GRID REFERENCE	STREET NAME	PAGE/GRID REFERENCE
St. Patrick's Place	71 A2	Stocking Avenue	56 D2	Strandmill Avenue	14 F2	Sutton	29 A1
*St. Patrick's Terrace	70 F3	Stocking Lane	56 D3	Strandmill Park	15 A2	Sutton Castle Apartments	29 B3
(Nth Brunswick St)		Stocking Wood	56 D3	Strandmill Road	15 A2	Sutton Court (off Sutton Downs)	28 D1 [1]
St. Stephen's Green East	75 C2	Stocking Wood Copse	56 D3	Strandville Avenue (North Strand)	72 E1	Sutton Downs	28 D1
St. Stephen's Green North	75 C2	Stocking Wood Drive	56 D3	Strandville Avenue East (Clontarf)	26 D4	Sutton Grove	28 D1
St. Stephen's Green West	75 B2	Stocking Wood Green	56 D3	Strandville House	26 D4 [4]	Sutton Lane	63 A3
St. Teresa's Gardens	74 E2	Stocking Wood Hall	56 D3	(off Strandville Ave East)		Sutton Lawns	28 D1
St. Ultan's Flats	75 B3	Stocking Wood Manor	56 D3	Strandville Place	72 E1	Sutton Park	28 D1
St. Vincent Street South	75 A3	Stocking Wood Rise	56 D3	Strangford Gardens	72 E2	Sutton Road	67 B2 [9]
St.Stephen's Green South	75 B2	Stocking Wood Way	56 D3	Strangford Road	72 E2	Sutton Villas	67 B2 [17]
St.Thomas Road (Ardee Street)	74 F2	Stockton Court	23 A3	Strasburg Terrace	39 A3 [21]	Swallowbrook	8 F4
Stable Lane (Smithfield)	70 F4	Stockton Drive	23 A3	(off Strand Street Ringsend)		Swallowbrook Crescent	8 F4
Stable Lane (Harcourt Street)	75 B2	Stockton Green	23 A3	Stratford	47 A2 [9]	Swallowbrook Park	8 F4
Stable Lane (Leeson St Lr)	75 C2	Stockton Grove	23 A3	(off Orwell Road Rathgar)		Swallowbrook View	8 F4
Stackstown	61 B1	Stockton Lawn	23 A3	Strathmore Road	60 E4	Swan Alley	74 F1
Stacummy Bridge	32 F4	Stockton Park	23 A3	Streamstown Lane	2 F4	Swan Grove	75 C4
Staffordstown	5 C2	Stokes Place	75 B2	Streamville Court	64 E1 [10]	Swan Hall	54 F1 [10]
Staffordstown Little	5 C1	Stone Mason's Green	57 A2	Streamville Road	27 A1	(off Belgard Square West)	
Stamer Street	75 A3	Stone Mews (off Rathgar Road)	47 A1 [8]	Strong's Court	71 B2	Swan Place	76 D4
Stanford Green	45 C1	Stonebridge	21 B2	Suffolk Street	75 B1	Swan Yard (off Harry Street)	75 B1
Stanhope Street	70 F3	Stonebridge Avenue	21 B2	Sugarloaf Crescent	67 C3	Swanbrook	67 C4
Stanley Street	70 F3	Stonebridge Close	64 E3 [2]	Sugarloaf Terrace	67 C3 [21]	Swan's Nest Avenue	27 B1
Stannaway Avenue	46 D1	Stonebridge Drive	21 B2	Suir Road	73 B2	Swan's Nest Court	27 B1 [2]
Stannaway Court	46 D2 [3]	Stonebridge Lane	64 D2 [1]	Sullivan Street	69 C3	(Swan's Nest Avenue)	
(off Stannaway Avenue)		Stonebridge Road (Clonsilla)	21 B2	Summer Arch	71 C1	Swan's Nest Road	27 B1
Stannaway Drive	46 E1	Stonebridge Road (Shankill)	64 D2	Summer Arch	71 C1	Swanville Place	47 A1 [4]
Stannaway Road	46 E1	Stonemasons Green	57 A2 [5]	(off Summer Street North)		(off Rathmines Road Lower)	
Stapolin	14 F4	(Broadford Crescent)		Summer Place	71 C2	Swanward Court	74 E4
Stapolin Avenue	14 F4	Stonemasons Green	57 A2	*Summer Row	71 C1	Sweeney's Terrace	74 F2
Stapolin House	14 F4	Stonemasons Way	57 A2	(off Summer Street North)		Sweetbriar Lane	58 D1
Stapolin Lawns	14 F4	Stonepark Abbey	46 F4	Summer Street North	71 C2	Sweetman House	14 F4
Station Close	35 A4	Stonepark Court	46 F4	Summer Street South	74 E1	Sweetman's Avenue	49 A3 [21]
Station Road (Dunboyne)	7 B3	Stonepark Orchard	46 F4 [17]	Summerfield (Blanchardstown)	22 E2	(off Frascati Road Blackrock)	
Station Road (Portmarnock)	14 E2	(off Stonepark Abbey)		Summerfield	39 A3 [33]	Sweetman's Avenue	49 A3
Station Road (Leixlip)	19 C4	Stoneview Place	50 D4 [13]	(off Irishtown Road)		Sweetmount Avenue	47 B4
Station Road (Raheny)	27 A2	(off George's Street Upper)		Summerfield	55 A2 [1]	Sweetmount Drive	57 B1
Station Road (Sutton)	29 A1	Stoney Park	52 F2	(off Watermeadow Park Tallaght)		Sweetmount House	47 B4 [18]
*Station Road (off Clover Hill Road)	35 A4	Stoney Road (Dundrum)	47 C4	Summerfield Avenue	22 E2	(off Beaumont Avenue)	
Station Road (Glenageary)	60 E1	Stoney Road (East Wall)	72 E2	Summerfield Close	22 E2	Sweetmount Park	47 B4
Station Road (Killiney)	60 E4	Stoneybatter	70 E3	Summerfield Close	60 F2 [10]	Sweetmount Park	57 B1
Station Road (Shankill)	64 E2 [6]	Stoneylea Terrace	67 C3 [10]	(off Dalkey Avenue)		Swift Hall	59 B4
Station View Apartments	22 E3 [3]	Store Street	71 C3	Summerfield Green	22 E2	Swiftbrook (Tallaght)	54 D1
(off Carpenterstown Road)		Stormanstown Road	25 A2	Summerfield Lawns	22 E2	Swiftbrook Avenue	54 D1
Station Way	14 D4	Stradbrook Close	59 B1	Summerfield Meadows	22 E2	Swiftbrook Close	54 D1
Stationcourt	22 D3	*Stradbrook Cottages (on	49 B4	Summerfield Rise	22 E2	Swiftbrook Drive	54 D1
Stationcourt Hall	22 D3	Stradbrook Road)		Summerhill	71 C2	Swiftbrook Park	54 D1
Stationcourt Park	22 D3	Stradbrook Gardens	49 B4 [8]	Summerhill Court	50 E4 [3]	Swift's Alley	74 F1
Stationcourt View	22 D3	(off Stradbrook Road)		(off Islington Avenue)		Swift's Grove	13 A3
Stationcourt Way	22 D3	Stradbrook Grove	49 B4	Summerhill Parade	50 D4 [6]	Swift's Row (off Ormond Quay)	71 A4
Steelstown	51 C3	Stradbrook Hall	49 B4 [20]	(off Summerhill Road)		Swiftwood	53 B1
Steelstown Interchange (N7)	51 B3	(off Stradbrook Road)		Summerhill Parade (Summerhill)	72 D1	Swilly Road	24 E4
Steeple Gate	39 A3 [46]	Stradbrook Hill	59 B1 [4]	Summerhill Place	71 C2	Swords	2 D1
(off Sandymount Road)		(off Abbey Road Monkstown)		Summerhill Road (Dunboyne)	7 A2	Swords Manor Avenue	1 B2
Steeven's Gate Apartments	74 D1	Stradbrook Lawn	49 B4	Summerhill Road (Dún Laoghaire)	50 D4	Swords Manor Court	1 B1
Steeven's Lane	70 D4	Stradbrook Park	49 B4	Summerseat	8 D4	Swords Manor Crescent	1 B1
Stella Avenue	25 A3	Stradbrook Road	49 B4	Summerseat Cottage	8 D4	Swords Manor Drive	1 B1
Stella Gardens	39 A3	Straffan Avenue	17 C4	Summerseat Court	8 D4	Swords Manor Grove	1 B2
Stella Maris Apartments	17 C4	Straffan Close	17 C4	Summerville	39 B1	Swords Manor View	1 B1
Stepaside	58 E4	Straffan Court	17 C4	Summerville Park	47 A1	Swords Manor Way	1 B1
Stepaside	62 E1	Straffan Crescent	17 C4	*Summerville Terrace	60 F2	Swords Road (Malahide)	3 A3
Stepaside Lane	62 E1	Straffan Drive	17 C4	(on Dalkey Ave)		Swords Road (Santry)	12 F4
Stepaside Park	58 E4	Straffan Green	17 C4	Sunbury Court	47 A2	Swords Road (Collinstown)	12 F2
Stepaside Park	62 E1	Straffan Grove	17 C4	Sunbury Gardens	47 A2	Swords Road (Santry)	25 B1
Stepaside Village	58 E3	Straffan Lawn	17 C4	Suncroft Avenue (off Strand Road)	14 F2 [3]	Swords Street	70 D3
Stephen Street Lower	75 B1	Straffan Park	17 C4	Suncroft Drive	54 D2	Sybil Hill Avenue	26 F3
Stephen Street Upper	75 B1	Straffan Place	17 C4	Suncroft Park	54 D2	Sybil Hill Road	26 F3
Stephen's Lane	76 D2	Straffan Road	17 C4	Sundale Avenue	54 D2	Sycamore Avenue (Castleknock)	22 E3
Stephen's Place	76 D2	Straffan Way	17 C4	Sundale Close	54 D2	Sycamore Avenue (Tallaght)	45 A3
Stephen's Road	73 B2	Straffan Wood	17 C4	Sundale Crescent	54 D1	Sycamore Avenue (Cabinteely)	59 B3
Sterling Square Apartments	8 D3	Straleek	41 B1	Sundale Green	54 D1	Sycamore Close (Kilnamanagh)	44 F3
Stewart Hall	71 A3	Stralem Court	21 B1	Sundale Grove	54 D2	Sycamore Close (Cornelscourt)	59 B3
Stillorgan	58 F1	Stralem Crescent	21 B1	Sundale Heights	54 D1	Sycamore Court (off Carriglea	59 C2 [3]
Stillorgan Court (off Upper	58 E1 [2]	Stralem Grove	21 B1	Sundale Lawn	54 D1	Avenue Kill O'The Grange)	
Kilmacud Road Extension)		Stralem Mews	21 B1	Sundale Meadows	54 D1	Sycamore Crescent	48 E4
Stillorgan Grove	48 F4	Stralem Terrace	21 B1	Sundale Parade	54 D1	(Mount Merrion)	
Stillorgan Heath (off Upper	58 E1 [3]	Strand Court	3 B2 [12]	Sundale Park	54 D2	Sycamore Crescent (Cabinteely)	59 B3
Kilmacud Road Extension)		Strand Lane (off St. John's Road East)	48 E1 [3]	Sundale Road	54 D2	Sycamore Drive (Castleknock)	22 E3
Stillorgan Heath	58 E1	Strand Road (Portmarnock)	4 D4	Sundale Villas	54 D1	Sycamore Drive (Tallaght)	45 A3
Stillorgan Park	48 F4	Strand Road (Portmarnock)	14 F2	Sundale Walk	54 D1	Sycamore Drive	57 B1 [1]
Stillorgan Park	49 A4	Strand Road (Portmarnock)	15 A1	Sundrive Park	46 E1	(off Sycamore Road Dundrum)	
Stillorgan Park Avenue	58 F1	Strand Road (Baldoyle)	15 A4	Sundrive Road	73 C4	Sycamore Drive (Cabinteely)	59 B3
Stillorgan Road (Donnybrook)	48 D1	Strand Road (Sutton)	29 B2	Sunnybank Apartments	69 B4	Sycamore Green (Cabinteely)	59 B3
Stillorgan Road (Mount Merrion)	48 E3	Strand Road (Sandymount)	39 B4	Sunnybank Court	47 C4 [1]	Sycamore Grove	59 A2 [7]
Stillorgan Road (Stillorgan)	58 F1	Strand Road (Merrion)	48 E1	(off Dundrum Road)		(off Pine Avenue Foxrock)	
Stillorgan Road (Foxrock)	59 A2	Strand Road (Ballybrack)	64 E1	Sunnybank Court	67 B1 [8]	Sycamore Grove (Cabinteely)	59 B4
Stillorgan Wood	58 E1	Strand Road (Bray)	67 C2	Sunnyside	62 F3	Sycamore House (Swords)	1 Inset
Stirling Park (off Orwell Road)	47 A3 [2]	Strand Street (Malahide)	3 B2	Sunville Green (off Moeran Road)	46 D1 [1]	Sycamore House (Sutton)	28 D1
Stirrup Lane (off Church Street)	70 F3	Strand Street (Ringsend)	39 A3	Susan Terrace	74 F2	Sycamore House (Shankill)	64 E2 [11]
St James Place	39 A4 [31]	Strand Street Great	71 A4	Susanville Road	25 B4	Sycamore House	76 D3
(off Sandymount Road)		Strand Street Little	71 A4	Sussex Road	76 D3	Sycamore Lawn (Castleknock)	22 E3
Stockhole	13 A2	Strand Terrace	47 B2 [2]	Sussex Street (off Eblana Avenue)	50 D4 [16]	Sycamore Lawn (Cabinteely)	59 B3
Stockhole Lane	12 F1	(off Milltown Road)		Sussex Terrace	76 D3	Sycamore Park (Castleknock)	22 E3

STREET NAME	PAGE/GRID REFERENCE	STREET NAME	PAGE/GRID REFERENCE	STREET NAME	PAGE/GRID REFERENCE	STREET NAME	PAGE/GRID REFERENCE
Sycamore Park (Finglas)	24 E1	Taney Road	47 C4	Templeview Square	14 D4	The Claremont Apartments	12 D4
Sycamore Park (Tallaght)	45 A3	Tangier Lane (off Grafton Street)	75 B1	Templeview Vale	14 D4 [1]	The Cloisters	25 B3 [5]
Sycamore Road (Finglas)	24 E1	Tara Crescent (off Kilakee Green)	55 B2 [3]	(off Templeview Rise)		(off Grace Park Road)	
Sycamore Road (Fox and Geese)	45 A1	Tara Hill Crescent	46 F4	Templeview View	14 D4	The Cloisters	46 F2
Sycamore Road (Mount Merrion)	48 E4	Tara Hill Grove	46 F4 [2]	Templeview Walk	14 D4	(Mount Tallant Avenue)	
Sycamore Road (Dundrum)	57 B1	(off St. Patrick's Cottages)		Templeview Way	14 D4	*The Close (Robswall)	3 C3
Sycamore Street	71 B4	Tara Hill Road	46 F4	Templeville Avenue	46 D3	The Close (Plunkett Hall)	7 A2
Sycamore View	22 E3	Tara Lawn	27 A1	Templeville Drive	46 D3	The Close (Dunboyne Castle)	7 A3
Sycamore Walk	59 B4	Tara Street	71 C4	Templeville Park		The Close (Lutterell Hall)	7 B2
Sydenham (off Corrig Avenue)	50 D4 [23]	Tassagard Greens	53 B2	(off Templeville Road)	46 E3 [1]	The Close (Moyglare Hall)	17 C1
Sydenham Court	39 A4 [53]	Tassagart Drive	53 A2	Templeville Road	46 D3	The Close (Manorfields)	21 B1
(off Sandymount Avenue)		Tay Lane	52 E2	Tenterfields	74 E2	The Close (Beaumont)	25 C1
Sydenham Mews	68 D3	Taylors Court	56 E1	Terenure	46 F2	The Close (Oldtown Mill)	31 C3 [2]
*Sydenham Place	47 C4	Taylor's Hill	57 A3	Terenure Park	46 F2	The Close (Celbridge)	31 C3
(on Kilmacud Rd Upr)		Taylor's Lane (Ballyboden)	56 E1	Terenure Place	46 F2 [3]	The Close (Temple Manor)	31 C4
Sydenham Road	39 A4 [4]	Taylor's Lane (Pimlico)	74 E1	(off Hannaville Park)		The Close (Grange Manor)	34 D3
(off Merrion Road)		Teeling Way	72 F2	Terenure Road East	46 F2	The Close (Tallaght)	44 F3
Sydenham Road (Dundrum)	47 C4	Temple Bar	71 B4	Terenure Road North	46 F2	The Close (Templeogue)	46 D3
Sydenham Villas (Dundrum)	57 C1	Temple Buildings	71 A2	Terenure Road West	46 E2	The Close (Mount Merrion)	48 E3
Sydenham Villas (Bray)	68 D3 [6]	Temple Cottages	71 A2	Terminal Road North	39 C2	The Close (off The Wood Tallaght)	55 A2 [2]
Sydney Avenue	49 A3	Temple Court (off Temple Road)	49 A3 [25]	Terminal Road South	39 C2	The Close (Ballyboden)	56 E2
Sydney Parade Avenue	48 E1	Temple Court (Arbour Hill)	70 D3	Termon Court (off Gallaun Road)	11 C4 [1]	The Close (Ballinteer)	57 C2
Sydney Terrace	49 A3	Temple Court	76 E1	Terrace Place (off Bella St)	71 C2	The Close (off The Wood Tallaght)	
Sylvan Avenue	45 A3	(off Hogan Place)		Tetrarch Grove	7 C1	The Coachworks	75 A3
Sylvan Close	44 F3	Temple Court Apartments	12 E4	Texas Lane	3 A2	The Coombe	74 F1
Sylvan Drive	44 F3	Temple Crescent	49 B4	*The Alders	12 E4	The Coppice (Palmerstown)	35 C1
Symphony House	75 C3	Temple Gardens (Santry)	12 E4	(off Northwood Avenue)		The Coppins (Celbridge)	32 D3
Synge House	47 A3	Temple Gardens (Milltown)	47 B2	The Alders (off Monkstown Valley)	49 B4 [6]	The Coppins (Foxrock)	59 B4
Synge Lane	75 A3	Temple Grove	32 D3	The Anchora Apartments	3 B2 [10]	The Copse (Drumcondra)	25 B3
Synge Place	75 B3	*Temple Hill (on Terenure Road West)	46 E2	*The Anchorage (Robswall)	4 D3	The Copse	33 B2 [1]
Synge Street	75 B3	Temple Hill	49 B4	The Anchorage	4 D3	The Copse	57 B2 [3]
Synge Way	35 C4	Temple Lane North	71 B2	The Anchorage (off Clarence	49 C4 [33]	(off The Heights Ballinteer)	
Synnott Place	71 B1	Temple Lane South	71 B4	Street Dún Laoghaire)		*The Court (Robswall)	4 D3
Synnott Row	71 B1	Temple Manor (Dunboyne)	7 B2	The Appian Way	76 D4	The Court (Lutterell Hall)	7 B2
Synnott Row	71 B1	Temple Manor (Celbridge)	31 C4	The Arches	17 C3	The Court (Plunkett Hall)	7 A2
Synnott Terrace	49 C4 [16]	Temple Manor (Greenhills)	45 C3	The Avenue (Plunkett Hall)	7 A2	The Court (Sadleir Hall)	7 A2
(off Dunleary Road)		Temple Manor Avenue	45 C3	The Avenue (Lutterell Hall)	7 B2	The Court (Dunboyne Castle)	7 B3
Synod Hall	75 A1	Temple Manor Close	45 C3	The Avenue (Dunboyne Castle)	7 B3	The Court (Mulhuddart)	9 A4
		Temple Manor Court	45 C3	The Avenue (Mulhuddart)	9 A4	The Court (Larch Hill)	12 F4
T		Temple Manor Drive	45 C3	The Avenue (Louisa Valley)	19 C4	The Court (Moyglare Hall)	17 C2
		Temple Manor Grove	45 C3	The Avenue (Manorfields)	21 B1	The Court	22 F2 [4]
Taaffe's Place	72 E1	Temple Manor Way	45 C3	The Avenue (Celbridge)	32 D3	The Court	25 A4 [20]
Tailors Court	75 A1	Temple Park	47 B3	The Avenue (St Wolston's Abbey)	32 D4	The Court (Whitehall)	25 C2
Tailor's Hall	75 A1	Temple Park Apartments	12 E4	The Avenue (Grange Manor)	34 D3	The Court (Clontarf)	26 D4
Talbot	2 F3	Temple Park Avenue	49 B4	The Avenue (Tallaght)	44 F3	The Court (off The Village Raheny)	27 B3 [2]
Talbot Avenue	2 F3	Temple Place	71 B2	The Avenue (Templeogue)	46 D3	The Court (Sutton)	29 A1
Talbot Court (Malahide)	3 A2	Temple Place	75 C4	The Avenue (Ballyboden)	56 E2	The Court (Celbridge)	31 C3
Talbot Court (Blanchardstown)	22 F2	Temple Road (Rathgar)	47 B2	The Avenue (Ballinteer)	57 C2	The Court (Oldtown Mill)	31 C3
Talbot Downs	22 F2	Temple Road (Blackrock)	49 A3	The Avenue (Carrickmines)	63 A1	The Court (Temple Manor)	31 C4
Talbot Hall (Swords)	1 Inset	Temple Square	47 B2 [5]	*The Barley Store Apartments	71 C1	The Court (Tallaght)	44 F3
Talbot Lane	60 E3 [4]	(off Orchard Road South)		(off Portland Street North)		The Court (Tallaght)	44 F4
(off Ballinclea Road)		Temple Street North	71 B2	The Bawn	3 B3	The Court (Templeogue)	46 D3
Talbot Lane (Talbot Street)	71 C3	Temple Street West	70 D3	The Bawn Grove	3 B3	The Court (Donnybrook)	47 C2
Talbot Lodge	48 F4	Temple Terrace	60 F2 [16]	*The Beaches	12 E4	The Court (Ballinteer)	57 B2
Talbot Memorial Bridge	71 C4	(off Coliemore Road)		(off Northwood Avenue)		The Court (Carrickmines)	59 B4
(River Liffey)		*Temple Villas	47 B1	The Beeches (Donaghmede)	27 A1	The Court (Ballybrack)	60 E4
Talbot Park	2 F3	(on Palmerston Road)		The Beeches	49 B4 [21]	The Court (Glenamuck Road)	63 A1
Talbot Place	71 C3	*Temple Villas (Arbour Hill)	70 D3	(off Monkstown Valley)		The Court (Shankill)	64 E3
Talbot Road (Swords)	2 F3	Templemore Avenue	47 A2	The Beeches	56 F1 [8]	The Courthouse	52 F2
Talbot Road	60 E3 [3]	Templeogue	46 D4	(off Barton Drive Willbrook)		*The Courtyard (Robswall)	3 C3
(off Killiney Hill Road)		Templeogue Lodge	46 D4	The Beeches (Kilmacud)	58 D1	The Courtyard (Clonsilla)	22 D3
Talbot Street	71 C3	Templeogue Road	46 E3	The Beeches (Abberley)	64 E1 [22]	The Courtyard (Celbridge)	31 C4
Tallaght	55 A1	Templeogue Wood	46 D4	The Belfry (Kilbarrack)	27 B1	The Courtyard (Templeogue)	46 E3
Tallaght Bypass	54 F1	Templeroan	56 D1	The Belfry (Citywest Road)	53 C2	The Courtyard (Rathfarnham)	46 F4
Tallaght Bypass	55 A1	Templeroan Avenue	56 D1	The Belfry (Inchicore)	73 A1	The Courtyard (Leopardstown)	58 E2
Tallaght Road	45 C4	Templeroan Close	56 E1	The Belfry Apartments	25 C2 [11]	The Courtyard (Bray)	67 B2
Tallaght Road	55 B1	Templeroan Court	56 D1	(off Collins Avenue West)		The Courtyard	71 B2
Tallow Hall	54 F1 [7]	Templeroan Crescent	56 D1	The Birch	57 C1 [12]	The Courtyard	76 D1
(off Belgard Square West)		Templeroan Downs	56 E1	(off Overend Way Dundrum)		The Coutryard (off Foxrock Park)	59 A2 [10]
Tamarisk Avenue	45 A3	Templeroan Drive	56 D1	The Birches	59 A3	The Cove	3 A2
Tamarisk Close	45 A3	Templeroan Green	56 D2	The Birches Apartments	23 C3 [3]	The Covert (off The Coppice)	35 C1 [1]
Tamarisk Court	45 A3	Templeroan Grove	56 D1	(off Pelletstown Avenue)		The Crescent (Swords)	2 D2 [4]
Tamarisk Dale	45 A3	Templeroan Lodge	56 D2	The Black Avenue	33 B1	The Crescent (Malahide)	4 D3
Tamarisk Drive	45 A3	Templeroan Meadows	56 E1	The Blackthorn	57 C1 [14]	The Crescent (Plunkett Hall)	7 A2
Tamarisk Grove	45 A3	Templeroan Mews	56 D1	(off Overend Way Dundrum)		The Crescent (Lutterell Hall)	7 A2
Tamarisk Heights	45 A3	Templeroan Park	56 D1	The Bramblings	26 E3	The Crescent (Dunboyne Castle)	7 B3
Tamarisk Lawn	45 A3	Templeroan View	56 D1	The Briars	35 C1	The Crescent (Mulhuddart)	9 A4
Tamarisk Park	45 A3	Templeroan Way	56 D1	The Bridge	64 E3	The Crescent (Larch Hill)	12 F4
Tamarisk View	45 A3	Templeview Avenue	14 D4	The Brokerage Apartments	71 C4	The Crescent (Moyglare Hall)	17 C1
Tamarisk Walk	45 A3	Templeview Close	14 D4	The Burgage	60 F2	The Crescent	22 F3 [1]
Tamarisk Way	45 A3	Templeview Copse	14 D4	The Castlelands	46 F4 [11]	(off Church Court Castleknock)	
Tandys Lane	33 C3	Templeview Court	14 D4	(off The Courtyard)		The Crescent	25 C2 [8]
Tandys Lane	34 D3	Templeview Crescent	14 D4	*The Cedars (off Northwood Avenue)	12 E4	(off Beaumont Road)	
Taney Avenue	47 C4	Templeview Downs	14 D4	The Cedars (off Monkstown Valley)	49 B4 [5]	The Crescent (Whitehall)	25 B3
Taney Court	47 C4	Templeview Drive	14 D4	The Cedars (Abberley)	64 E1 [21]	The Crescent (Sutton)	29 A1
Taney Crescent	47 C4	Templeview Green	14 D4	The Chandler Apartments	23 B3 [2]	The Crescent (Oldtown Mill)	31 C3
Taney Drive	47 C4	Templeview Grove	14 D4	(off Ashtown Road)		The Crescent (Abbeyfarm)	31 C4
Taney Grove	47 C4	Templeview Lawn	14 D4	The Charter	12 D4 [2]	The Crescent (Temple Manor)	31 C4
Taney Lawn	47 C4	Templeview Park	14 D4	The Charter	12 D4	The Crescent	32 D4
Taney Manor	47 C4	Templeview Place	14 D4	The Chase	58 F2	(St Wolston's Abbey)	
Taney Park	47 C4	Templeview Rise	14 D4	The Cherries (off Grange Wood)	57 A2 [2]	The Crescent (Lucan)	33 C2
Taney Rise	47 C4	Templeview Row	14 D4	The Claremont	12 D4 [6]	The Crescent (Grange Manor)	34 D3
						The Crescent (Tallaght)	44 E4

STREET NAME	PAGE/GRID REFERENCE
The Crescent (Tallaght)	44 F3
The Crescent	47 C1 [4]
(off Donnybrook Road)	
The Crescent (Ranelagh)	47 B1
The Crescent (Tallaght)	55 A1
The Crescent (Ballyboden)	56 E2
The Crescent	57 B2 [1]
(off The Walk Ballinteer)	
The Crescent (Carrickmines)	63 A1
*The Cresent (Robswall)	4 D3
The Croft	32 D2
The Dale (Dunboyne)	7 B2
The Dale (Moyglare Hall)	17 C2
The Dale (Manorfields)	21 B1
The Dale (Celbridge)	31 C3
The Dale (Kilnamanagh)	44 F3
The Dale (Belgard)	44 F4
The Dale	57 B2 [4]
(off The Heights Ballinteer)	
The Dale (Carrickmines)	63 A1
The Dale (Bray)	67 B2
The Deanery	31 C3 [1]
The Dell	57 A2
The Dingle	35 B2
The Distillery Building Apartments	25 B4 [17]
(off Distillery Road)	
The Downs (Dunboyne Castle)	7 A3
The Downs (St Wolston's Abbey)	32 D4
The Drive (Sadleir Hall)	7 A2
The Drive (Lutterell Hall)	7 B2
The Drive (Dunboyne Castle)	7 B3
The Drive (Mulhuddart)	9 A4
The Drive (Manorfields)	21 B1
The Drive (Oldtown Mill)	31 C3
The Drive (Abbeyfarm)	31 C4
The Drive (Temple Manor)	31 C4
The Drive (Grange Manor)	34 D3
The Drive (Kilnamanagh)	44 F3
The Drive (Tallaght)	55 A1
The Drive (Ballyboden)	56 E1
The Drive (Ballinteer)	57 B2
The Drive (Woodbrook Glen)	67 C1
The Drive Apartments	56 E1
The Dunes	15 A1
The Elm (Rockfield)	57 C1
The Elms (Dunboyne)	7 B2
*The Elms (off Northwood Avenue)	12 E4
The Elms (Celbridge)	32 D2
The Elms (Elm Park)	48 E2
The Elms (Loughlinstown)	64 E1 [4]
The Elms	64 E3
The Elms Apartments	23 C3 [2]
(off Rathbourne Avenue)	
The Fairways (Portmarnock)	14 E2
*The Fairways (Woodbrook Glen)	67 C1
The Fairways Apartments	8 D3
The Falls (off Dodder Road	46 F3 [5]
Lower Rathfarnham)	
The Forum	58 E2
The Fosters	48 E3
The Gables (Grange View Road)	43 B1
The Gables (Rathgar)	47 A2
The Gables (Nutgrove)	57 A1
The Gables (Dundrum)	57 B1
The Gables	59 A3 [5]
(off Torquay Road Foxrock)	
The Gables	70 D1
The Gallan	60 D3
The Gallops	58 E3
The Gardens	63 A1
The Garth (Cookstown)	44 E4
The Garth (Kingswood Heights)	44 F3
The Gasworks	76 F1
The Gate	44 D1
The Gate Lodge	30 E3
The Glade (Oldtown Mill)	31 C3
The Glade (St Wolston's Abbey)	32 D4
The Glade (Palmerston)	35 B2
The Glade (Kingswood Heights)	44 F3
The Glade (Ballinteer)	57 B2
The Glebe	34 E2
The Glen (Louisa Valley)	19 C4
The Glen (Raheny)	27 B3
The Glen (Ballyboden)	56 E1
The Glen (Ballinteer)	57 B2
The Glen	58 D3
The Glen	60 D1 [14]
(off Glenageary Road Lower)	
The Glens	63 A1
The Golf Links	3 C3
The Goulding	12 D4 [5]
The Goulding Apartments	12 D4
The Grainhouse	74 E2
*The Granary (Long's Place)	74 E1
The Grange (Malahide)	3 B4
The Grange (Terenure)	46 F2
The Grange (Deans Grange)	59 B1
*The Green (Robswall)	3 C3
The Green (Malahide)	3 B2
The Green (Lutterell Hall)	7 B2
The Green (Dunboyne Castle)	7 B3
The Green (Mulhuddart)	9 A4
The Green (Larch Hill)	12 F4
The Green (Moyglare Abbey)	17 B2
The Green (Moyglare Hall)	17 C2
The Green (Manorfields)	21 B1
The Green (Beaumont)	25 C1
The Green (Celbridge)	31 C3
The Green (Oldtown Mill)	31 C3
The Green (Tallaght)	44 F3
The Green (Templeogue)	46 D3
The Green (Ballyboden)	56 E1
The Green (Ballinteer)	57 B2
The Green (Carrickmines)	63 A1
The Green (Woodbrook Glen)	67 C1
The Green Road	60 Inset
The Greenlands	46 F4
The Grove (Plunkett Hall)	7 A2
The Grove (Sadleir Hall)	7 A2
The Grove (Dunboyne Castle)	7 A3
The Grove (Lutterell Hall)	7 B2
The Grove (Louisa Valley)	19 C4
The Grove (Whitehall)	25 B3
The Grove	27 B3 [1]
(off The Village Raheny)	
The Grove (Abbeyfarm)	31 C4
The Grove (St Wolston's Abbey)	32 D4
The Grove (Grange Manor)	34 D3
The Grove (Tallaght)	44 E4
The Grove (Tallaght)	44 F4
The Grove (Tallaght)	55 A1
The Grove (Dundrum)	57 A1
The Grove (Ballinteer)	57 B2
The Grove (Woodbrook Glen)	67 C1
The Haggard	30 D2 [6]
(off Main Street Howth)	
The Hall	46 F2
The Hampton	12 D4
*The Hardwicke Apartments	70 F3
(Church Street Upper)	
The Haven (Malahide)	3 B2
The Haven (off St. Mobhi Boithirin)	25 A3 [17]
The Hawthorns	12 E4
(off Northwood Avenue)	
The Hawthorns (Abberley)	64 E1 [20]
The Heath (Tallaght)	44 F4
The Heath (Templeogue)	46 D3
The Heath (Ballinteer)	57 B2
The Hedgerows	59 A3
*The Heights (Robswall)	3 C3
The Heights (Dunboyne Castle)	7 B3
The Heights (Ballinteer)	57 B2
The Hill (Malahide)	3 B3
The Hill (Mulhuddart)	9 A4
The Hill (Monkstown)	49 C4
The Hill (Ballinteer)	57 C2
The Hill	58 D3
The Hill (Stillorgan)	58 F1
The Hole in the Wall Road	14 E4
The Hollows	34 D2 [3]
(off Adamstown Road)	
The Holly (Rockfield)	57 C1
*The Hops (end Basin Street)	74 D2
The Island	36 E2
The Killigeen	52 D4
The Kilmore	12 D4 [4]
The Kilmore Apartments	12 D4
The Kilns	14 F2
The Lakelands	46 F4 [8]
(off Rathfarnham Wood)	
The Landey	12 D4 [7]
The Larches (Abberley)	64 E1 [16]
The Laurels (Dollymount)	26 F4
The Laurels	36 E4 [3]
(off Bluebell Avenue)	
The Laurels	41 B1
The Laurels	46 F4 [13]
(off Main Street Rathfarnham)	
The Laurels (Terenure)	46 F2
The Laurels (Churchtown)	47 B4
The Laurels	55 A1 [10]
(off Main Street Tallaght)	
The Lawn (Kinsaley)	2 E3
The Lawn (Plunkett Hall)	7 A2
The Lawn (Moyglare Abbey)	17 B2
The Lawn (Finglas)	24 E2
The Lawn (Oldtown Mill)	31 C3
The Lawn (Tallaght)	44 E4
The Lawn (Ballyboden)	56 E2
The Lawn (Ballinteer)	57 B2
The Lawn (Woodbrook Glen)	67 C1
The Lawns (Abbeyfarm)	31 C4
The Lawns (Temple Manor)	31 C4
*The Lighthouse (Robswall)	4 D3
The Lime (Rockfield)	57 C1
The Linden	57 C1 [13]
(off Overend Way Dundrum)	
The Links	14 F2
The Little Grove	32 D4
The Lodge (Balgriffen)	14 E3
The Lodge (Clontarf)	26 D4
The Lodge (Glenageary)	60 D1
The Lodge Apartments	23 C3 [6]
(off River Road)	
The Maieston	12 D4 [1]
The Maieston	12 D4
The Mall (Malahide)	3 B2
The Mall (off Main Street Baldoyle)	15 A4 [4]
The Mall (Leixlip)	33 A1
The Mall (Lucan)	34 D1
The Malt House	74 E2
The Maltings	67 C2
The Maltings Apartments	70 E4
The Manor	46 D2 [7]
(off Kimmage Road West)	
The Manor (Templeogue)	46 D4
The Maples (Bird Avenue)	47 C3
The Maples	49 B4 [4]
(off Monkstown Valley)	
The Mayne	8 E2
The Meadow	57 B2
The Meadows (Dunboyne)	7 B2
The Meadows (Killester)	26 F3
The Meadows (Oldtown Mill)	31 C3
The Meadows (Newtownpark Ave)	59 A1
The Meadows East	44 F4
The Meadows West	44 F4
*The Mews (Robswall)	4 D3
The Mews (Killester)	26 E3
The Mews (Clontarf)	26 E4
The Mews (off Clontarf Road)	27 A4 [5]
The Mews (Templeogue)	46 E3
The Mews (off Castlewood Avenue)	47 A1 [19]
The Mews (Hill Street)	71 B2
The Mews Apartments	23 C3 [5]
(off River Road)	
The Mill	74 E2
The Mill Pond Apartments	44 D1 [4]
(off Nangor Road)	
The Mills	22 F2
The Moorings (Malahide)	3 C3
The Moorings (Chapelizod)	36 E2
The Moorings	39 A3 [38]
(off Fitzwilliam Quay)	
The Moorings	75 B4
The Moorings Apartments	76 E3
(off Merrion Road)	
The New Road	23 B1
The Northumberlands	76 E2
The Nurseries (Swords)	1 C3
The Nurseries (Mulhuddart)	9 B4
The Nurseries	60 F4 [4]
(off Wyattville Road Ballybrack)	
The Nurseries (Oldcourt)	67 B3
The Oaks (Swords)	1 B3
The Oaks (Hollystown)	9 C1
*The Oaks (off Northwood Avenue)	12 E4
The Oaks (Dollymount)	27 A4
The Oaks (Celbridge)	32 D3
The Oaks (Belgard)	44 E4
The Oaks (Churchtown)	47 B4
The Oaks (Ballinteer)	57 B2
The Oaks (Rockfield)	57 C1
The Oaks (Loughlinstown)	64 D1 [1]
The Oaks (Abberley)	64 E1 [17]
*The Oar House Apartments	71 C1
(off Portland Street North)	
*The Observatory (Windmill Lane)	72 D4
The Old Forge	34 D3
The Old Presbytery	39 A3 [34]
(off Cambridge Park)	
The Orchard	14 D4
The Orchard	22 D3 [1]
(off Carpenterstown Road)	
The Orchard (Killester)	26 E3
The Orchard (Oldtown Mill)	31 C3
The Orchard	34 D1 [14]
(off Lucan Road)	
The Orchard (Palmerston)	35 B1
The Orchard (Kimmage)	46 E2
The Orchard	49 B3 [5]
(off Seapoint Avenue)	
The Orchard (Deans Grange)	59 A1
The Orchard Apartments	35 B3
The Oval	35 C2
The Paddock (Moyglare Abbey)	17 B2
The Paddock (Ashtown)	23 C4
The Paddock (Oldtown Mill)	31 C2
The Paddocks (Swords)	2 D2
The Paddocks (Dunboyne)	7 B2
The Paddocks	60 F1 [3]
(off Ulverton Road Dalkey)	
The Paddocks (Kilmainham)	73 B2
The Paddock's	26 E4 [6]
(off Seaview Ave North Clontarf)	
The Palms	48 D3
The Park (Plunkett Hall)	7 A2
The Park (Dunboyne Castle)	7 B3
The Park (Larch Hill)	12 F4
The Park (Louisa Valley)	19 C4
The Park (Beaumont)	25 C1
The Park (Celbridge)	31 C3
The Park (Oldtown Mill)	31 C3
The Park (Abbeyfarm)	31 C4
The Park (Grange Manor)	34 D3
The Park (Tallaght)	44 F3
The Park (Templeogue)	46 D3
The Park (Tallaght)	55 A2
The Park	58 D3
The Park Apartments	75 B4
The Park Lands	46 F4 [7]
(off Castleside Drive)	
The Pines (Castleknock)	23 A3
The Pines (Killester)	26 E3
The Pines (Ballinteer)	57 B2
The Pines	58 D1 [1]
(off Woodley Park Kilmacud)	
The Pines (Oldcourt)	67 B3
The Place (Dunboyne Castle)	7 B3
The Place (Carrickmines)	63 A1
The Plantation	76 D2
The Plaza Apartments	9 B2
The Poplars (off Monkstown Valley)	49 B4 [7]
The Priory (Malahide)	3 B2 [4]
The Priory (Cabra)	24 D4
The Priory (Grange Road)	56 F1
The Quarry	4 D4 [2]
The Ramparts	63 C1
The Rectory	27 A2
The Rectory	58 D4
*The Richmond Apartments	70 F3
(Brunswick Street North)	
The Rise (Malahide)	3 B3
The Rise (Manorfields)	21 B1
The Rise (Glasnevin)	25 A2
The Rise (Newcastle)	42 D4
The Rise (Tallaght)	44 E4
The Rise (Tallaght)	44 F3
The Rise (Mount Merrion)	48 E4
The Rise (Ballyboden)	56 E2
The Rise (Ballinteer)	57 B2
The Rise (Dalkey)	60 E2
The Rise (Carrickmines)	63 A1
The Road (Manorfields)	21 B1
The Rookery	56 D2
The Rose	9 B2
The Rowan (Rockfield)	57 C1
The Rowans (Abberley)	64 E1 [18]
The Sand Holes	22 F4 [1]
(off Carpenterstown Road)	
The Scalp	63 A4
The Slopes	49 C4
*The Spinaker (Robswall)	4 D3
The Spinnaker	4 D3
The Spruce	9 B2
The Square (Larch Hill)	12 F4
The Square (off Main Street Lucan)	34 D1 [5]
The Square (off Irishtown Road)	39 A3 [5]
The Square (Greenogue Ind Est)	42 E4
The Square (Tallaght)	54 F1
The Stables (off Hampton Crescent)	48 E3 [1]
The Stables Apartments	23 C3 [4]
(off River Road)	
The Steeple (Moyglare Abbey)	17 B2
The Steeples	36 E3
*The Steps Apartments	73 B1
(Kilmainham Lane)	
The Stiles Road	26 E4

STREET NAME	PAGE/GRID REFERENCE
The Summit (Howth)	30 E3
The Sweepstakes	39 A4[22]
(off Merrion Road)	
The Sycamore (Rockfield)	57 C1
*The Sycamores	12 E4
(off Northwood Avenue)	
The Sycamores	64 E1[3]
The Tallow Apartments	23 C3[7]
(off Ashtown Road)	
The Terrace	63 A1
The Thatch Road	25 C2
The Thicket	59 A3
*The Tower (Smithfield)	70 F4
*The Tramyard Apartments	36 F3
(off Thomas Davis Street West)	
The Turnpike	12 D4[3]
The Turnpike	12 D4
The Vale	35 C1
*The View (Robswall)	3 C3
The View (Dunboyne Castle)	7 A3
The View (Larch Hill)	12 F4
The View (Manorfields)	21 B1
The View (Celbridge)	31 C3
The View (Oldtown Mill)	31 C3
The View (St Wolston's Abbey)	32 D4
The View (Tallaght)	44 F3
The View (Tallaght)	55 B1
The View (Ballinteer)	57 B2
The View (Carrickmines)	63 A1[1]
The Village (Clonsilla)	21 C3
The Village	25 B3[2]
(off Drumcondra Road Upper)	
The Village (Raheny)	27 B3
The Village Centre	34 D1[12]
(off Lucan Road)	
The Village Court	34 D1[13]
(off Lucan Road)	
The Village Gate	60 F2
*The Walk (Robswall)	3 C3
The Walk (Dunboyne Castle)	7 B3
The Walk (Moyglare Hall)	17 C2
The Walk (Louisa Valley)	19 C4
The Walk (Manorfields)	21 B1
The Walk (Oldtown Mill)	31 C3
The Walk (Templeogue)	46 D3
The Walk (Tallaght)	55 A1
The Walk (Ballinteer)	57 B2
The Walk (Carrickmines)	63 A1
The Walled Gardens	32 D2
The Walled Orchard	33 B1
*The Warehouse Apartments	74 F2
(Clanbrassil Terrace)	
The Warren	2 F3
The Water Rill	2 E2
The Waxworks Apartments	23 C3[8]
(off Ashtown Road)	
The Way (Dunboyne Castle)	7 B3
The Weir	36 E2
*The Wheat Barn Apartments	71 C1
(off Portland Street North)	
The Wicklow Way	61 C4
The Willow	9 B2
The Willow (Rockfield)	57 C1
*The Willows (off Northwood Avenue)	12 E4
*The Willows (Glasnevin)	24 F3
The Willows (Celbridge)	32 D3
The Willows (off Claremont Road)	39 A4[45]
The Willows (off Orwell Road)	47 A3[1]
The Willows (off Monkstown Valley)	49 B4[3]
The Willows (Abberley)	64 E1[19]
The Wood (Tallaght)	55 A2
The Wood	58 D3
The Wood (Carrickmines)	63 A1
The Wood	64 E3
The Woodlands (Celbridge)	32 D3
The Woodlands	46 F4[9]
(off Rathfarnham Wood)	
The Woods (off Charlemont)	25 C3[9]
Theresa House	46 F4[20]
(off Stonepark Court)	
Third Avenue (Tallaght)	44 F4
Third Avenue (Seville Place)	72 E3
Thirlestane Terrace	74 F1
*Thomas Court Bawn	74 E1
(at School Street)	
Thomas Davis Court (off Bayside)	27 C1[4]
Thomas Davis Street (West)	36 F3
Thomas Davis Street South	74 F1
Thomas Lane	71 B3
Thomas Moore Court	27 C1[3]
(off Bayside Square South)	
Thomas Moore Road	45 C1

STREET NAME	PAGE/GRID REFERENCE
Thomas Street	74 F1
Thomas Street West	74 E1
Thomastown Crescent	60 D2[2]
(off Sallynoggin Road)	
Thomastown Road	60 D3
Thomond	64 E2[9]
Thomond Road	36 E3
Thompson's Cottages	71 C2
Thor Place	70 D3
Thormanby Grove	30 D2[10]
(Thormanby Road)	
Thormanby Lawns	30 D2
Thormanby Lodge	30 E2
Thormanby Road	30 E2
Thormanby Woods	30 E2
Thorn Wood	48 E3
Thornberry Apartments	8 F4
Thorncastle Court Apartments	39 A2[3]
(off Thorncastle Street)	
Thorncastle Street	39 A2
Thorncliff (off Dundrum Road)	47 B2[8]
Thorncliffe Park	47 B3
Thorndale Avenue	26 D2
Thorndale Court (off Collinswood)	25 C2[4]
Thorndale Crescent	26 D2
Thorndale Drive	26 D3
Thorndale Grove	26 D3
Thorndale Lawns	26 D2
Thorndale Park	26 D2
Thornfield Square	44 E1
Thornhill Gardens	31 C2
Thornhill Heights	31 C2
Thornhill Lane	27 A4
Thornhill Meadows	31 C2
Thornhill Road (Kilmacud)	48 E4
Thornhill Road (Bray)	67 A2
Thornhill View	67 B1[5]
Thornleigh Avenue	1 Inset
Thornleigh Close	1 Inset
Thornleigh Court	1 Inset
Thornleigh Green	1 Inset
Thornleigh Grove	1 Inset
Thornleigh Lane	1 Inset
Thornleigh Park	1 Inset
Thornleigh Place	1 Inset
Thornleigh Road	1 Inset
Thornleigh Row	1 Inset
Thornville Avenue	27 B1
Thornville Drive	27 B2
Thornville Park	27 C1
Thornville Road	27 B1
Thornville Terrace	27 B2[1]
(off Thornville Road)	
Three Rock Close (off Kipure Avenue)	45 B3[1]
Three Rock Grove	57 B3
Three Rock Road	58 E2
Thundercut Alley	70 F3
Tibradden Close	45 B2[1]
(off Tibradden Drive)	
Tibradden Drive	45 B2
Tibradden Grove	45 B3
Tibradden Lane	56 F4
Tibradden Road	56 F3
Ticknick	63 B2
Ticknock Avenue	57 C3
Ticknock Dale	57 C3
Ticknock Drive	57 C3
Ticknock Grove	57 C3
Ticknock Hill	57 C3
Ticknock Park	57 C3
Ticknock Road	57 B4
Ticknock Way	57 C3
Tiknock	61 B1
Tiknock Bridge	61 B1
Timard	17 A1
Timber Mills Apartments	26 E2
Tinkers Hill	21 A4
Tinkler's Path	36 E1
Tinnehinch	66 E4
Tinnehinch Bridge	66 E4
Tivoli Avenue	46 F1
Tivoli Close	59 C1
Tivoli Road	49 C4
Tivoli Terrace East	50 D4
Tivoli Terrace North	49 C4
Tivoli Terrace South	49 C4
Tobernea Terrace	49 B3[2]
(off Seapoint Avenue)	
Tolka Cottages	24 F3
Tolka Estate	24 F2
Tolka Estate Road	24 F3
Tolka Quay	39 A2

STREET NAME	PAGE/GRID REFERENCE
Tolka Quay Road	39 A2
Tolka Road	25 B4
Tolka Vale	24 E3
Tolka Valley Road	24 D3
Tolka Valley View	24 D2
Tolka View (off Main Street)	22 F2[2]
Tom Clarke House	25 B4[1]
(off Ballybough Road)	
Tom Kelly Road	75 B3
Tonduff Close	45 B3
Tonguefield Road	46 E1[1]
(off Blarney Park)	
Tonlegee Avenue	26 F1
Tonlegee Drive	26 F1
Tonlegee Road	27 A1
Tootenhill	52 D2
Tootenhill (Rathcoole)	52 E2
Tor an Ri Close	34 F3
Tor an Ri Court	34 F3
Tor an Ri Lane	34 F3
Tor an Ri Parade	34 F3
Tor an Ri Terrace	34 F3
Tor an Ri Walk	34 F3
Torca Road	60 F2
Torca View (off Sorrento Road)	60 F2[33]
Torcaill	3 C4
Torlogh Gardens	25 C4[8]
(off Philipsburgh Avenue)	
Torlogh Parade	25 C3[1]
(off Griffith Avenue)	
Torquay Road	58 F2
Torquay Wood	58 F2
Tory Square	22 F1
Tourmakeady Road	25 B2[1]
(off Innishmaan Road)	
Tourville Lodge (off Church Lane)	46 F3[6]
Tower Avenue	46 F2
Tower Road (Castleknock)	22 F4
Tower Road	36 D1
Tower Road (Clondalkin)	44 D1
Tower Terrace	73 B1
(off Kilmainham Lane)	
Tower View Cottages	24 F4[2]
(off Finglas Road)	
Townsend Street	71 C4
Townyard House Apartments	3 B2[9]
Townyard Lane	3 B2
Tracy Bonham Lane	70 E4
Traders Wharf	49 C3
*Traders Wharf Apartments	70 F4
(Ushers Quay)	
Trafalgar Lane	49 B4
Trafalgar Terrace (Blackrock)	49 B3
Trafalgar Terrace (Bray)	67 C2[31]
Tramway Court (Sutton)	29 A1
Tramway Court	55 A1[8]
(off Old Blessington Road)	
Tranquility Grove	26 D1
Traverslea Close	60 D1
Traverslea Woods	60 D1
*Traynor Place (O'Reilly Ave)	73 C1
Treepark Avenue	45 A3
Treepark Close	45 A3
Treepark Drive	45 A3
Treepark Road	45 A3
Trees Avenue	48 E4
Trees Road Lower	48 E4
Trees Road Upper	48 E4
Treesdale	48 F4
Tresilian	59 A3
Trideat Apartments	39 A4[33]
(off Claremont Road)	
Trim Road	26 D1
Trimelston Apartments	47 C3
Trimleston Avenue	48 E2
Trimleston Drive	48 E2
Trimleston Gardens	48 E2
Trimleston Park	48 E2
Trimleston Road	48 E2
Trinity Hall (Rathgar)	47 A2
Trinity Square	72 D4
Trinity Street	71 B4
Trinity Road	72 D1
Tristan House Apartments	36 E2[15]
(off Martin's Row Chapelizod)	
Tritonville Avenue	39 A3[8]
(off Cranfield Place)	
Tritonville Close	39 A3[22]
(off Sandymount Road)	
Tritonville Court	39 A4
Tritonville Crescent	39 A3[9]
(off Tritonville Road)	

STREET NAME	PAGE/GRID REFERENCE
Tritonville Mews	39 A3[45]
(off Sandymount Road)	
Tritonville Road	39 A3
Trosyrafon Terrace	68 D2[1]
Tuansgate Apartments	54 F1[1]
(off Belgard Square East)	
Tubber Lane Road	33 B2
Tubbermore Avenue	60 F2
Tubbermore Road	60 F2
Tuckett's Lane	30 D2
Tudor Court	2 F2
Tudor Lawns	58 F2
Tudor Road	47 B1
Tulip Court	13 C4
Tullyhall	34 D4
Tullyhall Avenue	34 D4
Tullyhall Close	34 D4
Tullyhall Court	34 D4
Tullyhall Crescent	34 E4
Tullyhall Drive	34 E4
Tullyhall Green	34 D4
Tullyhall Park	34 D4
Tullyhall Rise	34 E4
Tullyhall Way	34 D4
Tullyvale	63 C1
Turnapin Cottages	12 F3
Turnapin Green	12 F3
Turnapin Grove	12 F3
Turnapin Lane	12 F3
Turnberry	28 D1
Turnberry Square	28 D1
Turnpike Road	45 A2
Turnstone Apartments	48 E3
Turret Road	35 C2
Turrets Flats (off Summerville Park)	47 A1[9]
Turvey Avenue	73 B1
Tuscany Downs	27 A2
Tuscany Park	28 D1
Twin Cottages	49 A4[5]
(off Yankee Terrace)	
Tymon Close	55 A2
Tymon Crescent	54 F2
Tymon Farm	45 C4
Tymon Grove	55 A2
Tymon Heights	55 B2
Tymon Lane	45 B4
Tymon Lawn	55 A2
Tymon Lodge Apartments	45 B3
Tymon North	45 B4
Tymon North Avenue	45 B4
Tymon North Court	45 B4[1]
(off Tymon North Road)	
Tymon North Gardens	45 B4
Tymon North Green	45 B4
Tymon North Grove	45 B4
Tymon North Lawn	45 B4
Tymon North Park	45 B4
Tymon North Place	45 B4[2]
(off Tymon North Avenue)	
Tymon North Road	45 B4
Tymonville Avenue	45 B4
Tymonville Court	45 A4
Tymonville Crescent	45 A4
Tymonville Drive	45 A3
Tymonville Grove	45 B3
Tymonville Lawn	45 B4
Tymonville Park	45 B4
Tymonville Road	45 A4
Tynan Hall	44 F3
Tynan Hall Avenue	44 F3
Tynan Hall Grove	44 F3
Tynan Hall Park	44 F3
Tyrconnell Park	36 F3
Tyrconnell Road	36 F3
Tyrconnell Street	36 F3[6]
(off Tyrconnell Road)	
Tyrconnell Villas	36 F3[7]
(off Gratten Crescent)	
Tyrellstown Boulevard	9 B2
Tyrellstown Way	9 B2
Tyrone House	71 C3
Tyrone Place	73 A2
Tyrrell Place	71 C1
*Tyrrel's Lane	39 A3
(off Fitzwilliam St Ringsend)	

U

STREET NAME	PAGE/GRID REFERENCE
UCD Village Belgrove	48 D3
Ullardmor	60 F2[27]
(off Ardeevin Road)	

STREET NAME	PAGE/GRID REFERENCE
Ulster Street	24 F4
Ulster Terrace (off Stillorgan Grove)	58 F1 [4]
Ulster Terrace (North Strand)	72 D1
Ulverton Close	60 F1 [5]
(off Ulverton Road Dalkey)	
Ulverton Court	60 F1 [13]
(off Ulverton Road Dalkey)	
Ulverton Road	60 F1
*Ulysses House Apartments	71 A3
(Little Britain Street)	
University Village Apartments	17 C2
Upper Cliff Road (Thormanby Road)	30 E2 [2]
Upper Dargle Road	67 A2
Upper Garville Avenue	47 A2
Upper Glen Road	36 E1
Upper Kilmacud Road Extension	58 E1
Uppercross	34 F1
Uppercross Court	55 A1 [7]
(off Old Blessington Road)	
Uppercross Road	73 C2
Urney Grove	60 E2 [7]
(off Killiney Road)	
Usher Lane	1 A2
Usher Street	70 F4
Ushers Court Apartments	70 F4
Usher's Island	70 E4
Usher's Quay	70 F4

V

STREET NAME	PAGE/GRID REFERENCE
Vale Terrace	67 B2 [7]
(on lower Dargle Road)	
Vale View	67 B2 [21]
Vale View Avenue	59 B3
Vale View Close	59 B3
Vale View Grove	59 B3
Vale View Lawn	59 B3
Valentia House	71 B1
Valentia Parade	71 B1
Valentia Road	25 B3
Valeview Crescent	24 D2 [6]
(off St.Helena's Road)	
Valeview Drive	24 D2
Valeview Gardens	24 D2 [2]
(off St.Helena's Road)	
Valley Drive	63 C1
Valley Park Avenue	24 D2 [1]
(off Valley Park Drive)	
Valley Park Drive	23 C2
Valley Park Road	23 C2
Valley View	1 B1
Vanessa Close	31 C3
Vanessa Lawns	31 C3
Vauxhall Avenue	74 D2
Vavasour Square	76 F2
Venetian Hall	26 E3
Ventry Drive	24 D4
Ventry Park	24 E4
Ventry Road	24 E4
Verbena Avenue (Kilbarrack)	27 C1
Verbena Avenue (Foxrock)	59 A3
Verbena Grove	27 C1
Verbena Lawn	27 C1
Verbena Park	27 C1
Verdemont	22 D2
Vergemount (off Clonskeagh Road)	47 C1 [12]
Vergemount Hall	47 C1 [9]
(off Clonskeagh Road)	
Vergemount Park	47 C1 [6]
(off Clonskeagh Road)	
Verney House	62 F3
Vernon Avenue	26 F4
Vernon Court (Vernon Avenue)	26 F4
Vernon Court (off Clontarf Road)	39 C1 [3]
Vernon Drive	26 F3
Vernon Gardens	26 F4
Vernon Grove (Clontarf)	26 F4
Vernon Grove (Rathgar)	47 A2
Vernon Heath	26 F4
Vernon Park	26 F4
Vernon Rise	26 F3
Vernon Street	75 A2
Vernon Wood (off Vernon Avenue)	39 C1 [4]
Veronica Terrace	39 A3 [40]
(off Oliver Plunkett Avenue)	
*Veronica Terrace	39 A3
(off Oliver Plunket Ave)	
Verschoyle Avenue	53 C2
Verschoyle Close	53 C2
Verschoyle Court	76 D2
Verschoyle Crescent	53 C2
Verschoyle Drive	53 C2

STREET NAME	PAGE/GRID REFERENCE
Verschoyle Glen	53 C2
Verschoyle Green	53 C2
Verschoyle Heights	53 C2
Verschoyle Mews	76 D2
Verschoyle Park	53 C2
Verschoyle Place	76 E2
(off Lr Mount St)	
Verschoyle Rise	53 C2
Verschoyle Vale	53 C2
Verville Court	26 E4
Vesey Mews	49 C4
Vesey Park	34 D2
Vesey Place	49 C4
Vesey Terrace	34 D1 [2]
(off Main Street Lucan)	
*Vevay Arcade (on Vevay Road)	67 C3
Vevay Crescent	67 C2 [58]
Vevay Road	67 C3
Vevay Villas	67 C3 [18]
Vicar Street	74 F1
Vicars Court	8 F4
Vico Road	60 F3
*Vico Terrace (Off Vico Road)	60 F3
Victoria Avenue (Donnybrook)	47 C1
Victoria Avenue (Bray)	68 D2
Victoria Cottages (off Bath Street)	39 A3 [44]
*Victoria Cottages (off Irishtown Rd)	39 A3
Victoria Lane (off Botanic Avenue)	25 B4 [9]
*Victoria Lane	47 A2
(off South Zion Road)	
Victoria Quay	70 E4
Victoria Road (Clontarf)	26 E4
Victoria Road	46 F2
Victoria Road (Killiney)	60 E3
Victoria Road (Dalkey)	60 F2
Victoria Street	75 A3
Victoria Terrace (Clontarf)	39 B1
Victoria Terrace (Dundrum)	47 C4
Victoria Terrace	50 D4 [8]
(off Mellifont Avenue)	
Victoria Terrace (off Dalkey Avenue)	60 F2 [11]
Victoria Village (off Rathgar Avenue)	46 F2 [7]
Victoria Village (Rathgar)	47 A2
Victoria Villas (Clontarf)	26 D4
Victoria Villas	46 F2 [5]
(off Rathgar Avenue)	
Viking Harbour (Ushers Island)	70 E4
Viking Place	70 E3
Viking Road	70 E3
*Villa Bank (Royal Canal Bank)	71 A1
Villa Blanchard	22 F2
Villa Building Apartments	30 D1 [15]
(off Harbour Road)	
Villa Nova	48 F4
Villa Park Avenue	24 D4
Villa Park Drive	24 D4
Villa Park Gardens	24 D4
Villa Park Road	24 D4
Village Court Apartments	46 F4 [6]
(off Butterfield Avenue)	
*Village Gate Arcade	67 C2
(on Main Street Bray)	
Village Green	
(off Main Street Rathfarnham)	46 F3 [4]
Village Green (Tallaght)	55 A1
Village Heights	9 A4
*Village House (Reilly's Avenue)	73 D3
Village Square (Tallaght)	55 A1
Village Weir (off Main Street Lucan)	34 D1 [7]
Villarea Park	60 E1
Villiers Road	47 A2
Vintage Court	74 E2
Violet Hill Drive	24 F3
Violet Hill Park	24 F3
Violet Hill Road	24 F3
Virginia Drive	24 D2
Virginia Hall	54 F1 [8]
(off Belgard Square West)	
Virginia Heights	54 F1
Virginia Park	24 D2
Viscount Avenue	12 F4

W

STREET NAME	PAGE/GRID REFERENCE
Wadelai Green	25 A2
Wadelai Road	25 A2
Wade's Avenue	27 A3
Wainsfort Avenue	46 D3
Wainsfort Crescent	46 D3
Wainsfort Drive	46 D2
Wainsfort Gardens	46 D3
Wainsfort Grove	46 E3

STREET NAME	PAGE/GRID REFERENCE
Wainsfort Manor	46 D3
Wainsfort Manor Crescent	46 D3
Wainsfort Manor Drive	46 D3
Wainsfort Manor Green	46 D3
Wainsfort Manor Grove	46 D3
Wainsfort Park	46 E3
Wainsfort Road	46 D3
Waldemar Terrace	47 B4 [12]
(off Dundrum Road)	
Walker's Cottages	75 B4
Walker's Court	75 B4
Walkinstown	45 B1
Walkinstown Avenue	45 B1
Walkinstown Close	45 B1
Walkinstown Crescent	45 B1
Walkinstown Cross	45 C2
Walkinstown Drive	45 B1
Walkinstown Green	45 B1
Walkinstown Parade	45 B1
Walkinstown Park	45 B1
Walkinstown Road	45 C1
Wallace Road (off Bunting Road)	45 C1 [2]
Walnut Avenue (Whitehall)	25 B3
Walnut Avenue (Clondalkin)	44 F3
Walnut Close	44 F3
Walnut Court	25 B2
Walnut Drive	44 F3
Walnut Lawn	25 B3
Walnut Park	25 B3
Walnut Rise	25 B3
Walnut View (off Brookwood)	56 E2 [5]
Walsh Road	25 A3
Waltersland Road	58 F1
Waltham Terrace	48 F4
Walton Hall (Swords)	1 Inset
Waltrim Grove	67 B4
Walworth Road	75 A3
Warburton Terrace	68 D2 [7]
Ward's Hill	74 F2
Warner's Lane	75 C3
Warren Avenue	22 E3
Warren Close	22 E3
Warren Court	28 D1 [5]
(off Warrenhouse Road)	
Warren Crescent	22 E4
Warren Green (Carpenterstown)	22 E3
Warren Green (Sutton)	28 D1
Warren Manor	2 F3
Warren Park	22 E3
Warren Street	75 A3
Warrenhouse Road	28 D1
Warrenmount	74 F2
Warrenmount Place	74 F2
Warrenpoint (off Clontarf Road)	26 E4 [1]
Warrenstown	9 B4
Warrenstown Close	9 B4
Warrenstown Court	9 B4
Warrenstown Drive	9 B4
Warrenstown Garth	9 B4
Warrenstown Green	9 B4
Warrenstown Grove	9 B4
Warrenstown Lawn	9 B4
Warrenstown Park	9 B4
Warrenstown Place	9 B4
Warrenstown Rise	9 B4
Warrenstown Row	9 B4
Warrenstown Vale	9 B4
Warrenstown View	9 B4
Warrenstown Walk	9 B4
Warrenstown Way	9 B4
Warrington Lane	76 E2
Warrington Place	76 E2
Warwick Terrace	76 D4
Wasdale Grove	46 F2
Wasdale House	
(off Wasdale Park)	46 F3 [8]
Wasdale Park	46 F3
*Washington Grove	46 E4
(off Washington Lane)	
Washington Lane	46 E4
Washington Park	46 E4
Washington Street	74 F3
Waterfall Avenue	25 B4
Waterfall Road	26 F3
Watergate Estate	55 A1
Waterloo Avenue	72 E1
Waterloo Lane	76 D4
Waterloo Mews	76 E3
(off Shelbourne Road)	
Waterloo Road	76 D4
Watermeadow Drive	54 F2
Watermeadow Park	55 A2

STREET NAME	PAGE/GRID REFERENCE
Watermill	27 B3
Watermill Avenue	27 A3
Watermill Close	55 A2
Watermill Drive	27 A3
Watermill Grove	55 A2
Watermill Lawn	27 A3 [1]
(off Watermill Road Raheny)	
Watermill Lawn (Tallaght)	55 A2
Watermill Park	27 A3
Watermill Road	27 A3
Watermint Court	24 D3 [3]
(off Lockkeeper's Walk)	
Waterside Apartments	76 F1
Waterside Avenue	2 E2
Waterside Close	2 E2
Waterside Court	2 E2
Waterside Crescent (Swords)	2 E2
Waterside Crescent (Portmarnock)	3 C4
Waterside Drive	2 E2
Waterside Green	2 E3
Waterside Grove	2 E2
Waterside King's Hall	2 E2
Waterside Lawn	2 E2
Waterside Park	2 E2
Waterside Place	2 E3
Waterside Rise	2 E2
Waterside Road	2 E2
Waterside Walk	2 E2
Waterside Way	2 E2
Waterstown	35 C1
Waterstown Avenue	35 C1
Waterville Road	22 F1
Waterville Row	22 F1
Waterville Terrace	22 F1
Watery Lane (Swords)	1 C1
Watery Lane	2 D1
Watery Lane (Clondalkin)	44 E1
Watkins Buildings	74 F2
Watling Street	70 E4
Watson Avenue	60 D4
Watson Drive	60 D4
Watson Park	60 D4
Watson Road	60 D3
Watson's Estate	60 D3
Waverley Avenue	25 C4
Waverley Terrace	46 F1 [12]
(off Harolds Cross Road)	
Waverley Terrace (Bray)	67 C2 [28]
Waynestown	5 C1
Wayside Cottages	62 F2
Weaver Lane	71 A1
Weaver's Close	74 F2
Weavers Row (The Coombe)	74 E2
Weaver's Row (Clonsilla)	21 C2
Weaver's Square	74 F2
Weaver's Street	74 F2
Weaver's Walk	21 C2
Webster's Cottages	49 A4 [8]
(off Annaville Avenue)	
Wedgewood Estate	58 D2
Weirview	34 F1
Weirview Drive	58 F1
Weldon's Lane	15 A4
Well Road	2 D2 [2]
Wellesley Place	71 C1
Wellington Cottages	45 C3 [2]
(off Willington Green)	
Wellington Court	46 D2 [5]
(off Whitehall Road West)	
Wellington Court (Bray)	67 C2 [56]
*Wellington Gardens	47 B1
(off Oakley Road)	
Wellington House	76 E4
(off Seafort Avenue)	
Wellington Lane (Tallaght Road)	45 C3
Wellington Lane	76 E4
(Wellington Road)	
Wellington Lodge	39 A4 [52]
(off Serpentine Avenue)	
*Wellington Mews	76 E4
(Wellington Lane)	
Wellington Park	46 D3
Wellington Place (Leeson Street)	76 E4
Wellington Place North	71 A2
Wellington Quay	71 B4
Wellington Road	46 D3 [1]
(off Whitehall Road Templeogue)	
Wellington Road (Phoenix Park)	69 B4
Wellington Road (Ballsbridge)	76 E4
Wellington Street (off George's	50 D4 [1]
Place Dún Laoghaire)	
Wellington Street Lower	71 A2

STREET NAME	PAGE/GRID REFERENCE	STREET NAME	PAGE/GRID REFERENCE	STREET NAME	PAGE/GRID REFERENCE	STREET NAME	PAGE/GRID REFERENCE
Wellington Street Upper	71 A2	Weston Way	33 B2	Whitehall Road (Churchtown)	47 A4	William's Place Upper	71 B1
Wellmount Avenue	24 D2	Westpark (Coolock)	26 F2	Whitehall Road West	46 D2	(off Portland Place)	
Wellmount Court	24 D2	Westpark (Rathcoole)	52 F2	Whitehall Square	45 C2	Willie Bermingham Place	73 C1
Wellmount Crescent	24 D2	Westpark (Tallaght)	55 A1	Whites Gate (Phoenix Park)	23 A4	Willie Nolan Road	15 A4
Wellmount Drive	24 D2	Westview Terrace	67 C2 [29]	White's Lane North	71 A2	Willington Avenue	45 C3
Wellmount Green	24 D2	Westway Close	9 C4	White's Road	23 A4	Willington Court	45 C3
Wellmount Parade	24 D2	Westway Grove	9 C4	White's Villas (off Carysfort Road)	60 F1 [10]	Willington Crescent	45 C3
Wellmount Park	24 D2	Westway Lawns	22 F1	Whitestown	22 D1	Willington Drive	45 C3
Wellmount Road	24 D2	Westway Park	9 C4	Whitestown Avenue	22 D1	Willington Green	45 C3
Wellpark Avenue	25 B3	Westway Rise	9 C4	Whitestown Crescent	22 D1	Willington Grove	45 C3
Wellview Avenue	9 A3	Westway View	9 C4	Whitestown Drive (Blanchardstown)	22 D1	Willington Lawn	45 C3 [1]
Wellview Crescent	9 A3	Westwood Avenue	23 C2	Whitestown Drive (Tallaght)	54 E2	(off Willington Grove)	
Wellview Green	9 A3	Westwood Road	23 C2	Whitestown Gardens	22 D1	Willington Park	45 C3
Wellview Grove	9 A3	Wexford Street	75 B2	Whitestown Green	22 D1	Willow Avenue	32 E4
Wellview Park	9 A3	Wharton Terrace	74 F4	Whitestown Grove	22 D1	Willow Avenue (Clondalkin)	44 D2
Wendell Avenue	4 D4	Whately Hall	8 F4	Whitestown Park	22 D1	Willow Avenue (Loughlinstown)	64 D1
Wentworth Apartments	76 E1	Whately Hall	8 F4	Whitestown Road	54 F2	Willow Bank	49 C4
Werburgh Street	75 A1	Whately Place	58 E1	Whitestown Walk	22 D1	Willow Bank Drive	56 E1
Wesbury	58 E1	Wheatfield	67 C3	Whitestown Way	54 F2	Willow Bank Park	56 E1
Wesley Heights	57 C2	Wheatfield Grove	4 D4	Whitethorn	35 B3	Willow Brook	32 E4
Wesley House	76 D4	Wheatfield Road (Portmarnock)	4 D4	Whitethorn Avenue	26 D2	Willow Court (Clondalkin)	44 D2
Wesley Lawns	57 C2	Wheatfield Road (Palmerstown)	35 C2	Whitethorn Close	26 D2	Willow Court (Loughlinstown)	64 D1
Wesley Place	74 F3	Wheatfields Avenue	35 B3	Whitethorn Crescent (Artane)	26 D2	Willow Cove	32 E4
Wesley Road	47 A2	Wheatfields Close	35 B3	Whitethorn Crescent	35 B3	Willow Crescent	32 E4
West Park Drive	24 F2	Wheatfields Court	35 B3	(Coldcut Road)		Willow Crescent	64 D1
West Pier (Howth)	30 D1	Wheatfields Crescent	35 B3	Whitethorn Drive	35 B3	Willow Drive	32 E4
West Pier (Dún Laoghaire)	49 C3	Wheatfields Drive	35 B3	Whitethorn Gardens	35 B3	Willow Drive	44 D2
West Road	72 E2	Wheatfields Grove	35 B3	Whitethorn Grove (Artane)	26 D2	Willow Gate	57 B1
West Terrace	36 F3	Wheatfields Park	35 B3	Whitethorn Grove (Celbridge)	32 D3	Willow Green	32 E4
Westbourne Avenue	43 C1	Wheaton Court		Whitethorn Park (Artane)	26 D2	Willow Grove (Clondalkin)	44 D2
Westbourne Close	43 C1	(off Inchicore Terrace South)	36 F3 [20]	Whitethorn Park (Coldcut Road)	35 B3	Willow Grove (off Carriglea Avenue)	59 C1 [13]
Westbourne Court	46 F3	Whelan House Flats		Whitethorn Rise	26 D2	Willow Grove (Cornelscourt)	59 B3
Westbourne Drive	43 C1	(off Thorncastle Street)	39 A3 [29]	Whitethorn Road (Artane)	26 D2	Willow House	76 D3
Westbourne Grove	43 C1	Whelan's Terrace		Whitethorn Road (Milltown)	47 C2	Willow Lawn	32 E4
Westbourne Lodge	56 D1	(off Temple Road)	49 A3 [19]	Whitethorn Walk (off Carriglea	59 C2 [2]	Willow Lodge	23 A4
Westbourne Rise	43 C1	Whitaker Hall	71 A2	Avenue Kill O'The Grange)		Willow Mews	48 E1
Westbourne Road	46 F3	Whitchurch Drive	56 F2	Whitethorn Walk	59 A2 [8]	Willow Park (Dunboyne)	7 B2
Westbourne Terrace	67 C2 [52]	Whitchurch Road	56 F2	(off Pine Avenue Foxrock)		Willow Park	59 A2 [6]
Westbourne View	43 C1	White Gables	64 D2	Whitethorn Way	35 B3	(off Pine Avenue Foxrock)	
Westbrook	46 D2	White Hall (Ballymount Road)	44 F3	Whitton Road	46 F2	Willow Park (Loughlinstown)	64 D1
Westbrook Lawns	53 C2	White Oak	47 C3	Whitworth Avenue	71 C1	Willow Park Avenue	24 F1
Westbrook Park	33 C2	White Oaks	67 B4	*Whitworth Parade	25 A4	Willow Park Close	24 F1
Westbrook Road	47 B3	Whiteacre Close	25 B1	(off Saint Patrick's Road)		Willow Park Crescent	24 F1
Westbury	34 D3	Whiteacre Court	25 B1	Whitworth Place	25 A4 [16]	Willow Park Drive	25 A1
Westbury Avenue	34 D3	Whiteacre Crescent	25 B1	(off Drumcondra Road Lower)		Willow Park Grove	24 F1
Westbury Close	34 D3	Whiteacre Place	25 B1	*Whitworth Place	71 B1	Willow Park Lawn	24 F1
Westbury Drive	34 D2	Whitebank Road	39 B3	(off Binns Bridge)		Willow Park Road	24 F1
Westbury Grove	33 C3 [1]	Whitebarn Road	47 A4	Whitworth Road	25 A4	Willow Place (Booterstown)	48 F3
Westbury Park	34 D3	Whitebeam Avenue	47 C2	Whitworth Terrace	71 C1	Willow Place (Loughlinstown)	64 D1
Westcourt	74 D1	Whitebeam Road	47 C2	(off Russell Ave)		Willow Rise	32 E4
Westend Gate	22 F3	Whitebeams Road	58 D2	Wicklow Lane	75 B1	Willow Road (Fox and Geese)	45 A1
Westend Village	22 E2	Whitebrook Park	54 E1	(off Wicklow Street)		Willow Road (Dundrum)	57 B1
Western Parkway	35 B2	Whitechapel Avenue	22 D2	Wicklow Street	75 B1	Willow Terrace	48 F2
Western Parkway Motorway	22 E4	Whitechapel Court	22 D2	Wicklow Way	65 A4	Willow Vale	60 D4
Western Road	74 E3	Whitechapel Crescent	22 D2	Wigan Road	25 A4	Willow View	32 E4
Western Way	71 A2	Whitechapel Green	22 D2	Wikeford Hall (Swords)	1 Inset	Willow Wood Close	21 C2
Westerton Rise	57 C1 [1]	Whitechapel Grove	22 D2	Wilderwood Grove	45 C4	Willow Wood Downs	21 C2 [1]
(off Ballinteer Road)		Whitechapel Lawn	22 D2	Wilfield (off Sandymount Avenue)	39 A4 [15]	(off Willow Wood Grove)	
Westfield Park	68 D3	Whitechapel Park	22 D2	Wilfield Park	39 A4	Willow Wood Green	21 C2
Westfield Road	46 F1	Whitechapel Road	22 D2	Wilfield Road	39 A4	Willow Wood Grove	21 C2
Westfield Terrace	49 A3 [10]	Whitechurch Abbey	56 F1 [4]	Wilford Court	67 B1	Willow Wood Lawn	21 C2
(off Rock Road)		(off Grange Park)		Wilfrid Road	46 F1	Willow Wood Park	21 C1
Westhampton Place	46 F2 [2]	Whitechurch Avenue	56 F2	Wilfrid Terrace	46 F1 [5]	Willow Wood Rise	21 C1
(off Terenure Road North)		Whitechurch Close	56 F2	(off Tivoli Avenue)		Willow Wood View	21 C2
Westhaven	8 F4	Whitechurch Court	56 F2	Willans Avenue	21 A1	Willow Wood Walk	21 C1
Westland Row	76 D1	Whitechurch Crescent	56 F2	Willans Drive	21 A1	Willowbank	57 C1
Westmanstown	42 D3	Whitechurch Drive	56 F2	Willans Green	21 A1	Willowbrook Grove	31 C3
Westminster Court	59 A3 [6]	Whitechurch Green	56 F2	Willans Rise	21 A1	Willowbrook Lawns	31 C3
(off Brighton Road Foxrock)		Whitechurch Grove	56 F2	Willans Row	21 A1	Willowbrook Lodge	31 C3
Westminster Lawns	58 F2	Whitechurch Heights	56 F2	Willans Way	21 A1	Willowbrook Park	31 C3
Westminster Park	59 A2	Whitechurch Hill	56 F2	Willbrook	46 F4	Willowfield	39 B4
Westminster Road	59 A3	Whitechurch Lawn	56 F2	Willbrook Downs	56 F1	Willowfield Avenue	47 C4
Westmoreland Park	47 B1 [4]	Whitechurch Park	56 F2	Willbrook Estate	56 F1	Willowfield Park	47 C4
(off Sandford Road)		Whitechurch Pines	56 F1	Willbrook Grove	46 F4 [1]	Willowmount (off Willow Place)	48 F3 [3]
Westmoreland Street	71 B4	Whitechurch Place	56 F2	(off Willbrook Street)		Willows Court	21 C2
Weston Avenue (Leixlip)	33 B1	Whitechurch Road	46 F4	Willbrook House	75 C4	Willows Drive	21 C2
Weston Avenue	47 B4	Whitechurch Road	56 F2	Willbrook Lawn	46 F4	Willows Green	21 C2
Weston Close (Leixlip)	33 B1	Whitechurch Stream	56 F1	Willbrook Park	46 F4	Willows Road	21 C2
Weston Close (Churchtown)	47 B4	Whitechurch View	56 F2	Willbrook Road	46 F4	Willsbrook Avenue	34 E2
Weston Court	33 B2	Whitechurch Walk	56 F2	Willbrook Street	46 F4	Willsbrook Crescent	34 F1
Weston Crescent	33 B1	Whitechurch Way	56 F2	William Beckett House	76 D2	Willsbrook Drive	34 E2
Weston Drive	33 B1	Whitecliff	56 F1	William Dargan Bridge	47 B4	Willsbrook Gardens	34 E1
Weston Green	33 B1	Whitefriar Garden Flats	75 A1	William Pallister House	46 F4 [22]	Willsbrook Green	34 E2
Weston Grove	47 B4	(off Whitefriar Street)		(off Stonepark Court)		Willsbrook Grove	34 E1
Weston Heights	33 B2	Whitefriar Place	75 B1	William Street North	72 D1	Willsbrook Park	34 E1
Weston Lane (Leixlip)	33 B1	Whitefriar Street	75 A1	William Street South	75 B1	Willsbrook Place	34 E1
Weston Lawn	33 B1	Whitehall	25 B2	William's Lane	71 B3	Willsbrook Road	34 E2
Weston Meadow	33 B2	Whitehall Close	46 D3	William's Park	47 A1	Willsbrook View	34 E1
Weston Park (Leixlip)	33 B1	Whitehall Gardens	46 D2	Williams Place Lower	71 C1	Willsbrook Way	34 E1
Weston Park (Churchtown)	47 B4	Whitehall Mews	59 A2	(Buckingham Street Upper)		Wilmont Avenue	60 E1 [1]
Weston Road	47 B4	Whitehall Park	46 D3	William's Place South	75 A2	(off Glasthule Road)	
Weston Terrace (off Weston Park)	47 B4 [9]	Whitehall Road (Kimmage)	46 D2	William's Place Upper	71 B1	Wilson Crescent	48 D4

STREET NAME	PAGE	GRID
Wilson Road	48	E4
Wilson Terrace	74	F1
Wilson's Place	76	D1
Wilton Court	76	D3
Wilton Place	76	D3
Wilton Terrace	76	D3
Windele Road (off Joyce Road)	25	A3 [12]
Windermere	21	B2
Windermere (off Gilford Road)	39	B4 [8]
Windgate Rise	30	D3
Windgate Road	30	D3
Windmill Avenue (Swords)	1	C2
Windmill Avenue (Crumlin)	46	D1
Windmill Crescent (Swords)	1	A2
Windmill Crescent	46	D1 [2]
(off Windmill Road Crumlin)		
Windmill Lands	1	C2
Windmill Lane	72	D4
Windmill Lane Apartments	72	D4
Windmill Park	22	D3 [2]
(off St Mochtas Drive)		
Windmill Rise	46	D1
Windmill Rise	1	C2
Windmill Road	73	B4
Windmill Terrace	22	D3 [3]
(off St Mochtas Drive)		
Windmillhill	51	C3
Windrush	64	E2 [7]
Windsor Avenue	25	C4
Windsor Court	59	B1 [1]
(off Stradbrook Road)		
Windsor Drive	59	B1
Windsor Mews	3	B2 [5]
Windsor Park	59	B1
Windsor Place	75	C2
Windsor Road	47	B1
Windsor Terrace (Malahide)	3	B3
Windsor Terrace (Dún Laoghaire)	50	D4
Windsor Terrace (Ranelagh)	75	A4
Windsor Villas	25	C4 [3]
(off Philipsburgh Avenue)		
Windy Arbour	47	C3
Winetavern Street	71	A4
Wingfield	62	E1
Winston Ville	26	D4 [12]
(off Charlemont Road Clontarf)		
Winter Garden Apartments	72	E4
Winton Avenue	47	A2
Winton Grove	46	F2 [19]
(off Terenure Road North)		
Winton Road	76	D4
Wogansfield	33	A1
Wolfe Tone Avenue	50	D4 [4]
(off Cross Avenue)		
Wolfe Tone Close	71	A3
Wolfe Tone Quay	70	D4
Wolfe Tone Square East	67	C3
Wolfe Tone Square Middle	67	C3
Wolfe Tone Square North	67	C3
Wolfe Tone Square South	67	C3
Wolfe Tone Square West	67	C3
Wolfe Tone Street	71	A3
Wolseley Street	74	F3
Wolstan Haven Avenue	31	C3
Wolstan Haven Road	31	C3
Wolverton Glen	60	E2
Wood Avens	35	A3
Wood Dale Close	55	B2
Wood Dale Crescent	55	B2
Wood Dale Drive	55	B2
Wood Dale Green	55	B2
Wood Dale Green	55	C2
Wood Dale Grove	55	C2
Wood Dale Oak	55	C2 [1]
(Wood Dale Green)		
Wood Dale View	55	C2
Wood Lane	70	E4
Wood Quay	71	A4
Wood Street	75	A1
Woodbank Avenue	23	C2
Woodbank Drive	23	C2
Woodberry (Carpenterstown)	22	E3
Woodberry (Lucan)	34	D3
Woodbine Avenue	48	E2
Woodbine Close	27	A1
Woodbine Drive	27	A1
Woodbine House	48	E2 [4]
(off Woodbine Road)		
Woodbine Park (Raheny)	27	A1
Woodbine Park (Booterstown)	48	E2
Woodbine Road (Raheny)	27	A1
Woodbine Road (Booterstown)	48	E2
Woodbine Terrace	47	C4 [2]
(off Dundrum Road)		
Woodbrook Court	22	D3
Woodbrook Crescent	22	D3
Woodbrook Downs	64	E4
Woodbrook Glen	67	C1
Woodbrook Hall	22	D3
Woodbrook Lawn	67	C3
Woodbrook Park	22	D3
(Carpenterstown)		
Woodbrook Park (Templelogue)	46	D4
Woodbrook Square	22	D3
*Woodchester House	75	A1
(Golden Lane)		
Woodcliff Heights	30	E2
Woodfarm Avenue	35	C2
Woodfarm Cottages	35	C1 [6]
(off Lucan Road Palmerston)		
Woodfarm Drive	35	C2
Woodfield	56	D2
Woodfield Cottages	36	F3 [8]
(off Sarsfield Road)		
Woodfield Place	36	F3 [15]
(off Sarsfield Road)		
Woodford	58	E2
Woodford Avenue	44	F1
Woodford Close	44	F1
Woodford Court (Monksfield)	44	F1
Woodford Court	46	F1 [10]
(off Leinster Road West)		
Woodford Crescent	44	E1
Woodford Downs	44	F1
Woodford Drive	44	E1
Woodford Garth	44	E1
Woodford Green	44	F1
Woodford Grove	44	F1
Woodford Heights	44	F1
Woodford Hill	44	F1
Woodford Lawn	44	F1
Woodford Meadows	44	E1
Woodford Parade	44	E1
Woodford Park	44	F1
Woodford Park Road	44	F1
Woodford Rise	44	F1
Woodford Road	44	E1
Woodford Terrace	44	F1
Woodford View	44	F1
Woodford Villas	44	E1
Woodford Walk	44	F1
Woodford Way	44	F1
Woodhaven	47	C2 [10]
(off Milltown Bridge Road)		
Woodhazel Close	25	A1
Woodhazel Terrace	25	A1
Woodlands (Malahide)	14	F1
Woodlands (Maynooth)	17	B3
Woodlands	22	D1 [2]
(off Blakestown Road)		
Woodlands	47	A2 [1]
(off Orwell Road Rathgar)		
Woodlands Avenue (Stillorgan)	48	E4
Woodlands Avenue (Cornelscourt)	59	C3
Woodlands Court	15	A1
Woodlands Drive (Stillorgan)	48	E4
Woodlands Drive	59	C3
(Johnstown Road)		
Woodlands Park	48	F4
(Mount Merrion)		
Woodlands Park	59	C3
(Johnstown Road)		
Woodlands Road	59	C3
Woodlawn	12	F4
Woodlawn Avenue	12	F4
Woodlawn Close	12	F4
Woodlawn Court	12	F4
Woodlawn Crescent	12	F4
(Coolock Lane)		
Woodlawn Crescent	47	B4
(Churchtown)		
Woodlawn Drive	12	F4
Woodlawn Green	12	F4
Woodlawn Grove (Coolock Lane)	12	F4
Woodlawn Grove	47	B4 [7]
(off Churchtown Road Lower)		
Woodlawn Park (Coolock Lane)	12	F4
Woodlawn Park (Churchtown)	47	B4
Woodlawn Park (Tallaght)	55	C2
Woodlawn Park	59	C1 [4]
(off Mounttown Lower)		
Woodlawn Park Avenue	55	B1
Woodlawn Park Drive (Firhouse)	55	B1
Woodlawn Park Grove	55	C2
Woodlawn Rise	12	F4
Woodlawn Terrace	47	B4 [2]
(off Churchtown Road)		
Woodlawn View	12	F4
Woodlawn Villas	59	C1 [16]
(off Mounttown Road Lower)		
Woodlawn Walk	12	F4
Woodlawn Way	12	F4
Woodleigh	47	A2 [2]
(off Rathmines Road Upper)		
Woodley Court	58	D1 [4]
(off Woodley Park Kilmacud)		
Woodley Park	58	D1
Woodley Road	60	D3
Woodpark (Blanchardstown)	22	F2
Woodpark (off The Rise)	25	A3 [20]
Woodpark (Ballinteer)	57	B2
Woods End	22	F2
Woodscape	34	D3
Woodside (Leixlip)	19	C4
Woodside (Clontarf)	26	F4
Woodside (Howth)	30	D2
Woodside (Rathfarnham)	47	A3
Woodside Drive	47	A3
Woodside Grove	47	A3
Woodside Hall	57	C3
Woodside Road	57	C3
Woodstock Court	47	B1 [2]
(off Sandford Road)		
Woodstock Gardens	47	B1 [24]
(off Sandford Road)		
Woodstock Park	56	D1
Woodstown	55	C2
Woodstown Abbey	55	C2
Woodstown Abbey	56	D2
Woodstown Avenue	55	C2
Woodstown Close	55	C2
Woodstown Court	55	C2 [2]
(Woodstown Avenue)		
Woodstown Crescent	55	C2
Woodstown Dale	55	C2
Woodstown Drive	55	C2
Woodstown Gardens	55	C2
Woodstown Green	55	C2
Woodstown Heath	55	C2
Woodstown Height	55	C2
Woodstown Hill	55	C2
Woodstown House	46	F4 [21]
(off Stonepark Court)		
Woodstown Lane	56	D2
Woodstown Lawn	55	C2
Woodstown Meadow	55	C2
Woodstown Parade	55	C2
Woodstown Park	55	C2
Woodstown Place	55	C2
Woodstown Rise	55	C2
Woodstown Road	55	C2
Woodstown Vale	55	C2
Woodstown Walk	55	C2
Woodstown Way	33	C3
Woodthorpe	58	E1 [5]
(off Coolnevaun Kilmacud)		
Woodtown Way	56	D3
Woodvale Avenue	21	C1
Woodvale Crescent	21	C1
Woodvale Drive	21	C1
Woodvale Garth	21	C1
Woodvale Green	21	C1
Woodvale Grove	21	C1
Woodvale Park	21	C1
Woodvale Way	21	C1
Woodview (Celbridge)	32	D2
Woodview (Lucan)	33	C2
Woodview	48	F3
(Mount Merrion Avenue)		
Woodview	64	E2 [12]
Woodview Close	27	A1
Woodview Cottages	46	F3 [1]
(off Church Lane)		
Woodview Court (Dunboyne)	7	B3
Woodview Court	58	F1 [1]
(off Ard Lorcain Stillorgan)		
Woodview Court Apartments	33	C2
Woodview Drive	67	C3 [4]
Woodview Grove	22	E2
Woodview Heights (Dunboyne)	7	B3
Woodview Heights (Lucan)	33	C2
Woodview House	48	F3
Woodview Park (Castleknock)	23	A3
Woodview Park (Ardara Avenue)	27	A1
Woodville Avenue	34	E1
Woodville Close	34	E1
Woodville Court	26	E1
Woodville Green	34	E1
Woodville Grove	34	E1
Woodville House	26	D1 [4]
(off Kilmore Road)		
Woodville Lawn	34	E1
Woodville Road	25	A4 [7]
(off Botanic Avenue)		
Woodville Walk	34	E1
Wormwood Gate	70	F4
(off Bridge Street Lower)		
Wyattville	64	D1
Wyattville Close	64	D1
Wyattville Hill	64	D1
Wyattville Park	64	D1
Wyattville Road	64	D1
Wyckham Grove	57	C1
Wyckham Park Road	57	B1
Wyckham Place	57	C1
Wyckham Way	57	C1
Wynberg Park	49	B4
Wyndham Park	67	C2
Wynnefield Park	47	A1 [21]
(off Charleville Road)		
Wynnefield Road	47	A1
Wynnsward Drive	47	C2
Wynnsward Park	47	C2
Wyteleaf Grove	14	D4
Wyvern Estate	60	E3

X

STREET NAME	PAGE	GRID
Xavier Avenue	72	E1

Y

STREET NAME	PAGE	GRID
Yale	48	D3
Yankee Terrace	49	A4
Yarnhall Street	71	A3
Yeates Hall	59	B4
Yeates Way	35	C4
Yeats Court	39	A4 [54]
(off Sandymount Avenue)		
Yellow Meadows Ave	44	F1
Yellow Meadows Drive	44	E1
Yellow Meadows Estate	44	F1
Yellow Meadows Grove	44	E1
Yellow Meadows Lawn	44	E1
Yellow Meadows Park	44	E1
Yellow Meadows Vale	44	E1
Yellow Road	25	C2
Yellow Walls	3	A2
Yellow Walls Road	3	A2
Yellownook Avenue	59	C3
Yewlands Terrace	46	F2
York Avenue	47	A1
York Road (Ringsend)	39	A2
York Road (Rathmines)	47	A1
York Road (Dún Laoghaire)	49	C4
York Street	75	B2
York Terrace	49	C4 [4]
(off York Road Dún Laoghaire)		

Z

STREET NAME	PAGE	GRID
Zardoz Court	76	F4
(off Claremont Road)		
Zion Road	47	A2
Zoo Road	69	B3
Zuma Terrace (on Mount	74	F4
Drummond Ave)		

LIST OF STREETS NOT NAMED ON MAP BUT SHOWN AS SMALL NUMBERS

PAGE/GRID REF	STREET NAME
1 A2	1 Grove Court
1 C1	1 Elmwood Court
C1	2 Rathbeale Court
2 D2	1 St Columcille's Crescent
D2	2 Well Road
D2	3 Colmcille Court
D2	4 The Crescent
D2	5 New Road
2 F3	1 Blizzard Apartments
3 A2	1 Hillcrest
3 A3	1 Castle Oaks
A3	2 Ravenswood
A3	3 Oakleigh Court
3 B2	1 Fair Haven
B2	2 Haven View
B2	3 Railway Court
B2	4 The Priory
B2	5 Windsor Mews
B2	6 Fisherman's Green
B2	7 Broadmeadow Mews
B2	8 Ross Cottages
B2	9 Townyard House Apartments
B2	10 The Anchora Apartments
B2	11 James's Terrace Upper
B2	12 Strand Court
3 B3	1 Castle Court Apartments
3 C2	1 Seabank Court
C2	2 Clearwater Apartments
C2	3 Obelisk Court
4 D4	1 Alder Court
D4	2 The Quarry
7 B2	1 St Mary's Terrace
B2	2 Avondale Square
7 B3	1 Congress Park
B3	2 Hamilton Court
9 A4	1 Ashmount
A4	2 Ashfield Park
A4	3 Riverpark View
A4	4 Riverside
11 A4	1 St Margaret's Court
11 C4	1 Termon Court
12 D4	1 The Maieston
D4	2 The Charter
D4	3 The Turnpike
D4	4 The Kilmore
D4	5 The Goulding
D4	6 The Claremont
D4	7 The Landey
12 E4	1 Domville Court
13 A4	1 Newbury Terrace
13 B4	1 Greenlawns
B4	2 Clonshaugh Rise
B4	3 Ferrycarrig Green
B4	4 Clonshaugh Court
B4	5 Moatview Terrace
B4	6 Glin Close
B4	7 Glin Court
14 D4	1 Templeview Vale
D4	2 Elmfield Close
D4	3 Clonmellon Grove
D4	4 Beechbrook Grove
14 F2	1 St Lawrence O'Toole Avenue
F2	2 Church Avenue
F2	3 Suncroft Avenue
F2	4 St Brigid's Avenue
F2	5 St Ann's Square Lower
F2	6 St Anne's Square
F2	7 Hazel Court
15 A4	1 Seapoint Avenue
A4	2 Parochial Avenue
A4	3 Back Lane
A4	4 The Mall
A4	5 Breffni Gardens
A4	6 Brookstone Lane
A4	7 Seapoint Court
A4	9 Admiral Court
17 C3	1 Kelly's Lane
C3	2 Fagan's Lane
C3	3 Coates Lane
C3	4 Geraldine Court
C3	5 Court House Square
C3	6 Leinster Cottages
C3	7 Charter House
18 D3	1 Leinster Lodge Apartments
D3	2 Leinster Court
20 D4	1 Cypress Springs
21 C1	1 Meadow Dale
C1	2 Oakview Grove
21 C2	1 Willow Wood Downs
C2	2 Cedar Grove
22 D1	1 Briarwood Park
D1	2 Woodlands
D1	3 Briarwood Road
D1	4 Ashcroft Grove
D1	5 Ashcroft Court
D1	6 Rose Vale Court
D1	7 Blake's Court
22 D2	1 Coolmine Mews
D2	2 Kirkfield
22 D3	1 The Orchard
D3	2 Windmill Park
D3	3 Windmill Terrace
22 E3	1 Rosehaven
E3	2 Luttrell Park Heath
E3	3 Station View Apartments
22 F2	1 Herbert Crescent
F2	2 Tolka View
F2	3 Catherine's Well
F2	4 The Court
22 F3	1 The Crescent
F3	2 Castleknock Court
F3	3 Ashleigh Court
22 F4	1 The Sand Holes
23 A3	1 Beech Park Crescent
A3	2 Hadleigh Green
A3	3 Beechpark Close
A3	4 Park Court Apartments
A3	5 Castleknock Manor
23 B3	1 Mill Lane
B3	2 The Chandler Apartments
23 B4	1 Castleknock Gate
23 C2	1 Eastwood
23 C3	1 Rathbourne Court
C3	2 The Elms Apartments
C3	3 The Birches Apartments
C3	4 The Stables Apartments
C3	5 The Mews Apartments
C3	6 The Lodge Apartments
C3	7 The Tallow Apartments
C3	8 The Waxworks Apartments
23 C4	1 Baggot Terrace
C4	2 St Vincent's Cottages
C4	3 St Joseph's Cottages
C4	4 Ashtown Lodge
24 D1	1 Cardiffsbridge Grove
D1	2 Casement Close
24 D2	1 Valley Park Avenue
D2	2 Valeview Gardens
D2	3 Mellowes Court
D2	4 Mellowes Crescent
D2	5 Ravens Court
D2	6 Valeview Crescent
D2	7 Church View
D2	8 Patrickswell Court
24 D3	1 Clearwater Court
D3	2 Cassian Court
D3	3 Watermint Court
D3	4 Compass Court Apartments
D3	5 Riverstown Gardens
24 D4	1 Roosevelt Cottages
D4	2 Convent View Cottages
D4	3 Convent View Crescent
D4	4 Lyndon Gate
D4	5 Park Spring's
D4	6 Park Crescent House
D4	7 Parkside View
D4	8 Doreen House Apartments
24 E1	1 Georges Road
E1	2 Gofton Hall
E1	3 Heath Square
E1	4 Clearstream Court
24 E2	1 Ballygall Place
E2	2 Glenhill Villas
E2	3 St Helena's Court
E2	5 Johnstown Gardens
E2	6 Collins Row
E2	7 Glebe View
24 E4	1 Kilkieran Court
E4	2 St Finbarr's Court
E4	3 Rowan Hamilton Court
E4	4 Dunmanus Court
24 F2	1 Drapier Green
F2	2 Glasnamana Place
F2	3 Johnstown House
24 F3	1 Northland Grove
F3	2 Northland Drive
F3	3 Glasnevin Oaks
F3	4 Bellevue Cottages
F3	5 Cremore Villas
F3	6 Addison Hall
F3	7 Botanic Hall
F3	8 Addison Avenue
24 F4	1 St Philomena's Road
F4	2 Tower View Cottages
F4	3 Delvin Road
F4	4 Bengal Terrace
F4	5 Fertullagh Road
F4	6 Connaught Parade
F4	7 Clareville Court
F4	8 Shandon Green
F4	9 Shandon Mill
25 A1	1 Pinewood Grove
A1	2 Shanliss Gardens
A1	3 Oldtown Park
A1	4 Shangan Hall Apartments
A1	5 Gateway Apartments
25 A3	1 Claremont Avenue
A3	2 Church Avenue
A3	3 St David's Terrace
A3	4 Barron Place
A3	5 Comyn Place
A3	6 St Ita's Road
A3	7 St Malachy's Road
A3	8 St Michael's Road
A3	9 Addison Place
A3	10 St Mobhi Grove
A3	11 Clonmore Court
A3	12 Windele Road
A3	13 O'Brien's Place North
A3	14 O'Neachtain Road
A3	15 River Gardens
A3	16 Mobhi Court
A3	17 The Haven
A3	18 Glenavon Court
A3	19 Hillcrest Court
A3	20 Woodpark
A3	21 James Joyce Court
25 A4	1 Millmount Villas
A4	2 De Courcy Square
A4	3 Enniskerry Road
A4	4 Devery's Lane
A4	5 Prospect Square
A4	6 Glendalough Road
A4	7 Woodville Road
A4	8 St Teresa's Road
A4	9 St Teresa's Place
A4	10 Botanic Villas
A4	11 St Alphonsus Avenue
A4	12 St Brendan's Road
A4	13 St Clement's Road
A4	14 Botanic Park
A4	15 Lindsay Grove
A4	16 Whitworth Place
A4	17 Botanic Square
A4	18 Botanic Mews
A4	19 Prospect Court
A4	20 The Court
25 B1	1 Ailesbury
B1	2 Schoolhouse Mews
25 B2	1 Tourmakeady Road
25 B3	1 Clonturk Avenue
B3	2 The Village
B3	3 Clare Park Villas
B3	4 Beaucourt
B3	5 The Cloisters
B3	6 Clonturk Court
B3	7 All Hallows Lane
25 B4	1 Tom Clarke House
B4	2 St Joseph's Avenue
B4	3 Clonturk Gardens
B4	4 Kingston Lodge
B4	5 Holycross Avenue
B4	6 Robert Street
B4	7 Robert Place
B4	8 College Manor
B4	9 Victoria Lane
B4	10 Edgewood
B4	11 College Mews
B4	12 Richmond House
B4	13 Richmond Hall
B4	14 Brook House
B4	15 Distillery Loft Apartments
B4	16 Clonliffe Square
B4	17 The Distillery Building Apartments
25 C1	1 Ivy Court
C1	2 Beaumont Court
C1	3 Beaumont Wood
25 C2	1 Chestnut Court
C2	2 Dromnanane Road
C2	3 Dromnanane Park
C2	4 Thorndale Court
C2	5 Laragh Flats
C2	6 Collindale
C2	7 Beaumont Hall
C2	8 The Crescent
C2	9 Grace Park Lawns
C2	10 Riachville
C2	11 The Belfry Apartments
25 C3	1 Torlogh Parade
C3	2 Morrogh Terrace
C3	3 Calderwood Grove

PAGE/ GRID REF	STREET NAME
C3 4	Croydon Terrace
C3 5	Sion Hill Court
C3 6	Collins Court
C3 7	St Vincent's Court
C3 8	Collins Close
C3 9	The Woods
C3 10	Rosemount
25 C4 1	Annadale Avenue
C4 2	Shelmartin Terrace
C4 3	Windsor Villas
C4 4	St Joseph's Terrace
C4 5	St Declan's Terrace
C4 6	St Aidan's Park
C4 7	Fairview Green
C4 8	Torlogh Gardens
C4 9	Marino Mart
C4 10	Fairview Passage
C4 11	Fairview Terrace
C4 12	Caragh Court
C4 13	Marino Court
C4 14	Fairview Court
C4 15	Bushfield Square
C4 16	Melrose Court
C4 17	Elton Court
C4 18	Belmount Court
26 D1 1	Kilbarron Court
D1 2	Cromcastle Close
D1 3	St Luke's Court
D1 4	Woodville House
D1 5	Kilmore Court
D1 6	Cromcastle Court
26 D2 1	Newlands Court
26 D3 1	Cherrymount Crescent
D3 2	Cherrymount Grove
D3 3	Marino Villa
26 D4 1	Brighton Avenue
D4 2	Hollybrook Court Drive
D4 3	Hollybrook Court
D4 4	Strandville House
D4 5	Haddon Park
D4 6	Crescent House
D4 7	Kilronan Court
D4 8	Glenbrian Hall
D4 11	Hollybrook Mews
D4 12	Winston Ville
26 E1 1	Lismeen Grove
E1 2	Brookville Crescent
E1 3	Coolock Village Close
26 E2 1	Maryfield Avenue
E2 2	Artane Cottages Lower
E2 3	Artane Cottages Upper
E2 4	Brookwood Abbey
26 E3 1	St Brigid's Drive
E3 2	St Brigid's Court
E3 3	Quarry Cottages
E3 4	Killester Court
E3 5	Killester Park
26 E4 1	Warrenpoint
E4 2	St John's Wood
E4 3	Lambourne Village
E4 4	Knights Bridge
E4 5	St David's Court
E4 6	The Paddock's
26 F1 1	Elton Court
F1 2	Ayrefield Park
26 F2 1	Gorsefield Court
26 F4 1	Park View
F4 2	Hunter's Row
F4 3	Kincora Walk
27 A1 1	Elton Walk
A1 2	Glentworth Park
A1 3	Invermore Grove
A1 4	Curracloe Drive
A1 5	Laracor Gardens
A1 6	Gables
27 A3 1	Watermill Lawn
A3 2	St Anne's Court

PAGE/ GRID REF	STREET NAME
27 A4 1	Seafield Grove
A4 2	St Gabriel's Court
A4 3	Rinn na Mara
A4 4	Mount Prospect House
A4 5	The Mews
A4 6	Doyles Lane
27 B1 1	Howth Junction Cottages
B1 2	Swan's Nest Court
B1 3	Redmond's Court
B1 4	Briarsfield Walk
B1 5	Briarfield Villas
B1 6	St Berach's Place
27 B2 1	Thornville Terrace
B2 2	Greendale Court
B2 3	Roseglen Manor
27 B3 1	The Grove
B3 2	The Court
B3 3	Oakwood Apartments
27 C1 1	Bayside Crescent
C1 2	Emily Lawless Court
C1 3	Thomas Moore Court
C1 4	Thomas Davis Court
C1 5	James Joyce Court
27 C2 1	Mariners Court
C2 2	Del Val Court
28 D1 1	Sutton Court
D1 2	Seafield
D1 3	St Domhnach's Well Street
D1 4	Marine Cove
D1 5	Warren Court
D1 6	Moyclare Gardens
29 A1 1	James McCormack Gardens
A1 2	St Catherine's Terrace
A1 3	Radcliffe
29 B1 1	Corrbridge Terrace
B1 2	Avalon Apartments
B1 3	Corr Castle Apartments
B1 4	Offington Manor Apartments
29 B3 1	Shielmartin Park
B3 2	Martello Terrace
30 D1 1	Dunbo Terrace
D1 2	Evora Terrace
D1 3	Findlater Building Apartments
D1 4	Dunbo Hill
D1 5	Howth Terrace
D1 6	Harbour View
D1 7	Marine Villas
D1 8	St Lawrence Quay
D1 9	Island View Apartments
D1 10	Howth House Apartments
D1 11	Abbey Terrace
D1 12	Evora Crescent
D1 13	Cuan na Mara
D1 14	Howth Peninsula Apartments
D1 15	Villa Building Apartments
D1 16	St Lawrence Building Apartments
30 D2 1	St Lawrence's Terrace
D2 2	Seaview Terrace
D2 3	St Mary's Road
D2 4	St Mary's Place
D2 5	St Nessan's Terrace
D2 6	The Haggard
D2 7	Hillside Terrace
D2 8	Dungriffan Villas
D2 9	St Nessan's Close
D2 10	Thormanby Grove
D2 12	St Nessans Court
D2 13	Crosstrees Court
D2 15	Forge Court
D2 16	Campbell Court

PAGE/ GRID REF	STREET NAME
30 E2 1	Cannon Rock View
E2 2	Upper Cliff Road
E2 3	St Nessan's Apartments
31 C2 1	Crodaun Court
31 C3 1	The Deanery
C3 2	The Close
C3 3	St Judes Apartments
33 A1 1	Ralph Square
A1 2	Liffey View Apartments
33 B2 1	The Copse
33 C3 1	Westbury Grove
34 D1 1	Sarsfield Terrace
D1 2	Vesey Terrace
D1 3	Hanbury Lane
D1 4	Sarsfield Court
D1 5	The Square
D1 6	Dispensary Lane
D1 7	Village Weir
D1 8	Brookvale
D1 9	Mount Gandon
D1 10	Gandon Mews
D1 11	Old Rectory
D1 12	The Village Centre
D1 13	The Village Court
D1 14	The Orchard
D1 15	Mill Bank
D1 16	Gandon Court
D1 17	St Andrews Court
34 D2 1	Arthur Griffith Court
D2 2	Adams Town Court
D2 3	The Hollows
34 E1 1	Edmondsbury Court
34 F1 1	Latouka Apartments
34 F2 1	Liffey Hall
F2 2	Foxford Court
34 F3 1	Foxborough Hall
F3 2	Foxborough Crescent
35 A3 1	Neilstown Village Court
A3 2	Liscarne Dale
A3 3	Collinstown Crescent
35 A4 1	Ballymanagin Lane
A4 2	Moorfield Close
A4 3	Neilstown Cottages
A4 4	Rosebank Place
A4 5	Rosebank Hall
35 B4 1	Rosebank View
B4 2	Rosebank Court
35 C1 1	The Covert
C1 2	Glenside Villas
C1 3	Clarkeville Terrace
C1 4	Red Cow Cottages
C1 5	St Fintan's Terrace
C1 6	Woodfarm Cottages
35 C2 1	Culmore Park
C2 2	Glenaulin Green
35 C4 1	Cherry Orchard Way
36 D2 1	Rossaveal Court
36 D3 1	Le Fanu Drive
36 E2 1	Park Lane
E2 2	Maidens Row
E2 3	Hibernian Terrace
E2 4	St Laurence Grove
E2 5	St Mary's Terrace
E2 6	Isolde Gardens
E2 7	Liffey Terrace
E2 8	Clayton Terrace
E2 9	St Laurence Terrace
E2 10	Mullingar Terrace
E2 11	Riverview Court
E2 12	New Row
E2 13	Isolde House Apartments
E2 14	Distillery House Apartments
E2 15	Tristan House Apartments

PAGE/ GRID REF	STREET NAME
36 E3 1	O'Hogan Road
E3 2	Lynch's Lane
E3 3	St Lawrence Glen
E3 4	Convent Lawns
36 E4 1	Old Naas Road Cottages
E4 2	Millrose Estate
E4 3	The Laurels
E4 4	Hollybrooke
36 F3 1	Park Street
F3 2	Phoenix Street
F3 3	Inchicore Terrace North
F3 4	Murray's Cottages
F3 5	Partridge Terrace
F3 6	Tyrconnell Street
F3 7	Tyrconnell Villas
F3 8	Woodfield Cottages
F3 9	St Patrick's Terrace
F3 10	Abercorn Terrace
F3 11	Granite Terrace
F3 12	Ring Street
F3 13	Inchicore Square
F3 14	Oblate Drive
F3 15	Woodfield Place
F3 16	Hampton Court
F3 17	St James's Place
F3 18	St George's Villas
F3 19	Abercorn Square
F3 20	Wheaton Court
36 F4 1	Muirfield Drive
F4 2	Bernard Curtis House
F4 3	La Touche Court
F4 4	Grove Court
F4 5	Landsdowne Valley Park
39 A2 1	Fishermans Wharf
A2 2	Alexandra Quay
A2 3	Thorncastle Court Apartments
39 A3 1	Cambridge Street
A3 2	Fitzwilliam Street
A3 3	St Patrick's Villas
A3 4	Seapoint Terrace
A3 5	The Square
A3 6	St Brendan's Cottages
A3 7	Cambridge Avenue
A3 8	Tritonville Avenue
A3 9	Tritonville Crescent
A3 10	Seafort Gardens
A3 11	Leukos Road
A3 12	Clonlara Road
A3 13	Kyle-Clare Road
A3 14	Parkview Place
A3 15	Canon Mooney Gardens
A3 16	Caroline Row
A3 17	Havelock Terrace
A3 18	Dodder Terrace
A3 19	Ennis Grove
A3 20	Londonbridge Drive
A3 21	Strasburg Terrace
A3 22	Tritonville Close
A3 23	St James Terrace
A3 24	Cambridge Court
A3 25	Lansdowne Hall
A3 26	Sandymount Court
A3 28	O'Rahilly House Flats
A3 29	Whelan House Flats
A3 30	Ropewalk Place
A3 31	Kennedy Court
A3 32	Simpsons Lane
A3 33	Summerfield
A3 34	The Old Presbytery
A3 36	Fitzwilliam Quay
A3 37	Fitzwilliam Point
A3 38	The Moorings
A3 39	Magdalen Terrace
A3 40	Veronica Terrace
A3 41	Philomena Terrace
A3 42	Celestine Avenue
A3 44	Victoria Cottages
A3 45	Tritonville Mews

PAGE/GRID REF	STREET NAME
A3 46	Steeple Gate
A3 47	Fairfield Court
A3 48	Baggot Rath House
A3 49	Fairview Avenue
39 A4 1	Sandymount Green
A4 2	Sandymount Castle Road
A4 3	Sandymount Castle Drive
A4 4	Sydenham Road
A4 5	Sandymount Castle
A4 6	Churchill Terrace
A4 7	Prince of Wales Terrace
A4 8	Railway Cottages
A4 9	Martin White Chalets
A4 10	Gilford Court
A4 11	Homelee
A4 12	Lynton Court
A4 13	Spafield Terrace
A4 14	Adair
A4 15	Wilfield
A4 16	Park Court
A4 17	Dromard Terrace
A4 18	Seafort Cottages
A4 19	Seafort Terrace
A4 20	Seafort Villas
A4 21	Claremont Court
A4 22	The Sweepstakes
A4 23	Ballsbridge Park
A4 24	Lansdowne Square
A4 26	Ballsbridge Avenue
A4 29	Cannon Mews
A4 30	Cannon Place
A4 31	StJames Place
A4 32	Glenesk Court
A4 33	Trideat Apartments
A4 34	Merry Bush
A4 35	Oisin Court
A4 36	Claremont Court
A4 37	Argyle House Apartments
A4 38	Oaklands Court
A4 40	Anglesea House
A4 41	Elbin House
A4 42	Raglan House
A4 43	Clyde House
A4 44	Oakbury Court
A4 45	The Willows
A4 46	Gilford Pines
A4 47	Hollyrood Apartments
A4 48	Herbert Court
A4 49	St James Court
A4 50	Renoir Apartments
A4 51	El Greco Apartments
A4 52	Wellington Lodge
A4 53	Sydenham Court
A4 54	Yeats Court
A4 55	Avondale Mews
39 B1 1	Alverno
B1 2	Haddon Court
39 B3 1	Prospect Terrace
39 B4 1	Gilford Terrace
B4 2	Sandymount Castle Park
B4 3	Martello View
B4 4	Bethany House
B4 5	Hempenstal Terrace
B4 6	Martello Wood
B4 7	St Catheryn's Court
B4 8	Windermere
B4 9	Radcliff Hall
39 C1 1	Churchgate Avenue
C1 2	St Joseph's Square
C1 3	Vernon Court
C1 4	Vernon Wood
43 C1 1	Bawnogue Cottages
C1 2	Nangor Place
C1 3	St Catherines Grove
44 D1 1	St Patrick's Avenue
D1 2	Leinster Terrace
D1 3	Beech Row

PAGE/GRID REF	STREET NAME
D1 4	The Mill Pond Apartments
D1 5	Nangor Crescent
D1 6	Cherrywood Villas
44 D2 1	Church View
D2 2	Green Isle Court
44 E1 1	St Killian's Park
E1 2	Monastery Heights
E1 3	Bettysford
E1 4	Castle Crescent
E1 5	Friar's Walk
E1 6	Riverside
E1 7	Millview
44 E2 1	St Brigid's Park
44 F1 1	Knockmitten Close
F1 2	Knockmitten Lane North
44 F3 1	Pinetree Grove
F3 2	Belgard Close
F3 3	Shalimar Apartments
44 F4 1	Pinetree Crescent
45 A3 1	Parkhill Heights
A3 2	Parkview
45 B2 1	Tibradden Close
B2 2	Ballymount Cottages
45 B3 1	Three Rock Close
45 B4 1	Tymon North Court
B4 2	Tymon North Place
45 C1 1	Field Avenue
C1 2	Wallace Road
C1 3	Percy French Road
C1 4	O'Dwyer Road
C1 5	Esposito Road
C1 6	Landsdowne Valley
C1 7	Somerville Park
C1 8	Harty Court
45 C2 1	St Peter's Terrace
45 C3 1	Willington Lawn
C3 2	Wellington Cottages
45 C4 1	Spawell Cottages
46 D1 1	Sunville Green
D1 2	Windmill Crescent
D1 3	Father Kit Court
D1 4	St Agnes Terrace
D1 5	Rockmeade Court
D1 6	Brug Chroimlinn
D1 7	Looceville Court
D1 8	Somerville Court
46 D2 1	Muckross Drive
D2 2	Lorcan O'Toole Court
D2 3	Stannaway Court
D2 4	Beechfield Mews
D2 5	Wellington Court
D2 7	The Manor
46 D3 1	Wellington Road
46 D4 1	Hillcrest
D4 2	Hillcrest Manor
46 E1 1	Tonguefield Road
E1 2	Cloyne Road
E1 3	Faughart Road
E1 4	Clonmacnoise Grove
E1 5	Bedford Court
E1 6	Poddle Green
E1 7	Larrisa Court
46 E2 1	Riversdale Grove
E2 2	Hazel Park
E2 3	Kimmage Court
E2 4	Rathland Drive
E2 5	Brookfield Green
E2 6	Brookfield Court
E2 7	Hazelbrook Apartments
E2 8	Clonard Court
E2 9	Riverside
E2 10	Baroma

PAGE/GRID REF	STREET NAME
E2 11	Clonallen
E2 12	Cranford Court
46 E3 1	Templeville Park
E3 2	Fortfield Court
46 E4 1	Butterfield Meadow
46 E4 2	Brookmount Court
46 F1 1	Mount Harold Terrace
F1 2	Le Bas Terrace
F1 3	Mountain View Avenue
F1 4	Manor Villas
F1 5	Wilfrid Terrace
F1 6	Fitzpatrick's Cottages
F1 7	Ryan's Cottages
F1 8	Parkview Court
F1 9	Gandon Close
F1 10	Woodford Court
F1 11	Kenilworth Manor
F1 12	Waverley Terrace
F1 13	Smith's Lane
F1 14	Kengar Mews
F1 15	Mount Argus Square
F1 16	Mountain View Court
F1 17	Casimir Court
F1 18	Kerrygold House
F1 19	Kennilworth Lodge
46 F2 1	Ashdale Park
F2 2	Westhampton Place
F2 3	Terenure Place
F2 4	Eagle Hill Avenue
F2 5	Victoria Villas
F2 6	Maple Drive
F2 7	Victoria Village
F2 8	Frankfort Court
F2 9	Frankfort Flats
F2 10	Rathdown Court
F2 11	Rathgar Villas
F2 12	Greenlea Place
F2 13	Brighton Green
F2 14	McMorrough Road
F2 15	Earls Court
F2 16	Rathgar Park
F2 17	Olney Grove
F2 18	Eaton Hall
F2 19	Winton Grove
F2 20	Beechlawn Manor
F2 21	Beechlawn Mews
F2 22	Eaton Court
F2 23	Carlisle Court
F2 24	Fairfield House
F2 25	Beaumont House
F2 27	Loughmorne House
46 F3 1	Woodview Cottages
F3 2	St Agnes Terrace
F3 3	Dodder Park Drive
F3 4	Village Green
F3 5	The Falls
F3 6	Tourville Lodge
F3 7	Le Brett Terrace
F3 8	Wasdale House
F3 9	Crannagh Castle
F3 10	Crannagh Court
46 F4 1	Willbrook Grove
F4 2	Tara Hill Grove
F4 3	Beaufort Villas
F4 4	Glenann
F4 5	St Mary's Terrace
F4 6	Village Court Apartments
F4 7	The Park Lands
F4 8	The Lakelands
F4 9	The Woodlands
F4 10	Beaufort Court
F4 11	The Castlelands
F4 12	Rathfarnham Mill
F4 13	The Laurels
F4 14	Loftus Square
F4 15	Blackburn Square
F4 16	Otterbrook
F4 17	Stonepark Orchard
F4 18	Castle Court
F4 19	A.W. Pugin House

PAGE/GRID REF	STREET NAME
F4 20	Theresa House
F4 21	Woodstown House
F4 22	William Pallister House
F4 23	Frances Ball House
F4 24	De Bret House
F4 25	Hogan House
F4 26	Riversdale View
47 A1 1	Rathmines Park
A1 2	Leinster Square
A1 3	Prince Arthur Terrace
A1 4	Swanville Place
A1 5	Castlewood Terrace
A1 6	Castlewood Place
A1 7	Grosvenor Park
A1 8	Stone Mews
A1 9	Turrets Flats
A1 10	Purser Gardens
A1 11	Esker Villas
A1 12	Parker Hill
A1 13	Alma Terrace
A1 14	Observatory Lane
A1 15	Belgrave Place
A1 16	Cambridge Villas
A1 17	Salem Court
A1 18	Maxwell Court
A1 19	The Mews
A1 20	Roland Court
A1 21	Wynnefield Park
A1 22	Mount Anthony Estate
A1 23	Louis Lane
A1 24	Castlewood Close
A1 25	Rathmines Avenue Court
A1 26	Cosy Lodge
A1 27	Newington Terrace
A1 28	Rathgar Court
47 A2 1	Woodlands
A2 2	Woodleigh
A2 3	Highfield Court
A2 4	Cowper Mews
A2 5	Garville Place
A2 6	Garville Drive
A2 7	Rathgar Park
A2 8	Orwell Mews
A2 9	Stratford
A2 10	Garville Court
47 A3 1	The Willows
A3 2	Stirling Park
A3 3	Orwell Court
A3 4	Newtown Villas
A3 5	Newtown Court
A3 7	Orwell Bank
A3 8	Crannagh Way
A3 9	Landore
A3 10	Park View
A3 11	Ard Na Gréine
A3 12	Newtown House
A3 13	Dodder Vale
47 A4 1	Castle Court
A4 2	Nutgrove Court
47 B1 1	Sallymount Gardens
B1 2	Woodstock Court
B1 3	Collier's Avenue
B1 4	Westmoreland Park
B1 5	Field's Terrace
B1 6	Rugby Villas
B1 7	Beechwood Park
B1 8	Bushfield Avenue
B1 9	Charleston Court Flats
B1 10	Oakley Court
B1 11	Cullenswood Road
B1 12	Moran's Cottages
B1 13	Mountain View Cottages
B1 14	Sallymount Terrace
B1 15	Chelmsford Lane
B1 16	Belgrave Villas
B1 17	Bushfield Place
B1 18	Smith's Cottages
B1 19	Beechdale Mews
B1 20	Oakley Square
B1 21	Palmerston Close

PAGE/ GRID REF	STREET NAME
B1 22	Moyne Court
B1 23	Oakley Park
B1 24	Woodstock Gardens
B1 25	Marlborough Lane
B1 26	Castlewood Court
47 B2 2	Strand Terrace
B2 3	St Luke's Crescent
B2 4	Balnagowan
B2 5	Temple Square
B2 6	Milltown Grove
B2 7	Milltown Hill
B2 8	Thorncliff
B2 9	Shanagarry
B2 10	Dodder Bank
47 B3 1	St Columbanus Place
B3 2	St Gall Gardens North
B3 3	St Gall Gardens South
B3 4	Milltown Terrace
B3 5	Dartry Cottages
47 B4 1	Glenbower Park
B4 2	Woodlawn Terrace
B4 3	Beaumont Close
B4 4	Briarly Court
B4 5	St Nathy's House
B4 6	Ardtona Avenue
B4 7	Woodlawn Grove
B4 8	Henley Court
B4 9	Weston Terrace
B4 10	Frankfort
B4 11	Rosemount Terrace
B4 12	Waldemar Terrace
B4 13	Airfield Drive
B4 14	Nutgrove Avenue
B4 16	Annadale
B4 17	St Nathy's Villas
B4 18	Sweetmount House
B4 19	Camberley Oaks
B4 20	Camberley Elms
47 C1 1	St Broc's Cottages
C1 2	Pembroke Cottages
C1 3	Belmont Park
C1 4	The Crescent
C1 5	Harmony Avenue
C1 6	Vergemount Park
C1 7	Norwood Park
C1 8	Brookvale Road
C1 9	Vergemount Hall
C1 10	Sandford Gardens
C1 11	Auburn Road
C1 12	Vergemount
C1 13	Eglinton Square
C1 14	Mount Sandford
C1 15	Rowan Hall
C1 16	Cedar Hall
C1 17	Millbrook Village
C1 18	Simmonscourt Terrace
C1 19	Brookfield
C1 20	Harmony Court
C1 21	Riverside Walk
C1 22	Eglinton Wood
C1 23	Shamrock Hill Mews
C1 24	Donnybrook Castle
C1 25	Argyle Square
47 C2 1	Prospect Lane
C2 2	Beech Hill Villas
C2 3	Beech Hill Crescent
C2 4	Beech Hill Terrace
C2 5	Palmerston Grove
C2 6	Clonskeagh Drive
C2 7	Clonskeagh Square
C2 8	St Bridget's Flats
C2 9	Crannagh
C2 10	Woodhaven
C2 11	Richview Villas
C2 12	Byrne's Terrace
47 C3 1	Annaville Grove
C3 2	Olivemount Grove
C3 3	Friarsland Avenue
C3 4	Harlech Villas
C3 5	Gledswood Drive
C3 6	Olivemount Terrace
C3 7	Glenard Hall
C3 8	Belfield Close
C3 9	Roebuck Lawn
C3 10	Roebuck Crescent
47 C4 1	Sunnybank Court
C4 2	Woodbine Terrace
C4 3	Alexandra Villas
C4 4	Roseville Terrace
C4 5	Pembroke Cottages
C4 6	Pembroke Terrace
C4 7	Claremont Terrace
C4 8	Glenville Terrace
C4 9	St Joseph's Grove
48 D1 1	Merrion View Avenue
D1 2	Simmonscourt Avenue
D1 3	Simmonscourt View
D1 4	Ailesbury Close
D1 5	Simmonscourt Square
48 D2 1	Nutley Square
D2 2	Donnybrook Close
D2 3	Donnybrook Green
D2 4	Greenfield Manor
48 D3 1	Hopkins Square
D3 2	Finglas Square
D3 3	Hayden Square
D3 4	Hyde Square
D3 5	Meenan Square
48 D4 1	Edenwood
D4 2	Sophie Baret Residence
48 E1 1	Merrion Court
E1 2	Merrion Gates
E1 3	Strand Lane
48 E2 1	Seafield Park
E2 2	Bellevue Court
E2 3	Merrion Crescent
E2 4	Woodbine House
48 E3 1	The Stables
E3 2	Mountbrook
48 E4 1	Greygates
E4 2	Beaufield Mews
E4 3	Ashurst
48 F2 1	St Helen's Villas
48 F3 1	Martello Terrace
F3 2	Pembroke Cottages
F3 3	Willowmount
F3 4	Cherbury Mews
48 F4 1	St Helier's Copse
F4 2	Orpen Dale
F4 3	Park Villas
F4 4	Cedar Square
F4 5	Grove House Gardens
49 A3 1	Newtown Villas
A3 2	Maretimo Road
A3 3	Ben Inagh Park
A3 4	Maretimo Gardens West
A3 5	Craigmore Gardens
A3 6	George's Place
A3 7	St Anne's Square
A3 8	Bath Place
A3 9	Rockwell Cove Apartments
A3 10	Westfield Terrace
A3 11	Idrone Mews
A3 12	Brusna Cottages
A3 13	Collins Court
A3 14	Patrick's Row
A3 15	Eagle Hill
A3 16	Maretimo Terrace
A3 17	Maretimo Place
A3 18	Maretimo Villas
A3 19	Whelan's Terrace
A3 20	Carbury Place
A3 21	Sweetman's Avenue
A3 22	Lisalea
A3 23	Frascati Court
A3 24	Frascati Hall
A3 25	Temple Court
A3 26	St Anns Close
49 A4 1	Avondale Park
A4 2	Prince Edward Terrace Lower
A4 3	Prince Edward Terrace Upper
A4 4	Lindenvale
A4 5	Twin Cottages
A4 6	Fieldview Cottages
A4 7	Cullen's Cottages
A4 8	Webster's Cottages
A4 9	Rockville Estate
A4 10	Avoca Hall
A4 11	Brookfield Grove
A4 12	Brookfield Court
49 B3 1	Ardenza Terrace
B3 2	Tobernea Terrace
B3 3	Ardenza Park
B3 4	Seapoint Terrace
B3 5	The Orchard
49 B4 1	Montpelier Place
B4 2	Montpelier Manor
B4 3	The Willows
B4 4	The Maples
B4 5	The Cedars
B4 6	The Alders
B4 7	The Poplars
B4 8	Stradbrook Gardens
B4 9	Brighton Terrace
B4 10	Belgrave Place
B4 11	Belgrave Terrace
B4 12	Brooklawn Avenue
B4 13	Brooklawn Wood
B4 14	Rockford Terrace
B4 15	Beaupark Downs
B4 16	Drayton Close
B4 17	Heathfield
B4 18	Southdene
B4 19	Arundel
B4 20	Stradbrook Hall
B4 21	The Beeches
B4 22	Brighton Lane
B4 23	Knocknagow
49 C4 1	Rosary Gardens West
C4 2	Barrett Street
C4 3	Smith's Villas
C4 4	York Terrace
C4 5	St Mary's Street
C4 7	Oakwood
C4 8	Harbour Terrace
C4 9	Grosvenor Terrace
C4 10	Clifton Lane
C4 11	Clifton Avenue
C4 12	Richmond Green
C4 13	Clifton Terrace
C4 14	Alma Place
C4 15	Seaview Terrace
C4 16	Synnott Terrace
C4 17	Bentley Villas
C4 18	St Michael's Terrace
C4 19	St Brendan's Terrace
C4 20	Northcote Terrace
C4 21	Knapton Court
C4 22	Knapton Lawn
C4 23	Northcote Place
C4 24	Cambridge Terrace
C4 25	Primrose Hill
C4 26	Mounttown Cottages
C4 27	Knapton Terrace
C4 28	Pakenham
C4 29	Monkstown Gate
C4 30	Alma Park
C4 31	Clearwater Cove
C4 32	Marina House Apartments
C4 33	The Anchorage
C4 34	Smyth Gardens
C4 35	Eglinton Park
50 D4 1	Wellington Street
D4 2	Rosary Gardens East
D4 3	Desmond Avenue
D4 4	Wolfe Tone Avenue
D4 5	Charlemont Avenue
D4 6	Summerhill Parade
D4 7	Haddington Terrace
D4 8	Victoria Terrace
D4 9	Marine Terrace
D4 10	Northumberland Place
D4 11	Northumberland Park
D4 12	Dungar Terrace
D4 13	Stoneview Place
D4 14	Martello Avenue
D4 15	Crosthwaite Terrace
D4 16	Sussex Street
D4 17	Marine Court
D4 18	Charlemont Terrace
D4 19	Mill Street
D4 20	Anglesea Lane
D4 21	Park Lane
D4 23	Sydenham
D4 24	Oratory Mews Court
D4 25	Crofton Terrace
D4 26	Connaught Place
D4 27	Albert Terrace
D4 28	Crofton Mansions
50 E4 1	Mornington Avenue
E4 2	Martello Terrace
E4 3	Summerhill Court
52 F2 1	Eaton House
54 D1 1	Brookfield Court
D1 2	Jobstown Village Square
D1 3	Rossfield Court
D1 4	Rossfield Close
D1 5	Glenshane Dale
D1 6	Glenshane Place
54 D2 1	Elm House Apartments
D2 2	Montpelier Walk
54 F1 1	Tuansgate Apartments
F1 2	Abberley Square Apartments
F1 3	Aengus Hall
F1 4	Alen Hall
F1 5	Horan Hall
F1 6	Losset Hall
F1 7	Tallow Hall
F1 8	Virginia Hall
F1 9	Loftus Hall
F1 10	Swan Hall
55 A1 1	St Maelruans Park
A1 2	High Street
A1 3	Avonbeg Court
A1 4	St Dominic's Court
A1 5	Old Bawn Court
A1 6	College View
A1 7	Uppercross Court
A1 8	Tramway Court
A1 9	New Bancroft Place
A1 10	The Laurels
A1 11	New Bancroft Hall
A1 12	New Bancroft Square
A1 13	Courthouse Square Apartments
55 A2 1	Summerfield
A2 2	The Close
A2 3	Allenton Crescent
55 B1 1	Bolbrook Drive
B1 3	Bolbrook Avenue
B1 4	Bolbrook Close
B1 5	Avonmore Avenue
B1 6	Moynihan Court
55 B2 1	Oldcourt Lawn
B2 2	Killininny Court Apartments
B2 3	Tara Crescent
55 B3 1	Ely Crescent
B3 2	Ely Grove
B3 3	Ely Green
B3 4	Ferncourt Drive
B3 5	Ferncourt Crescent
B3 6	Beechdale Close
55 C1 1	Brookmount Lawns
C1 2	Knocklyon Mews

PAGE/GRID REF   STREET NAME

PAGE	GRID REF		STREET NAME
	C1	3	Homeville Court
	C1	4	Homeville
	C1	5	Balrothery Cottages
	C1	6	Prospect Lodge
	C1	7	Castle Side
55	C2	1	Wood Dale Oak
	C2	2	Woodstown Court
	C2	3	Knocklyon Gate Apartments
56	D1	1	Coolamber Court
	D1	2	Pine Grove
	D1	3	Ballyroan Court
56	E1	1	Orchardton
56	E2	1	Beechview
	E2	2	Cypress Avenue
	E2	3	Larch Drive
	E2	4	Beech Walk
	E2	5	Walnut View
56	F1	1	Sarah Curran Road
	F1	2	St Gatien Road
	F1	3	Fonthill Abbey
	F1	4	Whitechurch Abbey
	F1	5	Edenbrook Court
	F1	6	Forthill Court
	F1	8	The Beeches
57	A1	1	Marley Villas
	A1	2	Meadow Villas
	A1	3	Barton Court
57	A2	1	Priory Court
	A2	2	The Cherries
	A2	3	Elm Way
	A2	5	Stonemasons Green
57	B1	1	Meadow Avenue
	B1	2	Hawthorn Drive
	B1	3	Mount Albion Road
	B1	4	Sycamore Drive
	B1	5	Hillview Glade
	B1	6	Hillview Court
57	B2	1	The Crescent
	B2	2	Ballinteer Court
	B2	3	The Copse
	B2	4	The Dale
57	C1	1	Westerton Rise
	C1	2	Ashgrove Terrace
	C1	3	Eagle Terrace
	C1	4	Castle Court
	C1	5	McGrane Court
	C1	6	Ballyolaf Manor
	C1	7	Castleview
	C1	8	Ashgrove Court
	C1	9	Dundrum Gate Apartments
	C1	10	Riverbank
	C1	11	Riversdale
	C1	12	The Birch
	C1	13	The Linden
	C1	14	The Blackthorn
57	C2	1	Clonlea Wood
	C2	2	College Park Court
	C2	3	College Park Drive
58	D1	1	Drummartin Crescent
	D1	2	Carrick Lawn
	D1	3	The Pines
	D1	4	Woodley Court
58	D2	1	Balally Terrace
	D2	2	Moreen Lawn
	D2	3	Blackthorn Grove
	D2	4	Blackthorn Court
	D2	5	Rathdown Terrace
	D2	6	Blackthorn Green
	D2	7	Blackthorn Close
	D2	8	Olaf Hall
	D2	9	Rathdown Grove
58	D3	1	Churchlands
58	E1	1	Dale Close
	E1	2	Stillorgan Court
	E1	3	Stillorgan Heath

PAGE	GRID REF		STREET NAME
	E1	4	Convent Court
	E1	5	Woodthorpe
58	E3	1	Glencairn Garth
58	F1	1	Woodview Court
	F1	2	Ard Lorcain Villas
	F1	3	Grange Cottages
	F1	4	Ulster Terrace
	F1	5	Pear Tree Field
	F1	6	Dunstaffnage Hall Apartments
58	F2	1	Leopardstown Court
	F2	2	Leopardstown Lawn
	F2	3	Silver Pines
	F2	4	Ellesmere
	F2	5	Ballymoss Parade
	F2	6	Arkle Square
	F2	7	Sir Ivor Mall
	F2	8	Fey Yerra
58	F4	1	Ballyogan Park
59	A1	1	Orchard Cottages
	A1	2	Red Brick Terrace
	A1	3	Moore's Cottages
	A1	4	Hawthorn Manor
	A1	5	Rosehill
	A1	6	Ardagh Close
	A1	8	Newtown Park Court
	A1	9	Galloping Green
	A1	10	Avila Apartments
	A1	11	Newtownpark House
	A1	12	Obelisk Avenue
59	A2	1	Knocksinna Grove
	A2	2	Knocksinna Court
	A2	3	New Park Lodge
	A2	4	Foxrock Mount
	A2	5	Chestnut Park
	A2	6	Willow Park
	A2	7	Sycamore Grove
	A2	8	Whitethorn Walk
	A2	9	Birch Dale
	A2	10	The Coutryard
	A2	11	Kelston Hall
	A2	12	Sefton Hall
59	A3	1	Brighton Cottages
	A3	2	Kilteragh Pines
	A3	3	Avalon
	A3	4	Brighton Lodge
	A3	5	The Gables
	A3	6	Westminster Court
59	B1	1	Windsor Court
	B1	2	Grange Grove
	B1	3	Oliver Plunkett Villas
	B1	4	Stradbrook Hill
	B1	5	Springhill Cottages
	B1	6	Grange Terrace
	B1	7	Abbey Court
	B1	9	Faber Grove
	B1	10	Deans Court
	B1	11	Devon Close
	B1	12	Monkstown Square
59	B3	1	Kerrymount Close
	B3	4	Monaloe Crescent
	B3	5	Clonkeen Lawn
	B3	6	Monaloe Court
	B3	7	New Cornelscourt
59	C1	1	Oliver Plunkett Square
	C1	2	Patrician Park
	C1	3	Mounttown Park
	C1	4	Woodlawn Park
	C1	5	Oliver Plunkett Terrace
	C1	6	Fitzgerald Park
	C1	7	St Patrick's Terrace
	C1	8	Dunedin Drive
	C1	9	St Patrick's Close
	C1	10	Highthorn Woods
	C1	11	Aspen Park
	C1	12	Birch Dale
	C1	13	Willow Grove
	C1	14	Carriglea Court
	C1	16	Woodlawn Villas

PAGE	GRID REF		STREET NAME
	C1	17	Meadowlands Court
	C1	18	Meadowlands Mews
59	C2	1	Hillview Cottages
	C2	2	Whitethorn Walk
	C2	3	Sycamore Court
	C2	4	Hazel Lawn
	C2	5	Eaglewood Apartments
	C2	6	Rochestown House Apartments
	C2	7	Eaglewood House
	C2	8	Eaglewood Mews
	C2	9	Rochestown House
59	C3	1	Little Meadow
	C3	2	Cabinteely Court
	C3	3	Cabinteely Park
	C3	4	O'Shea's Cottages
	C3	5	Little Orchard
59	C4	1	Kilbogget Villas
	C4	2	Church Villas
60	D1	1	O'Donnell Gardens
	D1	2	Royal Terrace North
	D1	3	Myrtle Avenue
	D1	4	Emmet Street
	D1	5	Eden Villas
	D1	6	Laurel Hill
	D1	7	Granite Hall
	D1	8	Magenta Place
	D1	9	Marlborough Park
	D1	10	Royal Terrace Lane
	D1	11	Beechwood Grove
	D1	12	Rollins Court
	D1	13	Seven Houses
	D1	14	The Glen
	D1	15	Glengara Close
	D1	16	Silchester Wood
	D1	17	Carlisle Terrace
	D1	18	Durham Place
	D1	19	Rus-in-Urbe Terrace
60	D2	1	Honey Park
	D2	2	Thomastown Crescent
	D2	3	Pearse Close
60	D3	1	Auburn Road
	D3	2	Granville Crescent
60	D4	1	Annabeg
	D4	2	Meadow Court
60	D4	3	Oakton Green
60	E1	1	Wilmont Avenue
	E1	2	Congress Gardens
	E1	3	Albert Park
	E1	4	Claremont Villas
	E1	5	St Paul's Terrace
	E1	6	St Peter's Terrace
	E1	7	Findlater Street
	E1	8	Devitt Villas
	E1	9	Dixon Villas
	E1	10	Glen Terrace
	E1	11	Glasthule Buildings
	E1	12	Hastings Terrace
	E1	13	Brighton Terrace
	E1	14	Lawson Terrace
	E1	15	Killiney Terrace
	E1	16	Munster Terrace
	E1	17	Neptune Terrace
	E1	18	Cliff Terrace
	E1	19	Beaufort
	E1	20	Ballygihen Villas
	E1	21	Seabank Court
	E1	22	St Helen's
	E1	23	Chester Square
	E1	24	Dundela Haven
	E1	25	Arkendale Woods
	E1	26	Arkendale Court
	E1	27	Adelaide Villas
	E1	28	Adelaide Terrace
	E1	29	Atmospheric Road
	E1	30	St Margaret's Close
	E1	31	Avondale Court
60	E2	1	Barnhill Lawn
	E2	2	Killiney Towers

PAGE	GRID REF		STREET NAME
	E2	3	Barnhill Park
	E2	4	Kilcolman Court
	E2	5	Edwin Court
	E2	6	Fairlawns
	E2	7	Urney Grove
	E2	8	Marlborough Court
	E2	9	Castlepark Court
60	E3	1	Hill Cottages
	E3	2	Mount Auburn
	E3	3	Talbot Road
	E3	4	Talbot Lane
60	E4	1	Oakton Court
	E4	2	Dale View Park
	E4	3	Mountain Villa
	E4	4	The Nurseries
	E4	5	Mountain View Road
	E4	6	Rainsford Lane
	E4	7	Firgrove
60	F1	1	Carysfort Drive
	F1	2	Ormeau Drive
	F1	3	The Paddocks
	F1	4	South Winds
	F1	5	Ulverton Close
	F1	6	Rocklands
	F1	7	Bayswater Terrace
	F1	8	Bullock Steps
	F1	9	Liscanor
	F1	10	White's Villas
	F1	11	Mayville Terrace
	F1	12	Castlelands Grove
	F1	13	Ulverton Court
	F1	14	Pilot View
	F1	15	Bailey View
	F1	16	Castlelands
	F1	17	Churchill Mews
	F1	18	Bartra Rock Apartments
60	F2	1	St Patrick's Avenue
	F2	2	Railway Road
	F2	3	Anastasia Lane
	F2	4	St Patrick's Square
	F2	5	Cats Ladder
	F2	6	Dalkey Grove
	F2	7	Barnhill Grove
	F2	8	St Patrick's Road
	F2	9	Monte Vella
	F2	10	Summerfield Close
	F2	11	Victoria Terrace
	F2	12	Sorrento Drive
	F2	13	Sorrento Lawn
	F2	14	Coliemore Villas
	F2	15	Seafield Terrace
	F2	16	Temple Terrace
	F2	17	Grosvenor Terrace
	F2	18	Charlotte Terrace
	F2	19	Heany Avenue
	F2	20	Desmond Cottages
	F2	21	Ardbrugh Villas
	F2	22	Burmah Close
	F2	23	Dalkey Court
	F2	24	Kilbegnet Close
	F2	25	Sorrento Close
	F2	26	Craiglands
	F2	27	Ullardmor
	F2	28	Sorrento Mews
	F2	29	Sorrento Court
	F2	30	Sorrento Heights
	F2	31	Ardbrugh Close
	F2	32	Castle Cove
	F2	33	Torca View
63	A1	1	The View
64	D1	1	The Oaks
	D1	2	Cherry Court
	D1	3	Cois Coillte
64	D2	1	Stonebridge Lane
64	E1	1	Killiney Court
	E1	2	Killiney Oaks
	E1	3	The Sycamores
	E1	4	The Elms
	E1	5	St Aubyn's Court

PAGE/ GRID REF	STREET NAME	PAGE/ GRID REF	STREET NAME	PAGE/ GRID REF	STREET NAME	PAGE/ GRID REF	STREET NAME
E1	6 Ennel Court	B2	3 Dargle Court	C2	13 Milton Terrace	67 C3	1 Cherry Tree Drive
E1	7 Sheelin Grove	B2	4 Ashley Heights	C2	14 St Kevin's Terrace	C3	2 Roselawn Park
E1	8 Glencarr Court	B2	5 Dargle Crescent	C2	15 Darley Cottages	C3	4 Woodview Drive
E1	9 Domville Grove	B2	6 Copper Beech Grove	C2	16 Brabazon Cottages	C3	5 Kennedy Park
E1	10 Streamville Court	B2	7 Vale Terrace	C2	17 St Laurence's Terrace	C3	8 Newcourt Villas
E1	12 Bayview Glade	B2	9 Sutton Road	C2	18 St Columcille's Terrace	C3	9 O'Byrne Villas
E1	13 Sheelin Hill	B2	10 Dargan Street	C2	20 Seapoint Villas	C3	10 Stoneylea Terrace
E1	14 Sheelin Walk	B2	11 Fairgreen Road	C2	21 Dunbur Terrace	C3	11 Mountain View
E1	16 The Larches	B2	12 Pearse Road	C2	22 Elmgrove Terrace		Apartments
E1	17 The Oaks	B2	13 Mountpleasant Villas	C2	23 St Aidan's Terrace	C3	14 Putland Villas
E1	18 The Rowans	B2	15 Diamond Terrace	C2	24 Seapoint Terrace	C3	15 Oldcourt Terrace
E1	19 The Willows	B2	16 Parkview Terrace	C2	25 Goldsmith Terrace	C3	16 Lauderdale Terrace
E1	20 The Hawthorns	B2	17 Sutton Villas	C2	26 Prince of Wales Terrace	C3	17 Mayfield Terrace
E1	21 The Cedars	B2	18 Esmonde Terrace	C2	27 Novara Terrace	C3	18 Vevay Villas
E1	22 The Beeches	B2	20 New Ravenswell Row	C2	28 Waverley Terrace	C3	19 Orchard Terrace
E1	23 River Close	B2	21 Vale View	C2	29 Westview Terrace	C3	20 Bray Head Terrace
64 E2	1 River Lane	B2	22 Old Rathmore Terrace	C2	30 Augustine Villas	C3	21 Sugarloaf Terrace
E2	2 Clonasleigh	B2	23 New Rathmore Terrace	C2	31 Trafalgar Terrace	67 C4	3 Bentley Avenue
E2	3 Beechfield Haven	B2	25 Gertrude Terrace	C2	32 Fairgreen Terrace	C4	6 St Mary's Terrace
E2	4 Athgoe Drive	B2	26 Herbert View	C2	33 St Brigid's Terrace	68 D2	1 Trosyrafon Terrace
E2	5 Maryland	B2	27 Rivervale Apartments	C2	34 Loretto Avenue	D2	2 Montebello Terrace
E2	6 Station Road	B2	29 Bruce's Terrace	C2	35 Loretto Terrace	D2	3 Esplanade Terrace
E2	7 Windrush	B2	29 Old Ravenswell Row	C2	36 Sidmonton Gardens	D2	4 Brennans Terrace
E2	8 Shanganagh Wood	67 B3	1 Ballynoe Court	C2	37 Rosslyn	D2	5 Sidbury Court
E2	9 Thomond	B3	2 Rathclaren	C2	38 Shankill View	D2	6 Dargan Court
E2	10 Beechwood House	B3	3 St Clair's Terrace	C2	39 Florence Terrace	D2	7 Warburton Terrace
E2	11 Sycamore House	B3	4 Killarney Court	C2	40 Florence Villas	D2	8 Sloan Terrace
E2	12 Woodview	B3	5 Kilgrastor Court	C2	41 Carlton Terrace	D2	9 Belgrave Villas
E2	13 River Lane Grove	B3	6 Glenbrook	C2	42 Carlton Villas	D2	10 Belgrave Terrace
E2	14 Corbawn Glade	B3	8 Brickfield Lane	C2	43 Alexander Terrace	D2	11 Claremount Terrace
64 E3	1 Guilford Terrace	67 B4	1 Ballywaltrim Cottages	C2	44 Belton Terrace	D2	12 Richmond Terrace
E3	2 Stonebridge Close	B4	2 Ballymorris	C2	45 Church Terrace	D2	13 Milward Terrace
E3	3 Osprey Court	67 C1	1 St Patrick's Square	C2	46 Old Brighton Terrace	D2	14 Brennans Parade
E3	4 Cluain na Greine Court	C1	2 Martello Terrace	C2	47 New Brighton Terrace	D2	16 Marlborough Terrace
64 E4	1 Kiltuck Park	67 C2	1 Sidmonton Square	C2	48 Killarney Villas	D2	17 Marine Terrace
67 B1	1 Raverty Villas	C2	3 Eglington Road	C2	49 Market Square	D2	18 Jones Terrace
B1	2 St Peter's Terrace	C2	4 Rosslyn Grove	C2	50 Fairgreen Court	D2	19 Mount Norris Villas
B1	3 Myrtle Grove	C2	5 James Connolly Square	C2	51 Bayview	D2	20 St Marys Terrace
B1	4 Arbutus Grove	C2	6 Sidmonton Place	C2	52 Westbourne Terrace	D2	21 Fitzwilliam Terrace
B1	5 Thornhill View	C2	7 Novara Park	C2	53 King Edward Court	D2	23 Convent View
B1	6 Fernbrook	C2	8 St Cronan's Road	C2	54 Loretto Villas	68 D3	1 Eaton Court
B1	7 Roseville Court	C2	9 Cill Manntan Park	C2	55 Marie Villas	D3	2 Meretimo Villas
B1	8 Sunnybank Court	C2	10 Kilmantain Place	C2	56 Wellington Court	D3	3 Grosvenor Avenue
67 B2	1 Auburn Villas	C2	11 Father Colohan Terrace	C2	57 Novara Mews	D3	4 Brookfield Avenue
B2	2 Glenburgh Terrace	C2	12 Royal Marine Terrace	C2	58 Vevay Crescent	D3	5 Sidmonton Court
				C2	59 Bull Lane	D3	6 Sydenham Villas
				C2	60 Purcell Lane		